READING
DIFFICULTIES

sixth edition

READING DIFFICULTIES
their diagnosis and correction

GUY L. BOND

MILES A. TINKER

BARBARA B. WASSON
Moorhead State University

JOHN B. WASSON
Moorhead State University

PRENTICE HALL, Englewood Cliffs, New Jersey 07632

Library of Congress Cataloging-in-Publication Data

Reading difficulties : their diagnosis and correction / Guy L. Bond . . . [et al.]. — 6th ed.
    p.   cm.
    Includes bibliographies and index.
    ISBN 0-13-754987-3
    1. Reading—Remedial teaching.   2. Reading disability.   I. Bond,
Guy Loraine, [date]
LB1050.5.R377 1989
428.4′2—dc19

            88-22468
              CIP

Editorial/production supervision: *Edith Riker*
Cover design: *George Cornell*
Manufacturing buyer: *Peter Havens*

© 1989 by Prentice-Hall, Inc.
A Division of Simon & Schuster
Englewood Cliffs, New Jersey 07632

Printed in the United States of America

10 9 8 7 6 5 4 3 2 1

ISBN   0-13-754987-3

Prentice-Hall International (UK) Limited, *London*
Prentice-Hall of Australia Pty. Limited, *Sydney*
Prentice-Hall Canada Inc., *Toronto*
Prentice-Hall Hispanoamericana, S.A., *Mexico*
Prentice-Hall of India Private Limited, *New Delhi*
Prentice-Hall of Japan, Inc., *Tokyo*
Simon & Schuster Asia Pte. Ltd., *Singapore*
Editora Prentice-Hall do Brasil, Ltda., *Rio de Janeiro*

Contents

11   CORRECTING FAULTY PERCEPTUAL AND DECODING SKILLS IN WORD RECOGNITION   *176*

12   TREATING THE EXTREMELY DISABLED READER   *201*

13   ADAPTING INSTRUCTION TO THE HANDICAPPED CHILD   *218*

Preface

Deficiencies in reading ability among children and adults have become a serious national concern. Severe disability in reading, in modern times, makes finding employment difficult, changing employment problematical, and advancement in employment nearly impossible.

This sixth edition of *Reading Difficulties: Their Diagnosis and Correction* has been revised with major changes in emphasis.

Recent research findings have placed special emphasis in the areas of visual and auditory perception, brain hemisphere functioning, cognitive style, and emotional and behavioral aspects of reading difficulties. Increased emphasis has been given to informal diagnosis of all degrees of reading disability.

Other areas of increased emphasis include the instructional use of computers for children with reading difficulties, the involvement of the reading disabled students as active participants in all remedial efforts, and an emphasis on helping disabled readers develop awareness and control of their own reading.

In addition, expanded coverage has been given to suggestions for parents and development of student interest in reading.

The aim of this book is to help classroom teachers, resource teachers, and reading specialists to diagnose and to correct the various kinds of problems involved in preventing and correcting reading disabilities. The authors are keenly aware of the fact that learning to read is complex and that there are many possible confusions along the route. If the classroom teacher can detect and correct these difficulties early, many minor problems that could lead to a major reading disability may be prevented. This book is designed to give the teacher specific help by describing how to diagnose and correct reading difficulties in the formative stages.

Certain children will persist in their reading difficulties to the point that they will need more detailed diagnosis and individualized remedial training. The classroom teacher cannot be expected to make these more detailed and complex analyses, but this book discusses the various reading disabilities in a sufficiently detailed and direct manner that a thorough understanding of the most complex cases is possible. Finally, there are specific suggestions for diagnosing and correcting even the most stubborn kinds of problems of disabled readers so that all who are concerned with disabled readers will have the information necessary to understand the adjustments required.

For the sake of convenience and brevity in this book, we refer to the child as *he* and to the teacher as *she*. This does not mean that we do not recognize the equal importance of female readers and male teachers, and we regret that there is no neutral term that reflects our feelings.

The authors have extensively used the results of research on reading instruction and reading disability. We wish to thank all of the research workers who have made this book possible. We have drawn heavily on our own and many coworkers' clinical experience at the University of Minnesota Psycho-Educational Clinic and the Moorhead State University Reading Clinic. For their many suggestions, we wish to thank specifically Bruce Balow, Theodore Clymer, Robert Dykstra, Leo Fay, Bjorn Karlsen, Virginia McKinnon Deitz, Maynard Reynolds, Elynn Severson, and Carol Sibley, associates of the authors on the faculties of the University of Minnesota and Moorhead State University. We also wish to thank the many in-service teachers who presented their insights when discussing the problems of reading instruction while they were taking advanced courses and seminars. Finally, the authors wish to give special thanks to Fredericka H. Bond.

Guy L. Bond
Miles A. Tinker
Barbara B. Wasson
John B. Wasson

READING
DIFFICULTIES

1

Introduction

Being able to read well is a valuable attribute. At work, at home, at school, even at leisure, reading is required to some extent. Reading is a needed channel of communication with the global community.

Consideration of the daily activities of almost any adult reveals a need for reading. These activities are made possible or are aided by information gained from reading. Magazines, newspapers, books, maps, directories, pamphlets, signs, and catalogs all assist the reader in making plans and in carrying them out. People read to obtain information, to buy wisely, to solve problems, for pleasure, and for many other reasons. More people read now than ever read before.

NATURE OF READING DEVELOPMENT

Preparation for reading does not start when a child enters school for the first time. It has begun long before this. Even before an infant talks, there is communication between parents, the young child and with others. From infancy until the child enters school, a multitude of experiences and the child's reactions and adjustments to them help to prepare each youngster for the demands of learning to read. In a few short years, children progress from the point at which they can only pat the pictures in their books to learning to point out and name familiar objects in the pictures. Soon they willingly listen when read to, then recite little rhymes and talk about the stories in books. These steps are gains in verbalization and in recognition of form and meaning. Progress in *readiness* for reading can be extensive and significant during the preschool years.

When taught with any of the usual approaches used in learning to read, the child must understand the relationship of printed language to oral language, must understand that a printed word stands for a spoken word and has the same meaning as the spoken word. In beginning reading, the printed word should be in the child's speaking and meaning vocabulary, so the child will associate the printed word with both the sound and meaning of the spoken word.

The printed words in any writing are merely symbols for the meanings intended by the author. These symbols serve as cues to the reader, who must organize an understanding of what is meant. The ease with which a child can do this depends largely upon his background of experiences. For a beginning reader, these meanings are acquired through the reader's previous experiences and previously acquired facility with language. The child reads using his experience and language skill, interrelating them to derive meaning from printed symbols.

To a large degree, a child's thinking requires verbal manipulations. When the child begins to read, this is important to consider, for thinking is essential to reading at all stages of development. In fact, reading as a tool for learning will be ineffective unless it is accompanied by thinking. Learning to read and reading to learn should develop together throughout the school years.

Reading is both a subject of instruction and a tool for studying. Special skills should be taught as they are needed and they should be taught in the appropriate context. For example, the special skills needed for reading in science should be taught with material similar to that used in science instruction. Although this emphasizes reading as a tool, it also teaches reading.

Growth in reading abilities is developmental. Each new learning is an addition to or an expansion or refinement of previous attainments. This growth involves the gradual acquisition of skills which together enable the learner to interpret printed symbols correctly. This facilitates the learner's participation in meaningful communication through reading. These skills are developed concurrently with their use as part of reading itself. Reading development is the result of completion of tasks which are neither easy nor simple. Each new learning rests upon a child's previously acquired achievements. Each new learning requires that the child apply newly developing skills to increasingly more complex reading materials. Instruction must maintain balances among the various skills and abilities essential to growth and be geared to the needs and characteristics of the children being taught.

Definition of Reading

Our definition of reading is as follows: *Reading is the recognition of printed or written symbols which serve as stimuli to the recall of meanings built up through the reader's past experience.* New meanings are derived through manipulation of concepts already in the reader's possession. The organization of these meanings is governed by purposes clearly defined by the reader. In short, the reading process involves both the acquisition of meanings intended by the writer and the reader's own contributions in the form of interpretation and evaluation of and reflection on those meanings.

Description of Normal Reading Growth

To identify those children who have failed to make satisfactory progress in reading, it is necessary to have in mind some standards of reading growth. There are marked individual differences in rate of reading attainment. Some children begin to read early and progress rapidly. Others start late and move forward slowly. Between these are the average learners. It should also be noted that a child may progress at different rates during different stages in the development of reading abilities. Generally, however, growth in reading tends to be continuous and developmental in nature. At each stage, the skills essential to success at the next level are acquired. When this progress is continued without serious interruption, the child eventually becomes a mature reader.

The prereading period.   Soon after birth the child begins to acquire experience essential to learning to read. When, in addition, the child matures in mental ability and emotional adjustment and acquires increasing interests, he becomes ready to begin reading. A listening and speaking vocabulary develops gradually. In time sentences are understood and properly used. Meanwhile the child develops skill in auditory and visual discrimination. Varieties of concepts are formed. Under favorable circumstances the child is able to focus attention, enabling him to listen to and comprehend stories. If the child's experience has been extensive, if many clear concepts have been acquired, and if adequate facility in the understanding and use of language has been achieved, the child has a distinct advantage in getting ready for reading.

A child's experiences affect the rate of development of skills up to the time reading instruction is begun. To acquire auditory and visual skills and language facility, a child must have both appropriate experiences and guidance. The child must be encouraged to discriminate sounds and visual details and to listen to and use words. It is important for adults to talk to and with the child. Stories should be read with the child while he looks at the pictures and talks about them. The child who is accumulating extensive experience with such items as picture books, crayons, paper, scissors, and paint brushes is also preparing for reading.

Under favorable circumstances, provided that mental growth, personal adjustment, and physical development are normal, the child will not only be *ready* to read but should also be *eager* to read. There are marked differences in the rate at which children acquire reading readiness. A few are ready even before entering kindergarten, others by the time they enter first grade. Many become ready soon after beginning first grade, but a few are not ready until later.

Progress in reading readiness.   The child is ready to begin a reading program only after reaching sufficient mental maturity, achieving satisfactory classroom adjustment, maintaining normal physical development, acquiring an adequate background of experiences, and developing positive attitudes toward reading. As already noted, there are many degrees of readiness among children at the beginning of grade one. After an evaluation of each child, the teacher provides instruction to compensate for whatever deficiencies in reading readiness she discovers.

It should be pointed out here that the concept of readiness is basic to the development of reading ability at all levels, from kindergarten on. With each new unit of instruction, the child should be prepared to accomplish the reading and thinking activities involved in it. For success in any specific reading task, the pupil must possess the necessary concepts, the vocabulary knowledge, and the ability to handle the language relationships involved. The child must also select and organize ideas and details which are related to his purpose. All this implies instruction and guidance so that the student will be *ready to read* each new unit proficiently.

Introduction to reading.   After proper preparation, the child is introduced to reading in grade one. The child begins to accumulate a sight vocabulary and at the same time learns that printed and written symbols stand for meanings in a variety of situations. Training in auditory and visual discrimination continues. New word meanings are acquired. The teacher helps the child use elementary techniques and clues for word identification. Meanwhile the child is progressing naturally from reading labels, words standing for actions, short signs, and notes to reading a book, the preprimer. Such systematic training in reading a book leads to success at the primer level and so on to the first reader. All along, learnings are practiced through exercises suggested in manuals, through workbooks, and through other supplementary materials.

There will be noticeable individual differences in the reading progress made by first-grade students. By the end of the first grade, the average learners will have acquired a considerable stock of sight words, some independence in using techniques of word recognition, and much skill in both oral and silent reading of easy materials, including those in the public library.

Progress in the primary grades.   To a great extent, the reading instruction in grades two and three consists of extension, refinement, and amplification of the program begun in grade one. New techniques of reading are introduced, and the child begins to learn them when he is ready. Throughout the primary grades, there are no abrupt distinctions in progressing from one part of the program to the next. Under favorable circumstances, the average child will have achieved the following goals by the end of grade three: (1) marked progress in mastering techniques of word recognition and the other fundamentals of reading, (2) considerable independence in reading, (3) a degree of flexibility in the use of reading skills, (4) a sound basis for study-type reading, (5) greater speed in silent rather than oral reading, and (6) positive attitudes toward reading. With normal progress, by the end of grade three the child will have acquired a sound foundation for future reading, although there will be many skills in word recognition, comprehension, and techniques of study to be developed later.

Reading instruction in grades four through six is an extension of the developmental program begun in the primary grades. Besides improving the basic abilities, it focuses on developing the specialized abilities and study skills required for reading subject matter in content fields and other work-type materials. Beginning in grade four, children move into a phase of increasing diversification of learning in which reading is the essential tool. To an accelerating degree, reading becomes a means of gathering information and achieving pleasure. When there has been normal progress in the earlier grades, the consolidation of basic reading abilities and the extension of these abilities in specialized directions in the intermediate grades proceeds at a relatively rapid pace. The child reads more independently and more widely. Although the relative emphasis upon silent reading increases, oral reading should not be neglected. By the time the sixth grade is finished, the child who has made normal progress will have achieved the basis for reading in later years. Additional instruction in reading in the junior and senior high school years is necessary to assure proficiency. This is especially true in perfecting the special skills needed for serious study and for the comprehension of difficult materials.

Progress in the basic reading abilities.   Throughout the grades, there tends to be a steady growth in the acquisition of word knowledge, word-recognition skill, and comprehension skill. Progress is developmental or sequential, and each learning provides a basis for learnings similar to it. Reading readiness plays an important role. A child is ready to advance to a more complex level of a learning sequence only when mastery of previously taught skills is sufficient to ensure success in more mature learning. In word recognition, for example, the child learns letter and phonogram sounds in the early years. This equips the child for the more mature features of word recognition taught in the intermediate grades, which include syllabication, prefixes, suffixes, and word roots. Basic reading abilities are not acquired in isolation but as part of a well-integrated sequential reading program.

Progress in the special reading abilities.   Acquisition of the special abilities necessary for proficient reading in the content areas, such as reading to organize, begins early and progresses at a gradual pace for most students. Since the reading of some content material is introduced in grade one in many reading programs, it is necessary to teach the elementary features of the special abilities during the primary grades. By grade three, such guidance receives a good deal of emphasis. When the special abilities are stressed, the progress of the average pupil in reading to learn has advanced far enough by the end of the primary grades that a smooth transition to the major reading tasks in the intermediate grades will be achieved.

As the child moves through grade three and through the intermediate grades, the study skills are added to the special reading abilities. Mastery of the basic reading skills, together with continuing improvement in special reading skills and study skills, is coordinated into proficient reading. With normal progress, the child will have developed much flexibility in adapting these skills to the purposes and subject-matter requirements of each of the content areas. The child will also have learned the supplementary skills necessary for the reading problems unique to a particular subject. Although complete mastery of the special reading abilities cannot be achieved by the end of grade six, there will have been good progress in this direction. The child will have a sound foundation for further progress in the reading tasks in the junior and senior high school years. However, a sound foundation is not enough. Because the materials read in high school are more mature than those used in elementary school, the child must be taught how to meet more advanced reading demands.

Goals of Reading Instruction

An effective reading program does more than develop the abilities and skills, both basic and special, outlined in the preceding section. Nevertheless the broader goals of the reading program are built upon these foundations. Reading is more than skill in identification and recognition of words, in grouping words into thought units, and in noting details and following directions. It is more than the sum of all reading skills and techniques.

The overall goal of reading instruction is to help each pupil become as able and diversified a reader as his capabilities, the available facilities, and the instructional program permit. To achieve this, certain subgoals must be considered. These goals are present during early reading experiences and become more apparent as reading develops through the grades. It should be recognized that there is interdependence among the goals of reading instruction. One goal is not necessarily more important than another. These goals will be discussed in the paragraphs that follow.

Basic understanding of words, sentences, paragraphs, and entire selections. Growth in these understandings is essential if the student is to develop into a mature reader. Word meanings are derived from experience. As language facility increases and words are used with newly experienced situations, concepts are clarified and enriched. Growth is continuous but gradual. The instructional program for developing a child's understanding and use of words to express meanings provides a variety of appropriate firsthand and vicarious experiences, wide and extensive reading, and study of words in context. It also develops the habit of attending to the meaning of words, so that if an unusual or expressive word is used the child will note it and its meaning. An understanding of words is basic to an understanding of sentences, paragraphs, and selections.

The understanding of sentence structure affects reading comprehension. Besides knowing the meaning of words in a sentence, the reader must grasp the relationships between words and groups of words. The kind and amount of instruction are determined by individual needs. With one child, the instruction may involve proper phrasing and interpretation of punctuation. Another child may need instruction in interpretation of figures of speech and use of a word whose meaning fits the verbal context. A third may need help in sorting out and properly relating several ideas incorporated in one sentence.

Along with understanding words and sentences, comprehending a paragraph requires understanding the relationship among sentences in that paragraph. The instructional task involves guiding the student in identifying the topical sentence containing the key idea and in interpreting its relationship to the explanatory or amplifying sentences. In a similar manner, attention should be devoted to the relationship between paragraphs in longer selections.

Word, sentence, and paragraph understanding are essential to comprehension of reading selections. Also involved is a child's ability to listen to and understand a selection read aloud. Some children, when they begin school, are skilled at listening to and understanding stories. Others have acquired little or no story sense by that time. These will need guidance and instruction in how to listen carefully to what is said and in how to follow a sequence of events in stories. Story sense is never completely developed for any child by the time reading instruction is begun, and guidance in listening attentively and in following sequences of events should be an integral part of reading instruction at least through the primary grades. After the primary grades, because of the more complex plots and more complicated organization of ideas encountered, the child must learn to sense the author's organization in order to grasp the meanings of the longer selections.

Maturity in reading habits and attitudes.   Development of reading habits and attitudes begins early and continues for as long as the child is growing in reading capability. The child learns to appreciate and to care for books. The child develops intellectual curiosity and comes to realize that books can help satisfy the need to know, to solve problems, and to contribute to group enterprises. The habit of attending to words and of demanding an understanding of their meanings should be encouraged at all levels. Finally, the habit of relying on one's own resources and of energetically attacking reading material should be encouraged early, to establish a realistic amount of independence throughout the instructional program.

Independence in reading.   To begin to read well and to be able to continue developing as a reader after formal education is finished, the child must develop independence in reading. There are several aspects to achieving this independence. The child must be able to recognize words quickly and easily in order to understand and consider content. Independence in reading depends on the ability to work out the pronunciation and understanding of new words. The independent reader also knows appropriate sources where new information can be found, is able to select relevant subject matter from these sources, and can judge the suitability of that subject matter. Independence in reading is also shown by the ability of the child to initiate reading activities, to appreciate reading problems, and to set reading purposes. Reading programs organized into important experience units that require related reading and activities encourage growth in independence. The teacher's guidance plays an important role in the development of independence in reading.

Efficiency in the use of basic study skills.   A number of skills are needed for attaining this goal. Efficiency in locating information through such aids as tables of contents, indexes, and the card catalog is one example. Instruction in the elementary techniques of finding information begins early. The more complex skills are taught in sequential order. Proficiency in the use of general reference material is a second example of study skills. Beginning with simple alphabetizing, the child progresses to use of such reference sources as dictionaries and encyclopedias.

Additional skills include the interpretation of pictures, maps, graphs, and charts. Teaching begins in kindergarten and progresses in a developmental manner through the school years.

Finally organizational skills must be included as essential study skills. This important group of skills includes outlining, classifying materials under main and subheadings, organizing sentences in experience charts in sequential order, and ordering selected materials in sequence. Constructing time lines, two-way charts, and classification tables are other examples. The ability to organize materials is essential to well-rounded growth in reading proficiency.

Maturity in five major classes of comprehension abilities.   The development of five interrelated types of comprehension, each corresponding to a different though related ability, is a major goal of reading instruction. These types are (1) reading for specific information, (2) reading to organize, (3) reading to evaluate, (4) reading to interpret, and (5) reading to appreciate. These varieties of comprehension are the ever present goals of reading instruction. They should not be postponed so that they have to be initiated in the more advanced grades.

Maturity in adjusting to the reading demands of the various disciplines.   To communicate their ideas to readers, authors write in ways appropriate to their purposes. To mature in reading proficiency, a child must learn to adjust his reading to the requirements of the specific type of material being read. An example is the contrast between the adjustment needed for reading and solving an arithmetic story problem and that for reading an easy short story. Such adjustments are made through coordination of the basic reading proficiencies, the different abilities involved in comprehension, and the study skills. The reader must choose from his repertory of skills those that are best for reading effectively a particular selection for a specific purpose.

A young child starts to develop a differential attack upon various types of reading material as soon as he reads a science unit in his basic reader or in a supplementary book. Versatility in this sort of adjustment improves from grade to grade. The teacher should help in making these adjustments. The achievement of facility in this differential attack is a goal of reading instruction at all grade levels.

Breadth of interest in reading and maturity of taste.   To be successful, a reading program must go beyond development of the basic and special abilities and the study skills. The child must also want to read widely. The amount, the variety, and the quality of what is read reflect the quality of the teaching program.

POINT OF VIEW

The authors believe that reading problems develop because one or more factors within the child or in the environment, or both, prevent him from reaching his learning capacity. Reading difficulty may occur at any stage of a child's school career from the first grade through the grades. The writers believe that reading disability can be corrected through proper diagnosis and remedial instruction. Nothing is accomplished by blaming the disability on low intelligence, lack of interest or laziness, or the home. For one reason or another, school instruction has not capitalized on the child's mental ability nor developed motivation by appealing to the child's interests.

If all the skills and abilities necessary for growth toward reading maturity are to be acquired, the learner must be motivated and energetic, work smoothly at his own level of accomplishment, and also be a comfortable learner. Each child must be able to sense that his proficiency in reading is increasing and that the enterprise is worth the effort.

In recent years, the teaching of reading has gained an important position in our schools. Research has been carried out, teachers are better trained, reading materials have multiplied, and techniques and devices for teaching have improved. Nevertheless, a surprising number of pupils fail to make the progress in reading expected from their potential.

The presence of reading disability in our schools is a serious problem at all grade levels. Many reading difficulties can be prevented. The classroom teacher can correct others in their initial stages, when correction is relatively easy. A sound preventive program stresses at least three kinds of instruction: (1) a thoroughgoing reading readiness program to prepare the child for beginning reading and for reading at successively higher levels; (2) proper adjustment of instruction to individual differences; and (3) systematic developmental programs at all levels.

A well-organized instructional program works to prevent reading disabilities. If it were possible in day-to-day classroom teaching to instruct each student according to his exact instructional needs, there would be less need for remedial work. Even with the best teaching and the best-organized, systematic program, certain children will experience serious difficulties. With less than the best teaching, the incidence of reading disability will increase. In any case, there will be an appreciable number of pupils who have serious difficulty with their reading, and there must be remedial help available to correct these difficulties.

View on Causes

The writers know that the causes of reading disability are multiple and tend to be complex. In the more difficult cases, a pattern of interacting factors usually operates, each contributing its part to the disability and each impeding future growth. The reading specialist must search out as many as possible of these limiting conditions operating in a particular case and apply the proper corrective measures.

In general the writers believe that most reading disabilities are created and are not inherent. Reading disabilities are sometimes the result of unrecognized, predisposing conditions within the child, but for the most part they are caused by elements of the child's environment at home, at play, and at school. Without appropriate guidance or proper instruction, the child fails to acquire the skills needed to develop normal reading ability.

Reading difficulties vary from minor to very severe. When minor difficulties occur and are not recognized and promptly corrected, their deleterious effects become cumulative and may result in a severe disability.

Although the writers emphasize educational factors as causes of reading disability, they also recognize that there are others which may and often do contribute as parts of a complex pattern of causes. These include immaturity, associated sometimes with low socioeconomic status; personal adjustment problems; physical deficiencies; and excessive pressure for achievement from home or school. There seldom is a single factor that causes reading disability, but one factor may be relatively more important than others.

The writers are aware that failure to recognize a child's handicaps and failure to adjust instruction to lessen their effects upon learning can contribute to a reading disability. Unless all educational, physical, and behavioral factors that can hinder normal progress in learning to read are identified early and corrected if possible, along with proper instructional adjustments, reading disability is apt to develop.

View on Remedial Instruction

The writers maintain that remedial instruction in reading is essentially the same as good classroom teaching, but is more individualized. The teacher works with the child, using essentially regular teaching methods, but concentrates on the skill in which the child is deficient. Effort is concentrated on the pupil's needs, assuming that there has been a thorough diagnosis of his strengths and weaknesses.

The authors believe the best results in remedial instruction are attained by designing an *individual instructional plan* that utilizes a combination of approaches. The remedial plan, however, should include any one or any combination of approaches suggested by the results of the diagnosis.

Effective remedial instruction is given by a good reading teacher, a teacher who is familiar with the principles and practices of sound reading instruction. Above all, the teacher must be versatile in adapting materials and techniques to specific needs based on formal and informal diagnosis and on the specific events of daily instruction. Instructional tasks may need to be broken down into small manageable units. Extra effort is usually needed to give clear introductions to activities for students who have difficulty understanding what to do and to insure that students are actively involved in learning. The teacher must employ patience, understanding, and empathy.

Success in remedial work is achieved only when there is a positive interaction between teacher and child and when the student is strongly motivated toward reading improvement. Even in group remediation, some individual attention by the teacher is important. To help the student view reading as enjoyable and worthwhile, the teacher must present lessons and activities which are as pleasant, interesting, and meaningful as possible. Sufficient variety helps maintain interest. However, it is not simply instructional methods which impart positive attitudes and motivation for reading improvement to children. Of great importance are the expressed attitudes and observed actions of the teacher; enthusiasm is essential.

A good many poor readers dislike reading due to previous failures. The wise remedial reading teacher knows how to dramatize progress in order to demonstrate success. Spoken remarks, written comments or evaluations, even the use of stickers or stars provide valuable information to the child about progress and success. Such feedback should be frequent and honest and should always stress what the child has done well or any evidence of improvement. Progress charts may be used on which units of improvement are small enough that progress can be frequently recorded. Take-home samples of the child's work, sight-word files, progress charts, and similar materials which illustrate to parents the child's improvement in reading also help demonstrate success.

The writers are convinced that well-conceived remedial instruction results in improved reading. Theoretically the instruction should bring the child up to the reading grade that is consistent with his learning potential. This should be possible except in those cases that are complicated by factors beyond the ability of the teacher to correct. It is, however, most unusual when a skilled teacher is not able to bring about a significant improvement in reading, given a reasonable amount of time.

PLAN OF THIS BOOK

This book discusses a practical approach to reading which is based on research findings and sound instructional procedures. Our chief concern is the child who experiences difficulty in his attempts to learn to read. We are convinced that both the classroom teacher and the reading specialist must be equipped to diagnose and correct reading deficiencies whenever they arise.

We will present the treatment of learning problems in ways that apply to both the classroom teacher and the reading specialist. Chapter 2 is concerned with the extent of individual differences and the problems of adjusting instruction to meet these differences.

The next four chapters deal with diagnosis of reading disabilities. Chapter 7 discusses the principles and levels of diagnosis and treats questions to be answered by the diagnostician in analyzing reading difficulties. Chapter 8 describes specific standardized and informal diagnostic procedures. Chapter 9 examines the principles involved in using the diagnostic findings to formulate an appropriate educational plan of remediation.

The techniques used in the treatment of word-recognition difficulties are described in the next four chapters. The techniques used to overcome deficiencies in basic meaning clues necessary for successful word recognition are discussed in Chapter 10. Remedial techniques used for faulty decoding skills in word recognition are presented in the following chapter. Chapter 12 concentrates on the remedial teaching necessary for the complex reading problems of extremely disabled readers, and Chapter 13 presents the adjustments needed to assist the disabled reader who is handicapped physically, emotionally, intellectually, or environmentally.

The last four chapters focus on the problems of basic comprehension abilities and more specific types of disabilities related to comprehension. Chapter 14 identifies remedial techniques for correcting basic comprehension difficulties. Chapter 15 deals with remedial treatment for weaknesses in specific comprehension abilities and basic study skills and with various reading materials of the content fields. Chapter 16 is concerned with improving inefficient rates of comprehension and overcoming ineffective oral reading, and Chapter 17 covers ways to encourage continuous growth in reading by expanding interests in reading, increasing independence, and providing follow-up help.

To help the readers of this book identify antecedents, we have chosen to use *he* for the disabled reader, and *she* for the teacher. We have also used the labels *remedial teacher* and *reading specialist* according to the phase of work being done, whether it be by resource teachers, reading specialists, or classroom teachers. Although we have tended to use the word *child* in our writing, the principles of diagnosis and treatment are equally applicable to all disabled readers from the early grades to adult.

2

Adjusting Instruction
To Individual Differences

The teacher's goal is to provide instruction and learning opportunities in the classroom which will encourage maximal growth in reading development and in achievement in all the other outcomes of the curriculum for each child she instructs. The organization of classroom activities and the adjustment of methods and materials to the wide variations found among children is one of the most crucial and complex problems which education must solve.

In any plan of school organization, the teacher is the main contributor to adjusting instruction in reading to the individual differences among the children she teaches. The teacher must know the nature of reading growth, the types of reading difficulties that might impede growth, and the characteristics of each child that might predispose the child to reading difficulties.

INDIVIDUAL DIFFERENCES IN THE CLASSROOM

The classroom teacher needs to be a keen observer and student to follow the reading growth of all the children. The knowledge she has of each child's general level of reading capability, while important, is not sufficient for maximum accomplishment nor for prevention of serious reading problems. The teacher must also study the attainment of specific skills and abilities, so that any faulty learning can be detected and corrected early and so that any omissions or overemphasis can be avoided.

A class made up of 25 to 30 children cannot be taught as though all members of the class had the same interests, desires, intellectual capabilities, or physical characteristics; nor can it be taught as though they had reached the same levels of attainment in reading or possessed identical instructional needs. Each child must be given material that is as nearly suitable to his level of reading growth as is possible. The child must be taught by methods compatible with his characteristics and capabilities. For him, those phases of reading instruction that demand immediate attention must be emphasized. Reading instruction, to be effective, must proceed on an individual basis.

The teacher, however, is teaching a class and not just one child. Her problem is one of organizing instruction so that a class may be taught as a community, with all members engaged in educationally worthwhile activities. At the same time, instruction must be adjusted to meet the needs and characteristics of individuals. It must be organized so that, for at least part of the time, the teacher is free to devote attention to those children needing special guidance. Adjusting instruction to individual differences in large classes is probably the most difficult instructional problem faced by the teacher.

Improved Methods and Materials

Fortunately, today's teachers are better prepared to adjust instruction to individual differences in reading than were teachers in the past. As a result of research and classroom practice, the teacher of today is equipped with more and better teaching techniques. The teacher is an effective caring professional who realizes that reading growth is developed gradually over the years in an orderly, systematic manner and is facilitated by businesslike, energetic, and organized instruction.

Today's teachers are more aware of the individual instructional needs of children than were teachers of the past because there is an ever-increasing diversity of instructional needs in every classroom. Fortunately, children's individual needs can be far better diagnosed today than formerly. As a result, many serious reading problems are prevented and those reading problems that do develop are more successfully corrected. It is also true that more information is available to teachers so that they may adjust instructional programs to meet the known needs of the class.

Basic reading programs, supplementary reading materials, library and media center materials, as well as opportunities to work with computers and other special equipment provide the resources needed for carefully planned systematic instruction and for attention to individual needs.

Reasons for Increased Attention to Differences in Reading

The contemporary teacher is better equipped to adjust instruction to individual differences than was the teacher of the past. There are several reasons why this is good. First, awareness of the importance of education and of reading ability in modern society has caused a greater concern for the reading capability of the growing child than there has ever been before. Second, children who have difficulty in reading are no longer allowed to drop out of school. Every child who enters the first grade is expected to go on developing reading proficiency up to the level of his capabilities as the child progresses through the elementary and secondary schools. Third, because practically all children are retained in the school, reading ability is no longer used as the sole criterion for promotion. Children now, for the most part, are promoted in school so that they will be with other children of their own age, interests, and stage of development. This policy, in some respects, makes the problem of adjusting reading instruction to individual differences more difficult. Fourth, improved instruction has increased the need for adjusting instruction to individual rates of growth. The only way to make children equal in reading ability is not to teach any of them. Then they would all have the same stature in reading— none of them would be able to read. But instruction that allows each child to grow as rapidly as he is able encourages differences in reading capability. Under improved instruction, a wide range in reading ability can be expected at any grade level. It would be unrealistic to expect children with divergent interests, with different backgrounds, and with unequal linguistic ability, physical stamina, hearing ability, vision, and intellect to grow at the same rate in a complicated set of skills and abilities such as those used in learning to read.

Range in Reading Ability to Be Expected

At any grade level, then, it is reasonable to expect that there will be a wide range in reading ability. In the fifth grade, for example, it is quite normal to find a six- or seven-year difference between the least and the most competent reader. This range of reading ability within a fifth-grade class cannot and should not be prevented, but it must be recognized and adjustments must be made.

Failure to adjust the material and the instruction to the range of reading capability found within the classroom is a major cause of reading disability. This failure limits the usefulness of the printed page as a tool of learning throughout the curriculum. The teacher must know the reading capability and the varying instructional needs of each child. The teacher must know how to make appropriate adjustments in class organization and in instruction to meet the range of reading talent and the variety of instructional needs.

Every teacher is aware that children grow in reading capability at different rates and that in any class there is a wide range of reading capabilities. Teachers know that there is a vast difference in the difficulty of a paragraph that can be read and understood by the most able and the least able within the class. Teachers know that some children read extensively and that others read very little. They know that many children initiate their own reading activities and that others must be urged to read. They know that some read books of high quality and others appear to be satisfied with relatively immature writing. They are aware that some children read broadly and others confine their readings to a single type or to what satisfies a single interest.

It is little wonder that children grow at different rates. A child learns to read with his eyes, ears, energy, background of experience, interests, drives, emotional stamina, and intelligence. Any differences found within children in any of these traits will affect the rate at which they learn to read. The teachers know that it is quite normal for children to have differences in auditory acuity, in physical stamina, and in intelligence. The problem of adjusting to individual differences is one of recognizing these differences and the varying rates of growth, and thus of adjusting materials and instruction so that the child may be an energetic, comfortable learner, absorbed in the learning situation. The instructional program should allow the child neither to dawdle nor to be placed in situations that are so difficult that the child may become confused and discouraged.

Most teachers quickly recognize that individual differences in reading exist within their classrooms. Teachers also are aware that each child varies in his own reading capabilities. They know that just because a certain child excels in reading and understanding science, it does not necessarily follow that the same child will also excel at oral reading of poetry. It is often evident that a child, by grasping the overall meaning of a sentence, is able to recognize unfamiliar words, even though his knowledge of phonics remains limited. Another child may have a high degree of independence in working out words but is unable to group them into thought units. The extent of these variations, the ways of diagnosing them, and the importance of making adjustments for individual differences is frequently not fully understood.

Figure 2-1 illustrates the range of reading ability found within selected classrooms at various grade levels for students whose reading instruction was the responsibility of the classroom teacher.

As shown, the range of reading capability increases as pupils progress through school. The total range between the best and the poorest reader in the second-grade class is two years and five months; in the third grade, the range is three years and six months; in the fourth grade, four years and eight months; in the fifth grade, six years and one month; in the sixth grade, seven years; and at the secondary school level, the range of reading becomes very large indeed. These data approximate the range in reading ability that is usually found and that the teacher must be prepared to handle at the various grade levels.

Probably the most important information about a typical class is *the great range in reading talent that is to be found in the upper and lower third of the class.* Also, the fact that the middle third is relatively homogeneous in reading capability is important. In grade five, for example, the difference between the best and the poorest reader in the upper third of the distribution is spread over about two years and six months. Some members of this upper third will find themselves comfortable with books suited to typical students halfway through the fifth grade, while others can profitably read books appropriate to the early months of grade eight.

The problem of adjusting to this wide range of reading capability makes it important for the teacher to diversify instruction for the superior readers. Similarly, the lowest third of a fifth-grade class has a great range in reading ability—a range of about two years and five months. A few of these pupils will find material suited to the typical beginning second-grader somewhat difficult. There are others within this

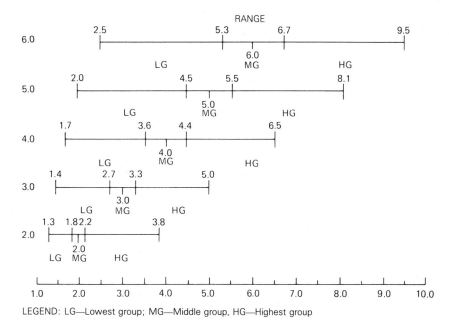

LEGEND: LG—Lowest group; MG—Middle group, HG—Highest group

FIGURE 2-1   Range of reading ability found in selected classrooms of grades two through six at the beginning of the school year.

same lowest third who can profitably read material suited to pupils halfway through the fourth grade. The lowest group also needs diversification of instruction to meet the wide range of reading capability.

The problem of adjusting instruction to fit the large range of reading capability found in the upper third and in the lowest third of a fifth-grade class is, however, quite different. The pupils in the upper third of the distribution are competent, independent readers, and the teacher, in adjusting to their individual differences, can depend upon their proficiency and their independence. Adjustment to the large range found in the lowest third of the distribution is complicated by the fact that these pupils are somewhat less than competent and are not independent readers at all. The problem is still more difficult in planning for the poorer readers, because there are not as many reading materials suitable to their age and interest level, or to their reading level. The teacher is fortunate that superior readers have little difficulty in selecting materials suitable to their reading abilities, interests, and intellectual capacities.

Most teachers who use grouping to adjust to individual differences vary the number of pupils in the reading groups. A teacher might make the middle group the largest because they are more homogeneous; the advanced group next largest because they are more independent; and the lowest group quite small, because they need closer diagnosis and more help.

BASIC CONSIDERATIONS IN ADJUSTING TO INDIVIDUAL DIFFERENCES IN READING

The problem of adjusting to the wide range of reading capability, resulting from the different rates of growth found in any classroom, has many dimensions. Each of these dimensions must be considered in formulating programs for adjusting to individual differences in reading. Among the more important facts to be considered when formulating an instructional approach are the following:

1. Children are alike in many ways.
2. Children grow in many ways other than in reading capability.
3. A child's general development in reading is not necessarily uniform.
4. Reading is a complex learning.
5. Adjustments to individual differences change with advancement through the curriculum.
6. Adjustment to individual differences change according to the phase of the reading curriculum considered.
7. Adjustments to individual differences change with changes in school organization.
8. Adjustment to individual differences must be realistic in the time required.
9. Teacher energy and time for preparation are not unlimited.

These facts must be recognized in formulating classroom organization and procedures to adjust to individual differences in reading. They are so crucial that neglecting any one of them limits the adequacy of the adjustment. Quite obviously, an adjustment that so dissociates one child from another so that learning is no longer a shared experience is unwise; or an approach that takes more of the teacher's time in preparation than is reasonable must be rejected; or a method that freezes a child in a less advanced group so that he cannot advance if his rate of learning accelerates cannot be recommended. Adjustments to individual differences in reading, then, must recognize and provide for the many dimensions of the problem.

Children Are Alike in Many Ways

A program of adjustment to individual differences in reading must recognize the similarities as well as the differences among children. Each child in the classroom is an important individual. Each child has many drives, motives, and desires. Children of any given age, for example, are likely to be interested in many of the same things. Each child in a class needs to be recognized as an important member of the classroom community. The poor reader, as well as the good one, must have friends and be an integral part of the class, must make contributions to the class, and must not be forced into a position of inferiority. Every child should be helped to preserve feelings of personal worth. All children need to feel that they are progressing and continually becoming better readers, even though some may recognize that their rate of growth in reading is somewhat slower than that of other children. When each child is of recognized personal worth, each child will have a feeling of confidence, security, and well-being that will encourage comfortable and efficient growth in reading for all children.

Children Grow in Many Ways Other Than in Reading Capability

Any adjustments must take into account the many characteristics of child growth and development besides level of attainment in reading. Children are changing in physical size, in social adaptability, and in interests. They are developing proficiencies in many skills and abilities.

It is sometimes suggested that within a school system children could be grouped placing all those with the same reading needs in the same classroom. The teacher could then use more uniform approaches in teaching them. The problem with this grouping plan is that differences between children within classrooms would soon become apparent. Children might be equal in reading capability at the onset of instruction, but they would soon become heterogeneous. The differences in rates of reading growth would show up almost immediately. Moreover, children grouped according to reading ability would not be similar in many other characteristics. There would be almost as great a range in chronological age within a group classified according to reading ability as there is now in reading ability among children classified according to chronological age. Methods of adjustment, then, which place children of different ages and interest levels within the same classroom are unfortunate. Programs of adjustment that keep children, as nearly as possible, with others of their own levels of *overall* development are the ones that are most likely to succeed. Adjustment to individual differences in reading will have to be done in ways other than homogeneous grouping according to reading ability at any level of instruction.

A Child's General Development in Reading Is Not Necessarily Uniform

Any adjustment that does not provide for moving the child from one group to another is unwise. One child, for example, may find reading a very difficult undertaking at the outset, but as the child progresses, rate of growth may be accelerated. This child may have high general intelligence but be limited in auditory acuity. At the beginning the child would find establishment of word-recognition techniques somewhat difficult. As a result, his growth in reading would be slow. But as the program advanced and as the role of reasoning became increasingly important, his rate of growth in reading would accelerate. Another child might start out being relatively good in the reading program as long as the building of basic sight vocabulary and word-recognition techniques were the important determinants of success. But if this child was somewhat limited in the more complex reasoning abilities, such as ability to make accurate judgments and to visualize what is read, his rate of growth would taper off as the program, at more mature levels, began to emphasize these capabilities.

The correlation between ingelligence and reading ability at the end of the first grade is approximately .50 (Bond & Dykstra, 1967). The relationship rises through the grades (Rubin, 1982, p. 50) to approximately .70 at the upper elementary level and .80 at the high school level. To the extent that organization within the classroom allows the child to grow comfortably and energetically in reading, and remains flexible enough to adjust to varying rates of growth, progress can be optimized.

Reading Is a Complex Learning

Reading ability is not a specific or single attribute. It is made of a hierarchy of many skills and abilities, attitudes, and tastes. A well-rounded basic reading program encourages relatively uniform growth in the many components of reading ability. Nonetheless, a study of reading profiles indicates that no child develops skills, abilities, attitudes, interests, and tastes in the same manner. There will be marked differences in degree of maturity of reading development in the various outcomes of reading instruction.

A fifth-grade child, for example, may show as great a difference as three or four years between his most mature reading capability and his least mature one. He may have a high degree of proficiency in using word-recognition techniques, but his ability to read to understand the fundamental idea in a selection may be relatively immature. Or the child may, given an unlimited time, be able to work out words independently as well as the usual seventh-grader, while his fluency in understanding what the passage is about may only be equal to that of the beginning third-grader. Another child may be relatively efficient in reading material of the narrative type, but may be relatively ineffective in reading materials in the content fields. Uneven profiles of reading, produced by the complex nature of learning, are unfortunate and indicate the need for corrective work.

The child would be rare whose areas of best and worst performances in the complex task of learning to read are separated by less than a year. The reading program must be flexible enough to adjust to the differences in reading capabilities found in the individual child. The program cannot be so formalized that the adjustments cannot vary according to the type of reading done at a given time. The child with poor ability to understand the general idea of a passage should get considerably more exposure to that type of reading than he does to the word-recognition exercises in the basic program. The child who reads narrative material satisfactorily but is poor at reading material of a content field must have the level of difficulty of the latter material adjusted to the development of his comprehension abilities and to the application of these to reading content material.

A reading program designed to meet the individual needs of children must take into account not only the range of general reading achievement found within a classroom, but also the characteristics of each child's reading growth pattern. Undoubtedly, the complex nature of reading and the resultant unevenness in child growth in reading make adjusting to individual differences in reading difficult.

Teachers who are successful in meeting the individual reading needs of their students must be aware of the reading attainments of each student and must employ teaching methods that allow for individual adjustments.

Adjustments to Individual Differences Change with Advancement through the Curriculum

The problem of adjusting to individual differences changes in at least three ways during the school years. First, the range of reading capability found within any classroom increases as the pupils become more and more proficient in reading. You will recall that a beginning second-grade class has a range of reading capability of about two and a half years, while a beginning sixth-grade class has a range of approximately seven years. The range increases at each higher grade level through high school and beyond. This difference in range does not necessarily mean that the teacher at higher grade levels has more difficult problems of adjusting to individual differences than do teachers at lower grade levels. It does mean, however, that there will have to be a greater difference between the level of difficulty in the materials used. An inspection of the difference between the material that the average fourth-grader can read and the material that the average sixth-grader can read will not be as apparent as the difference between material that an average second-grade child can read and the material that a child approximately halfway through the first grade can read. The rate of reading growth during the early grades is very rapid, and the fineness of adjustment required to meet the reading capabilities within a second-grade class is more demanding than the adjustment needed to meet the range of reading capabilities in the sixth grade or beyond.

The second way in which adjustment to individual differences changes through the grades is found in the relative independence of students at the higher levels, as contrasted with children in the second grade. Teachers in the first and second grades have very few who can be called independent readers, while teachers at higher grade levels find an increasing proportion of independent readers. Although there are many independent readers at upper grade levels, this does not mean that adjustment to individual needs is not necessary, but it does mean that teachers can rely more upon individual assignments that can be done independently. In the basic reading program, in which skills and abilities are developed, the problem of the sixth-grade teacher, for example, is similar to that of the second-grade teacher.

The need for basic reading instruction is not diminished as the child advances. The teacher of the intermediate grades must be alert to the need for adjusting to the level of development in each child's reading skills and abilities. The teacher must be aware of the need for adjusting to the child's range of capabilities, of the importance of identifying his reading needs, and of giving systematic instruction to ensure balanced growth. It cannot be overemphasized that a systematic, well-organized program of instruction in reading is essential to the intermediate grades. Incidental reading instruction with social studies material, for example, will not suffice.

Another way in which adjustment to individual differences changes as students progress is in the amount of available and suitable reading material. The teacher in the intermediate grades has more material, at various levels, for the range of reading talent found within these grades than does the primary teacher. The secondary teacher has an even wider range of materials from which to choose. It must be remembered that even the poorest group of readers in a sixth-grade class are just as mature readers as the most competent readers in a beginning second-grade class.

In formulating programs for adjusting to individual differences, it is essential to recognize the changes that occur throughout the school years. It is fortunate that as the range of reading capability increases, the independence of the children in the class is increasing and that there is a wider selection of suitable materials available. It also should be remembered that at all levels of instruction there is an abundance of materials suitable for the capable readers. The problem is difficult only for the poor readers. Fortunately, the number of materials suitable for poor readers increases in the higher grades.

Adjustments to Individual Differences Change According to the Phase of the Reading Curriculum Considered

The child, at all levels of advancement, must have at least four types of reading experiences to become a proficient reader. First, the child must progress through a systematic set of reading experiences designed to show him how to read. Second, the child must participate in those reading experiences in which reading is used as an aid in gaining understanding and knowledge within subject matter areas. Third, the child must have reading experiences designed to enhance personal development, interests, and tastes. These are experiences that give broad contacts with children's literature, enhance understanding of self, enlarge awareness of social relationships, and develop aesthetic appreciations. Fourth, the child must have experiences designed to correct reading faults. This phase of the program can be described as reeducative or corrective. There is probably no child who, from time to time, does not have reading faults, or who does not need more practice in some reading skill or ability.

The adjustment to individual needs and capabilities in each of these phases of the reading program is a different problem. Adjustments suitable for one phase of the reading curriculum are not necessarily good for another. If the child's goal is to develop skills and abilities in reading, the adjustment to individual differences in reading is different than if the goal is to understand the content. The goals set by the teacher in these two situations are different. When the teacher is teaching social studies, her primary concern is developing the outcomes of social studies instruction, even though the children are using books for this purpose. When the teacher is teaching reading, her primary concern must be the development of skills and abilities in reading, even though the children may be reading in their basic readers material of the social studies type. It would be unfortunate if teachers thought that reading skills and abilities could be learned incidentally when the basic purpose is learning the subject matter of any of the content fields. It would be equally unfortunate if the basic reading program failed to give systematic instruction in the skills and abilities necessary to read materials of the content areas.

In summary, adjustment in the four types of reading experience is dictated by the results expected and the use of reading. In the basic reading program, some form of group instruction is advisable. In the second type—reading in other branches of the curriculum—it is likely that the experience curriculum or topical unit approach is desirable. In reading for personal development, a high individualized approach emphasizing the "right book for the right child" is most feasible.

In the reeducation or corrective phase of the program, the skill that needs attention prescribes the type of instruction needed and who among the children should work together. Much of the controversy over the most effective way to adjust to individual differences stems from the fact that proponents of one type of adjustment over another are actually concerned with one particular phase of the reading program which especially interests them. It should be remembered that these phases are not completely discrete. For example, when the children have a social studies lesson, the teacher may discern that certain ones are having difficulty in finding places on a map, and may surmise that the cause of their difficulty is that they are ineffective in interpreting the marginal key numbers and letters. The teacher would then call these children aside and reeducate them in the skill needed in map reading. Although this skill was covered in the basic reading program, these children failed to learn it.

Adjustments to Individual Differences Change with Changes in School Organization

As the child progresses through the grades, the school organization changes. The usual type of organization in the primary grades is a self-contained classroom. A single teacher is responsible for learning activities in the primary class. This changes in the intermediate grades. In most school systems, there are special teachers for music, art, physical education, and other specialized areas. In some school systems, there are departmentalized arrangements in which teachers devote their entire day to teaching arithmetic, reading, or some other subject. In most secondary schools, the students have different teachers for each subject.

In the secondary school, understanding a student as fully as is necessary for adjusting to his reading needs is more difficult than in the primary grades. This is so because the secondary school teacher may be teaching as many as 150 different students in five classes for an hour a day, while the primary teacher lives rather closely with some twenty-five or more children during the day. It is fortunate that reading growth begins when the teacher and children live and work together throughout the entire day, because a detailed understanding of the child's interests, needs, drives, and levels of reading competency is necessary if proper provision for his reading needs is to be made. The application of this detailed information is crucial when the child is a relatively immature and dependent learner.

As stated, differences in school organization can complicate the problem of recommending adjustments to individual differences. In the secondary school, the need for guidance programs to collect information about the students and to see that it reaches the teachers who must make the adjustments must be fulfilled. This is not so essential a recommendation in the primary grades, for the teacher in this case can observe the children throughout the year.

Adjustment to Individual Differences Must Be Realistic in the Time Required

In considering suitable methods of adjusting to individual differences in reading, the time it requires becomes exceedingly important. The time that can be devoted to basic instruction in reading, for example, is limited. At all levels of instruction, other learning is taking place during the school day, and the efficient use of time in all school activities is fundamental. Reading is no exception. Those methods of adjustment, then, that make undue demands on either the teacher's instructional time or the class's working time must be rejected. A teacher must organize her class in the most efficient way. She cannot, for example, devote her entire time to developing reading skills and abilities for just one child at the expense of the other members of the class, no matter how urgent the child's need.

Programs that recommend that each child have a different book for his individual needs for basic instruction are unrealistic. It is necessary for the teacher, in developing reading skills and abilities, to introduce the material, to establish purposes, to develop background, to introduce new vocabulary, to guide reading through pertinent questions, to discuss the selection after it is read, and to give comprehension exercises related to the selection. The new words must be related to previously learned words in order to develop word-recognition techniques, and the selection must be used creatively so that the children feel they have completed the experience. Faced with such instructional demands, it is apparent that the teacher cannot have each child reading a different book while she is teaching the class to develop skills and abilities in reading. There simply would not be enough time. If we assume that the teacher devotes an hour a day to systematic instruction in reading development, she would have somewhat less than two minutes in which to accomplish the fundamentals of reading instruction for each different selection that some twenty-five children were reading.

Because of the time factor, some form of grouping for basic reading instruction is recommended. It must be recognized that even if the class is divided into three groups, each reading a different topic, the teacher who devotes an hour a day to basic reading instruction must divide her time among each of the three groups. Whatever method of adjusting to individual differences in reading is adopted, the efficient use of teacher and class time must receive careful consideration.

Teacher Energy and Time for Preparation Are Not Unlimited

Methods of adjusting to individual difference and of adopting a class organization must be realistic in their demands on the teacher. Sometimes it is suggested, for example, that teachers prepare the exercises to correct a faulty learning or to reinforce skills and abilities that the children have only partially learned. These recommendations are justified. But if the teacher were to prepare materials to meet all of the reeducative or practice needs of a class of twenty-five pupils, she would need more than a twenty-four hour day. The use of commercially prepared supplementary materials suitable to the child's level of development is recommended as one means of saving the teacher's energy and preparation time.

In certain methods of group instruction in the basic reading program, the teacher is expected to teach three discrete sections in reading and therefore is expected to make three preparations. These involve the collection of pictures and other means of developing readiness, background, interest, and understanding of word meanings. They also include analysis of the stories or selections to be read by each group and the preparation necessary to develop the specific comprehension abilities and word-recognition techniques for three separate lessons. They entail finding three separate sets of related reading materials and planning three separate activities related to what is being read.

Though there are many plans for adjusting to individual differences in reading, whichever is used, the fact that the teacher is a person whose time and energy are not unlimited must be taken into account. The fact that children like to work and do things together must also be recognized. It must be remembered when formulating the approach to basic reading instruction that they are growing in many ways other than in reading capability, that their reading development is not necessarily uniform, that reading is a very complex learning, and that class time is limited. All these considerations have to be taken into account when planning adjustments to individual rates of growth in reading.

MEETING INDIVIDUAL DIFFERENCES IN READING

A major responsibility of the school is to help each child develop to the limit of his capability. Any failure in the instructional program to adjust to individual differences in reading has two effects: first, failure to adjust materials and methods in reading instruction to the range of reading capability found within any classroom impedes growth in reading; second, failure to adjust the difficulty of reading material to the known reading capabilities of individual pupils in the classroom reduces the usefulness of printed material as an aid to learning in all areas. In addition, material which does not challenge the capable learners in the various content areas limits the possibility of superior achievement in those areas for the brighter children and also limits their growth in reading. Exposing the less able readers to materials that are too difficult reduces for them the usefulness of printed material as an aid to learning, and it can cause serious confusions and rejection of reading, thereby causing reading disabilities.

The entire reading curriculum of the children in a classroom must be adjusted to their individual reading capabilities, if the printed page is to become an effective tool of learning, and if reading disability is to be prevented. A fifth-grade child, for example, who can read material of seventh-grade difficulty with ease and profit should have many reading experiences at that level of difficulty. A fifth-grade child who is unable to read third-grade material comfortably will not profit much from holding a fifth-grade book in his hands and staring at it. This child would profit from reading a book more in keeping with his reading capabilities.

Individual differences in reading must be provided for throughout the curriculum, if printed material is to become an effective aid to learning for all the members of the class and if maximum growth in reading is to be achieved. The adjustment of instruction to individual differences in reading is more than just an approach. It is a combination of approaches and adaptation of methods of instruction that encourage individual rates of growth.

The various approaches to meeting individual differences in teaching reading are difficult to discuss and to evaluate, because each phase of the reading curriculum has special problems. The basic program in reading is probably the most complex in the curriculum in adjusting to individual differences. This phase of the curriculum must assume responsibility for developing in an orderly, sequential manner the skills and abilities needed for success in all other reading activities. Adjustment to individual differences in the basic reading program must be such that there is little chance for gaps in learning, for overemphases resulting in loss of balance among the skills and abilities, and for persistence of faulty habits with consequent confusion and deterioration of reading progress. When reading is used as an aid to learning, adjusting to individual differences is considerably less complex and resolves itself into bringing children and books realistically together so that the topics under consideration can be effectively studied. In personal development reading, the problem is still less complex. This phase of the reading curriculum can be individual, with guided reading programs in which children and books are brought together according to each child's level of reading maturity, interests, personal growth and needs. Neither an orderly sequence of skill development nor the knowledge and understanding of a curricular field need to be considered. The sole problem here is that of guiding each child into books that can be read comfortably and with pleasure and that develop him as a person.

The importance of finding suitable material for every situation cannot be overemphasized. In all reading, the child must have material that he can read effectively. At times there should be material with which he must struggle, but he must be able to win. In this way the child will increase stature in reading. More often, the child must read material which causes little or no difficulty. It is through such reading that the child gains fluency and the ability to understand the ideas of the author.

In the basic reading program, the difficulty of the material is ever-increasing. As soon as the child is comfortable in reading, the difficulty is increased so that the learner is continually challenged. Fortunately, material is well-introduced, difficulties are anticipated, and instruction on how to proceed is given.

Materials that the child reads independently in other phases of the curriculum should be somewhat less difficult than those in his basic reading program. This is especially true of the guided reading program. The teacher does not have time to give the necessary instruction in reading for twenty-five different references. The materials for both the content fields and for personal development should be at such a level of difficulty that they can be studied and read independently without faulty reading.

There are many ways in which the problem of adjusting to individual differences in the program of basic instruction in reading can be attacked. Many administrative and curricular plans involving schoolwide adjustments have been tried. Some of the better known are *ability grouping* among the classes according to intelligence, reading capability, or average achievement; yearly *retention or advancement* based upon overall educational advancement or reading achievement; *continuous growth* or *ungraded primary* plans in which the child is advanced to a higher reading level upon completion of the current reading program; *team teaching* which involves a large group of children taught together by several teachers in one large room for many lessons, then separated for reading instruction according to level of advancement; and *special rooms* where children of like reading maturity are taught reading, but for the rest of the day are in the regular classroom with other children of their own ages. As yet an adequate solution to the problem has not been found and maybe never will be.

Flexible grouping plans are very likely the best and most widely used approaches in adjusting to individual differences in reading. In the basic reading program, in which an orderly introduction of reading skills and abilities is essential and a gradual expansion of vocabulary load is demanded, it is likely that for certain parts of the instruction three reading groups are desirable. There can be no method of promotion nor any static method of grouping that will solve the problem. When grouping is flexible, many of the difficulties are avoided, and grouping becomes one of the best single means of individualizing instruction in reading.

Grouping procedures must be flexible in three ways. First, the group formed for basic reading instruction should be used for that phase of the curriculum only, and the children should be regrouped according to need in other phases of the curriculum. Second, the children who need instruction in a certain reading skill or ability should form a temporary instructional group even if they come from different basic reading groups. Third, a child should be able to move readily from one group to another if he improves in reading ability enough to be better suited to a more advanced group. A child also should be able to move to a less advanced group without stigma if he has been absent, or if for any other reason needs to be with a less mature reading group. A child may even meet with two groups for a time.

When the children use reading as an aid to learning in the content fields, the class sometimes profits from working together as well as in groups. There is a great need for material, differentiated in difficulty, in the content fields, so that the individual differences in reading can be met realistically and practically. When reading children's literature, it is often wise to have the entire class working together. A book shared through reading aloud parts of a favorite story or showing a new book added to the room library could involve the entire class. In the reeducative phase of the reading program, the entire class might profit from a demonstration of a word-recognition technique and could be taught together.

Instruction with multiple, flexible grouping and with materials that allow the whole class to participate while each child is working with material he can read will do much to allow children to grow in reading at the rate best for each. When adjustments to levels of reading capability are combined with attention to individual needs, the teaching of reading can be adjusted to individual differences. This instruction will do much to prevent minor misunderstandings from accumulating to the point at which the child becomes confused and develops reading difficulties.

This administrative plan for meeting individual differences is designed to give a good teacher a more reasonable chance of making these adjustments. But no matter what arrangement is adopted, the crux of the adjustment lies in the ability of the teacher to diagnose the needs of the children and to be ready to provide whatever corrective help is needed.

DIAGNOSTIC TEACHING IN THE CLASSROOM

The effectiveness of diagnostic teaching is based on the extent to which the teacher knows each child within the classroom. In order to attain maximum growth in reading and to avoid confusions in learning, the teacher must be aware of and adjust to each child's capacities, physiological condition, emotional and social adjustments, interests, attitudes, and general level of reading ability.

Besides these personal, cognitive, and physical characteristics, the teacher must know the child's reading development. It is to the child's growth in the specific skills and abilities in reading, above all else, that the instructional program must be geared. Diagnostic teaching is based on an understanding of the *reading* strengths and needs of each child. This knowledge must be used to modify instructional procedures so that teaching, adjusted to the changing needs of the children, can be maintained. This teaching centers on continuous diagnosis of the skill development of each child and on flexibility in instruction so that the teacher can alter the general procedures or methods to meet the specific needs of the individual.

One child may find most of the learnings relatively easy but some difficult and time-consuming. One child may find the knowledge of sound-symbol relationships relatively easy to learn, whereas he may acquire little skill in using meaning clues to word recognition. In the same class with the same instruction, another child may quickly develop too much dependence upon meaning clues and too little skill in sound-symbol relationships. Fortunately, most children maintain a rather consistent balance among the essential skills and abilities of reading and need only a small and infrequent amount of attention to maintain growth. Even for these children, the teacher should be alert to neglected skills or knowledges. Sometimes serious disabilities are simply the result of minor confusions which have been allowed to continue.

Most children maintain consistent reasonable achievement in reading. These children are helped if the teacher recognizes their minor deviations from effective, balanced reading growth and gives added or modified instruction to overcome any faulty or inadequate learning. Some children require more careful and continuous diagnosis than do others. Children who have more complex difficulties in learning to read make up only a small percentage of those being taught. Usually there are no more than two or three in a classroom of twenty-five children. In these instances, more thorough and time-consuming appraisals may be needed. These children may also require a more intensive program of remediation. Some of their difficulties may be too time-consuming or too complex to be diagnosed and corrected by the classroom teacher. However, a thorough diagnosis of a particular child's reading problem, accompanied by an *appropriate individual educational plan of remediation* made by a reading specialist, will enable the classroom teacher to correct the difficulty without interfering with the progress of the rest of the class. In other cases, the child can be served best in a reading center. These are decisions that must be made cooperatively by the classroom teacher and the reading specialist.

Every child's reading growth must be appraised continuously if his progress is to be at a high level and if any confusion is to be detected before the more stubborn problems develop. Work samples, always present in the day-by-day teaching and learning activities of a class, enable the expert teacher to gain familiarity with each child's needs. More systematic observations may be made through informal diagnosis or standardized testing. In studying the children's reading patterns, the teacher uses many sources of available information to decide on the instructional modifications. These sources will be discussed later in this book.

Many teachers keep a diagnostic notebook in which they list the children within each instructional group. As the teacher studies each child's reading pattern, she makes a notation of any reading characteristic that might limit the child's reading growth and of any indication of visual difficulty, auditory limitation, negative attitude, tendency toward fatigue, or anything else she observes. For example, a teacher might notice that one child, poor in comprehension, is a word-by-word reader; another child, good in using analytical skills, is ineffective in using context clues as an aid to word recognition; a third child has a limited meaning vocabulary; another reads rapidly, but with many inaccuracies, because of uncertainty about initial blends and digraphs; still another child reads slowly because he overarticulates as he reads; another has excellent word-recognition capabilities, is able to comprehend all the details in a passage, but is relatively ineffective in organizing, evaluating, and reflecting on what he has read. The teacher rightly feels that all of these types of problems can be corrected while teaching the group as a whole.

The expert teacher makes individual adjustments in the regular reading lessons. As the children progress through the reading lesson, the teacher has many opportunities to give each one the necessary experiences needed to overcome particular problems.

Knowing the results of all the appraisals, including her daily observations, the teacher is able to modify the general approach to reading so as to adjust instruction. The more diversified the approach, the greater the opportunity for the teacher to make such adjustments. This may be one reason why combined approaches to reading prove more effective than do narrow programs.

Most reading lessons can be separated into introductory, guided reading, and follow-up phases. During the introductory phase, which includes introducing the lesson, developing concepts and word meanings, introducing unknown word patterns, and setting purposes for reading a selection, instructional adjustments can be made to help children with certain types of reading problems. In the guided silent reading and discussion phase, other types of instructional modifications are possible. During the follow-up phase of teaching the lesson, which includes exercises to develop specific skills and abilities and related recreational and self-selected reading, there are many other opportunities for fulfilling individual needs.

During the introductory phase of teaching a selection, the teacher gives the child who is weak in the use of context clues more opportunities to select from among the new words being introduced those that fit the context of either oral sentences or those presented on the chalkboard. The teacher gives the child having difficulty with initial blends more opportunities to work on those presentations that emphasize similarity of initial blends in known and unknown words. The child with a limited meaning vocabulary should discuss the pictures and concepts for clarification of word meanings. He should be encouraged to attend to the meanings of all words introduced, so that the habit of attending to words and their meanings is fostered. When the purposes for reading are being developed, children limited in specific types of comprehension should be given more opportunities to discuss how to read for a specific purpose. The teacher might even adjust the purpose for reading. For example, the child who reads to note the details but is poor in reflecting on what is read, might be asked to read the selection in order to tell in one sentence what the selection was about, or to write a title for the selection.

During the guided reading and discussion phase, the teacher might call upon the children to relate some of the content of the selection. If there is a misconception, the teacher should use this as an instructional opportunity to correct the faulty reading instead of calling upon another child for the correct response. The teacher should have the child who made the mistake find the place where the idea was presented and then determine with him how the error came about. In this way, the error could be used to help the child overcome the problem.

In the follow-up phase, the teacher has unlimited scope in adapting to individual needs. In the skill and ability exercises prepared by the teacher, emphasis can be placed where it is needed. In the skill development workbooks, the teacher may excuse a child who depends too much on context clues from those exercises emphasizing their use. Or the word-by-word reader may be excused from word-drill exercises and be encouraged to prepare a conversational selection for reading aloud, stressing reading the selection in the way people talk.

Most of these adjustments are made by the classroom teacher who is sensitive to the needs of each child and who makes modifications to correct any confusion before it becomes seriously limiting to his future growth. Such a teacher is a *diagnostic teacher*. If this teaching is coupled with a flexible grouping plan, the broad use of children's literature, and a stimulating learning environment in which children feel free to participate and express themselves, the reading program will provide maximum growth for all and will limit the frequency of reading disablity because *it is the teacher who makes the difference* in adjusting to individual differences. The classroom teacher, however, cannot be expected to solve all problems in reading instruction. Her work must be supplemented, for each child who needs it, with a diagnostic and remedial program. The classroom teacher cannot spend the time necessary to correct the more complex reading problems. Therefore, every school should have the services of a reading specialist. The reading specialist has three responsibilities, those of a consultant, a diagnostician, and a remedial teacher. The classroom teacher's responsibilities are to prevent disabilities, to aid in their early detection, and to carry out those corrective procedures appropriate to the classroom. It is the hope of the authors that this book will aid both the classroom teacher and the reading specialist in helping all pupils to become more effective readers.

SUMMARY

One of the most complex problems confronting the teacher is that of adjusting instruction to individual differences in reading. The children within any classroom vary greatly in reading maturity, reading habits, intellectual capabilities, and physical characteristics. The teacher must organize the class and the instruction so that each child can work up to capacity. The teachers of today are better equipped with better professional training, improved materials, and more effective assessment procedures necessary for making these adjustments than were the teachers of the past.

The range of reading ability found in any classroom is large. The better the instruction and the longer it continues, the greater will be the range in reading achievement. If instruction is excellent, not only will the average reading performance of the class be raised, but also the range of reading achievement within the class will become greater. Each succeeding year of instruction increases the range of reading achievement within the class. There will be extensive overlapping in the reading capabilities found in the various grades. Indeed, there is so much that the teacher, at any grade level, must be able to fulfill the reading needs of the children for grades above and below the one she is teaching. If the teacher organizes the class into three instructional groups, the range within the upper and the lower group will still be so great that further grouping is required. Adjustment to the upper group is somewhat easier than it is to the lower group because of the reading competence and independence of the children and the greater availability of appropriate materials.

Among the more important considerations in meeting individual differences in reading are the similarities and differences in children, the nature of individual reading development, the complexities in learning to read, the changes of approaches due to differences in curriculum and school organization, the differences at the various grade levels, and the need for realistic use of class time and teachers' energies.

The need for adjusting to individual differences in reading throughout the entire curriculum makes adaptation somewhat more complicated than adjusting to the basic reading program alone. The methods and class organization effective for one type of reading will not always be good for another. The types of reading may be classified roughly as basic instruction in reading, reading and study in other phases of the curriculum, independent personal development or recreational reading, and reeducative or remedial reading. These phases of reading are not completely separate. In general, the approaches to individual differences used in these phases are different, and much of the controversy over methods stems from the fact that the proponents of one approach over another are emphasizing different phases of reading instruction.

Some approaches that have been tried include retention, curriculum adjustment plans, fixed grouping plans, and flexible grouping plans. Among these, the flexible grouping plans, utilizing materials written on many levels of difficulty, seem to have the most promise. Whatever approach is used, the teacher should be sure that groups are not fixed but can be adjusted to facilitate the outcomes expected from the instruction. Also the number and size of the groups should be compatible with the maturity and independence of the children. In many instances, the groups should be reading about a topic of concern to the entire class, and the best and the poorest readers should have opportunities to work together.

Despite the type of school and classroom organization used to aid the teacher in adjusting to differences in reading growth, the skill of the teacher is the most important factor. The crux of meeting the individual differences found among children lies in the ability of the teacher to diagnose the needs of the children and to correct their minor confusions in reading before these confusions become major disabilities. Even under the best classroom instruction, a limited number of pupils develop reading difficulties that can be solved only by special diagnostic and remedial procedures.

STUDY QUESTIONS

1. Why is adjusting to individual differences important?
2. Why might accommodating individual differences in reading be easier for a teacher in the higher grades than for a teacher in the

lower grades, even though the range of reading achievement is much greater as the students reach the higher grades?

3. If students were grouped according to their reading achievement, why would individual differences still be an important concern?

4. What are the four types of reading experiences necessary for proficient reading? Describe a classroom activity which would provide a reading experience for each of the four types.

5. Why should children be grouped for reading instruction?

6. What is a diagnostic teacher?

SELECTED READINGS

BOND, G. L. "Employ More Diagnostic Teaching in the Classroom." *Reading Improvement,* 1976, *13,* 35–39.

BURMEISTER, L. E. *Reading Strategies for Secondary School Teachers,* Chaps. 1–4. Reading, Mass.: Addison–Wesley Publishing Co. Inc., 1974.

HARRIS, A. J., AND E. R. SIPAY. *How to Increase Reading Ability,* 8th ed., Chap. 5. New York: Longman, Inc., 1985.

HEILMAN, A. W., T. R. BLAIR, AND W. H. RUPLEY. *Principles and Practices of Teaching Reading,* 6th ed., Chap. 11. Columbus, OH: Charles E. Merrill Publishing Company, 1986.

MUESER, A. M. *Reading Aids through the Grades,* 4th ed., sec. 1. New York: Teachers College Press, 1981.

3

Description
of Disabled Readers

Most children grow in reading with relatively desirable and consistent patterns of proficiencies. They develop reading capacities consistent with their general learning capability. Children's instructional needs can be met effectively by the classroom teacher using the approaches suggested for adjusting to individual differences in reading. There are some children, however, whose reading growth is so atypical, so different from that of the usual child, that they constitute an instructional challenge. Often the classroom teacher can diagnose these difficulties and give these children the corrective or reeducative help that they need, so that they can continue to progress in reading growth. At other times, these disabled readers become so confused that they require more time for individual help than the classroom teacher can devote to them. In both instances, the child is a disabled reader, but the nature and severity of the disability determines the best approach.

In considering the nature of reading disability, it is necessary to isolate the group of children to be discussed, define the disabled reader, explain the characteristics that set the child apart from the general population, and describe the categories into which disabled readers fall.

The child who is a disabled reader cannot be described as one whose reading ability is below his achievement in other school subjects. Although some disabled readers can be so described, the majority will be low both in reading and in general achievement. This is true because poor reading ability so limits other achievement that it is the rare child who can attain success in school in spite of having a reading disability. It also is important to note that the child who is low in both reading and general achievement may or may not be a disabled reader. A child may be poor in reading and poor in the other school subjects for reasons other than disability in reading.

The disabled reader is the child who is so handicapped in reading that his educational career is in jeopardy. Not only is the child's educational growth imped-ed, but frequently his reading patterns are so confused that future growth in reading becomes improbable. This child is ineffective in using print as an aid to learning. This child is often a discouraged student who thoroughly dislikes reading. In many cases, this child becomes so frustrated over the inability to read that personal adjustment suffers. This child may feel quite anxious while reading or may some-times demonstrate maladaptive adjustment in general.

George illustrated the former type of poor adjustment when he said, "I don't want to learn to read. I don't want to read about a boy that has a boat. I want to have one myself." Many children who have trouble with reading complain about the material not meeting their needs, but when they can read that same material, they find a new interest.

Amy displayed a functional disorder when it became apparent that she could not read even for two or three minutes without developing a headache and an upset stomach. She claimed to have eye trouble, although this could not be detected by thorough examination. She would work on puzzle-type material and numbers for long periods of time with no sign of visual discomfort or stomach unrest. After she attained success in reading by careful, individually planned work based on a com-plete diagnosis, she showed no signs of her former disorders. Not all children who have both poor reading and poor personal adjustment can be said to have them as a result of poor growth in reading. Sometimes the child is disturbed for other reasons and reading suffers along with other achievements.

Typically, the disabled reader is a child of intellectual capability who has (for reasons to be discussed in the following chapters) failed to grow in reading. The child is not living up to potential as a learner in reading. The child is likely to be ineffective in all that is expected in school. The child may reject reading, become discouraged, acquire maladaptive adjustment patterns, and become increasingly less able to learn. The child is in need of educational help.

IDENTIFYING THE DISABLED READER

The problem now confronting us is different from the one discussed in the preceding chapter. The identification of reading disability is much more complicated than sectioning a class into reading groups or even finding the right level at which to start instruction for each child in a class. A reading test alone is not enough to identify the reading disabled children in a school. There are many poor readers in every class who cannot be classified as disabled readers, and there are some seemingly ade-quate readers who are truly disabled. Therefore we must discuss the factors that need to be considered in order to determine whether a pupil is disabled in reading or is just a poor reader.

Opportunity to Learn

The child who is classified as disabled in reading must be distinguished from the child who has not had an opportunity to learn. If we did not take into account the opportunity of a child to learn, we would have to say that nearly all children are disabled readers before they enter the first grade. Although it is true that their ability to find meaning in the printed page is negligible and in no way in keeping with their ability to listen, they cannot be disabled because they have not yet been taught. They have had no opportunity to learn. They may have a relatively large listening vocabulary, but the typical child entering the first grade cannot read many more words than his own name. Most children, for example, cannot read the word STOP if it is taken off the octagonal sign on which they are accustomed to seeing it. In a way, they have had the opportunity to learn, because there has always been printed matter before them. But they did not receive systematic organized instruction, so, in reality, they have not had the opportunity to learn. Even though the child entering the first grade is not able to read as well as he can listen, he is not disabled because he is doing as well as could be expected of him.

The older child who has come from a non-English-speaking country to the United States would not be considered to have a reading disability, even though he did have an instructional problem. He may need to start learning to read elementary English, but he cannot be called a disabled reader. He should have material different from that for the six-year-old beginner, and he will need special methods of instruction. But he is not a disabled reader. He is a child who cannot read English because he did not have the opportunity to learn.

The lack of opportunity to learn is even more complicated than is indicated in the case of the child who has not yet entered school or is non-English-speaking. Some children will be disabled in reading in comparison to their other intellectual achievements, because they did not start to learn to read as early as they started other verbal learnings. A gifted child, for example, who is just entering the third grade may have the verbal facility of the usual sixth-grade child. He could not be expected to read as well as a typical sixth-grade child, because he has received reading instruction for only two years, while his general language has developed over a period of eight years.

Verbal Competency

The listening ability of a child is frequently used to indicate the level at which we could expect him to read. If the child has a superior listening vocabulary, he may be expected to read at a higher level than can other children of his age. If the child is able to understand paragraphs of more than usual difficulty read aloud to him, he should be able to read better than those children who have less listening ability. The child's verbal ability is measured by a test such as listening comprehension on the Diagnostic Reading Scales, Spache (1981).

There are two considerations the diagnostician must recognize in using the child's general verbal competence as an indicator of the reading level which he can be expected to attain. The first is that it may not be safe to assume that a child who is low in both reading and verbal ability does not have a reading disability. Poor performance on listening comprehension tests may indicate that the child has had one avenue of developing verbal ability closed to him. A child, for example, who has been a poor reader from the first grade to the sixth will not have had an opportunity to develop language equal to that of his natively equal counterpart who has always been a good reader. The poor reader will not have had as much experience with words because he has not read as widely. Nor will he have had as much experience in understanding paragraphs.

Disabled readers have been found to score lower on the Verbal Scale of the Wechsler Intelligence Scales (Revised) than they do on the Performance Scale (Brock 1982; Moore and Wielan 1981; and Roberts 1983). These findings could indicate either that these children have native limitations in verbal ability compared to their general intelligence and are therefore poor readers, or that they are limited in developing language because they are poor readers and therefore lack verbal experience. An able child who is a poor reader cannot be expected to develop as extensive a vocabulary and other verbal abilities as can a good reader. The use of verbal ability alone as a criterion for classifying children as reading disabled might classify certain children as verbally inept although, in truth, they are reading disabled and would benefit from remedial instruction.

The second problem in using a discrepancy between verbal ability and reading to classify a child as a disabled reader is that it does not take into account the opportunity of the child to learn. Two children, for example, may have the same measured verbal ability. One, however, is only a second-grade child while the other is a sixth-grade child. The second-grader has had only one year of reading instruction while the other child has had five. The younger child cannot be expected to read as well as the older child, who has had five times as much reading instruction, even though they measure the same on an oral vocabulary test or a test of ability to understand paragraphs read aloud.

Verbal competency should be one consideration in classifying a child as a disabled reader, but it will often mislead the teacher or diagnostician if used as the only criterion. The length of time in school and the opportunity to learn to read must also be considered. The accuracy of the estimate of verbal aptitude also must be taken into account if all the children who are in need of specific help in reading are to be located and if a child is not to be misjudged.

In identifying the child who is a disabled reader, teachers often compare the child's reading achievement with his degree of success in subjects requiring a minimum of reading. Arithmetical computation is used frequently as one subject in which success is less influenced by reading achievement. If the child is doing well in arithmetic and poorly in reading, the child is likely to be a disabled reader. Such information adds to the accuracy of locating children who are disabled readers rather than poor readers who are doing almost as well as can be expected.

Success in nonreading fields does indicate in most cases how well children are able to apply themselves to learning situations other than reading. If they are not motivated to achieve, they are likely to show ineffective learning in these fields as well as in reading. If they have limited ability to learn they will do as poorly in nonreading fields as in reading. But when children are successful in nonreading fields, yet have difficulty in reading, they are likely to be able, motivated children who are disabled readers because of faulty learning. These children can usually be helped a great deal by remedial instruction in reading. Although success in nonreading fields is insufficient evidence in itself to classify children as disabled readers, it is often used as one fact to be considered in making such a classification.

Monroe (1932), also cited in Harris and Sipay (1985), used arithmetic achievement as one of the criteria for selecting children who would profit from remedial instruction in reading. She used a reading index (R.I.) to find those children who were farther behind in reading than was reasonable to expect. The index was determined by using the child's average reading age (R.A.), chronological age (C.A.), arithmetic age (A.A.), and mental age (M.A.). The reading index (R.I.) can be calculated by using the following formula:

$$\text{R.I.} = \frac{\text{R.A.}}{(\text{C.A.} + \text{M.A.} + \text{A.A.}) \div 3}$$

Experience shows that a child with a reading index of 0.80 or below practically always has a reading disability. Those with indexes between 0.80 and 0.90 tend to be borderline. Some of the latter will need remedial instruction, others will not. All of those who are borderline should be tested further to see if irregularities in their reading profiles indicate serious problems.

Mental Ability

Mental ability is related to reading achievement. The mere fact that the child has high intellectual ability itself does not guarantee that he will be successful in reading, especially in the early years. Nor does the fact that a child has trouble in reading indicate that the child is mentally limited. Evidence shows that the relationship between intelligence and reading success becomes greater when populations are sampled at successively higher grade levels (Bond & Dykstra, 1967; Rubin, 1982, p. 50) ranging from approximately .50 at the end of the first grade to .80 at the high school level. These correlations indicate that factors in addition to mental age influence a child's success in reading. Some children, who begin relatively slowly in the primary grades, later increase their rate of learning and surpass some of their contemporaries. Thus, early success does not necessarily indicate ultimate reading achievement.

These comparative relationships seem reasonable. In the early stages of their reading development, children are concerned with the mechanical aspects of reading. For instance, word-recognition skills lean heavily upon visual and auditory discrimination. In the higher grades, the complexities of reading and study demand fine verbal discrimination, logical reasoning, abstract analysis, and other comprehension skills which require a high level of mental ability. It is not surprising that mental age and reading capability become more and more closely related as the reader progresses into more and more mature materials and reads for more and more mature purposes.

The mental ability of the child is often used as the basic criterion with which to compare reading capacity in order to judge the existence of a reading disability. The customary method of making this comparison is to use the mental age of the child as the key to reading expectancy. When the child's average reading is felt to be significantly lower than his mental age, the child is thought to be a disabled reader. While undoubtedly the true mental ability of the child should be used as a basic consideration in classifying a child as a disabled reader, caution is necessary for two reasons. First, the determination of mental capacity of a poor reader is difficult. Second, the problem is complicated by the fact that although mental age is calculated from birth, the child is not introduced to systematic instruction in reading until he is six or more years old.

In an attempt to consider age factors as well as mental age factors Harris and Sipay (1980) proposed the following formula for reading expectancy age:

$$\text{Reading Expectancy Age (R Exp A)} = \frac{2MA + CA}{3}$$

Using a division process, one can compare a child's present reading level with his expected reading level, to assess reading disability.

Assessing mental age. There are many types of tests which may be used to assess mental age. Four general types of measurement are commonly used. They are verbal group mental tests, nonverbal group mental tests, individual verbal mental tests, and individual performance mental tests. Each of these tests has its advantages and limitations. In classifying a child as a disabled reader, the particular measure of mental ability used must be considered carefully.

Verbal group mental tests. These are of little use in selecting children who will profit from remedial work in reading. These tests are, to a great extent, reading tests, and therefore the poor reader cannot demonstrate his true mental ability. Clymer (1952) has shown that at the fifth-grade level certain group intelligence tests gave no valid measure of the mental ability of the children who are reading in the lowest 40 percent of the class. To show the extent of misinterpretation possible by the uncritical use of such tests for disabled readers, the following example can be cited. At the end of kindergarten Mary was given an individual intelligence test, which indicated that she had an I.Q. of 115. In grade four, she was given a verbal mental group test and appraised to have an I.Q. of 80. Inasmuch as her reading achievement and general school performance were consistent with the 80 I.Q., no mismeasurement was suspected. She went into junior high school and in the ninth grade was given a verbal mental group test. Because of her reading difficulties, Mary could read neither the questions nor the answers. She marked her answer form mostly by guessing. She received an I.Q. of 56. The result, while somewhat consistent with her scholastic performance, seemed unreasonable to the counselor, so a complete assessment of Mary was made. When an individual intelligence test was given, the results indicated that she had an I.Q. of 104. Mary, in reality, had a marked reading disability. Her reading achievement measured at a third-grade level. She had ineffective decoding skills. She could comprehend but little and therefore could not show her true mental ability on a test that required reading.

Verbal group mental tests are often inappropriate for making comparisons between reading growth and mental growth. The one advantage to such tests is that they can be given to large groups. The results are useful in making comparisons among typical students. But they are worse than worthless in the case of poor readers, because the results are often considered accurate.

Nonverbal group mental tests. These tests can be used as a criterion for determining reading expectancy. They can be given to large groups and therefore save a great deal of testing time. They are useful in selecting children who have a notable discrepancy between their mental age and their reading age. These tests, although paper and pencil tests, do not require reading matter as a means of presenting the items. Therefore the disabled reader can take these tests unhampered by poor reading ability. The major difficulties with these tests are two: first, they are not as accurate in measurement as desirable for individual diagnosis; second, they do not appear to measure the type of mental ability needed for success in reading. They are, to some degree, performance tests rather than tests of reasoning ability. Nonetheless, they have merit as screening tests and can be administered by the classroom teacher, thus saving testing time. When reading disability is suspected, however, the results should be checked by more accurate, individual tests.

Individual verbal mental tests.   These are the most suitable measures of mental growth to be used with disabled readers. The Wechsler Intelligence Scale for Children, Revised and the Stanford-Binet Intelligence Scale are popular and useful tests of this type. They give an accurate measure of mental ability for able readers and have been shown to be affected only slightly by the lack of reading ability of disabled readers.

Individual performance mental tests.   These are useful in diagnosis of certain types of reading problems. They aid in measuring the mental ability of children who are hearing-impaired, those who have marked oral-expressive problems, or those who have other handicaps. These tests have the same limitations as other individual tests, since they are time-consuming and require trained examiners. Another limitation is that they do not emphasize the verbal aspects of intellectual growth.

Relating Mental Growth to Reading Expectancy

The problem of relating a child's mental growth to reading growth in order to estimate the level at which the child should be able to read is a complicated one. The usual way in which this judgment is made is to consider that the child should have reached a reading age or grade roughly comparable to his mental age or grade. Then, if a given child's reading grade is significantly lower than his mental grade, the child is classified as a disabled reader. The amount of discrepancy between reading grade and mental grade considered significant increases as the child grows older. In the primary grades from one-half to three-quarters of a grade difference is taken to be enough to classify the child as a disabled reader. In the intermediate grades, a difference of 1 to 1¾ grades is used. A second-grade child whose mental grade is 2.8 and whose reading is 2.2 would be thought a disabled reader. Similarly, in the second grade, a very able child whose mental grade is 4.0 and whose reading grade is 3.4 would be considered disabled. There is serious question, however, as to whether this latter conclusion is justified.

For example, the child with an I.Q. of 150 who enters the first grade at the age of 6.5 cannot be expected to read at a 4.3 grade level even though that would be about his mental grade. As a matter of fact, this child would be able to read little, if anything, because he has not yet been taught. The child has had no real opportunity to learn to read.

There are many possible ways of using the general intelligence of the child as a yardstick against which to judge reading growth. The results of mental tests in classifying a child as a disabled reader have been used with the mental age or grade as the level at which the child is expected to read. Most studies of overachievement and underachievement have used the mental age criterion to estimate who were the good and who were the poor achievers. These studies have universally found that bright children underachieve and dull children overachieve in comparison to their mental age.

The assumption that a child should be achieving up to his mental age needs careful inspection. Although it is true that learning such as listening or speaking vocabulary can be so judged, other learning cannot be expected to be related in the same way. The child of 150 I.Q. who is ten years old has a mental age of fifteen. For example, this means that he should, on the basis of his mental grade, be doing mathematics equal to that of about a tenth-grader instead of a fifth-grade child. But it is doubtful if such a child would know algebra and geometry, because the child has not yet met them. Reading achievement acts in much the same way.

Systematic instruction in reading is usually not begun before the first grade. The typical child, regardless of I.Q., has little if any measurable reading ability when starting the first grade. At this time, the child would be said to read at the 1.0 grade level. If we assume that the I.Q. is, in one respect, an index of rate of learning, we can estimate the reading potential of each child by means of the *reading expectancy* formula:

$$\left(\frac{\text{I.Q.}}{100} \times \text{years of reading instruction}\right) + 1.0 = \text{Reading Expectancy}$$

The 1.0 is added because the child who is just starting to learn to read is given a 1.0 grade score, and after one year of instruction the typical child will be classified as a 2.0 reader.

By this formula, the typical child with an I.Q. of 70 could be expected to read at the level of 1.7 at the end of one year of instruction, and at the end of two years of reading instruction, he should read at 2.4 grade level. Still using the same formula, the child with 100 I.Q. would be expected to read at 3.0 after two years of reading instruction, and the able child with 150 I.Q. would be expected to read at 4.0. At the end of 3½ years, a child with a 130 I.Q. could be expected to read at a 5.6 grade level, placing the numbers in the formula (130/100 × 3.5) + 1.0 = 5.55, which is the reading expectancy for that child. To the extent that all other elements that influence reading success are favorable, he could learn somewhat faster, thus exceeding reading expectancy. If, on the other hand, these other conditions were unfavorable, he would not read up to expectancy level and might even be so far behind that he would be considered a disabled reader.

Experience and research have shown this formula to be surprisingly accurate in estimating the potential reading ability of the typical child. As can be seen, the formula is easy to calculate, but the following considerations should be kept in mind:

1. The time of reading instruction is the years and months in school from the time systematic reading instruction was started. This typically begins with first grade. (Some slower learning children may have a delay of a year or so in starting to learn to read.)
2. Readiness training in kindergarten is not counted, even though such instruction does much to diminish the chances of disabilities from occurring once reading instruction has started.
3. If an I.Q. obtained from a Binet or Wechsler intelligence test is not available, it is suggested that a Slosson Intelligence Test given by the teacher or a group performance intelligence test score be substituted temporarily.

We must now consider the extent of discrepancy between the child's reading expectancy grade level and actual average reading grade, which would indicate that he is a disabled reader. Table 3-1 shows that this discrepancy increases grade by grade. In the first grade, for example, one-half year is a sufficiently large difference between reading expectancy and reading achievement to indicate a serious problem. Even children who are three-tenths of a year lower in reading achievement than we would expect them to be are considered seriously enough behind to be studied further as having a possible disability. At grade seven or above, the difference must be two or more years to be classified as a disability, and there must be a 1.3- to 2-year lag to indicate a possible disability, if supported by other evidence.

A child of superior intellect with a possible reading disability may appear to be progressing reasonably well in reading in comparison with the other children in his grade. The child may appear, for example, to be an efficient reader of third-

TABLE 3-1   Discrepancies Between Reading Expectancy and Achievement Which Indicate Disability at Each Grade Level

GRADE SCORE DISCREPANCY	GRADE IN SCHOOL						
	1	2	3	4	5	6	7 and Above
Indicating Disability	0.5 or more	.66 or more	.75 or more	1.0 or more	1.5 or more	1.75 or more	2.0 or more
Indicating Possible Disability	.3–.5	.4–.66	.5–.75	.7–1.0	.9–1.5	1.1–1.75	1.3–2.0

grade material even though he is only just finishing the second grade. His achievement in reading in comparison with his reading expectancy would place him in the region of doubt (a possible disability), but not significantly low enough to classify him as disabled. A study of his reading skill development might show irregularities, indicating that he was using faulty skills which, if allowed to persist, would limit him at more advanced levels.

Many reading disabilities that could have been discovered early do not become apparent until faulty reading techniques have become so entrenched that they interfere with reading at a more mature level. The tasks involved in reading change as materials become more difficult in structure and content, increasing demands are placed upon the reader. A reader's dependence upon use of immature skills can preclude the development of more advanced skills, eventually resulting in a reading disability. Yet such a disability might have been avoided easily if faulty reading techniques were identified and corrected early.

The disabled reader is, in general, one who has had an opportunity to learn to read but who is not reading as well as could be expected according to verbal ability, mental capacity, and success in nonreading learnings. He is, in reality, the child who is at the lower end of the reading distribution when compared with other children of the same age and general capability. The disabled reader is at the lower end for reasons which will be discussed in the following chapters. It should be noted, however, that there are other children of the disabled reader's general capability who are as far advanced in reading as the disabled reader is behind. These advanced readers have been fortunate and probably have been favorably endowed in other ways that influence effective reading growth.

CATEGORIES OF READING DISABILITIES

Children with reading difficulties can be classified into four categories.

1. General reading immaturity.   This category is composed of children who are significantly behind in reading when compared with other children of their general reading expectancy. There are no unusual characteristics about their reading patterns. Although these children are immature in reading, there is nothing especially wrong with the reading they do.

John, a fifth-grade boy of average intelligence, has always been disinterested in reading. As a result, he has read very little, far less than most of his classmates. Currently, he has great difficulty reading fifth-grade material, but reads third-grade material well and possesses reading skills typical of a normal third-grade child. John may be classified in the general reading immaturity group. Many disabled readers show general reading immaturity due to a variety of causes.

Remediation. Instruction should involve giving more experience in reading and systematic instruction at the child's level of reading achievement. These children do not require a reeducation in reading, but they do need adjustment in materials and instruction. If they are asked to read books that are too difficult for them, or if they are not given systematic instruction in reading at their level, they will very likely develop more complex reading disabilities.

2. Specific reading immaturity.

This classification is used for children who have specific limitations in their reading patterns.

Joan is able to read and understand the general significance of paragraphs difficult enough to challenge the reading skill of children of her age and intelligence. She cannot, however, read to follow directions or to organize longer selections. She has acquired general basic reading skills, but she has not learned to adapt them to all her reading purposes.

Remediation. Instruction should involve specific training in the areas in which the child is weak. Other adjustments will depend on the child's overall reading achievement. Many children with specific reading immaturity read at an acceptable level in general and require few adjustments other than the provision of specific training. Others may require adjusted materials.

3. Limiting reading disability.

This classification concerns those disabled readers who have serious deficiencies in their basic skills that limit their entire reading growth. Children who have a word-recognition deficiency, limiting mechanical habits, or inability to sense thought units, for example, fall into this category.

David has a limiting disability. He is a capable fifth-grade boy who is quite low in all types of reading. His intelligence enables him to grasp the significant ideas in a reading passage relatively well, even though he reads less well for specific detail. His ability to recognize words is even more immature. He is low in recognizing words in isolation, although in sentence and paragraph reading he does get aid from context clues. His basic problem, as detected through his oral reading and written work, appears to involve an inadequate approach to word attack. This limitation is not only the probable cause of David's reading disability, but it also threatens to impede any future growth unless corrected by careful remedial work.

Remediation. Children in this group need reeducation. Instruction must serve to help them unlearn some of the reading approaches they are currently employing and to teach them some new basic approaches to reading. Often these children are compensating in an unproductive manner because they failed to learn skills basic to continued reading growth. These children need the help of well-planned systematic remedial programs to correct their faulty reading approaches and to develop the previously unlearned skills that they need.

4. Complex reading disability.   This classification is really a subtype of limiting reading disability. These children not only have deficiencies in their reading, which limit further growth in reading, but in addition instructing them in reading is complicated by their avoidant attitudes toward reading and by their undesirable adjustments to their reading failure. Reeducating these children may be complicated further when they have sensory, physical, or other handicaps.

Remediation. Children in this group need careful assessment by a team of professionals in order to provide an appropriate remedial program. These childrens' learning handicaps must be recognized and planned for in order for successful reading remediation to be achieved. Constitutional and environmental factors will be discussed in the next three chapters. Modifications needed in the remedial treatment of complex reading disabilities are discussed in Chapter 13.

SUMMARY

Disabled readers are more than just children who cannot read well. They are children who are not reading as well as could be expected from their intellectual or verbal maturity. No two disabled readers are the same, and it is likely that no two disabilities are caused by the same set of circumstances. Many disabled readers become discouraged and frustrated when they read.

The classification of a child as a disabled reader rather than as just a poor reader must be based upon learning opportunity, verbal ability, achievement in learning situations other than reading, and the child's general mental ability. The mental ability of the child is used most often in assessing his reading expectancy. Care must be taken in measuring the mental ability of the disabled reader, because most tests require reading ability. For this reason, individual mental tests are the most suitable instruments.

The problem of using mental growth as a means of assessing reading expectancy is a complicated one. The use of mental age or grade as the sole criterion of expected attainment in reading is of questionable validity. A more sensible and useful approach would be to depend on calculations based on years of reading instruction and the child's I.Q.

Disabled readers can be grouped into descriptive categories according to the seriousness of the problem and the nature of the adjustment needed. General reading immaturity refers to those children whose reading ability is generally immature but otherwise well-balanced. Children with specific reading immaturity are low in one or more types of reading but are competent in basic reading skills and abilities. Children with limiting reading disability are deficient in basic reading abilities that preclude further growth in reading. Children with complex reading disability are those who cannot grow further in reading because of deficiencies in basic reading abilities. Their problems are complicated by learning handicaps such as rejection of reading, accompanying personality problems, and sensory or physical limitations.

STUDY QUESTIONS

1. How does verbal competency relate to reading competency? How is verbal competency measured?
2. Success in nonreading fields and mental ability are used to predict reading success. What are the advantages and disadvantages of each as a predictor?
3. What is the reading expectancy of a child with an I.Q. of 80 who is just beginning sixth grade and has had five years of reading instruction (grades one through five)? If this child's reading achievement is at a beginning third-grade level, is reading disability indicated?
4. Ralph was a pleasant cooperative seventh-grade student of average intelligence. He participated in many school activities and had many friends. However, he seemed to have unusual difficulty understanding and completing reading assignments in social studies. In other course work he did well, especially in math. When the reading teacher assessed Ralph's reading skills, she found that he was excellent in all aspects of word recognition and in understanding the details of his reading. However, he was a somewhat slow reader and quite poor in isolating major ideas and themes in longer selections. Which classification seems to best suit Ralph—general reading immaturity, specific reading immaturity, limiting reading disability, or complex reading disability?

SELECTED READINGS

HARRIS, A. J. AND E. R. SIPAY. *How to Increase Reading Ability*, 8th ed., Chaps. 1 and 6. New York: Longman, Inc., 1985.

KIRK, S. A., J. M. KLIEBHAN, AND J. W. LERNER. *Teaching Reading to Slow and Disabled Learners*, Chap. 1. Boston: Houghton Mifflin Company, 1978.

MCCORMICK, S. *Remedial and Clinical Reading Instruction*, Chaps. 5–8. Columbus, OH: Merrill Publishing Co. 1987.

SEARLS, E. F. *How to Use WISC-R Scores in Reading/Learning Disability Diagnosis*, Chaps. 1 and 6. Newark, DE: International Reading Association, 1985.

WILSON, R. M. AND C. J. CLELAND. *Diagnostic and Remedial Reading for Classroom and Clinic*, 5th ed., Chap. 3. Columbus, OH: Merrill Publishing Company, 1985.

4

Causes of Reading Disability: Physical Factors

Causes of reading disability are numerous. Rarely will a teacher or clinician find that a single factor has caused a child to be disabled in reading. It is almost always true that a reading disability is the result of several factors working together to impede successful reading progress. Reading is a complex process. Proficient reading depends upon the acquisition and versatile application of many intricately coordinated skills. These skills are acquired only through long, motivated practice under good guidance. Because the reading process is so complex, there are many opportunities for unfortunate complications to retard its growth. Various factors, operating singly or more often together, can block further progress in reading until they are discovered and eliminated, or until corrective instructional procedures can be devised to adjust to, or to circumvent, their effects.

Labels, such as dyslexia, sound serious, but do not provide so much as a hint of how to help a child, do not even have an accepted meaning, and certainly do more harm than good. Labeling usually does not provide useful remedial information. Finding out as precisely as possible what is needed to teach a child to read and then providing that help is more beneficial. A further complication in some cases is that it is difficult or impossible to distinguish cause from effect. It is easy, for example, to mistake emotional stress or behavioral problems as the cause of reading failure, when they are often the effect of a child's awareness of his failures in reading.

This chapter will discuss and evaluate the roles of various physical deficiencies or conditions as contributing causes of reading disability. Visual, auditory, and speech impairments and conditions of general health and neurological status will all be considered.

VISUAL IMPAIRMENT

Rutherford (1967, pp. 503–7) cites an extreme case of visual impairment. Janice seemed to be a well-adjusted child before entering first grade but then had great difficulty learning to read. Professional examination revealed severe visual impairment. On the way home, after receiving her corrective lenses, she asked her mother about the signboards along the street, the rear lights of cars, and even the leaves on trees. Of course Janice had seen them before, but not in the form and dimension in which they now appeared to her, which made them look so different that she could not identify them. It is no wonder that Janice was not able to learn to read before getting glasses.

It seems axiomatic that ocular comfort and visual efficiency are prerequisite to easy reading. When a child shows signs of becoming disabled in reading, the tendency of both teachers and parents is to think of visual problems. It is true that a child's eyesight may be so poor that it is practically impossible to read. There are a number of less severe eye defects which handicap children in the reading situation. When they attempt to read, they become uncomfortable, squirmy, fatigued, and so distraught that they can continue for only a short time. They may refuse to read at all. Although certain mild defects may not interfere with learning to read, they may make reading for a lengthy period fatiguing. It is not surprising, therefore, that many studies have concentrated upon visual impairments as causes of reading disability.

Considerable historical research relating visual deficiency to reading difficulty has resulted in conflicting findings. For a selective bibliography of research associating vision problems and reading problems see Weintraub and Cowan (1982). In general, research does not support a strong relationship between visual problems and reading problems (Poostay and Aaron, 1982). In the midst of disagreement and controversy, however, a few fairly consistent findings have been established:

1. There is a slightly greater percentage of visual defects among children with reading disability than among children without reading disability.
2. Children with visual defects, as a group, tend to read more poorly than children without visual defects.
3. On the other hand, many children with visual defects learn to read as well as or better than children without visual defects.
4. No matter what kind or type of visual deficiency is studied, some children can be found who have that specific kind or type of visual deficiency and who are making good progress in reading.

Most types of visual defects appear to increase the possibility of reading disability, but none of these appear to be sufficient in itself to preclude reading success. Perhaps the answer is that some children with visual defects fail to learn to read because of the extra effort required of them to master reading, whereas other children with the same visual defects do learn to read successfully because they, for one reason or another, try so hard that they overcome their handicap. In any event, children with visual deficiencies who do read well probably have learned under conditions of visual stress and fatigue. The wise teacher is alert to signs of fatigue among visually impaired children when they are required to complete demanding visual tasks and make appropriate adjustments. The appropriate educational adjustments for these visual problems will be discussed in Chapter 13.

Types of Visual Deficiency

Faulty focus of light rays that enter the eyes, *refractive errors,* may be associated with reading disability. However, certain types of refractive errors are more closely associated with reading disability than others (Eames, 1935; Young, 1963; Wharry and Kirkpatrick, 1986). The farsighted—*hyperopic*—child, who can bring far targets into clear focus easily but finds it difficult to focus clearly on near targets, is more likely to be reading-disabled than is the child with normal vision. On the other hand, the nearsighted—*myopic*—child who can easily bring near targets into clear focus but finds far targets difficult, is less likely to be reading-disabled than is the child with normal vision. According to research by Wharry and Kirkpatrick, even among learning disabled children, myopic children outperform normal and hyperopic children in reading. This seems reasonable when one considers the nature of the reading task, which involves prolonged periods of close visual inspection of near targets. However, if the teaching method relies heavily on the use of experience charts and chalkboard work, the nearsighted child may have difficulty.

Problems in focusing the two eyes precisely and simultaneously on a target, *binocular difficulties,* are more common among disabled readers than among successful readers. Lack of binocular coordination because of muscular imbalance of one or both eyes, *strabismus,* causes images to be blurred, or in more severe cases, causes two images of a single object to be seen. The result is confusion, fatigue, or suppression of one eye when the child attempts to read. It has been demonstrated that one-eyed students progress better in reading than those with muscle imbalance.

Another binocular characteristic connected with success in reading is precision of focus so that images may be fused into a single, clear picture. Fusion difficulties are associated with reading difficulties (Eames 1935; Spache and Tillman 1962). Not only accuracy of fusion, but also speed of fusion seem to be related to reading success. Ocular images of a fixed target that are unequal either in size or shape in the two eyes, *aniseikonia,* have also been found to be related to reading difficulties.

Many children with visual defects are successful in reading. Although visual defects may contribute to reading problems, even children with very poor vision can learn to read (Martin, 1971). Children with visual defects are more likely to get into difficult in reading and are more difficult to teach. Correction of visual defects is essential for all children with visual deficiencies, whether they are experiencing reading difficulties or not. Correction of visual defects enables children to learn to read more easily, but rarely, if ever, is such correction sufficient to relieve reading disability. Once correction has been made, however, most students are able to progress more easily when given appropriate remedial instruction.

Identification of Visual Defects

Accurate identification of all visual defects depends on the cooperation and coordinated efforts of home, school, and eye-care professionals. For an overview of vision screening, including screening of preschool children, see Lin-Fu (1971); for a simple pamphlet for parents, Eberly (1972) is recommended; and for excellent practical suggestions for organizing visual screening programs in the schools, see Jobe (1976).

Extensive research by Knox (1953) and Kozlowski (1968) strongly suggests that observation by the teacher, combined with visual screening tests by the school, provides more accurate identification of children in need of visual care than either teacher observation or school-administered visual screening tests alone.

However, as Jobe cautions, visual screening tests must be given only for the purpose of identification. Pupils who already have, or may develop, problems requiring the care of a specialist must be referred to a vision-care specialist. Screening tests are not diagnostic, and neither teachers nor school nurses should ever attempt to diagnose or treat visual problems.

Visual Screening Devices

Some of the more widely accepted school-administered visual screening devices are:

Keystone Visual Survey Tests, Keystone View Company, 2212 E. Twelfth Street, Davenport, Iowa
    52803
School Vision Tester, Bausch and Lomb, Rochester, New York 14602
Titmus School Vision Tester, Falvey Company, 1312 W. Seventh Street, Piscataway, New Jersey 08854

Teacher Observation

Based on extensive research on the identification of children with visual problems through observation, with subsequent validation by an eye specialist, Knox (1953) believes that the following behavioral symptoms are most useful:

1. Facial contortions
2. Book held close to face
3. Tenseness during visual work
4. Head tilting
5. Head thrust forward
6. Body tenseness while looking at distant objects
7. Poor sitting position

8. Head moving excessively while reading
9. Eyes rubbed frequently
10. Tendency to avoid close visual work
11. Tendency to lose place in reading

When two to four of these symptoms are noticeable and persistent, it is the teacher's responsibility to work with the parents, the school, and the eye-care professional to ensure that the child receives a proper vision examination. If a vision defect is diagnosed by a vision-care specialist, cooperative efforts must be made to provide proper vision care for the child and to make appropriate educational adaptations within the school. Suggestions will be found in Chapter 13.

Visual Processing Defects

Research on the relationship between visual perception, visual memory, visual sequencing, and reading disability has been contradictory and confusing (Waintraub and Cowan, 1982). Vernon (1969) concluded from a review of research relating deficient visual perception to severe reading difficulties that deficient visual perception is one of the characteristics of severely disabled readers, but that deficient visual perception is so often associated with a general maturational lag that it may be but one symptom of a general immaturity which also includes language development and personality development.

Robinson (1972) found that students with deficiencies in visual perceptual abilities also had lower I.Q.s than children who did not. Bryan and Bryan (1978, pp. 169–72) found from a review of research on visual processing—specifically visual memory and visual sequencing—that the relationship between these abilities and reading disability was not clear. Two major reasons for the ambiguity were cited. The first was a validity problem, specifically that researchers could not convincingly measure visual processing abilities. The second was that among the children studied, visual processing abilities were so intermingled with other factors usually considered detrimental to reading success that determining the cause of reading difficulty was not possible. Vernon and Robinson also expressed concern for the contamination of results of research on children with visual processing problems.

Kavale (1982), on the basis of a meta-analysis of 161 studies, concluded that visual perception is an important component of reading achievement, but that its importance varies depending on the combination of visual and reading variables considered in individual studies. On the other hand, research by Hare (1977) points out that all children with visual processing impairment are not poor readers. According to her research, among beginning readers individuals can be identified who are both visually and auditorially disabled, yet are achieving at grade level in reading.

Training children in visual perception does not improve their reading achievement according to research by Seaton (1977). In the clinic, however, children who have visual processing problems, as well as extreme reading disability often do benefit from a kinesthetic-auditory emphasis in reading instruction as described in Chapter 12.

AUDITORY IMPAIRMENT

Sustained hearing loss, even mild hearing loss, results in poor reading achievement, which becomes increasingly pronounced as children become older (Blair, Peterson, and Viehweg, 1985; Bockmiller, 1981; Quinn, 1981; Serwatka, Hesson, and Graham, 1984). In addition, even for children with very slight hearing loss or no hearing loss, but with a history of recurring middle ear disease, reading is adversely affected (McDermott, 1983; Silva, Chalmers, and Steward, 1986; Zinkus, Gottlieb, and Schapiro, 1978).

The importance of auditory abilities can be appreciated when one considers that children learn to read utilizing the language they understand and use, which is influenced by the language they have heard. Both the ability to pronounce words correctly and the ability to understand what they mean, as used in various sentences, is based on a child's language ability, which has been acquired through listening. The effect on reading of auditory deficiencies depends on the severity and type of auditory impairment; the quickness with which it was detected; the quality of the educational program; the coordination of the efforts of parents, specialists, and others; the desire of the child to read, and other causal factors that all work together to determine the eventual outcome.

Types of Auditory Deficiency

Weintraub (1972) identifies three major areas of concern.

1. Auditory acuity (hearing)
2. Audition (listening)
3. Auditory processing (working with sounds)

Much of the confusion in research, clinical work, and teaching results from the difficulty in separating the effects of hearing loss, listening skills, and auditory processing. Often a student may have difficulty with all three aspects of hearing, but sometimes the difficulty may be specific. For example, some children with no measurable hearing loss have difficulty hearing sounds in words but no difficulty understanding the meaning of spoken sentences. Other children with hearing loss have difficulty with all the auditory aspects of language, speech, and reading. Still other children have specific difficulty blending sounds into whole words and recognizing the meaning of the words. There are many kinds and types of auditory deficiency and what is best for one child with an auditory impairment may not be best for another child with a different auditory impairment.

Although research studies disagree, apparently because of dissimilar techniques of measurement and lack of uniform standards for differentiating hearing-impaired from non-hearing-impaired children, it is safe to say that a large number of schoolchildren—about 5 percent—have serious hearing losses. Apparently, many more children have slight hearing losses, which may become more serious unless proper medical treatment is given.

The relationship between hearing loss, especially a high-frequency hearing loss, and reading difficulty is well documented (DeChant and Smith 1977, p. 140; Savage and Mooney 1979, pp. 118–20; and Spache 1976, pp. 49–50). Although children with severe and extreme hearing losses always have great difficulty learning how to read, those with lesser impairments often do reasonably well if the hearing loss is identified early and appropriate medical and educational measures are taken. From the teacher's or the reading specialist's point of view, proper management of phonics instruction is crucial. For appropriate educational adjustments see Chapter 13.

Research shows a direct, though low, correlation between auditory processing and reading success. See Kavale (1981) for a meta-analysis of 106 studies relating auditory perceptual skills and reading ability.

Identification of Auditory Defects

As with vision, successful identification of all auditory defects depends upon the cooperation and coordinated efforts of home, school, and auditory specialists. Early screening of very young children has been very beneficial in many cases. Auditory screening programs in the schools are very important.

Auditory Screening Devices

Hearing loss is determined most accurately by means of an audiometer such as one of the following

Beltone Audiometers, Beltone Electronics Corporation, 4201 W. Victoria Street, Chicago, Illinois 60646
Grason-Stadler Audiometers, 537 Great Road, Box 5, Littleton, Massachusetts 01460
Maico Audiometers, Maico Electronics, Inc., 7375 Bush Lake Road, Minneapolis, Minnesota 55435

All companies have models especially adapted to school use.

Teacher Observation

An alert teacher notes signs of hearing difficulty through careful observations of children's behavior. Hearing impairment may be suspected if a child shows behavior such as:

1. Inattention during listening activities
2. Frequent misunderstanding of oral directions or numerous requests for repetition of statements
3. Turning one ear toward the speaker or thrusting head forward when listening

4. Intent gazing at the speaker's face or strained posture while listening
5. Monotone speech, poor pronunciation, or indistinct articulation
6. Complaints of earache or hearing difficulty
7. Insistence on closeness to sound sources
8. Frequent colds, discharging ears, or difficult breathing

For informal screening, a whisper or low-voice test can be used. Four or five children are lined up in a row in a quiet room about five feet from the examiner and with their backs to him. The examiner stays in one place and gives directions to the children, speaking in a distinct, low tone. Directions include items like: "Take five steps forward; raise your right arm; take two steps forward; hold up three fingers." By watching the children, the examiner can see those who hesitate, turn to see what other children do, look back at the examiner, or fail to follow directions. The children who get to a position approximately twenty feet from the examiner without signs of seeking help have normal hearing. Hearing-impaired children can be detected readily. Whisper tests may be given by softly saying single words with the child standing about twenty feet away with one ear turned toward the examiner. This is the distance at which most children can hear in the particular room used. The child tries to repeat each word as he hears it. If necessary, the examiner moves closer until responses are correct. Each ear is tested separately.

Although whisper or low-voice screening tests are valuable when they can identify a child with a hearing loss, these methods sometimes miss children with less severe hearing losses. For this reason, routine audiometric screening of all children before entering school, and from time to time during the school years, is preferable to total reliance on any informal method.

As with vision, the purpose of identification of hearing loss is to refer the child to a hearing specialist for proper treatment. In addition, educational services and instructional adaptations, as discussed in Chapter 13, must be provided.

SPEECH IMPAIRMENT

Defective speech is associated with reading difficulty, according to research by Bond (1935), Lyle (1970), and Monroe (1932). Usually, inaccurate formation of speech sounds, *articulation disorders,* are found to be more closely associated with reading disability than are the faulty rate of production or repetition of speech sounds, *fluency difficulties*. It is agreed that in many cases both inaccurate articulation and reading difficulties are associated with other factors such as slow intellectual development, neurological involvement, or inability to discriminate sounds in words. Nevertheless clinical experience suggests that for some children defective speech itself is a causal factor.

Monroe notes that faulty articulation may directly affect reading by causing confusion between the sounds the child hears others make and the sounds the child hears himself make when he is asked to associate print symbols with sounds in reading. Clinical experience and research by Bond show that reading methods that require individual letter-by-letter sounding and blending can cause difficulty for a student with faulty articulation. If the student has auditory limitations as well, the difficulty is augmented. Methods stressing visual-mental word analysis enable such a student to progress in reading more successfully.

Confusion may also arise when a student hears words spoken one way when *he* reads orally but another way when he sees the words in his book while *others* read them aloud. This confusion not only affects sound-symbol associations but also may interfere with the student's understanding of what is read. The child may thus become increasingly confused not only about how words are pronounced but also about what they mean.

Some children with speech defects become obviously upset when they are asked to read aloud. This is usually because the student is sensitive about articulation errors and dislikes displaying them in an oral reading situation. Clinical experience reveals that many children with speech defects, even very minor, barely noticeable problems, insist that they do not want to read aloud but are willing to read silently. In fact, clinical experience shows that insistence upon oral reading has been known to turn some children with speech defects against all reading.

Research by Bond and Monroe suggests that speech defects are not associated with silent reading achievement but are associated with oral reading disability. Some evidence suggests that the strongest association of all may be between speech defects and poor oral reading when it occurs together with adequate silent reading.

The child with speech defects usually needs the assistance of a speech specialist to remedy his speech problem, plus an appropriate reading program. Emphasis on visual-mental word analysis and silent reading usually is best. Planning a suitable reading program for a child with speech defects becomes more complicated when other factors such as slow intellectual development, neurological impairment, or auditory discrimination difficulties are also present. Suggestions for educational adjustments are made in Chapter 13.

NEUROLOGICAL IMPAIRMENT

Among children who have not yet acquired the ability to read, there are a very few who have sustained known brain damage before, during, or after birth. Some of these children suffer severe handicaps, such as aphasia, cerebral palsy, marked mental retardation, or debilitating motor problems. They obviously require highly specialized medical assistance and educational programming. Other children with known brain damage are much less handicapped. They, too, require medical assistance and educational programming. However, for reading instruction, appropriate educational programming may or may not be much different from good reading instruction for the typical learner, depending on the needs of the individual child. Case studies from the Geneva-Medico-Educational Service (1968) suggest that known brain lesions, unless very severe, often do not retard learning and that many children with verifiable brain damage do make good progress in reading. Educational adjustments for such children are discussed in Chapter 13.

Besides the concern for the child with known brain damage, there has been a great deal of recent concern, research, speculation, opinion, and clinical data reported regarding *suspected* brain damage and reading difficulties. Such terms as developmental dyslexia, primary reading retardation, minimal brain damage, maturational lag, and others have been used to refer to suspected brain damage in the absence of medically verifiable brain pathology. Bender (1957), Critchley (1970), and Rabinovitch (1962), among many others, have argued persuasively in favor of some type of neurological impairment, other than known brain pathology, as a probable cause of reading difficulty. A careful and perceptive review of relevant research by Balow, Rubin, and Rosen (1975) suggests that subtle, often undetected, neurological impairment associated with complications of pregnancy and birth is a cause of later reading disability among some children. Rourke (1975) also presents compelling evidence for the view that neurological dysfunction, in the absence of known brain damage, is a common associate of reading disability.

On the other hand, Spache (1976b) provides a highly critical review of the overwhelming abundance of literature relating suspected neurological impairments to reading disability. He warns that some specialists appear to be attributing almost all reading difficulties to suspected neurological impairment, not only in the absence of known brain damage, but even in the absence of *any* signs of abnormal neurological functioning. Isom (1968) cautions that the assessment of a child's neurological development and its relationship to reading is extraordinarily complex. His thoughtful review of neurological research relevant to reading indicates that among children who show signs suggestive of neurological impairment, some have no reading difficulty, some have moderate reading difficulty, and some have serious reading disability. He emphasizes the critical need for competent research comparing the frequency of occurrence of presumably abnormal neurological signs found in reading-disabled children with the frequency of occurrence of the same signs among their non-reading-disabled peers. In a somewhat related study, Larsen, Tillman, Ross, Satz, Cassin, and Wolkin (1973) found that among a group of 100 children referred to a center for learning disabilities, signs of neurological impairment were no more common among those who were reading-disabled than among those who were making normal progress in reading.

In a study comparing reading-disabled children with and without clinical signs of neurological dysfunction, Black (1973) found no real differences among the groups in severity of reading problems, overall cognitive functioning, or behavior. He concluded from his research that suspected neurological dysfunction was *not* an important factor in planning proper remediation of reading disability. Black (1976) also compared children who were suspected of neurological dysfunction with children with known brain damage. Once again, patterns of behavior, cognitive abilities, and academic difficulties noted for these groups were similar enough to suggest that specialized remedial programs differentiating between children with documented brain damage and suspected brain dysfunction are probably unwarranted.

Black concluded that remedial programs should be based *not* on probable neurological causation, but rather on the instructional needs of each child.

In the authors' opinion, a medical referral for neurological assessment should be made when:

1. There is an extreme discrepancy between a child's reading expectancy and reading achievement in spite of appropriate educational experiences.
2. Despite a wide discrepancy between expectancy and achievement, a child's progress in a carefully planned and well-taught reading program is persistently and unexplainably slow.

Practically speaking, what should the reading teacher or reading clinician do about suspected neurological involvement among poor readers? The best initial referral for neurological assessment is usually to a cooperative pediatrician who has had extensive experience with both normal and neurologically impaired children. Often no real evidence of neurological impairment will be found, sometimes an unexpected physical deficiency of a different sort will be uncovered, and sometimes evidence of neurological impairment will be revealed. If any type of physical condition which requires medical assistance is found, appropriate measures should of course, be taken. Any suggestions a physician offers which might serve to enhance a child's learning should be followed. However, reading instruction for the disabled reader who shows medical signs of neurological impairment, as for any other disabled reader, should proceed according to a careful plan based on a diagnosis of the child's particular reading deficiencies and instructional needs. Methods of proper diagnosis and treatment of reading difficulties are included in Chapters 7 through 17.

Based on an ambitious review of clinical and research evidence concerning neurological correlates of reading disabilities, Duane (1983) suggests there is a biological preference for verbal tasks to be performed with maximum fluency and accuracy within the left hemisphere of the brain. Yet some children with reading disabilities appear, by observing their learning strategies, to be using right hemisphere processing when reading. As Helfeldt (1983) points out, right hemisphere processing, more typical of boys, tends to be visually-oriented and is facilitated through active manipulation of the learning environment. Academic learning tasks that demand a great deal of attentive listening and long periods of quiet sitting are not suited to right hemisphere processing. Neither is a major emphasis on language- or phonics-based methods of reading instruction. Procedures that emphasize the perceptual aspects of the visual stimuli in reading instruction are more beneficial.

According to research by Bakker, Teunissen, and Bosch (1976), early reading proficiency is associated with dominant processing of information in either hemisphere. For children using right hemisphere processing, reading tends to be slow and accurate while for those using left hemisphere processing reading tends to be more rapid, but less accurate. Eventually, however, advanced reading, which is both rapid and accurate, is favored by left hemisphere dominance.

GENERAL HEALTH IMPAIRMENT

Learning to read is a difficult, even arduous, task. To succeed, the learner must be an attentive, active participant in the learning process. General health factors such as endocrine disorders, cardiac conditions, allergies, and other physical problems make it difficult for children to be effective learners (Carner, 1981). Any physical condition that lowers a child's vitality makes it difficult for the child to sustain active attention to learning.

Chronic Illness and Malnutrition

Chronically ill or malnourished children are often unable to sustain attention to demanding learning tasks. These children are likely to miss much instruction due to frequent absences, which makes learning even more difficult. When learning to read becomes a matter of having to catch up on a week's missed work, while feeling insecure about how to proceed and feeling tired, unwell, and perhaps hungry, it is little wonder that some children begin to dislike and avoid reading.

What is the teacher's responsibility in regard to poor general health, malnutrition, and frequent absence?

1. When a general health problem is suspected, the teacher, school nurse, parents and others should discuss the matter and decide what to do. Often the appropriate action is to refer the child for a medical diagnosis. In this case, it is important to alert the doctor or diagnostic team to the nature of the behavior in the home and in the school which prompted the referral.

2. Although malnutrition is still an important problem for many children, the schools have taken an increasingly important role in combating it through various lunch, milk, and breakfast programs. Some teachers, especially those who use behavior modification techniques, may also provide some students with tiny amounts of nutritious food as part of their teaching procedures.

3. In the case of absenteeism, it is the teacher's responsibility to provide special assistance to ensure that children have not missed essential skill development and that they do not feel confused or insecure about proceeding with their work. Depending upon the circumstances, the teacher can provide this assistance directly, use other resource personnel within the school, or enlist the parents' aid.

General Fatigue

In a reading clinic, it is often discouraging to hear a chronically fatigued and disabled reader give a detailed rendition of last evening's late, late television movie. It is especially so when follow-up questioning reveals that the student watches a great deal of television, usually far into the night. In this case, the child's television viewing habits must be discussed with his parents and the child himself. Often viewing habits will be changed; sometimes they will not. It is tempting to believe that extensive television viewing or other factors which seem to be interfering with proper rest are causing a student's reading difficulty, and in some cases this is true.

In other cases, overuse of television or other activities may be a child's way of escaping from the frustrations the child feels, including the frustration of reading failure.

SUMMARY

This survey suggests that any one of a number of physical conditions may be a contributing factor in reading disability. Much of the evidence is equivocal. It is obvious that any single factor seldom, if ever, causes reading disability. As emphasized throughout this chapter, reading disability tends to be caused by many factors. Several hindering factors combine into a pattern to produce the disability.

Although the evidence concerning the relation between specific eye defects and reading disability is ambiguous, there are certain relevant trends. (1) Eye defects appear frequently among both good and poor readers and can be a handicap to either group. Comfortable and efficient vision should be provided for all children whenever possible. (2) There is evidence that farsightedness, binocular incoordination, fusion difficulties, and aniseikonia may contribute to reading disability. When there is a visual defect, there are usually other associated contributing causes. (3) Visual examinations are essential in the diagnosis of certain reading disabilities.

Hearing impairment can be a handicap in learning to read. This is particularly true when the hearing loss is severe enough to interfere with normal auditory discrimination. There is evidence that hearing impairment may be associated with reading disability as a contributing cause when (1) the hearing loss is severe, (2) the child has high-tone deafness, and (3) pupils with hearing loss are taught reading by predominantly auditory methods.

Defects in articulation, which complicate word discrimination and recognition, may contribute to reading disability. Any emotional involvement created by speech defects tends to inhibit progress in learning to read. Brain damage is seldom a cause of reading disability, but when it is present a very difficult instructional problem exists. Various conditions associated with poor health can be detrimental to normal progress in reading.

STUDY QUESTIONS

1. What is the association between visual defects and reading disability?
2. How can a teacher identify a child with hearing difficulty?
3. How might articulation disorders interfere with reading progress?
4. What generalizations can be made about teaching reading to neurologically impaired children?
5. What do you feel is the proper role of a teacher regarding the health needs of children?

SELECTED READINGS

DeChant, E. V. *Diagnosis and Remediation of Reading Disabilities,* Chap. 3. Englewood Cliffs, NJ: Prentice-Hall, Inc., 1981.

Harris, A. J., and E. R. Sipay. *How to Increase Reading Ability,* 8th ed., Chap. 9. New York: Longman, Inc., 1985.

McCormick, S. *Remedial and Clinical Reading Instruction,* Chap. 3. Columbus, OH: Charles E. Merrill Publishing Company, 1987.

Roswell, F., and G. Natchez. *Reading Disability: Diagnosis and Treatment,* 2nd ed., Chap. 1. New York: Basic Books, Inc., 1971.

Savage, J. F., and J. F. Mooney. *Teaching Reading to Children with Special Needs,* Chaps. 4 and 5. Boston: Allyn & Bacon, Inc., 1979.

Spache, G. D. *Investigating the Issues of Reading Disabilities,* Chaps. 2, 3, 4, and 7. Boston: Allyn & Bacon, Inc., 1976.

Vernon, M. D. *Backwardness in Reading.* New York: Cambridge University Press, 1960.

Wilson, R. M. and C. J. Cleland. *Diagnostic and Remedial Reading for Classroom and Clinic,* 5th ed., Chap. 3. Columbus, OH: Charles E. Merrill Publishing Company, 1985.

5

Causes of Reading Disability: Cognitive and Language Factors

In the preceding chapter a number of physical conditions possibly affecting reading disability were surveyed. In this chapter various cognitive and language factors and their relationship to reading disability will be considered.

INTELLECTUAL LIMITATIONS

Although reading achievement is related to intelligence, according to Beldin (1976), Bond and Wagner (1966), Kirk and Elkins (1975), and Sewill and Severson (1975), intellectual development alone does not determine how well a given child will or should read. See also Black (1971) and Durrell (1955). The precise assessment of reading achievement and intelligence is complex and difficult. Both are influenced by other factors, and both are difficult to measure fairly and accurately. Nevertheless, for proper diagnosis of reading disability, the relationship between intelligence and reading achievement is very important. This is especially true for children with below-average intelligence.

As Durrell cautions, the relationship between intelligence and reading achievement must never be used to set any limit on how much or what a child can learn. The relationship between intelligence and reading achievement should be used to identify the child who is failing to progress in reading commensurate with what is most reasonable to expect of him. Discrepancies between reading expectancy and achievement which indicate disability by grade level can be found in Chapter 3.

The implication for the intellectually limited child is that if educational adaptations are made which are suited to his needs he can and will make continuous, appropriate progress in reading. Clinical experience shows that children and youth of quite limited intelligence can and do learn to read if the proper educational adaptations are made. Although their achievement remains very low in comparison with others of their age, they are able to master reading skills useful to them throughout their lives.

But as Buttery and Mason (1979), Cegelka and Cegelka (1970), and Kirk, Kliebhan, and Lerner (1978) point out, low intelligence can be a cause of reading disability when appropriate educational adaptations are not made. For example, if children with low intelligence are expected to read before they have been taught appropriate prereading skills, or if they are expected to progress through sequential reading instruction without adequate opportunity to securely learn essential reading skills, then they are likely to fail to make reasonable progress in reading. Research by Cummins and Das (1980) suggests that among educably mentally retarded adolescents poor reading skills may not be entirely attributable to their low intelligence, but also due to their failure to effectively apply their intellectual abilities to reading. Such students are reading-disabled not because their reading achievement is low but because it is unreasonably low. Methods of adapting reading instruction for the intellectually limited child will be described in Chapter 13.

When a child progresses in reading much more slowly than his peers, it is natural for his teachers to think that he may have low intelligence, especially when there are no other obvious reasons for his slow progress. However, it is not correct to assume that the child's intelligence is low, rather, it is imperative to refer the child to a specialist, such as a school psychologist; for further assessment. Either the Wechsler Intelligence Scale for Children (Revised) or the Revised Stanford-Binet Intelligence Test should be used for most children for this assessment. Results from group intelligence tests requiring the child to read as a part of the intelligence testing procedure must not be used, because the child who cannot read well cannot do well on these tests, no matter how well he might have performed if proper testing procedures had been used.

COGNITIVE FACTORS

Cognition, the process of gaining knowledge, and reading are related in two important ways. First, specific cognitive abilities are essential for the acquisition of reading skills. Second, for the competent reader, reading becomes a powerful means for knowledge acquisition, structuring, and application.

Researchers who have attended to cognitive factors in learning emphasize the central importance of the learner in all teaching-learning situations (Reid and Hreska 1981). From this point of view, effective reading instruction is that which facilitates the learner's ability to construct meaning from reading. As Smith (1978) suggests, ''Reading is asking questions of printed text. And reading with comprehension becomes a matter of getting your questions answered.'' Rystrom (1977) emphasizes the mental activity required in reading when he speaks of readers as ''both information receivers and information generators.''

Specific Cognitive Abilities

The relationships of specific cognitive abilities to reading retardation have been investigated through analysis of performance by disabled readers on individual intelligence tests and tests of cognitive abilities.

According to independent reviews of this research by Huelsman (1970), Kendler (1972), and Sattler (1974), poor readers as a group show higher abilities on performance measures than on verbal measures. They tend to have difficulty recalling specific information and working with symbols, although according to research by McConaughy (1985), poor readers are capable of high quality story comprehension when they read structurally simple narrative stories. Cohen (1969) and Kaufman (1975) have presented evidence that whereas successful readers can avoid being distracted during cognitive tasks, unsuccessful readers are less able to maintain concentration.

Bannatyne (1974) and Rugel (1974) both conducted research suggesting that poor readers are weak in sequencing ability, but strong in spatial abilities, such as quickly understanding how to put a complex puzzle together. According to an analysis of results of cognitive factors research, Spache (1963) has speculated that disabled readers may have unusual difficulty in recognizing that words have meaning and in recalling specific word meanings. They may also have difficulty recognizing the types of relationships within the structure of the paragraph and summarizing the facts of the paragraph in the reader's own words with due attention to order.

In teaching it may be well to keep in mind that for certain poor readers attention to having the children work with activities, games, and other *hands on* projects would be beneficial. Emphasis on relating reading to discussion and other verbal outcomes puts many poor readers at a considerable disadvantage.

Most teachers would agree that poor readers understand text better through listening than through reading. When Sannomiya (1984) presented the same text to children with good and poor comprehension at a fixed pace using a tape recording or an overhead projector, he found the tape presentation resulted in better comprehension for the poor readers for whom the text was difficult but not for the good comprehenders for whom it was easy. He suggests that auditory versus visual modality effects arise when the text is difficult and when children are not allowed sufficient time to process the text.

Poor readers may be at a special disadvantage when asked to work with the specific symbols used in reading and arithmetic. These symbols must be mastered, but the children may need extra understanding and encouragement as they attempt to achieve learnings which are specifically difficult for them. Also, recall of specific information from reading may be difficult for poor readers; whereas finding information, telling about the story, or drawing a picture about it, may be much more satisfying. Certain children need to be protected from too many distractions in the busy classroom or they will find themselves unable to concentrate on demanding tasks. They may also need instruction emphasizing order and structure in reading.

Cognitive Style

Cognitive style, or preferred manner of intellectual functioning, has been investigated widely in nonreading contexts (Kogan 1980). As a result of this research, it has been determined that consistent individual differences in cognitive style can be demonstrated. Certain instances exemplifying cognitive style include field dependence versus field independence, amount of reliance on the learning environment, tendency toward complexity versus simplicity in classification tasks, leveling versus sharpening in memory, focusing versus scanning as an attention strategy, and analytical versus global view of causation.

Recently, research concerning the relationship of several aspects of cognitive style and reading has been conducted. Field dependence-independence has been related to reading ability and achievement. Strongly field-dependent children process information in a generally global fashion and appear to be easily influenced by their environment, whereas strongly field-independent children typically process information in an analytical manner and tend to be individualistic.

Field-independence was found to be related to reading achievement by Blaha (1982), based on his study of 324 inner-city fifth-grade children. On the other hand, Roberge and Flexer (1984) who studied 450 suburban children, found that field-independent, analytic, sixth, seventh, and eight graders did *not* score higher in reading achievement than their field-dependent, globally-oriented peers. Their results did show that students' cognitive levels were related to reading achievement. Further research conducted by Blake (1985) involving 121 sixth-grade students similarly failed to find a relationship between field independence-dependence and passage comprehension. She did find a strong relationship between intelligence and passage comprehension. Research by Paradise and Block (1984) who studied 200 urban fourth-grade children suggested that students who closely match their teachers on field dependence-independence make greater gains in reading achievement than students who are dissimilar.

These conflicting results suggest that the effect of factors such as type of school, grade level, cognitive level, and teacher cognitive style need to be understood before the relationship of field dependence-independence to reading achievement can be established.

Dunn, Price, Dunn, and Saunders (1979) and Price, Dunn, and Saunders (1981) studied how students prefer to learn when provided with an opportunity to choose from among environmental, sociological, and physical conditions. It was argued that the kinds of decisions a student makes concerning instructional choices should be related directly to his learning style, because specific learning style characteristics appear to interact with instructional methods and environmental resources.

In reviews of research on learning style and reading, Marie Carbo (1983,

1985) has characterized poor readers, in contrast to good readers, as learning best (1) under conditions of quiet, (2) when allowed intake of food or drink, (3) if given opportunities to move about, (4) under carefully structured instruction, (5) in informally designed classrooms, (6) when provided chances to work with peers, (7) if provided tactile-kinesthetic learning experiences, and (8) when given major instructional emphasis at other times during the day than early morning.

Another aspect of cognitive style which has been related to reading achievement is conceptual tempo (Kogan 1980). Reflexive children, those who respond more slowly than average with fewer than average errors, in most studies achieve at a higher level in reading than do impulsive children who respond more quickly than average with more errors. In a study of 170 second-grade children, Readence and Baldwin (1978) found that while reflexive children achieved higher in reading than impulsive children overall, the method of reading instruction affected the specific aspects of reading on which the reflexive children performed better. On the other hand, a study of conceptual tempo as a predictor of first-grade reading achievement for a group of kindergarten children (Margolis, Peterson, and Leonard 1978) did not support the reading superiority of reflexive children. An additional study, conducted by Halpern (1984), involving 168 second-grade children only supported a relationship between conceptual tempo and performance on some types of word recognition and comprehension tasks.

LANGUAGE FACTORS

The importance accorded listening-speaking language as a basis for reading can be judged by statements made by Wilkerson (1971), who wrote that the ability to read is largely dependent on the skill in spoken language the learner already possesses, and by Lundsteen (1976), who felt that reading may depend so completely upon a basis in listening that it appears to be a special extension. Research by Blachman (1984), Edmiaston (1984), Fletcher, Staz, and Scholes (1981), Rosenblum and Stephens (1981), and Rosenthal, Baker, and Ginsburg (1983) demonstrates a positive relationship between children's language ability and their reading achievement. Among first-grade children, verbal fluency and phonics awareness appear to be associated with early reading success according to research by Blachman (1984).

Longitudinal research evidence (Ruddell, 1979) suggests that primary-grade listening ability may be a better predictor of total reading performance in grades eight, nine, and ten than primary-grade measures of reading comprehension and word analysis skills. Additional longitudinal research conducted by Aram, Ekelman, and Nation (1984) demonstrates an association between preschool language disorders and later adolescent reading deficits.

Syntactic Abilities

Language problems are commonly implicated in reading difficulties. The complexity of syntax, or sentence structure, has been shown to be highly related to reading difficulty (Dalgleish and Enkelmann 1979; Evans 1979). Studies on children's language and reading comprehension have yielded findings about the role of sentence structure in reading. Inability to understand written text is often the result of differences between a child's oral language facility and written language structure (Barnitz 1980). A review of ten years of research by Evans (1979) supports a probable relationship between difficulty of reading comprehension and complexity of written syntax.

Although most children are skilled in listening-speaking language before they are taught to read, the comprehension of certain oral language syntactic structures has not yet developed (Barnitz 1980). Chomsky's classic research (1969) on the acquisition of grammatical structures among children from ages five to ten demonstrated that the use of syntax continues to develop among children who are beginning readers. Chomsky also found that the development of syntax is variable from child to child and that errors in syntax persisted even among the oldest children in her group.

Research concerned with the structural difficulty of written materials and the language competencies of children who read them has been done by Glazer and Morrow (1978). In a study of ninety children, the use of syntax by six-, seven-, and eight-year-old children was compared with the use of syntax in reading texts used with children of the same ages. It was found that the reading materials were syntactically more complex than was the language of the children.

Studies dealing with good and poor readers' use of syntax, specifically pronouns, indicate that poor readers are less successful in using syntax in context reading and have less knowledge of English syntax than normal readers. When Chapman (1979) investigated good and poor readers' abilities to deal with pronouns in text reading, he found that good readers were more successful with pronouns than were poor readers, even in materials which did not cause either group difficulty with word recognition. Dalgleish and Enkelmann (1979) found that poor readers (ages eight through twelve) have less knowledge than normal readers of English syntax. Similar results were reported by Fletcher, Staz, and Scholes (1981) for eleven-year-old poor readers.

Semantic Abilities

From a logical basis, reading is highly related to oral language, since the printed word is a graphical representation of spoken language. Myklebust, among others, has contended that the hierarchical relationship between listening, speaking, and reading makes proficiency in the latter dependent on success with the former (Johnson and Myklebust 1967). In a 1969 review of the verbal ability correlates of reading failure, Chalfant and Scheffelin (1969, p. 95) could only identify a single report on the subject. Recently, Hammill and McNutt (1980) completed a selective review of studies relating language abilities and reading. In 31 studies relating receptive semantics (contextual listening) to reading proficiency they found 170 correlation coefficients with a median value of .44. This would suggest that a moderate degree of relationship exists between listening understanding and reading performance. On the other hand, of 82 coefficients from 23 studies relating expressive semantics (contextual speech) to reading, the median coefficent was not significant. This would suggest a low order of relationship between expressive vocabulary and reading proficiency. Taken in its totality, the reviewed research would indicate that a higher degree of relationship exists between receptive oral language and reading than between expressive oral language and reading. Additional research conducted by Edmiaston (1984) with third grade children confirmed a higher degree of relationship between receptive language and reading than between expressive language and reading. Her research also supported a stronger relationship between oral language and reading than was obtained by Hammill and McNutt. Edmiaston speculated that the relationship between oral language and reading may increase with age.

When intelligence was partialled out, Gray, Saski, McEntire, and Larsen (1980) found no significant relationship among seventy four- five- and six-year-olds between semantic ability in oral language and measures of reading readiness.

Miscue Analysis of Reading Errors

A miscue is an unexpected response to language that causes the reader's pronunciation to be at variance with the writer's words. In miscue analysis of oral reading, inaccuracies are analyzed according to the reader's use of syntactic and semantic information (Goodman and Watson 1977). Such analysis provides some insight into the language correlates of specific errors.

Hood (1978) cites three examples of oral reading errors. In the first example, a reader may try to use sounding to pronounce a word, resulting in a real or nonsense word which does not fit the sentence, or may make no attempt to pronounce the word. As a result, the meaning of the sentence is impaired. In the second example, a reader may guess a word that makes sense, though it may not look much like the text word. In this instance, the meaning of the sentence is less impaired. In the third example, a reader might glance at the entire sentence and even at more of the paragraph in order to determine an unknown word. In this example, the reader may use a word that fits in so well that the meaning of the sentence is retained. When these errors are analyzed for semantic acceptability, errors of the first type are considered more serious than errors of the second type and errors of the third type are considered the least serious.

In a complete miscue analysis, errors are analyzed and evaluated for seriousness using eighteen categories, including correction of miscues, graphic proximity, evaluation of how closely the miscue resembles the physical appearance of the words, syntactic acceptability, evaluation of how closely the miscue fits the structure of the sentence. For a complete detailed taxonomy that includes all eighteen categories and specific scoring rules and examples, see Allen and Watson (1976, pp. 157–224). For a simpler version, see Goodman and Burke (1972) and Burke (1973).

PSYCHOLINGUISTIC ABILITIES IN READING

Psycholinguistics, the study of language behavior, is useful in the understanding of reading (Smith 1973). General interest in psycholinguistics and reading is demonstrated by the 396 entries contained in the annotated bibliography entitled *Linguistics, Psycholinguistics and the Teaching of Reading* (Goodman and Goodman 1980). Much early research on the relationship of psycholinguistic abilities to reading performance has been based on subtests of the Illinois Test of Psycholinguistic Abilities (Kirk, McCarthy, and Kirk 1968; McCarthy and Kirk 1961).

In early research with the ITPA, Kass (1966) found a significant relationship between difficulty in learning to read and deficits in perceptual speed, closure, and visual memory. Ragland (1964) and McLeod (1965) found similar deficits among children with reading disability. Less enthusiasm for results of this type was found in a comprehensive review in 1976. Newcomer and Hammill, in reviewing the psycholinguistic correlates of academic achievement, concluded that the forty studies reviewed gave no support to the contention that visual tests of the ITPA showed a significant relationship to academic achievement. Among the auditory tests, three (grammatic closure, auditory association, and sound blending) showed a significant relationship with skill in reading. The strongest relationship was demonstrated for grammatic closure, emphasizing the persistent association between syntax in spoken language and reading proficiency. Later research by Backman (1983) suggested that sound blending ability is not necessary for early reading success. The general relationship between sound blending and reading achievement may be a consequence of teaching rather than a prerequisite for learning to read.

Modality Research

Teachers of reading-disabled children have long tried to match teaching style to the way in which the disabled reader learns best. This intuitively logical approach suggests that if the child's preferred learning modality (usually visual or auditory) could be identified the child could be taught better.

Hammill (1972) reviewed the research on training visual perception and the effect this might have on reading performance. On the basis of this review, Hammill concluded that visual perception training had no positive effect on reading performance. More recent research conducted by Seaton (1977) also showed that training children in visual perception does not improve their reading achievement. Hammill and Larsen (1974) reviewed 33 studies that utilized correlational procedures to examine the relationship between auditory perceptual skills and reading. The median correlation coefficient between specific auditory skills and general reading was not of sufficient magnitude to be useful in educational programming.

Foster, Reese, Schmidt, and Orthman (1976) conducted a study to determine if children who demonstrate strength in the auditory or visual channel could perform better if instructional strategies were matched with modality preference. The children were taught a series of sight words through methods designed to be predominantly auditory or visual. The visual preference subjects retained more when taught under visual conditions, while the auditory learner did as well under either teaching condition. Although the results have some implications for teaching reading, they provide an insufficient basis for placing children in reading programs based on their modality preference. In a 1978 review of the literature, Derevensky (p. 14) concluded that

> while the conceptualization of matching instructional strategies to individual differences via information about an individual's modal preference has great intuitive appeal, little empirical evidence in support of such a proposition can be found.

SUMMARY

This review has considered various cognitive and language factors and their association with reading success and reading difficulty. Although one specific deficit may be of essential importance in educational planning for an individual child, no one factor has been isolated as the single cause of reading difficulty in general. Some of the most recent and most carefully performed research studies available for review yielded the most ambiguous results.

Lower than normal intelligence need not be a cause of reading disability, in that reading achievement can be as advanced as is reasonable to expect for the slow-learning child. But when instructional procedures are not adjusted to a child's slow learning ability, an accumulation of partial learnings makes it impossible for him to profit from regular class instruction.

In a review of studies involving specific cognitive variables related to reading disability, a number of factors have been identified for groups of reading disabled children. The results of cognitive assessment give promise of providing additional information about the reading-disabled individual that will prove useful in planning an appropriate remedial program. Cognitive style also appears to be of promise in planning for reading-disabled youngsters.

Consideration of language and psycholinguistic factors revealed surprisingly little relationship between these variables and reading difficulty. The single variable which was persistently associated with reading difficulty was the children's use and knowledge of syntax.

STUDY QUESTIONS

1. Under what conditions can a child with low intelligence be considered reading disabled?
2. How do cognitive abilities differ from cognitive styles?

3. Why has the search for a single pattern of cognitive abilities as a predictor of reading difficulty proven largely unproductive?
4. Which language factor reviewed has been shown to be better developed among successful readers and more poorly developed among children experiencing reading difficulty?
5. Why is it helpful to analyze the types of miscues in oral reading?
6. What has been the overall research finding regarding the relationship between visual processing and reading achievement?

SELECTED READINGS

DeCHANT, E. *Diagnosis and Remediation of Reading Disabilities,* Chap. 5. Englewood Cliffs, NJ: Prentice-Hall, Inc. 1981.

GOODMAN, K. S., ed. *Miscue Analysis: Applications to Reading Instruction.* Urbana, IL: National Council of Teachers of English, 1973.

HARRIS, A. J., AND E. R. SIPAY. *How to Increase Reading Ability,* 8th ed., Chap. 8. New York: Longman, Inc., 1985.

KIRK, S. A., J. M. KLIEBHAN, AND J. W. LERNER. *Teaching Reading to Slow and Disabled Learners.* Boston: Houghton Mifflin Company, 1978.

NEWCOMER, P. L., AND D. D. HAMMILL. *Psycholinguistics in the Schools.* Columbus, OH: Charles E. Merrill Publishing Company, 1977.

SMITH, F. *Psycholinguistics and Reading.* New York: Holt, Rinehart and Winston, Inc., 1973.

6

Causes of Reading Disability: Emotional, Environmental, and Educational Factors

In the two preceding chapters a number of physical, cognitive, and language attributes possibly affecting reading disability were surveyed. In this chapter, various emotional, environmental, and educational factors and how they may contribute to reading disability will be examined.

PERSONAL AND SOCIAL ADJUSTMENT

When the behavior of disabled readers is compared with that of pupils making normal progress, it becomes obvious that there are differences in personal and social adjustment. Children who are failing to learn to read well are more likely to show indications of disturbed behavior than are their more successful peers (Jorm, Share, Matthews and Maclean 1986; Gentile and McMillan 1987). Although many children with reading difficulties manifest some indications of disturbed behavior, it is difficult to determine the relationship of behavioral problems, emotional problems, and reading problems.

When working with reading-disabled children in a one-to-one or small group setting, it soon becomes apparent that they are laboring to learn under stress. In the classroom, children with reading problems also manifest symptoms of stress. According to a substantial review of research reported by Gentile and McMillan (1987), the stress associated with reading difficulties can seriously limit some students' ability to concentrate, and can cause a range of behavior from anger and aggression to avoidance and apprehension. This is why some children with reading problems appear shy or listless, some appear unable to concentrate, and many appear to lack self-confidence. These children become discouraged easily and tend to give up when work becomes difficult. Other children with reading problems appear easily irritated, may argue with the teacher, or even become aggressive in the classroom. These children actively avoid reading.

It is the teacher's responsibility to aid and assist these children in proper classroom behavior for their own benefit and that of the rest of the class. It is crucial, as Gates noted many years ago (1947), not to assume that a child's instability is permanent or inalterable. It is necessary, if emotional or adjustment problems appear severe enough, to seek the aid of professionals, such as teachers of emotionally disturbed/behaviorally disordered children, school psychologists, or social workers. It is important to remember that many children with serious emotional or adjustment problems learn to read and to read well.

When groups of poor readers are compared to good readers, the results usually show a somewhat larger percentage of pupils with signs of personality maladjustment among the poor readers. In most instances, the differences are not great. According to Sornson (1950), children who become reading-disabled in the primary grades develop feelings of insecurity and show less satisfactory forms of personal and social adjustment than do their more successful peers.

A study of 90 second-graders in which behaviors were used to predict achievement scores was done by McKinney, Mason, Perkerson, and Clifford (1975). The results suggest that observable classroom behavior is an important determinant of academic progress. Swanson (1984), who studied 96 first-grade children, found observable classroom behavior to be highly related to reading achievement. In a study of 108 students enrolled in grades one, three, five, nine, and eleven, poor readers were off task more and volunteered to participate in class less than did good readers (Wasson, Beare, and Wasson 1988). Classroom behavior was also observed systematically by Camp and Zimet (1975). Their study of 45 first-grade children revealed that poor readers exhibited more deviant behavior and less on-task behavior than did good readers. When Harris and King (1982) studied 242 fourth- and fifth-grade children, they found that children who were selected by their teachers as having low achievement were less preferred by their classmates, were less intelligent, and less emotionally stable than children viewed by their teachers as having no academic problems.

Self-concept, which can be thought of as one's perception of self, also appears to be related to reading difficulty. Eldredge (1981) concluded on the basis of her review of research that although a number of studies have shown no significant relationship between self-concept and reading achievement, most of the evidence supports a strong relationship. She also notes that one reason for this may involve the importance of reading in our society. Failure to master reading may interfere with the development of a child's positive self-concept. In a study of 800 nine-year-old children, Chapman, Silva, and Williams (1984) found that poor readers' self-perceptions of ability were significantly lower than for normal readers. Stevens

(1971) found that fourth-grade students, identified as remedial readers, were less accepted than others in their classrooms and that they had poor self-concepts. Using various measures of self-concept, Herbert (1968) and Prendergast and Binder (1975) report that ninth-grade students with low reading achievement also tend to have poor self-concepts.

In these group comparisons, poor readers, in general, felt less adequate than did good readers, they demonstrated more behavior problems, and were less well-accepted by their classmates. It should be remembered that some good readers can also show signs of personality maladjustment, feel inadequate, demonstrate behavior problems, or can experience rejection by classmates.

There is some evidence that certain types of disabled readers exhibit more unfavorable traits than others. Karlsen (1954) found that word-by-word readers rated low in attention, motivation, and social confidence, while context readers rated high on these characteristics.

Some studies have been concerned with the possible effect of adjustment difficulties on progress in reading. Feldhusen, Thurston, and Benning (1970) identified a group of aggressive-disruptive children for comparison to a group of children who behaved more appropriately. When the school achievement of the two groups was compared five years later, the school grades of the maladjusted group were found to be significantly lower than those of the normally adjusted children. Harris (1970), in summarizing a study by Margolin, Roman, and Harori from the Children's Juvenile Court in New York City, reported "Among those tested . . . 76% were found to be two or more years retarded in reading, and more than half of those disabled five or more years" (p. 37). Wattenberg and Clifford (1966) studied the relationship of self-concept of kindergarten children to beginning reading achievement. They found that the children's attitudes about themselves were more closely related to success in beginning reading than was intelligence. The researchers suggested that self-concept is causally related to reading achievement. Swanson (1982), however, found a positive, but very low, relationship between reading attitude and reading achievement among first-grade students. Black (1974) found that children with reading difficulties tend to hold a negative view of themselves. He also noted that older children with reading problems felt more negatively toward themselves than did younger children.

Although case studies of children often find an intimate relation between a child's emotional problems and his reading difficulties, most research studies comparing the personality characteristics of retarded readers to those of good readers have failed to show any consistent group differences. Harris and Sipay (1975) suggest that "this is probably due to the mistaken attempt to find a common personality type or problem in the reading disability cases" (p. 301).

Successful reading requires application and sustained concentration. Whatever emotional problems prevent a pupil from paying attention and concentrating also interfere with the child's learning to read. Harris and Sipay outline several types of emotional problems that may contribute to reading disability: conscious refusal to learn, overt hostility, negative conditioning to reading, displacement of hostility, resistance to pressure, clinging to dependency, quick discouragement, extreme distraction or restlessness, and absorption in a private world (daydreaming). Although in some cases the underlying emotional difficulties may be similar, the symptoms or forms of expression may differ so widely that attempts to place them in useful categories would be futile. It should also be kept in mind that reading problems tend to have several causes rather than just one. The more inhibiting factors present, the greater the possibility that a reading disability will occur.

Effects of Lack of Success

The inability to learn to read satisfactorily usually means severe frustration for the child. When his unsuccessful attempts to read make him conspicuous in a socially unfavorable way, the child is hurt and ashamed. His continued lack of success with attendant frustration and feelings of insecurity brings on emotional maladjustment (Sornson 1950). Some of these children become easily convinced that they are stupid. This feeling is frequently enhanced by the attitudes of their classmates, their parents, and even the teacher, if she fails to understand the real problem. The reading-disabled child comes to dislike reading and seeks opportunities to avoid it. Sometimes failure leads children to become timid, withdrawn; they frequently daydream. In other cases, children show their insecurity through nervous habits such as nail-biting, or through avoidant-motivated illnesses such as headaches. Still others may compensate for their feelings of inferiority by developing various forms of antisocial behavior.

Most children who enter school with well-integrated personalities are eager to learn to read. Such children thrive on success and approval. For some of them, though, learning to read will mean only the failure and frustration of reading difficulties. When success is denied and approval withheld, as failure and frustration increase, an emotional reaction is a natural consequence. From this, personal and social maladjustment often follow. Reading disability has led to personal maladjustment.

Maladjustment as a Cause

Some children are emotionally unstable even before they begin school. The basis of this maladjustment may be constitutional or environmental or may be due to a series of unfortunate incidents during the preschool years. Whatever the basis, some children exhibit impulsive responses, negative attitudes, irritability, attention difficulties, and lack of energy. These children are unable to achieve the cooperation and sustained effort required in learning to read. Until their adjustment is improved, there is little progress in learning to read.

Jorm, Share, Matthews, and Maclean (1986) who studied 453 kindergarten children through second grade, found that upon school entry, children who later developed reading difficulties were more likely to exhibit behavior problems than children who progressed normally in reading. The researchers attributed the behavior problems of the children they studied principally to attentional deficit.

McMichael (1979) also studied young children. She investigated the sequential relationship of antisocial emotional disorders and reading difficulties among 168 boys in their first two years at school. Her results indicated that antisocial behavior was apparent from the first months and was associated with reading difficulties through the first two years. Both studies suggest that the behavioral problems associated with reading disability may precede, and not just be a reaction to, difficulty with reading.

The personality patterns of backward readers in two special classes were explored by Frost (1965). He found that 40 percent of the children rated as maladjusted and another 40 percent were unsettled or likely to become maladjusted. The outstanding characteristic of these children was depression. Weinberg and Rehmet (1983) also found a high rate of depression in children with severe reading difficulties.

In a study of 108 emotionally disturbed boys ages 9 to 14, Graubard (1971) found their reading retardation to be about as much as for regular class students of the same ages. The greatest degree of retardation was found for the conduct-problem groups.

On the basis of research into the relationship of reading achievement and behavioral disorder involving 130 children from grades 2 through 6, Glavin and Annesley (1971) warn that learning problems do not disappear after the treatment of emotional problems unless the learning problems receive specific attention. They do not feel that conduct problems must be changed before academic achievement can be stressed, and they suggest that academic achievement can be required from conduct-problem children without causing additional conduct problems.

Maladjustment: Cause and Effect

When reading disability is accompanied by emotional involvement, the question arises whether the personality maladjustment is primary or secondary. There is no consensus among writers and investigators on this point. Examination of reported evidence and the views of writers and clinical workers suggest that although in some instances a previous emotional or behavioral difficulty prevents a child from learning to read, in most instances emotional or behavioral difficulties are reactions to reading failure. There are no data available that can assign exact percentages to the proportion of instances in which emotional or behavioral difficulties are causes rather than effects. The view that such maladjustments are most often results rather than causes is supported by the fact that in most instances emotional and behavioral difficulties improve as reading disability is alleviated by remedial instruction.

When emotional and personality maladjustment involves both cause and effect of reading disability, as previously noted, the interaction tends to become circular. In many cases, it is probable that there is a reciprocal relationship. Lack of success during early attempts to learn to read causes tension, stress, and frustration, usually accompanied by feelings of inadequacy and often by negative behavior. Resulting personal and social adjustment difficulties then handicap further progress in learning to read. Thus a vicious circle is formed. The reading disability and the emotional and behavioral reactions to the reading disability interact, each making the other more intense. For a more in-depth review of stress and reading difficulties, with suggestions for reducing stress during instruction of reading disabled children, see Gentile and McMillan (1987). Suggestions on how to help poor readers attend to and complete reading tasks are given in Chapter 13.

ENVIRONMENTAL FACTORS

Achievement in reading depends on the child's personal strengths and the demands of the reading program. Children with a background of family tension may approach reading as unhappy and insecure learners. Children from a culture different from that of the teacher and different from that portrayed in the materials they read may experience unusual difficulty in learning. Children who feel comfortable listening to and speaking a language or dialect different from the teacher's and different from that in their books may find learning to read unusually demanding.

Some of the children who are from unstable homes, or who must make cultural or language adjustments, do learn to read. Many teachers are sensitive to the students' needs and adapt instruction accordingly. Many students can adjust to the school's demands, even though they must try harder than the typical child.

Home Environment

Some children come from a home environment which provides love, understanding, an opportunity to develop individuality, and a feeling of security. Others do not. Quarreling parents, broken homes, child neglect, child abuse, overprotection, parental domination, anxiety, hostility, or destructive rivalry among siblings are likely to produce stress and feelings of insecurity. There is more evidence of family conflict in the homes of poor readers than in those of children with no reading difficulties, according to Seigler and Gynther (1960). Disturbed parent-child relations, marked sibling jealousy, and unfavorable attitudes toward school were characteristic of the poor readers studied by Crane (1950). Thayer (1970) counseled disabled readers and their parents, and then compared the reading progress of these pupils to that of those who had had no counseling. The former had made large gains while the latter had made none. These results suggest that improvement of home conditions facilitates improvement in reading.

Neglect or lack of sympathetic understanding may cause a child to feel that he is not loved or wanted. Apparent indifference on the part of a parent or overconcern for a child's difficulties in learning may cause anxiety, lack of confidence, and perhaps attention-seeking behavior.

Overprotection or domination of a child by his parents can lead to adjustment difficulties. Too much parental control can prevent a child from developing initiative and cause him to become so dependent on others that he is unable to learn independently. If a parent attempts to dominate all of a child's activities, including learning to read, the child may rebel against such domination and against reading as well. A parent's solicitude for every phase of a child's reading activities may produce anxiety to the point at which the child may reject reading entirely.

When a child's reading achievement is compared unfavorably to that of a brother or sister, it may have a bad effect. A child who cannot compete successfully may attempt to escape from competition and may refuse to continue to learn to read. Any conflict between parent and teacher over a child's reading is likely to have negative consequences. A study by Klein, Altman, Dreizen, Friedman, and Powers (1981) found that parental attitudes, such as being openly critical of the teacher, principal, or school, do affect a child's learning. These researchers also point out that some parents believe and communicate to their children the view that it is unnecessary to be concerned about school success. Learning is viewed as unimportant. Other parents hold the attitude that "high academic achievement is crucial to survival." These parents pressure their children for outstanding success in all school learning.

A child under unusual stress from conditions at home may become an anxious, insecure learner or give up much too easily when reading becomes demanding. Some children react to home stress by disrupting the classroom. In certain other instances, the result is quite different. Some children find reading alleviates personal anxiety and insecurity, and they use it and school success as an escape from environmental pressures. But usually home tension and pressures hinder rather than help reading progress.

Results of a national assessment of educational progress have been reported by Walberg and Tsai (1985). Among the 1,459 nine-year-old students surveyed, home environmental factors most associated with reading achievement were favorable attitude toward reading, reading materials available in the home, the use of English in the home, and kindergarten attendance. Neuman (1986) reports on the basis of a questionnaire administered to the parents of 84 fifth-grade students that frequency of reading to young children and availability of magazines in the home are related to the amount of children's leisure reading.

Austin, Bush and Huebner (1961) point out that, although certain home factors have been shown to be partly responsible for a child's success or lack of success in reading, these can almost never be cited as the single causal factor.

Attitudes

It is important that the child develop a favorable attitude toward school, classmates, and reading. While positive attitudes foster progress in learning to read, negative attitudes can result in reading difficulties. Personal and social adjustment, home conditions, peer relationships, teacher-pupil relations, and the instructional program all influence attitudes toward reading.

Although most children begin school eager to learn to read, some do not. Occasionally there will be a beginner who, for one reason or another, is antagonistic toward learning in general or toward reading in particular. It requires tact, patience, and sympathetic understanding and guidance from the teacher for these children to form positive attitudes toward reading.

In most instances, unfavorable attitudes toward reading come after, rather than before, the child is exposed to reading instruction. That is, successful achievers form positive attitudes toward reading and school, while slow-progress pupils and reading-disabled children have negative attitudes. Sound reading instruction emphasizing each child's successes does much to ensure that the child will maintain and acquire positive attitudes toward reading and other school activities--in short, that the child will like school.

Cultural and Language Differences

There is little doubt that the child who approaches reading from a cultural or language background different from that of his teacher and different from that of the material he is expected to read is at a disadvantage.

When cultural and language differences are also accompanied by poverty, poor food, poor sanitation, poor housing, and poor medical care, the disadvantage is compounded (Birch and Gussow 1970). When home conditions prompt the teacher to expect little from the student, the pathway to failure has been prepared (Rist 1970). Although, as Cohen and Cooper (1972) argue, it is not the role of education to eradicate all social ills, a major contribution can be made by teaching poor children adequate reading skills. The best way to do this, according to Cohen (1969), is to provide intensive, quality instruction, based not on race or social condition but on the learning needs of each child.

There are many kinds and types of cultural differences. They can affect the teachers' perceptions of their students and the childrens' perceptions of their teachers, their behavior in school, and the nature and importance of reading. For example, there are cultural differences in how a child should behave when an adult is speaking, the desirability or undesirability of answering when unsure, the amount of competition or cooperation displayed to peers, the amount of physical aggression that should be used, and the amount of control asserted over his own destiny. A child may be misunderstood by a teacher with a different cultural heritage, unless the teacher is aware of the differences and of the implications of such cultural differences.

If reading materials deal with events, activities, ideas, and ideals quite different from those in the child's own experiences, reading itself may seem to be for someone else, and may be rejected or considered unimportant for that reason. If a child's books negatively portray people from his culture, the child may reject reading, or may learn to read but develop adverse feelings about himself or his family. Spache (1970) provides a list of realistic yet positive books from which appropriate selections could be made for children from various minority groups. But, as Vick (1973) points out, there are many excellent materials available which have content suitable for all children.

Language differences pose an additional problem in instruction. Some children may speak a dialectal variation of the standard English used in the classroom. Other children may speak a foreign language. These language differences increase the difficulty of learning and of teaching reading.

Simons (1973), commenting on the mismatch between dialect and standard English, states that this causes reading interference. He criticizes both the unsystematic attempts to teach standard English along with reading and readers in which the stories are written in dialect. He feels that teaching standard English as a part of the reading lesson interferes with learning to read. Dialectal readers are unpopular because not all children who speak a dialect speak the same one. Simons and others, including Venezky and Chapman (1973) and Rystrom (1973), believe that the teacher's knowledge of dialectal differences and her attitude toward children who do not speak standard English are more important than dialect or materials.

Although dialectal differences interfere with learning to read standard English, language differences create even more serious problems. There is a great need for bilingual teachers who understand the positive qualities and are sensitive to the real needs of the non-English-speaking child. In an extensive review of the literature, Engle (1975) was unable to determine whether minority children in a bilingual culture should be taught to read in their native language or the dominant language. She pointed out that any method which undermines a child's pride in his native language or culture, or places a child in a situation in which he cannot understand the teacher's instruction, will be unsuccessful. Thonis (1976) is a valuable resource for those teaching Spanish-speaking children.

In summary, most authors agree that teachers of children with cultural or language differences must understand these differences in order to be effective in teaching reading. A positive attitude is also necessary, as is the ability to communicate to each child a sense of his dignity and worth.

The educational problems in improving the reading growth of children with cultural and language differences belong to the developmental reading program rather than to the remedial program. The educational program of these children should be adjusted to meet their individual needs.

Children from homes in which a language other than English is spoken may know little or no English. They may be unable to understand or to speak English well enough to participate in ordinary classroom activities. These children may appear to be of low mental ability, because it is difficult to obtain a fair estimate of a child's intelligence when he can neither understand nor speak English, no matter which type of test is used.

The reading difficulties of children who are learning English as a second language tend to be due to their inability to understand or speak English. The procedures ordinarily used in teaching beginning reading in our schools assume that each child has already learned to understand and speak the language. These children first need a program to strengthen their English. A preparatory instructional period ordinarily should have three simultaneous activities: first, building up a basic vocabulary for understanding and speaking; second, improvement of facility in oral communication; and third, providing a background of meaningful experiences. Words and concepts associated with experiences must be in English. Thus the child learns to speak and understand a vocabulary before he encounters it in reading. It is probable that much of the training in the understanding and use of spoken English should be carried out in sessions not concerned with reading. In general, lessons in reading should not be complicated by simultaneous training in pronunciation. All this does not mean that no reading is done while the child is being taught English. Although the two can be done concurrently, they should be in separate class periods.

These children do not become reading disabled if an appropriate teaching program is organized early in their school lives. Nevertheless, the development of an adequate background in English will be gradual. Until this is achieved, these children are at a disadvantage in all school activities. The program may need to be continued throughout the elementary school years.

Children from culturally different environments and speaking a dialect other than standard English have a somewhat different problem. Preschool-level programming is especially beneficial to culturally different children. As Lloyd (1965) points out, language patterns are established firmly by the time a child is six years old. Therefore, it is desirable to encourage early language development and build essential concepts in young preschool children. Such development of language and of necessary concepts is especially important for the culturally different child. This is part of the role of programs for preschool children. Preschool programs are important in helping disadvantaged children prepare for reading and other learning. Special teaching is also needed to help the disadvantaged child progress through the elementary grades.

Continued emphasis upon real experiences, field trips, audiovisual presentations, storytelling, puppetry, and role playing should be maintained throughout the school years. The language used as a by-product of these experiences is beneficial to disadvantaged children and is an important part of beginning reading instruction. The language experience approach may be used in a major or supplementary role in reading instruction. In this approach, children tell a story, immediately tied to a real experience, which the teacher writes down verbatim. The children then review the story and work on activities associated with the story, such as reading sentences, matching words, or drawing pictures to illustrate the story. For a child with experiential differences, language differences, or dialectal differences, this approach is useful in that it deals with experiences he has had, and it uses words and language structures with which he is familiar and comfortable.

Some children with dialectal differences or those for whom English is a second language have reading difficulties that can be corrected by specific remedial training. They should receive immediate help. These children should be treated like others disabled in reading; their reading patterns should be diagnosed, their basic reading problems isolated, and individual remedial plans formulated.

The fact that a given child, for example, has a dialectal difference itself should be taken into account in the remedial plan, and the techniques used should include the language experience approach. Silent reading exercises should always use interesting, meaningful material. Any oral reading errors related to the child's dialect should be ignored.

It should be remembered that children with dialectal differences understand radio and television well, although when they discuss what they have heard or seen, they tend to use their own dialect rather than the standard English used in the radio or television programs. This should not be criticized or belittled.

We suggest that these children do much independent reading of material written in standard English. The material should be very easy for each child to read, and the child should be allowed to discuss it as he likes. We also suggest that the child, for example, select parts of a story best liked, most exciting, most humorous, or well-written. The child then might choose a part of the story to read aloud to others. The child should read this material as it is written. It might be even more helpful if he pretended to be a television personality and read as he would on a real television program.

EDUCATIONAL FACTORS

Among all the factors that are considered possible causes of reading disability, the group of conditions classed as educational stands out as tremendously important. Careful consideration of various learner characteristics which predispose children to experience difficulty in learning to read does not diminish the importance of the educational program as the major cause of reading difficulty. Rather, it shows how necessary it is for each child's instruction in reading to meet his individual learning needs. In the vast majority of reading disability cases, careful diagnosis reveals that there is faulty learning or a lack of educational adjustment in the student's instructional program.

As discussed earlier, reading is a complex process made of many interrelated skills and abilities. As a child progresses through the reading program there is constant danger that he may fail to acquire these essential learnings or that he may get into difficulty because he may over- or underemphasize any one of them. Under the broad category of educational causes, several educational practices must be considered. Although this book discusses them separately, it should not be supposed that they operate in isolation, but rather are related and interacting.

School Administrative Policies

Success in teaching children to read depends on the teacher. Thus we must examine the role that certain administrative policies play in determining how effectively a teacher can organize and carry out her reading program. Some of the policies which hinder even the best of teachers will be considered briefly.

Reading versus pupil development.   Whether reading or child development should be the chief concern of the school during the early grades is controversial. Some educators believe that the emphasis should be almost entirely on developing reading skills. Others object to this and feel that the school's chief concern should be the happy, balanced development of each child's personality. Many teachers are not only aware of the issue but also may be under pressure to stress one approach at the expense of the other. The argument of those opposing effective reading in the primary grades is that putting pressure on the children to read may produce maladjustment. They claim that emphasis upon reading destroys interest in learning since, they believe, reading is an activity foreign to the real interests of children in these grades. Actually, there need be no serious conflict between well-balanced child development and all-around development which includes reading, if reading is taught properly. With individualized instruction, including reading readiness, development of reading can become an integral part of a well-balanced total program. In this program only those who are ready begin to read early in grade one. Other children start later, when they are capable of succeeding. When frustrations arise, it is likely to be because of the method of instruction. Reading instruction suffers when administrative pressure overemphasizes or underemphasizes reading in the primary grades.

Promotion policy and curriculum rigidity.   In 1938 Cole stated that the reason for the prevalance of remedial reading classes was the failure of schools to adjust the curriculum to the current promotion policy. To some degree this indictment is still valid. She was referring to promoting children mainly by age rather than by achievement, with no accompanying change in curriculum requirements. This produces a wider and wider range in reading ability in successively higher grades. At the same time, curriculum requirements remain fairly rigid. When pupils are promoted by age, not achievement, and there are no instructional adjustments made, then much of the material assigned to pupils in the higher grades is too advanced for the poorer readers' level of reading competence. The poorer readers also do not receive needed instruction in certain reading skills, because these skills are not usually emphasized in the higher grades. For some pupils, the result is reading disability. Yet it is not the yearly promotions per se which have caused the reading difficulty, but rather the failure to adjust instruction to the individual needs of certain students. If alternative materials are assigned and if essential skills are taught, then reading disability need not result from promotion by age.

Lack of Readiness for Beginning Reading Instruction

Success in beginning reading largely depends on the child's overall level of maturity. The pattern of growth entails many types of abilities, acquired behaviors, and specific knowledges. Although some aspects of reading readiness come with maturation, many of the most important ingredients are learned and can therefore be taught. This means that when a child approaches beginning reading lacking certain essential skills and knowledges these can and should be taught before or during beginning reading instruction. Research by Spache (1965) has demonstrated the effectiveness of appropriate training in visual and auditory perceptual skills for children who needed such skill development to succeed in beginning reading. The evidence suggests that the training was effective in developing visual and auditory perceptual skills before beginning reading instruction, and that in addition, such prereading skill development facilitated initial reading success. Other beginning reading achievements, such as knowledge of word meanings, attention to oral directions, ability to work independently and to work cooperatively in groups, and even the desire to read, can be taught.

Many first-grade children are not ready to learn to read in the typical program and therefore instructional modifications must be made if they are to experience initial success in learning to read. Reading disability is frequently caused by starting a child in a standard reading program before the child is ready. Because of lack of experience, verbal facility, visual or auditory perceptual development, overall immaturity, or a combination of these, the child is unable to achieve what is expected of him daily and therefore does not succeed. Instead of learning to read, the most the child can do is acquire only bits of reading skills which he is unable to use. Thus he falls farther and farther behind. The outcome will not be reading well, but frustration and failure, perhaps leading to feelings of inadequacy, inferiority, insecurity, and even rebellion. Such a child may even come to hate reading and all persons and activities connected with it.

The many failures in reading during the primary grades are due in part to the lack of instructional adaptation to differences in readiness for beginning reading instruction. Any educational program or administrative policy which provides exactly the same formal reading instruction for all pupils at the beginning of grade one causes reading failure for many pupils.

Lack of Adjustment to Individual Differences

Beginning in grade one and continuing in every grade thereafter, reading instruction can be effective for all pupils only when there is satisfactory adjustment to individual differences. Without such adjustment, reading difficulties arise. This topic has been considered in detail earlier.

Methods of Teaching

Most reading difficulties are caused by childrens' failure to acquire necessary learnings, or by faulty learnings, as they go through the reading program. The complexity of the reading process offers many opportunities for children to experience difficulties. Sometimes this is coupled with *ineffective teaching*. For one reason or another, there may be a lack of educational adjustment to the needs of certain students, so that they do not acquire essential learnings.

A number of factors may lead to ineffective teaching. Curriculum requirements may take so much of the teacher's time that the teacher is unable to individualize the program satisfactorily. Concurrently, the methods or materials used may be too difficult for certain youngsters. Under these conditions, it is probable that certain students are pushed through the program too rapidly to learn what the program is designed to teach.

Using materials and methods that seem dull and unimportant *to the student* is another part of ineffective teaching. In beginning reading, for instance, it is important that the child develop the attitude of insisting on understanding what is read. To do this, the reading material should either tell a story (have a plot) or give some information. This cannot be done by excessive use of badly constructed and insipid experience charts, nor by reading dull and anemic materials made of almost meaningless sentences, or by isolated drill on word parts. One youngster, on being exposed to such material, said to his teacher, "That sounds silly." It is not surprising that some children react to such reading and acquire negative attitudes which become obstacles to learning to read.

Similarly, procedures which do not tie class activities to the reading program can lead to reading disability. When reading is taught separately from activities the child enjoys, it is no wonder that the child sees no reason for learning to read. In contrast, if there is a relationship between reading and class activities, so that reading itself is a tool for those activities, the child becomes motivated to learn to read. It is desirable that reading activities affect some of of the important things the child is doing in the class, and that many of the class activities grow out of the reading program. Then the child can see a reason for reading, and interest and motivation are maintained at a high level.

It should be emphasized here that interest is not synonymous with entertainment. Real interest backed by strong motivation is not found by flitting from one amusing incident or story to another. Much better is a program in which reading is tied carefully to activities in the classroom.

This program would imply coordination among the language arts, speaking, writing, listening, spelling, and reading. Difficulties arise, for instance, when a youngster is expected to spell a word and use it in his writing when he has not learned to recognize it in his reading.

Excessive emphasis on isolated drill kills interest. As we shall see later, some drill is desirable and necessary. Sometimes, however, drills are so far removed from the act of reading that the child cannot bridge the gap. Not only is the child unable to transfer what is learned in the drill to actual reading, but he also cannot see the reason for the drill. Methods concentrating on isolated drill, rather than sharing stories and experiences, lead to loss of interest and inhibit the desire to learn to read.

Inappropriate emphasis on the basic reading skills can prevent effective reading. The basic skills include a sight vocabulary, word-recognition techniques, word meanings, reading by thought units or phrasing, comprehension, and study skills. Either underemphasis or overemphasis can lead to difficulties. Probably more children have difficulties due to underemphasis than to overemphasis. The basic skills underlie efficiency in reading. Stories and other reading matter in books are simply materials enabling the teacher to teach the child how to read. To do this, the skills and abilities should be properly stressed and systematically ordered.

Many youngsters are in trouble because progressive tendencies in teaching are not well thought out. It should not be forgotten that methods which ignore systematic, orderly development of the essential skills and abilities are not beneficial to the student. It is difficult to imagine proper emphasis on these skills and abilities without an orderly, sequential, reading program. Perfunctory, unorganized, and meaningless teaching of the content subjects contributes to the reading difficulties of some students. Teaching of the content subjects can contribute to effective reading if training in the basic skills and abilities is an integral part of that instructional program. The introduction to reading content materials should be made in a well-organized program that shows the child how to read by teaching the essential skills and abilities.

When emphasis upon mechanics of reading leads to neglect of meanings, children run into serious difficulty. Undue stress on word recognition, perfection of enunciation, and speed may lead to verbalism, the pronunciation of words without understanding their meanings. A girl in one of our remedial reading groups could read aloud fourth-grade materials without error, but she could comprehend practically nothing of what she "read." To pronounce words without understanding their meaning is not reading. It is merely word-calling. This girl was reading-disabled.

Overemphasis on phonic analysis as a word-recognition technique frequently causes disability. The child is so intent upon sounding out most of the words he encounters that he cannot attend to meaning. Or he laboriously separates a new word into its component sounds and then is unable to blend the separate sounds into a recognizable pronunciation of the word. Such children usually have an insufficient sight vocabulary and are unable to make adequate use of context clues for word recognition.

To progress satisfactorily in learning to read, there must be a proper balance among many skills and abilities. A sight vocabulary, various techniques for word recognition, concepts and word meanings, reading in thought units, comprehension and study skills, and many other abilities must not be taught separately. They are all part of an integrated sequential program. There is a balanced relationship between them that must be striven for. The student who gets into difficulty is quite frequently the child for whom a balance among them has not been maintained.

We grant that it is difficult to imagine a teacher who is able to handle a class of thirty children and at the same time keep account of all the essential balances while carrying out her sequential program in a systematic and orderly fashion. But the teacher should never forget the importance of the balanced program and do what is possible to achieve it. The smaller the class, the greater the possibility of maintaining the balance.

Role of the Teacher

The role of the teacher is important. She can have a positive or negative influence upon progress in learning to read. Students are fortunate if their teacher is so able, well-trained, and sympathetic that she maintains good student-teacher relationships and is able to achieve a proper balance in developing skills and abilities in the reading program. When teachers deviate from this, reading instruction is apt to suffer. The teacher who is inept because of either poor training, lack of experience, or a slavish devotion to inflexible routine, is unable to adjust reading instruction to the varied needs of her students.

A teacher's personality, especially when she has a negative attitude toward a particular student, may cause or intensify the stress associated with failure in reading. Apparent indifference, hostility, or obvious anxiety in the teacher when a student has difficulty in reading intensifies the child's emotional reactions and feelings of insecurity. We have to face it—too often the teacher is not without blame when a child becomes reading-disabled.

Role of the Library or Media Center

The school library or media center also plays an important part in the total reading program. Although the teacher develops the child's reading skills by means of the formal program of instruction in the classroom, it is through the school library or media center that the child's interests in reading are pursued and expanded. The librarian can provide teachers with materials for developmental reading programs as well as for individual and remedial programs. Within the library or media center, there can be attractive book displays, book talks, and storytelling hours to make reading exciting to the students. The library's varied book collections offer students opportunities for reference reading, research, and additional reading at each grade level.

Secondary schools lead in library services for their pupils; many elementary schools have been much less fortunate in their library facilities. In fact, some elementary schools have no books at all, other than textbooks. Other schools have small classroom collections, while still others, fortunately, have a library room or media center with a trained librarian or media expert.

The value of a library or media center to the elementary pupil's advancement in reading cannot be overemphasized. Gaver (1961) evaluated six school libraries and their services, as well as quantity and quality of reading done by the students. She found that higher educational gains were made when there was a school library, and students read more and better books when there was a library.

SUMMARY

The possible causes of reading disability are numerous. A single factor seldom causes reading disability. In all but the mildest cases, the difficulty is due to a composite of related conditions. The contributing factors interact in a pattern. The view taken in this book, therefore, is that reading disability is due to multiple causation.

Reading disability is usually accompanied by emotional involvement adversely affecting the child's personal and social adjustment and classroom behavior. This maladjustment may be due to constitutional factors, to environmental factors, or to failure in reading. In some cases a child may be emotionally upset or behaviorally disordered upon school arrival. Such a child is apt to have difficulty in reading. For many children, frustration arises from reading difficulty. In these instances the reading difficulty causes emotional upset often expressed by a wide variety of reading avoidant behaviors. It seems that emotional maladjustment may be both effect and cause. When an emotional reaction arises from reading disability, it may then become a handicap to further learning. There is, in such cases, a reciprocal relationship between emotion, behavior, and reading disability. When maladjustment is due to reading failure, it tends to disappear when the child learns to read satisfactorily. When maladjustment is the primary problem, the child should be served by an appropriate specialist.

For children who are learning English as a second language, ordinary reading instruction is usually not productive until they have made some progress in spoken English. Just as soon as the teacher considers it feasible, however, they can be taught reading concurrent with continued instruction in spoken English.

Disadvantaged children benefit greatly from preschool programming. Good health, sound nutrition, a positive self-concept, and language development are all helpful. In the preschool and the school years, opportunities to participate in real experiences and to utilize audiovisual presentations are especially beneficial to many disadvantaged children. The language experience approach can be an important part of beginning reading instruction for many children with experiential, language, or dialectal differences.

Frequently, reading disability is due largely to educational factors. Any administrative policy which prevents sufficient individualization of instruction, including emphasis upon reading readiness, prevents effective progress in reading. Failure to acquire the necessary learnings or the acquisition of faulty learnings is most frequently due to ineffective teaching. One or more of the following factors may be involved in the ineffective teaching which brings about reading disability; too rapid progress in the instructional schedule, isolation of reading instruction from other school activities, inappropriate emphasis on some technique or skill, or treating reading as a by-product of content studies. Frequently, the difficulty occurs because the instructional program has failed to maintain a balance in the growth of the large number of skills and abilities involved in learning to read.

If one conclusion were to be made, it is that there is no one cause for all reading disabilities. Each case is unique. Only when there is a valid diagnosis will there be a sound basis for planning an individual remedial program to alleviate the disability.

STUDY QUESTIONS

1. How do emotional and behavioral problems interfere with learning to read?
2. How do problems with reading affect a child's adjustment and behavior?
3. How do parental attitudes affect a child's progress in learning to read?
4. What should the teacher emphasize in teaching children with cultural or language differences?
5. What should be done if a first-grade child is not ready to learn to read in the typical program?
6. Why is it bad practice to emphasize the mechanics of reading to the extent that it leads to neglect of meaning?

SELECTED READINGS

GENTILE, L. M., AND M. M. McMILLAN. *Stress and Reading Difficulties.* Newark, DE: International Reading Association, 1987.

GILLET, J. W., AND C. TEMPLE. *Understanding Reading Problems,* 2nd ed., Chap. 10. Boston: Little, Brown, & Company, 1986.

HARRIS, A. J., AND E. R. SIPAY. *How to Increase Reading Ability,* 8th ed., Chap. 10. New York: Longman, Inc., 1985.

LAFFEY, J. L., AND R. SHUY, EDS. *Language Differences: Do They Interfere?* Newark, DE: International Reading Association, 1973.

McCORMICK, S. *Remedial and Clinical Reading Instruction,* Chap. 21. Columbus, OH: Charles E. Merrill Publishing Company, 1987.

QUANT, I. *Self-concept and Reading.* Newark, DE: International Reading Association, 1972.

SPACHE, G. D. *Investigating the Issues of Reading Disabilities,* Chaps. 5, 8, and 9. Boston: Allyn & Bacon, Inc., 1976.

7

Basic Considerations in Diagnosing Reading Difficulties

Remedial work not based on a thorough diagnosis is likely to waste time and effort for both the student and the remedial teacher. Moreover, remedial work done without adequate diagnosis is likely to fail. A student who has had difficulty with reading may already be insecure. Continued failure in the remedial program would be unfortunate. The person responsible for the remedial program should be aware of the possible results of failure, and should make every effort to ensure that each child will be successful and recognize that success.

GENERAL PRINCIPLES OF DIAGNOSIS

An adequate diagnosis determines in no small measure the success of the remedial program. Since reading is a complex process, there is no one single or simple cure for reading disability. Remedial training that is effective in one case might be detrimental or wasteful in another. It is only through understanding the underlying factors of disability for any given child that an adequate remedial program can be formulated. For example, two students have difficulty with reading. Appraisal shows that both are low in reading comprehension. Further analysis of the difficulty indicates that one student is low in comprehension because of inadequate recognition vocabulary. The other student is low because he is a word-by-word reader who is so conscious of individual words that he is unable to group them into thought units. The first student needs remedial work to build up awareness of words and ability to inspect them in detail. Obviously, this procedure would be detrimental to the second student's need for overcoming his overemphasis on isolated words.

The problem of helping the disabled reader is complicated further by the many characteristics of the child and his learning environment that affect his reading growth. It is necessary to adjust to some of the variations within the physical, emotional, educational, intellectual, and environmental factors if reading growth is to progress smoothly or at all. Sometimes these same factors need to be corrected before remedial programs can be effective.

It is little wonder, then, that the classroom teacher, attempting to correct disabilities in this intricate learning for a wide variety of children in trouble, finds that no two cases have the same instructional needs. Any attempt to give a child remedial instruction must be based on a thorough diagnosis of the child's unique reading needs and personal characteristics. This diagnosis is the very core of successful correction programs, whether they are for the less complex problems met in the classroom or for the more complicated problems which require the specialist teacher.

The classroom teacher may need special help in diagnosing or correcting some of the more complex disabled readers, or when limitations in reading are so subtle that a diagnosis, more detailed and more penetrating than the teacher has time or training to give, is required. Frequently it is necessary to study the reading pattern of a disabled reader by means of individual appraisals that take several hours to administer. It is expedient to have the more detailed diagnoses conducted by someone who can work individually with the children over a long period of time. In many cases of disability in reading, it is necessary to obtain evaluations and corrective help from other specialists, such as social workers, psychologists, or physicians.

Of course the teacher should diagnose and correct as many of the reading difficulties as she can. The early detection and correction of these problems will prevent many from becoming more complex. There are many diagnostic procedures that the classroom teacher can use in studying the moderately disabled reader. In the more subtle cases, an outside diagnosis may be needed to help the teacher formulate the kinds of remedial treatment she can provide in the classroom. In some instances, both the detailed diagnosis and the corrective treatment should be given by specialists. But in every reading disability case, whether simple or complex, a diagnosis is necessary.

A diagnosis is always directed toward formulating methods of improvement.   The diagnosis of a disabled reader should collect information necessary for planning a corrective program. There are two types of diagnosis— etiological and therapeutic. Etiological diagnosis finds out what originally caused a child to get into difficulty. This is often impossible and frequently useless for formulating a remedial program. It is of little use, for example, to search the records and find that a child is in difficulty in reading in the fourth grade because he was absent from school with the measles when he was in the first grade. Nothing can be done now to give him the help that should have been available when he returned to school after a month's absence during the first grade. This information, collected and summarized for research purposes, would be useful to prevent reading difficulties, but it is not useful for the immediate job of correcting a reading disability that began several years earlier.

Therapeutic diagnosis is concerned with the conditions now present in the child in order to plan a program of reeducation. The therapeutic diagnostician searches for the reading strengths and limitations of a child and for any characteristics within this child's present environment or makeup that need to be corrected before remedial instruction can be successful, or for conditions that need to be adjusted to before he can be expected to make progress. The reading specialist is more concerned about a current hearing loss, for example, than about finding out that the child was in difficulty because he had a temporary hearing loss several years ago.

Diagnosis is more than appraisal of reading skills and abilities.   The complex nature of reading disability and the many factors related to achievement in reading make it necessary to explore the child's many traits and reading skills and abilities for an adequate diagnosis. Besides discovering the deficiencies in reading that are at the root of the disability, it is often necessary for the reading specialist to appraise the physical, sensory, emotional, and environmental factors that could impede progress. Frequently, the diagnosis requires other expert help. The specialist should be alert to the possible effect of conditions within the child or his environment that require specialized help. All appraisals made in more complex cases should be extensive enough to pinpoint the existence of such limitations. The measurements used in a reading diagnosis will be discussed in the following chapters. It is enough to say here that the diagnosis should supply all the information pertinent to correct the disability.

The diagnosis must be efficient.   The diagnosis of some disabled readers is often lengthy and intricate. In other cases, the child's instructional needs can be isolated relatively easily and quickly. A diagnosis should proceed as far, and only as far, as is necessary to formulate a remedial program for each specific case. The diagnosis should proceed from group measurements to the more detailed individual measurements needed for the case under study. The diagnosis should be reached by measuring first the relatively common types of problems and then the more unusual ones.

It would be expected, for example, that one would routinely give to all suspected reading disability cases measurements of general reading capability and of general mental ability. It would only be in an unusual case that a complete neurological examination would be required. The procedures in diagnosis are much like successive screenings in which only the more complex and subtle cases are retained for further measurement and study. There are, then, various levels of diagnosis: (a) appraisals which are made routinely for all children in the schools or for all children referred for special study, (b) appraisals more detailed in character and made only in those instances when more analytical study is warranted, and (c) appraisals which are individual in nature, made only in more subtle cases.

In reading diagnosis, as in all educational diagnosis, there are three levels of study. The level reached in any one case depends on the characteristics of that particular case. The three levels through which some cases must be carried are general diagnosis, specific diagnosis, and child-study diagnosis.

General diagnosis has three purposes. First, it gives information necessary to adjust instruction to meet the needs of groups of children in general. For example, a fifth-grade class as a whole may be found to be relatively weak in reading achievement. If so, the conclusion may be that more attention should be given to reading instruction than had been given in the past. Second, the general diagnosis can give the information necessary for adjusting instruction to individual differences in reading found within the class. It can, for example, indicate the range of general reading capability with which the instruction must cope and also indicate the individuals that would profit from modifications usually made within a class to adjust to individual differences. Third, a general diagnosis can help to find the children in need of a more detailed analysis of their reading disability.

Specific diagnosis makes two important contributions to the correction of reading disability. First, it locates those areas of limited ability that need to be explored more fully. Second, it can often indicate by itself the instructional adjustments required. Many children, however, need a more detailed study of their reading problems and limiting characteristics than can be made at the specific level of assessment.

Child-study diagnosis is necessary for many disabled readers. This level of assessment involves a more detailed, thorough, and time-consuming study than is warranted for children with less complex reading problems. Many children's learning problems may require only a general study of their educational achievement and intellectual capacity. Other children's difficulties may require differential or specific study to locate the precise areas of limitation. Some of these children's problems may be so subtle or complex that detailed child study is required before a remedial program can be designed.

Information found in cumulative records should be used.

The yearly records of the school will give the specialist information about the progress the student has made throughout his school life. They will also indicate the subjects that have been difficult for the student. They will tell, too, about any periods of prolonged absence or changes of school. These records help to establish the grade level at which the trouble with reading may have started. The examiner should make a careful study of the school history of the student and should record those circumstances that are related to reading. Such a study often eliminates duplicate testing and gives information not available from other sources.

Only pertinent information should be collected.   There is a tendency for reading specialists to add tests to their routine diagnostic procedures on an experimental basis. This is as it should be, but when such tests are found to have little diagnostic value, they should be discontinued. The time, energy, and expense involved in obtaining valid diagnostic information is so great that persons making diagnoses should appraise the measuring instruments being used to make sure they are efficient and that they add to the understanding of the children's instructional needs. Unnecessary duplication should be avoided.

The child should be given every consideration when tests are administered in diagnosis. Indiscriminate testing may set a child against the whole procedure or even may cause him to doubt his ability to learn. The specialist should investigate thoroughly the specific reading pattern of each disabled reader, obtain a valid estimate of the child's learning capability, and be satisfied that the child's sensory abilities are normal or have been corrected so far as is possible. The child's classroom behavior should be considered. In addition, any special psychological and neurological characteristics should be noted when there is an indication that this information is pertinent to the optimal adjustment of the child being studied. It is advisable to intersperse reading measures with other activities since many children who are seriously disabled become resistant in reading situations. They easily become discouraged or even uncooperative if they are subjected to a long, uninterrupted series of reading tests.

Whenever possible, standardized test procedures should be used.   In diagnosing the learning difficulty of a disabled reader, his reading, physical, sensory, behavioral, and environmental factors must be analyzed. The authors of this book wish to make it clear that they fully appreciate the interrelationships which exist among the child's development, his other achievements, his personal qualities, his environment both in and out of school, and his reading capabilities. However, after a child has had reading disability identified as his major problem, it becomes necessary to investigate thoroughly his reading pattern to establish the exact nature of his difficulty. This is always one of the major concerns of the specialist, because without locating the particular reading anomalies, little, if anything, can be done to correct the reading disability.

It may be, for example, that a disabled reader is found to be farsighted, and correction is made with glasses. He is now comfortable visually. He stands a more reasonable chance of learning to read, but he is still a disabled reader. His reading should be analyzed to locate the faulty learnings, which may have been caused in part by his visual difficulty, in order to plan instruction to correct his reading disability. No matter what physical, environmental, or behavioral problem caused the reading difficulty, it is necessary to study and correct the reading disability. The other factors associated with the reading difficulty also need to be studied so that the correction in reading can be made most efficiently and so that the other conditions can be improved.

There are two general types of assessment used in diagnosing reading disability. The first involves the application of precise units and numerically expressed norms, such as age or grade norms, percentile norms, or standard score norms requiring measurement by standard procedures. The second is qualitative assessment for which norms expressed in numerical terms either are not available or are not appropriate. This second kind of assessment is limited in that the procedures are not systematic and the diagnostician's personal bias may enter into the appraisal. These procedures gain their merit from the fact that they allow the diagnostician to obtain information about things for which no standardized measures are available.

Standardized tests are valuable instruments for analyzing the child's reading strengths and weaknesses. They are also needed to collect facts useful in the formulation of a remedial program. Methods of appraisal involving accurate measurement should be used whenever possible. When using standardized tests it is necessary for the diagnostician to follow precisely the procedures for giving and scoring the instruments as specified in the accompanying manuals. Any variation from standard procedures may affect the use of the norms supplied.

The results of normative data obtained from standardized tests, both survey and diagnostic, must be interpreted carefully. The norms supplied for such tests indicate the performance of typical pupils in a sample of typical learnings within the field being measured. Therein the standardized tests have their strength and also their weakness. Disabled readers are far from being typical learners. They are designated disabled readers because they are atypical. Standardized tests allow the diagnostician to compare a disabled reader with the average learner. This is how strengths and weaknesses can be located with a minimum of bias.

The measurements should be interpreted carefully. A child of sixth-grade age, for example, with a reading expectancy of 6.0 may measure 3.0 in reading. An uninitiated examiner might assume that this child needs the reading materials and methods suitable for the typical third-grade child. This is usually not the case. This sixth-grade child is not a typical third-grade reader. He is a sixth-grade child with sixth-grade interests, drives, motives, and friends. He is not even a third-grade reader, for further study would very likely indicate that his basic reading skills and abilities, and therefore his instructional needs, are closer to those of a second-grade child. His degree of mental maturity enables him to use his limited basic reading skills better than does the typical child with 2.0 reading ability. He has 6.0 potential to which to apply his 2.0 reading skills. He is able to measure somewhat higher, namely 3.0, because of his greater mental maturity, than the second-grade child with 2.0 reading ability, 2.0 potential, and 2.0 chronological age and experience. This is but one illustration of the care with which the reading diagnostician must work. The standardized test is usually, however, the most reliable instrument of measurement. Standardized tests provide normative data, which can be used in reading diagnosis. The accuracy of diagnosis is increased through the use of numerical data.

Informal procedures should be used.   The need often arises to study areas for which standardized tests have not been developed. The diagnostician should explore further, by informal means, any insights into the nature of the particular reading disability discovered during the standardized procedures. Often informal assessment procedures supply more insight for planning a remedial program than does standardized testing. Most reading specialists combine formal testing with informal inventories of reading skills, abilities, interests, and attitudes for optimal understanding of a child's difficulty.

Decisions in diagnosis must be based on patterns of scores. When the information about a disabled reader has been collected, it must be arranged so that the various numerical scores can be compared with one another. An adequate diagnosis is made from these comparisons. High as well as low scores must be considered in estimating the instructional needs of the disabled reader. Disability in reading may be the result of an overemphasis in the child's program. One child's sight vocabulary may be low because he has always been so good at using word-attack techniques that he has found little need to remember words at sight. Another child may have such a compulsive need to be accurate in reading that he cannot become a fluent reader. He is always 100 percent accurate, and even if more detail about a passage was required, he would know that too. These lacks of balance can be detected by making comparisons with standardized norms.

If the diagnostician fails to compare the child's performance in the separate skills with his general reading ability, there will be many mistakes in planning remedial work. For example, when a fifth-grade child has only third-grade ability in syllabication, the diagnostician may think his lack of ability to break words into syllables is at the root of the difficulty. But when it is noted that the child's general reading ability is only that of the typical second-grade child, his ability to syllabify becomes a strength rather than a weakness.

After numerical data are compared and judgments are made, decisions should be modified in accordance with the qualitative data gathered from informal approaches. The diagnostician should be careful not to let isolated observations or bits of information alter drastically the judgments he has made from reliable and valid measurements.

Diagnosis should be continuous. Occasionally a child fails to respond to remedial instruction based upon the original diagnosis. In this case, after two or three weeks of instruction, the diagnosis should be reevaluated, perhaps with additional measurements and other appraisals. Something may have been overlooked in the original diagnosis.

When the remedial program is successful, the child's needs change. The original diagnosis indicated the instructional needs of the disabled reader at the time remedial instruction was undertaken. The remedial program based on it was designed to alter the child's reading profile in ways that would encourage better overall growth in reading. As remedial work progresses, study of the child should be continued. If the remedial instruction has been effective, the needs of the child will have changed and the remedial program may require modification. Diagnosis must therefore be continuous.

At the start of remedial instruction, a child may have been insecure in reading situations. The diagnostician may have recommended that a chart be kept to show him his progress. After a time, as the child gains security, the chart can be discontinued. Another child may have been relatively poor at using context clues as aids to word recognition and was depending solely upon analytical approaches. The remedial instruction may have been directed toward encouraging the use of context. After a time, it may be noted that the child is neglecting careful inspection of the words and making seemingly random guesses. The guesses make sense but not the correct sense. By continuous diagnosis, the remedial worker can detect when the problem changes and thus maintain a better balance between the word-recognition techniques. In these two examples, the remedial work had to be altered because the instructional needs of the child changed.

ANALYZING READING DIFFICULTIES

This chapter will not go into the diagnosis necessary to solve the many types of problems sometimes confused with reading disability. Our present concern is limited to the diagnostic procedures needed to locate and analyze reading disabilities of various kinds.

Sometimes, the diagnosis of reading disability points out other areas to be studied which, if not tended to, interfere with the correction of the reading problem. For example, a child's reading disability may be difficult to correct because of a serious behavior problem. It is not the province of this book to describe how to deal with the behavior problem. Nevertheless, the reading specialist has to be alert to such problems and should identify related problems needing further study by other specialists. In formulating a remedial program, the specialist must always take into account the presence of conditions that need treatment by other professionals.

A reading specialist needs to find the answers to some specific questions about the disabled reader before an effective remedial program can be formulated. Our discussion of the analysis of reading difficulties will be in terms of these questions:

1. Is the child correctly classified as a disabled reader?
2. What is the nature of the instruction needed?
3. Who can give the remedial work most effectively?
4. How can improvement be made most effectively?
5. Does the child have any limiting conditions that must be considered?
6. Are there any environmental conditions that might interfere with progress in reading?

Is the child correctly classified as a disabled reader?   Poor reading ability is so interrelated with other characteristics of child growth and development that it is often extremely difficult to determine whether the reading disability or some other condition is the basic problem. Not all children who are poor readers are reading disability cases. There are many children low in reading ability who cannot be considered reading disability cases. A few children who are disabled readers have a more important problem that should be remedied before correcting the reading. First, the teacher or specialist must identify the true nature of the problem and decide whether the child will profit from remedial instruction in reading or whether some other adjustment is required.

The child who is considered disabled because he is not as good in reading as other children the same age may be reading as well as could be expected. An example of this is the child with low verbal intelligence. This child cannot be expected to grow as rapidly in reading as can other children. His problem will not be solved by a remedial reading program, but it can be eased by curricular changes, language development training, and methods better suited to his learning ability. No child should be considered disabled in reading unless there is a discrepancy between his learning capacity and his reading performance. A classification system for reading disability is given in Figure 7-1.

Physical anomalies may cause a child to be classified as a disabled reader when the real need is to see a doctor, not a remedial teacher. For example, children with neurological problems cannot be expected to develop reading capabilities as rapidly as can their equally intelligent but neurologically sound contemporaries. Some neurological problems are more difficult for the educational diagnostician to

FIGURE 7-1 Classification System for Reading Disability

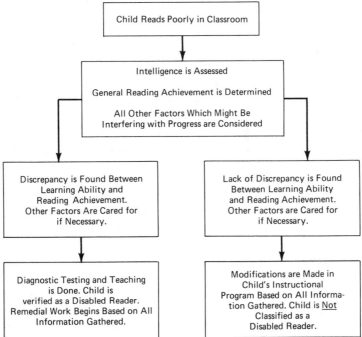

detect and are suspected only after considerable remedial instruction has been given with unsatisfactory results. The diagnostician should be alert to the possibility of neurological limitations, especially in those children high in intelligence and low in other organized learnings such as arithmetical computation. The reading diagnostician and remedial worker must be aware that not all human deficiencies can be corrected by education.

When children have neurological impairments, the reading teacher must often be satisfied with a less than usual rate of progress. The remedial reading program for neurologically impaired children is designed to give the child the individualized help needed. His problem is usually not a misbalanced reading growth pattern, but rather a restricted overall reading development, produced by the neurological limitation. A more detailed treatment of the visual and perceptual problems encountered by the neurologically impaired child will be given in Chapter 13.

The relationship between reading disability and behavior problems often makes it difficult to classify a child's major problem as a reading disability. Sometimes the poor reader is a behaviorally disordered child, and reading achievement suffers along with other school learnings. Or, the behavioral disturbance is brought about by the failure to make normal progress in reading. Here immediate attention to the reading problem will correct the reading problem and improve the behavior problem. Even in those cases in which deep-seated emotional problems are suspected of making the child an inefficient learner, emotional therapy and remedial instruction in reading can be given concurrently, to their mutual benefit.

What is the nature of the instruction needed?   The training needed by a disabled reader is indicated by the child's reading strengths and weaknesses. Establishing reading deficiencies is the most important phase of diagnosis for formulating a program of correction. The specialist's main problem is that of finding just what, in the reading pattern of the disabled reader, is hindering reading growth. The diagnostic study of what is really wrong with the child's reading, what faulty techniques he is using, what abilities he is overemphasizing, what abilities he lacks, is essential to formulating a remedial program.

There are some limitations in the child's reading profile which have little effect on reading growth in general. A child may be unable to read science materials or may be weak in one of the study skills. Under such circumstances, the limitation can be found readily and work begun to overcome the specific limitation. Many children have these minor and easily corrected reading limitations. A general and specific diagnosis can and should discover such problems. Once found, the training needed becomes clear: the child should have training in the weak area indicated by the diagnosis. This type of limitation is specific. Therefore, the diagnosis and planning of remedial instruction is relatively simple.

There are other limitations in disabled readers' reading patterns that have far-reaching effects. Failure to establish certain skills and abilities, overemphasis of others, failure to learn essential knowledges, or adoption of faulty approaches may interfere with the child's entire reading development. Lack of flexibility and adaptability may seriously limit the child's ability to adjust his reading skills to the needs of particular reading material or to certain purposes for reading.

Who can give the remedial work most effectively? The regular classroom teacher can and should give remedial instruction to most children moderately disabled in reading. The size of the class, other responsibilities, and her training limit the teacher to the solution of only the less complicated reading problems. The teacher must always decide just how much attention can be given to one child at the expense of many. In the well-managed classroom many reading difficulties can be detected early and corrected by the classroom teacher. Even under these circumstances, the teacher frequently needs the help of a reading specialist to aid her in the formulation of a classroom remedial program.

The second place in which remedial work in reading is given is at a reading center or resource room within the school. This center is usually a room well-stocked with materials for reading and for special practice exercises. Here a remedial teacher works with individual children or groups of children needing more specialized and individual attention than can be given by the classroom teacher.

In general, the smaller the group, the greater the returns for each child. Remedial teachers working in school reading centers need special training to handle the problems they meet. These remedial teachers should be able to diagnose complex reading cases and offer remedial suggestions for those children who are to be treated by the classroom teachers. The teachers in charge of remedial rooms or centers within a school should be successful classroom teachers who have had additional training in reading and in diagnosing and treating reading disability. Reading disability is no simple thing to be solved by a novice or merely by a set of exercises purporting to be suitable for all cases.

To decide where the child with a reading difficulty can most effectively be treated, the diagnostician first needs to decide into which of the general descriptive categories the child fits. These are described in Chapter 3.

Recommendations for general reading immaturity. Children who are significantly delayed in reading but show no unusual or limiting characteristics in their reading patterns and no personal rejection of reading can be treated effectively in the regular classroom. They are generally immature in reading but need no marked reeducation. They do need instruction for their level of advancement, a rigorously motivated reading program, and an opportunity to read a lot.

Some children in this category are better treated in the school reading center. If the child is so low in reading ability that he cannot profit from most of the instruction given in group work in class, he would be taught more productively by the remedial teacher in the school reading center. Most poor readers of secondary school age should be assigned to a remedial teacher. It is difficult for the secondary teacher, who works with more than 150 pupils a day, to know any one child well enought to assist the extremely immature reader.

The generally immature reader can usually be discovered by general diagnosis, using achievement tests and nonverbal group mental tests. He may not be isolated until the specific level of diagnosis is reached. The child with simple immaturity in reading is one who has a low but relatively uniform reading profile and no adverse reactions to his poor reading. He is disabled only because he is not reading as well as he could be expected to read. A study of his reading scores shows that he has normal reading patterns for the typical child of equal reading attainment. There is no interfering habit nor faulty attitude present to impede future growth.

Recommendations for specific reading immaturity.   Children best described as cases of *specific immaturity* are those who are limited severely in one or more areas of reading but who demonstrate that they have developed the general basic skills and abilities well enough to be able readers in other areas. Practically all of these children can be given the remedial work they need by the classroom teacher. The skills or abilities in which the child needs further training and experience have been found. Then, as the child participates in the regular developmental reading program, the teacher increases emphasis on specific areas in which the child is weak. If there are two or three children needing the same emphasis, from time to time the teacher can given them remedial training as a small group. In some instances, children with specific limitations from several classes of about the same grade level can be sent to the school remedial center for group instruction, but for the most part, they should be given training by the classroom teacher. The prognosis for overcoming specific reading immaturity is exceedingly good even though the degree of disability is sometimes great.

A child with specific immaturity in reading is discovered through reading tests that are more analytical than are those customarily used in general diagnosis. Tests that give scores in various important areas of reading, as well as informal measures, can be used to diagnose the child with specific reading problems. Indications of attainment in the more common types of comprehension and study skills are needed to pinpoint the areas of specific limitation. If a child scores high on some comprehension tests but low on other tests, he is correctly described as a case of specific reading immaturity and no further diagnosis is needed. The child's high scores indicate that there is no basic limitation in his reading. His low scores isolate the areas needing attention.

Recommendations for limiting reading disability.   The child who has serious deficiencies in basic reading skills and abilities which impede his entire reading growth is best described as having a *limiting disability*. Such a child is low in all types of reading, because he has acquired interfering habits or has failed to learn one or more essential skills. His reading profile does not indicate the healthy reading growth of the child with simple reading immaturity but rather a nonproductive reading pattern.

Most children with limiting disability should be given remedial work in a school reading center or resource room. A few could be corrected by the classroom teacher, but usually reeducation takes more time and careful planning than she is able to devote to it.

Recommendations for complex reading disability. Children who are best described as *complex disability* cases include the disabled readers whose problems are more subtle and complicated. These children are always severely delayed in reading. They may be bright, capable youngsters who demonstrate antagonism toward reading and who feel embarrassed about their inability to read. They sometimes make a good adjustment to their reading difficulty by doing outstanding work in fields such as art or arithmetic computation, which do not require reading ability. More often, they make a negative adjustment to their lack of success in reading which spreads to general ineffectiveness in other schoolwork. In many cases they lack persistence and tend to avoid school in general and from reading situations in particular. They are absent from school frequently and sometimes they become delinquent.

Complex reading disabilities include not only those children who have made a faulty adjustment to their reading problems, but also those who have other handicaps. Remedial programs are further complicated when they must be modified to adjust to physiological, emotional, intellectual, environmental, or other atypical conditions.

Many children with complex reading disability become blocked and so tense that they are ineffective learners. A child with a complex disability in reading is often found to have anxiety and worry about reading and fear of reading. He tends to be insecure and defeated. Children who are classified in this category need careful, individual attention. A child with complex reading disability needs a comprehensive diagnosis of his problem, and often the reading diagnostician must enlist the services of other specialists to appraise the child's needs accurately and thoroughly.

The remedial work for such children should be done in the school reading center or resource room, where there is time to give the child the necessary individual help that he requires.

How can improvement be made most effectively? The answer to this question is extremely important because the corrective program must be efficient in order to develop reading at an accelerated rate. Extensive diagnosis of the nature of the reading problem will have pointed out the type of instruction that is necessary. The specialist must now make several decisions that will increase the efficiency of actual remedial instruction. First, instructional material must be chosen at the optimal level of difficulty; second, material must be chosen that deals with topics that are interesting to the child, or at least as compatible as possible with interests of children of the same age; third, the specialist must suggest the methods by which progress will be demonstrated to the child; fourth, the specialist must estimate the length of the instructional period; and fifth, the specialist must give the necessary information for planning the independent work that the child needs.

Determining the proper level of difficulty of material. The specialist must make a careful estimate of the level of difficulty of the material that is to be used at the start of remedial instruction. Usually the child who is in difficulty with reading has been having trouble for some time. It thus becomes vital to select material at the appropriate level of difficulty. This material should be that in which the child can feel competent. The problem of selecting material of the right difficulty is complicated by the fact that the disabled reader cannot read as well as would be expected of a child of the same age. Some specialists think that the correct approach for estimating the difficulty of material is to study the results of standardized tests and thus ascertain the child's general reading level. They think that if a child measures, for example, 2.5, he should start remedial instruction in material suitable for the typical child halfway through the second grade. But research and experience have shown that for most disabled readers this would be an overestimation of the level at which their instruction should start.

Let us suppose that a child who obtains a grade score of 2.5 on a standardized reading test is one with a reading expectancy of 5.0. The child is really not a typical 2.5 reader. He is often a reader with considerably less skill development than a typical 2.5 child. This child is able to bring to the reading scene a much broader background of experience, a keener evaluation of the concepts, a higher level of reasoning ability than can the typical child who is halfway through the second grade. He may measure as much as a year higher in general comprehension than he would in basic reading abilities such as the ability to recognize words or to phrase them effectively for comprehension.

In judging the level of difficulty for initial remedial instruction, the specialist must consider, in addition to standardized tests, other evidence of the child's level of skill development. Such evidence as ability to read material aloud should be investigated. In oral reading situations, does the child make more than one error in every twenty running words? What is the child's skill in phrasing? What word-recognition techniques does the child use? What about his ability to answer various types of comprehension questions about the material read? The level at which the child can read comfortably and effectively can be estimated by trying him out in a series of basic readers and finding the level most suitable for him. The child may be started, for example, in a book at the second-grade level of difficulty. If this book proves to be too difficult, a first-grade book can be tried. If this is still too difficult, a primer could be used. The specialist may find that the first book he chooses is too easy—that the child can read the second-grade book with great fluency. Then he would try a third-grade reader. The specialist would sample books in the series until the level was found at which the child could read with reasonable ease. This informal approach gives a rough estimate of the level of difficulty suitable for a given child.

A second consideration in selecting material is the nature of the disability. The diagnostician must consider the instructional outcomes to be gained from its use. For example, if the child's major problem is developing greater speed, the material selected should be easier than that which would normally be used with a child of that general level of reading. If the child can comfortably read material of fourth-grade level, then material that is from a half-year to a year easier should be selected for increasing speed of reading. The material should contain no more than one word that would cause the child difficulty, in every hundred running words. If the child's problem is developing knowledge of visual, structural, and phonics elements, he should be given material that is rather difficult, material in which he is likely to meet one word that he needs to analyze in every twenty running words. He may be given exercises that require phonics analysis for a high percentage of the words. Such exercises would be too difficult for general reading purposes but would be suitable to this specific problem. It should be noted that in these exercises the child must have a reasonable chance for success. The selection of materials at the appropriate level of difficulty for a specific case is probably one of the most important decisions the specialist makes.

Estimating what material is suitable in interest and format. An important consideration in selecting material to be used for remedial treatment is that it should be suitable to the child in both interest and format. Securing this material is another major problem. Material must be found in which the child will be interested and which is presented in an appropriate format. Material must be found that will be relatively mature in content and format but which is at the reading level of the disabled reader. Published material contains exercises which could be used appropriately in remedial instruction. Or, the teacher may have to prepare materials. More frequently, the problem can be handled successfully by using material of appropriate difficulty and by enabling the child to use the results of his reading in ways important to him. For example, a boy of high school age may be willing to read in a fourth-grade science book an account of the way to connect a battery to a bell in order to make it ring, if he is actually allowed to do it.

The task of the specialist is that of estimating the difficulty level at which the child should be expected to read, the areas of interest that seem to be most acceptable to him, and the degree to which he will tolerate immature format. Estimates of all these conditions are made on the basis of reading tests, interest inventories, informal appraisals, and work samples with various types of materials.

Selecting means of demonstrating progress. The teacher should suggest appropriate means of demonstrating to the child that he is making progress in reading. She should also estimate the amount of attention that should be given to demonstrating reading progress to the child. The method of demonstrating this growth is determined by the remedial training to be given. If, for example, the child's problem is one of oral reading, a tape recording of the child's oral reading could be made at intervals throughout the remedial instruction. Then from time to time, the child would listen to his tapes and note the growth that is taking place. The amount of time that should be devoted to demonstrating success to the child depends upon the child and his reactions.

Estimating desirable length and frequency of remedial lessons. The teacher must estimate the length of time for each training period and also the frequency with which training should be given. These estimates are made from three types of appraisals. First, the results expected from remedial instruction must be considered. If the child needs to increase his speed of reading, the actual lesson should be relatively short and highly motivating. Between lessons the child may continue independently to emphasize speed of reading.

The second consideration used in judging the length of the remedial sessions is the age and physical stamina of the child. If he tires easily, or cannot concentrate for long periods of time, the length of each training period should be short. If he is an older child, physically strong and able to attend well, the training periods can be longer.

Third, any condition, such as poor vision, that limits the child's ability to pay close attention to reading instruction over a period of time shortens the length of remedial sessions. It is often better to have two short sessions a day than to have one longer one.

A careful inspection of all information available about the child is necessary to make a reasonable estimate of the length of time for each training period and the frequency of the remedial lessons.

Planning for independent work.   The child's reading disability will not be corrected in the remedial periods alone. He must extend his remedial reading experiences into his independent work. The level of difficulty of material used for independent work should be considerably easier than that studied during the remedial lessons. The independent work should be somewhat different from work done in remedial lessons. In planning independent work, the diagnostician must judge how best to motivate the child and what type of exercises would be most beneficial for the child to work on independently. For example, if the child is trying to build a larger sight vocabulary, would it be best for him to have a pack of word cards with which he drills himself, stories containing words in contextual settings, or workbook-type exercises? These decisions are made by the teacher on the basis of the nature of instruction needed, the characteristics of the child, and the characteristics of his general environment.

Does the child have any limiting conditions that must be considered?   In formulating a remedial program, the causes of reading disability considered in Chapters 4, 5, and 6 must be appraised by the specialist. The help of other experts must be employed, if needed. For the reeducation program to be effective, any limitations within the child which might detrimentally influence his reading growth must be located. If the child has poor vision, an examination by a competent expert is required. Whenever possible, the visual defect should be corrected. Whether corrected or not, modifications in the remedial program will be necessary. Such modifications are described in Chapter 13, which deals with the handicapped child.

If poor hearing is suspected, a hearing specialist should be consulted. Again, the mere correction of the auditory limitation will not improve the child's reading. It will, however, allow the child to profit from remedial instruction. The child with poor auditory capacity will need modifications in his instructional program. See Chapter 13 on the handicapped child.

Any factor that causes a reading disability may become a condition which needs correction or a condition to which the program must adjust. Whenever possible, such conditions should be corrected before the start of remedial training. When no correction is possible, the program must be altered to allow for the known limitation. It should be recognized that the correction of a limiting condition does not alter the reading needs of the child. If the child, for example, has third-grade reading skills and abilities in reading before the visual correction, he will still have third-grade skills and abilities in reading after the visual correction. The correction of a limiting condition does not alter the need for remedial reading instruction. However, it does improve the child's chances for learning to read efficiently and effectively.

Are there any environmental conditions that might interfere with progress in reading? The diagnostician must study the child's entire environment, for it may have limitations that could influence the success of the remedial program. Sometimes in their zeal to help their children, parents create emotional tensions that do not help the reading and disturb a child greatly. Or parents may try to help their child in ways that are detrimental to his reading growth. Parents can contribute much to the success of a remedial program by remembering that they should:

1. Take an interest in the independent reading work that the child brings home.
2. Give the child a good place in which to work without interruption.
3. Secure materials that will be the child's own, in consultation with the remedial teacher.
4. Hide their anxieties about the child's reading problem.
5. Tell the child a word if he has difficulty doing independent reading at home.
6. Read the independent material and discuss it with the child.
7. Avoid ridicule or making comparisons among siblings.
8. Let the child know that they appreciate his many accomplishments and that they have confidence in him.
9. Recognize that the child's "don't care" attitude toward reading is often a "do care very much" one and that it is wise to let him adopt this apparent attitude as a "safety valve."

Not only the home conditions and child-parent relationships but also the school situation should be studied. Frequently improvement of reading is left to the remedial program alone. The school environment may not be conducive to effective reading development for the disabled reader. The child's entire reading environment should be coordinated if he is to progress. Sometimes a teacher does not fully recognize the seriousness of having a child try to read material that is so difficult that it can be nothing but frustrating to him. At other times, the teacher is not aware that a child's lack of attention may be the result of a hearing loss. The specialist must try to find any problem in the child's environment which might impede his progress in learning to read.

ILLUSTRATION OF AN ANALYSIS OF READING DIFFICULTIES

The following illustration of reading diagnosis shows how the study of children from a fifth-grade class can be made, progressing from general diagnosis to specific diagnosis to child-study diagnosis.

General Diagnosis in Reading

The first level of diagnosis can be called *general diagnosis*. It is concerned with appraisal of all the children's levels of achievement on major indicators of reading growth. To adjust instruction to individual differences, teachers may note each child's facility in oral reading, amount of understanding from silent reading, daily performance on work sheet exercises, and observable enjoyment, dislike, or avoidance of reading. In addition, progress on unit tests from the child's reading series and standardized group achievement tests should also be used to assess reading progress.

The teacher can compare each child's progress in reading with his level of progress in nonreading academic areas. General alertness, level of knowledge brought to the classroom, and level of participation in instruction based on nonreading sources such as film or television should also be compared with performance on reading tasks.

If the teacher is concerned that the child may be a disabled reader, further assessment should be done which includes intelligence testing, based on an individually administered intelligence test, and reading level, based on a standardized individual reading test. At this point, if the child's reading achievement is about the same as his reading expectancy and as his success in other fields of learning, he is probably progressing as well in reading as can be expected. This is true even if he reads somewhat poorer than the other children in his class. This child will need no further diagnosis in reading even though he may need certain adjustments for the slow learner, to be described in Chapter 13. The classroom teacher should be aware of each child she teaches in the developmental reading program. In regular classwork, the teacher systematically studies every child's reading in a diagnostic manner.

If a child's achievement in reading is considerably lower than his reading expectancy, or if he achieves significantly better in nonreading classroom activities than in reading, further diagnosis is needed. General diagnosis helps identify those who are educationally handicapped by ineffective reading and those who need curricular adjustments. Standardized survey tests, achievement tests, intelligence tests, reading series tests, informal teacher-made tests, and teacher observations are all used in making these judgments.

At the general level of diagnosis, the teacher can study the results of standardized tests, reading series tests, and informal observations, to indicate the average reading achievement of the entire class. Is the class as a whole progressing at a below average, average, or above average rate? Is there any particular aspect of reading, such as knowledge of word meanings or following written directions, which appears to need extra attention?

From this study of the class as a whole, the teacher should consider the problem of adjusting materials and methods to individual differences. For example, in a fifth-grade class of 35 children, 13 were found to be instructionally suited to a fifth-grade reader. Ten of the children required simpler material. Twelve children were reading at a sixth-grade level or beyond and needed an expanded reading program. Three members of the class who were reading at a middle fourth-grade level or below were assessed further.

Alice was one such child needing further consideration. She was older than most of the children in the class, as she had repeated one year of school. Alice's reading expectancy was at the middle fourth-grade level, while her average reading achievement was also at the middle fourth-grade level. She did not display negative attitudes toward reading and was making adequate daily progress in reading. Her achievement in arithmetic calculations was at a middle third-grade level. Considering what is reasonable to expect of her, Alice is doing a creditable job learning to read. She has continued to make progress in developing reading skills, but at a somewhat slower pace than her classmates. Alice needs the type of instruction, described in Chapter 13, suitable to a slow-learning child.

Frank, another one of the children, is a disabled reader. He is more than two years behind in his reading development, compared to his reading expectancy. He is of average intelligence, so he should be reading at a beginning fifth-grade level. He needs to be studied further in order to plan a remedial program to improve his reading. Frank is relatively successful in arithmetic, which shows that he is able to achieve in areas other than reading. He shows dislike and avoidance of reading tasks in the classroom.

The third child, Henry, is reading-disabled, even though he is reading only two months below his grade placement. He is one of the youngest members of the class, but he is the most capable intellectually. His reading expectancy, based on a suspected high level of intellectual ability, is probably closer to the seventh-grade level than his current reading grade of 4.8. His achievement in arithmetic (7.5 grade level) is high and more in keeping with his inferred level of mental ability. Henry has a reading disability. A further diagnosis of Henry's reading disability, including an assessment of his level of mental ability, is needed in order to plan appropriate programming for him.

Specific Diagnosis in Reading

Specific diagnosis separates the reading act into some of its more precise skills and abilities. It enables the diagnostician to detect the areas of a child's difficulty. It shows whether the child's difficulty is in a specific type of comprehension, in word-recognition techniques, in reading efficiency, in oral reading, or in basic study skills. A specific diagnosis also might indicate how well the child is able to adapt his reading abilities to the demands of the specific content fields. There are many tests which give the type of information needed for specific diagnosis. Some of the more useful ones are mentioned in Chapter 8.

The general diagnosis revealed that Frank and Henry were disabled readers needing further diagnosis. Another child, Barbara, has not shown such an overall deficiency, but did show a specific immaturity. Barbara is, in general, a competent reader. She has great difficulty in one type of reading—reading to follow directions. She is one of the lowest members of the class in this skill, much lower than would be expected of her on the basis of grade placement, mental ability, and general reading achievement. This is not a serious matter, but it is probable that a short period of emphasis on this type of reading would make Barbara as proficient in reading to follow directions as she is in other comprehension abilities. She needs no further diagnosis.

Henry has a very uneven profile. Henry's specific diagnosis shows that he is low in the more general types of reading comprehension. It also shows that he is considerably better at recognizing words in isolation than he is at recognizing words in context. He is a very slow reader. It is reasonable to suspect that Henry is an overanalytical reader, and that he fails to use the more rapid word-recognition techniques. The precise nature of instruction he needs will have to be determined by further study in child-study diagnosis.

Frank is low in all types of reading and must be studied further. The specific diagnosis shows him to be a reading-disabled child, with only his speed-of-reading score approaching what could be expected of him. Even his speed of reading cannot be considered good performance because his reading is so inaccurate. It is apparent, on the basis of the specific diagnosis, that Frank has something basically wrong with his reading. The difficulty appears to be in the word-recognition area, but even this suspicion awaits child-study diagnosis before it can be verified.

Child-Study Diagnosis in Reading

Standardized tests for general and specific diagnosis, individual standardized tests, detailed reading diagnostic tests, and informal study of a child's approaches to the various aspects of reading are used in a thorough child-study diagnosis. This diagnosis also includes an analysis of the child's strengths and limitations as an individual—his sensory capacities, emotional reactions, and attitudes toward reading. A child-study diagnosis should also study the child's general school environment, the methods of instruction used in school, and the home conditions that might be specifically related to reading and that might influence his reading growth. The last kind of appraisal should find out how the parents feel about their child's reading problem and how much they will cooperate in overcoming the difficulty. A child-study diagnosis must give answers to the specific questions concerning the disabled reader that have been discussed in this chapter.

The first question, *whether the child is correctly classified as a disabled reader,* is answered frequently by the general diagnosis. In some cases, the child-study approach does indicate that a child's major problem is not disability in reading. The detailed studies of Henry and Frank did not reveal any condition which would lead to a classification other than reading disability. The general diagnosis showed, on the other hand, that Alice's problem was one of low intelligence and that she could not be classified as a disabled reader because her reading achievement seemed reasonable for her ability.

The second question, dealing with the problem of *who can give the remedial instruction most effectively,* can sometimes be answered in the general diagnosis and at other times in the specific diagnosis, but frequently must await the completed child study. The general diagnosis showed that Alice's problem could be remedied more adequately by an adjusted program and realistic expectations. Certainly her basic problem was not reading disability, nor could it be expected that she would be helped by remedial training in reading.

The specific diagnosis showed that Barbara was weak in just one type of reading. She had a specific immaturity in reading which could be handled adequately by the classroom teacher.

As a result of a thorough child study, it was judged that Henry would profit from group instruction remedial reading, while Frank's problem was so complex and charged with rejection of reading that it was felt that he would need to get his remedial work on a one-to-one basis in the resource room.

The third question, dealing with *the nature of the training needed,* was answered for Alice in the general diagnosis. She needed training in reading suitable to a slow-learning child. The training needed for Barbara was decided by the specific diagnosis, which showed that Barbara needed training in following exact directions. The child-study diagnosis showed that Henry was indeed an overanalytical reader. He had a high score in knowledge of phonic elements, and he attempted to use this means of word recognition even with words that he could recognize at sight when they were flashed before him with a speed that allowed him only a glance at the word. He also demonstrated a tendency to pay marked attention to word endings and to neglect somewhat the beginning of elements of words. In addition he was very poor at making adequate use of context clues. Henry has a marked limiting disability in word recognition. The remedial work that Henry needs will be described in Chapter 10.

The training needed by Frank was also indicated by the child-study diagnosis. Frank's problem is complex. He has failed to develop a systematic attack on words. He has difficulty with reversals and has rejected reading. In addition there was evidence that Frank had a visual handicap which had to be corrected before remedial work could be undertaken. The necessary remedial work is one of the types discussed in Chapter 12, dealing with left-to-right orientation in reading and word perception, and in Chapter 13 on the handicapped child. He also needed more work on word recognition as described in Chapters 10 and 11.

The fourth question that must be answered by the diagnosis deals with *how improvement can be brought about most effectively.* This question could have been answered for Alice in the general diagnosis and for Barbara in the specific diagnosis. Alice should be given material at approximately the middle of the third-grade level. She needs encouragement, success, and many opportunities to use the results of her reading in constructive activities such as building models or helping make displays and things of that sort. She needs concrete illustrations of what she is reading. Alice should read for only one well-defined purpose at a time because she finds it difficult to attend to several purposes at the same time.

For general purposes, Barbara should read material at middle fifth-grade level of difficulty. In the exercises designed to increase her ability to follow exact directions, her remedial instruction should be started with material somewhat less difficult. The purposes for which Barbara reads this material should be to organize, to get the sense of a sequence of ideas, and to follow exact directions. It would be desirable to keep a chart indicating her speed and accuracy in completing these materials. As she increases in accuracy, she can be encouraged to read somewhat more rapidly, and the difficulty of the material can be increased. Barbara can be expected to develop readily the ability to organize and to follow exact directions.

Complete child-study diagnoses were necessary to find out how improvement could be brought about most efficiently in the cases of Henry and Frank. Henry should have a time chart indicating the speed at which he reads during exercises designed to increase his speed. He should be given remedial instruction in material about halfway through the fourth grade in difficulty. Henry should do a lot of recreational reading. He should be given exercises designed to encourage the use of context clues at approximately a fourth-grade difficulty level.

Frank's problem is much more difficult. He needs to read material at approximately the second-grade level of difficulty. It would be desirable to use material that is as mature in format as possible—work sheets might be used. The remedial teacher must be optimistic and demonstrate to Frank that he is growing in his reading. He should make a card file so he can see that the number of words he recognizes is increasing. He could dictate some stories of his own and if his tendency to reverse words persists, it may be necessary to use sound tracing methods, described in a later chapter.

The fifth question is concerned with *limiting conditions within a child* that must be considered in formulating the remedial program. From a thorough case-study diagnosis, it became clear that Henry had no limiting characteristics to which the program needed to adjust or for which there had to be a correction made before remedial instruction. Frank was found to have two limiting conditions. The first was his rejection of reading. This must be taken into consideration in formulating his remedial program. The fact that Frank's arithmetic score was nearly equal to his reading expectancy indicated that in situations not involving reading Frank was able to apply himself reasonably well. Frank's second limitation was his eyesight. There was some indication that Frank was farsighted and that he found it difficult to focus on the printed page at reading distance. A thorough visual examination was recommended before Frank began remedial instruction.

The sixth question deals with *environmental conditions that might interfere* with the progress of remedial work. It was found that for three of the children,

Henry, Frank, and Alice, the school would have to make some adjustments to their needs. For Alice, the adjustments would be those expected in general adjustment to individual differences in any class. It was found, for example, that in science and social studies the same textbooks were used by all the children in the class. Alice could not be expected to use this material. A thorough study of Alice's placement will need to be made, but from the information available, a further diagnosis of her reading is not indicated.

Henry, who had been in the middle-reading group, should be kept there. But it was found that he could not effectively read some of the material of the content fields. Somewhat less mature reference material should be made available to him.

The school adjustments necessary for Frank are more complicated. Frank should not attempt to read the materials in the content fields, but he should use this reading time to read materials at his level of advancement. He may listen to the discussions in the classroom and participate in the creative activities.

There were no indications of unfortunate circumstances in any of the homes of these children, with the possible exception of Frank. Frank's parents were very concerned about his poor reading. They had attempted to teach him to read using information presented in a series of articles in their local newspaper. After about a month of instruction, they wisely judged that Frank was not only getting worse in reading, but that he was becoming highly upset by their instruction and by his own seemingly inadequate response. Frank's parents were eager to cooperate with the school. They agreed to set aside a place in their house for Frank to keep his reading materials, and they were happy to cooperate with his teacher's suggestion that they discuss with Frank the stories he read and pronounce for him words he found difficult.

Each child we have discussed from this fifth-grade class was different. Some of the children needed no further study beyond general and specific diagnoses. Two needed detailed child-study diagnoses. It was necessary for the reading specialist to have consultations with both the classroom teacher and the parents of two of the children.

In making the child-study diagnoses of the reading disabled children, both standardized and informal procedures were used, and in one case the services of an outside expert were needed. Selected reading diagnostic tests useful in child-study diagnosis will be described in the next chapter.

SUMMARY

The correction of reading disability is complicated by the intricate nature of the reading process and by the many differences in children and their environments influencing reading growth. It is little wonder that no two cases of reading disability confront the teacher or specialist with exactly the same problem. It is apparent that any remedial instruction must be based on adequate diagnosis. The more complex and the more subtle cases of reading disability often require more detailed and more penetrating study than the classroom teacher has the time or training to give. Sometimes the services of a reading specialist are required. In such instances, it is sometimes necessary to enlist the services of other specialists as well, such as social caseworkers, psychologists, or physicians.

The diagnosis of a disabled reader must be directed toward improvement of instruction. Therefore, the therapeutic type of diagnosis is better than the etiological, that is, the one that seeks causes only. The diagnosis is more than an appraisal of reading skills and abilities. It must also assess the mental, physical, sensory, emotional, and environmental factors that could impede progress.

The diagnosis must be efficient and should proceed only as far as necessary to formulate a remedial program. Some children's instructional needs can be found through general diagnosis, others will need a more thorough study by specific means, and still others may need a complete study of their reading disability. Since diagnosis of reading disability is detailed and time-consuming, only pertinent information should be collected and this by the most efficient means available.

Standardized measurements are essential to reliable diagnosis of reading disability. Even the results of standardized tests must be interpreted with care, because the disabled reader has an atypical and subtle problem. It is often necessary to use informal procedures for information not obtainable from standardized measurements.

The remedial program is planned by first taking into account the numerical data and then modifying it in accordance with whatever other information is obtained. The specialist should treat the data objectively so that the case can be judged accurately. After a reasonable period, if the remedial work proves unsuccessful, a reevaluation should be made to find the correct diagnosis. Even in successful cases, diagnosis should be continuous because reading disability is one aspect of a dynamic process which alters during remedial instruction, and the remedial program must be changed to meet the new needs of the disabled reader.

Decisions must be made in six essential areas.

1. Classification. Is the child correctly classified as a disabled reader or is some other problem of child growth and development the basic difficulty?

2. Training needed. What is the nature of the training needed? Identification of the particular character of the reading limitation is the most important part of the reading diagnosis. The reading pattern of the child must be studied to isolate the specific faulty learning impeding reading progress. This requires a thorough appraisal of the skills and abilities involved in reading.

3. Setting. Where can the remedial work be given most effectively? Should the child be reeducated in the classroom, school reading center, or resource room? The answer to this question lies in the nature of the reading problem. Most general immaturity and specific immaturity cases should be given remedial training in the classroom or school reading center. Children with limiting disability should be corrected at the school reading center, while complex disability, for the most part, should be corrected in the resource room.

4. Methods. What are the most efficient methods for improving the child's reading? These include levels and types of material to be used, ways of demonstrating progress

in reading to the child, and plans for extending the reading instruction that can be accomplished by the child independently.

5. Limitations. Are there any conditions within the child that might be detrimental to reading growth? Help of additional experts should be utilized whenever it is needed for diagnosis and correction of these limitations. Modifications in the remedial program must be made to adjust to any limitations.

6. Learning environment. Are there any conditions within the child's entire learning environment that might interfere with progress in reading? Cooperation from home and school will contribute to the solution of the child's reading problem.

STUDY QUESTIONS

1. Why is therapeutic diagnosis considered more essential than etiological diagnosis in assessment of reading difficulties?

2. What are the major purposes of general, specific, and child-study diagnoses? Why are all three needed for some children, while only general diagnosis is needed for others, and only general and specific for still others?

3. Why should standardized test procedures always be used in diagnosis of reading difficulties? In which instances are informal procedures more appropriate?

4. Why should one be concerned about whether or not a child is correctly classified as a disabled reader?

5. How do the reading needs of the child classified as each of the following differ: simple reading immaturity, specific reading immaturity, limiting reading disability, or complex reading disability? In what ways are they the same?

6. Which would you choose as most important to a disabled reader: material of the proper level, of appropriate format, or of suitable interest? How might one compensate for material which is too difficult, too immature in appearance, or too uninteresting?

SELECTED READINGS

DECHANT, E. *Diagnosis and Remediation of Reading Disabilities,* Chaps. 3 and 4. Englewood Cliffs, N.J.: Prentice-Hall, Inc., 1981

HARRIS, A. J., AND E. R. SIPAY. *How to Increase Reading Ability,* 8th ed., Chaps. 6 and 7. New York: Longman, Inc., 1985.

ROSWELL, F. AND G. NATCHEZ. *Reading Disability: Diagnosis and Treatment,* 2nd ed., Chap. 2. New York: Basic Books, Inc., Publishers, 1971.

WILSON, R. M., AND C. J. CLELAND. *Diagnostic and Remedial Reading for Classroom and Clinic,* 5th ed., Chap 2. Columbus, OH: Charles E. Merrill Publishing Company, 1985.

8

Use of Specific Assessment Procedures

The preceding chapter discussed six questions that should be answered in any diagnosis of reading disability. In addition, an illustrative analysis was given to show how the sequence of general, specific, and child-study levels of diagnosis helped to answer each question. The question that is the major responsibility of the reading specialist is the one concerned with the nature of the specific types of training needed to correct reading disabilities. The following classification of the more prevalent reading difficulties includes the types of deficiencies that must be found if a diagnosis is to indicate clearly the precise kinds of instruction needed.

CLASSIFICATION OF READING DIFFICULTIES

    A. Faulty word identification and recognition
         1. Failure to use context and other meaning clues
         2. Ineffective visual analysis of words
         3. Limited knowledge of visual, structural, and phonic elements
         4. Lack of ability in auditory blending or visual synthesis
         5. Overanalytical
             a. Analyzing known words
             b. Breaking words into too many parts
             c. Using a letter-by-letter or spelling attack
         6. Insufficient sight vocabulary

      7. Excessive locational errors
         a. Initial errors
         b. Middle errors
         c. Ending errors

B. Inappropriate directional habits
    1. Orientational confusions with words
    2. Transpositions among words
    3. Faulty eye movements

C. Deficiencies in basic comprehension abilities
    1. Limited meaning vocabulary
    2. Inability to read by thought units
    3. Insufficient sentence sense
    4. Lack of paragraph organization sense
    5. Failure to appreciate author's organization

D. Limited special comprehension abilities
    1. Inability to isolate and retain factual information
    2. Poor reading to organize
    3. Ineffective reading to evaluate
    4. Insufficient ability in reading to interpret
    5. Limited proficiency in reading to appreciate

E. Deficiencies in basic study skills
    1. Inability to use aids in locating materials to be read
    2. Lack of efficiency in using basic reference material
    3. Inadequacies in using maps, graphs, tables, and other visual materials
    4. Limitations in techniques of organizing material read

F. Deficient in adapting to reading needs of content fields
    1. Inappropriate application of comprehension abilities
    2. Limited knowledge of specialized vocabulary
    3. Insufficient concept development
    4. Poor knowledge of symbols and abbreviations
    5. Insufficient ability in using pictorial and tabular material
    6. Difficulties with organization
    7. Inability to adjust rate to suit purposes and difficulty of material

G. Deficiencies in rate of comprehension
    1. Inability to adjust rate
    2. Insufficient sight vocabulary
    3. Insufficient vocabulary knowledge and comprehension
    4. Ineffectiveness in word recognition
    5. Overanalytical reading
    6. Insufficient use of context clues
    7. Lack of phrasing
    8. Use of crutches
    9. Unnecessary vocalization
   10. Inappropriate purposes

H. Poor oral reading
    1. Inappropriate eye-voice span
    2. Lack of phrasing ability
    3. Inappropriate rate and timing
    4. Frustration in oral reading

These defects in reading patterns that must be appraised in a thorough diagnosis show that reading disability is not a simple condition that can be corrected by a single approach. Information on a child's strengths and weaknesses in these areas is obtained from a variety of evaluative techniques. A competent diagnostician uses both standardized and informal procedures in studying the nature of reading deficiencies, so that appropriate remedial programs can be designed. Detailed procedures for overcoming each of these specific deficiencies will be discussed further, beginning with Chapter 9.

Many testing and evaluation procedures are used in appraising the needs of the disabled reader. The diagnosis usually starts with giving achievement tests, a reading survey test, and an individual intelligence test. It may continue until such details as how many independent letters are unknown to the child or which of the important digraphs that are not known have been measured. A study of strengths and weaknesses should be evaluated in the detail necessary to formulate an appropriate plan of instruction.

In this chapter a variety of specific approaches to reading diagnosis will be considered. In order to plan appropriately for the disabled reader, all pertinent information obtainable must be collected and studied.

TESTS USED IN GENERAL DIAGNOSIS IN READING

In general diagnosis, standardized tests of general achievement, skill area achievement, and survey reading are used. General achievement tests are used to measure the relative strengths and weaknesses of students in various areas of the curriculum. They are commonly administered to all the children in the school. Individual tests of development in several academic skill areas are selectively administered to those children who are experiencing learning difficulties. Reading survey tests are used to obtain an estimate of the students' overall reading achievement and to determine their relative strengths and weaknesses in such attributes as vocabulary, comprehension, word analysis, and reading rate. The teacher can use these results to aid in adjusting to individual differences within the classroom and to help find the areas of reading that need corrective treatment.

General Achievement Tests

A profile of the disabled reader's relative performance in major areas of the curriculum, as measured by general achievement tests, enables the reading specialist to isolate the academic areas in which a student may be experiencing difficulty in application of reading to specific content. The specialist can also see whether or not the disabled reader scores significantly higher on the nonreading subjects in comparison to the reading section of the test. If so, reading might be a basic problem. A marked variation in the profile might suggest that the student was deficient in a certain specific comprehension ability or in some basic study skills. All of these irregularities would indicate that further diagnosis is needed. A few typical examples of *general achievement tests* useful in general diagnosis are listed next. For examples and evaluations see Buros (1985).

California Achievement Tests.   Forms E and F. Grades 0–K.9, K.6–2.2, 1.6–3.2, 2.6–4.2, 3.6–5.2, 4.6–6.2, 5.6–7.2, 6.6–8.2, 7.6–9.2, 8.6–11.2, 10.6–12.9: Reading (vocabulary, comprehension, sound recognition, visual recognition, and word analysis); Language (mechanics and expression); Spelling; Mathematics (computation, concepts, and applications); Study Skills; Science; Social Studies (CTB/McGraw-Hill, 1985, 1986).

Iowa Tests of Basic Skills.   Primary Battery, Multilevel, and Separate Level Editions. Grades K.1–1.5, K.8–1.9, 1.7–2.6, 2.7–3.5, 3, 4, 5, 6, 7, 8–9: Listening; Word Analysis; Vocabulary; Reading/Reading Comprehension; Language (spelling, capitalization, punctuation, usage, and expression); Work Study (visual materials and reference materials); Mathematics (concepts, problem solving, and computation); Social Studies; Science; Listening; Writing (Hieronymus, Hoover, and Lindquist, 1986).

Metropolitan Achievement Tests (6th edition).   Survey Battery. Grades K.0–K.9, K.5–1.9, 1.5–2.9, 2.5–3.9, 3.5–4.9, 5.0–6.9, 7.0–9.9, 10.0–12.9: Vocabulary; Word Recognition Skills; Reading Comprehension; Math (concepts, problem solving, and computation); Spelling; Language; Science; Social Studies (Prescott, Balow, Hogan, and Farr, 1985).

SRA Achievement Series.   Grades K.5–1.5, 1.5–2.5, 2.5–3.5, 3.5–4.5, 4.5–6.5, 6.0–8.5, 8.0–10.5, 9.0–12.9: Reading (visual discrimination, auditory discrimination, letters and sounds, listening comprehension, vocabulary, and comprehension); Mathematics (concepts, computation, and problem solving); Language Arts (mechanics and usage); Spelling; Reference Materials; Social Studies; Science (Naslund, Thorpe, and Lefever, 1983, 1984).

Stanford Achievement Test (7th edition).   Grades 1.5–2.9, 2.5–3.9, 3.5–4.9, 4.5–5.9, 5.5–7.9, 7.0–9.9: Word Study Skills; Word Reading; Reading Comprehension; Vocabulary; Listening Comprehension; Spelling; Language/English; Concepts of Number; Mathematics Computation; Mathematics Applications; Environment; Science; Social Science (Gardner, Rudman, Karlsen, and Merwin, 1982, 1983, 1984).

Skill Area Achievement Tests

A comparison of the disabled reader's relative performance in overall reading, spelling, and mathematics attainment assists the specialist in determining whether the child's academic difficulties are limited to reading disability or are more general. Because these tests are individually administered they also serve to identify the child with satisfactory skill area development who performs poorly in group tests. For additional examples and evaluations see Buros (1985).

Kaufman Test of Educational Achievement.   Brief Form. Grades 1–12: Mathematics; Reading; Spelling (Kaufman and Kaufman, 1985).

Woodcock-Johnson Psycho-Educational Battery, Part Two: Tests of Achievement.   Grades 0.0–12.9: Reading; Mathematics; Written Language; Knowledge (Woodcock and Johnson, 1977).

Reading Survey Tests

Reading survey tests provide a general measure of some of the most important components of reading such as power of comprehension, word recognition, and speed of reading. Performance of a child on a reading survey test suggests how the pupil might perform in a real-life reading situation. This information can be used to verify or negate the existence of a reading difficulty.

The complex nature of reading growth and development requires that no single type of test be used as the sole criterion of a child's reading stature. Each subtest of a survey test is in itself a measure of an important reading outcome. The score of each subtest can be compared with the average reading score of the survey test to see if a child is weak in power of comprehension, word recognition, speed, or accuracy. If a given score were significantly lower than the average reading score, an area of reading needing further study would be identified.

The tests listed next are examples of suitable reading survey tests for general diagnosis. They also have some analytical value. For more examples and evaluations of these tests, see Buros (1985).

California Achievement Tests, Reading.   Forms E and F. Grades K.0–K.9, K.6–2.2, 1.6–3.2, 2.6–4.2, 3.6–7.2, 6.6–12.9: Vocabulary; Comprehension; Sound Recognition; Visual Recognition; Word Analysis (CTB/McGraw-Hill, 1985).

Gates-MacGinitie Reading Tests (2nd edition).   Forms 1, 2, 3. Grades 1–12. Vocabulary; Comprehension (MacGinitie, 1978).

Nelson-Denny Reading Test.   Forms E and F. Grades 9–16, Adult: Vocabulary; Comprehension; Reading Rate (Brown, Bennett, and Hanna, 1981).

TESTS USED IN SPECIFIC DIAGNOSIS IN READING

Specific diagnosis explores systematically particular areas of reading weakness. Specific diagnosis, for example, will indicate that a disabled reader's problem is a deficiency in the area of basic comprehension abilities, but it will not isolate the exact limitations involved. A specific diagnosis might indicate the instruction needed for the first two types of reading cases, that is, simple and specific reading immaturity. The tests used in specific diagnosis do not go into enough detail to plan remedial instruction for those children classified as having a limiting or complex reading disability.

Many standardized tests are available that can make a systematic analysis of the various areas of reading growth. Some reading problems can be identified clearly enough to enable the diagnostician or the classroom teacher to develop an individual remedial plan to overcome the specific difficulty. Other problems indicated by the specific diagnosis will need further study, using child-study techniques, before a suitable remedial plan can be formulated.

If the diagnosis requires a child-study approach, the diagnostician will need to include all of the information acquired in the general and specific levels of diagnosis and any other data required to complete the case study. The reading specialist will need to make comparisons among the various measures of reading proficiency. The chronological age and I.Q. of the disabled reader will also need to be taken into consideration.

A few examples of tests for specific diagnosis are listed next. The list is not complete. For more examples and critical evaluations, see Buros (1985).

Kaufman Test of Educational Achievement. Comprehensive Form. Grades 1–12: Reading Decoding (prefixes and word beginnings, suffixes and word endings, closed syllable short vowels, open syllable long and final e pattern vowels, vowel digraphs and dipthongs, r-controlled patterns, consonant-le patterns, consonant clusters and digraphs, single and double consonants, and whole word errors); Reading Comprehension (literal comprehension and inferential comprehension) (Kaufman and Kaufman, 1985).

Stanford Diagnostic Reading Test. Grades 1.5–12 (four levels: red, green, brown, blue): Word Reading; Reading Comprehension; Auditory Discrimination; Phonetic analysis; Structural Analysis; Auditory Vocabulary; Vocabulary; Word Parts; Reading Rate; Scanning and Skimming (Karlsen, Madder, and Gardner, 1984).

Test of Reading Comprehension, Revised. Ages 7–17: General Vocabulary; Syntactic Similarities; Paragraph Reading; Sentence Sequencing; Supplementary Subtests (reading math vocabulary, reading science vocabulary, reading social studies vocabulary, reading the directions of schoolwork, sentence sequencing) (Brown, Hammill, and Wiederholt, 1986).

Woodcock Reading Mastery Test, Revised. Forms G and H. Grades K–14 and adult: Visual Auditory Learning; Letter Identification; Word Identification; Word Attack; Word Comprehension (antonyms, synonyms, analogies); Passage Comprehension (Woodcock, 1986).

TESTS USED IN CHILD-STUDY DIAGNOSIS IN READING

The tests used in the general and specific levels of diagnosis form the basis of the child-study diagnosis. For some disabled readers, these tests give the diagnostician sufficient information to develop an *appropriate individual plan of remediation,* and further diagnosis is not needed. For the disabled readers who have not yet been diagnosed adequately, a study of their test results usually indicates the areas of reading limitation that should be explored further. The techniques used are confined mostly to individual testing procedures that require special training and some supervised clinical experience for valid results. The specific standardized tests used at three levels of diagnosis in reading are summarized in Figure 8-1.

The techniques of individual diagnosis described here are representative but by no means inclusive of all the programs described in the literature. The reader should bear in mind that each of these techniques (and others not described) has had successful use in the field.

The descriptions in this chapter are designed to give the reader a general impression of the main characteristics of the diagnostic tests. Actual use of any

FIGURE 8-1 Sample Standardized Tests Used in Reading Diagnosis

GENERAL DIAGNOSIS IN READING

General Achievement Tests—relative strengths and weakness in various areas of the curriculum (group testing).

> *California Achievement Tests*
> *Iowa Tests of Basic Skills*
> *Metropolitan Achievement Tests*
> *SRA Achievement Series*
> *Stanford Achievement Test*

Skill Area Achievement Tests—relative strengths and weakness in various academic skill areas (individual testing).

> *Kaufman Test of Educational Achievement, Brief Form*
> *Woodcock-Johnson Psycho-Educational Battery, Part Two: Tests of Achievement*

Reading Survey Tests—overall reading achievement, relative strengths and weaknesses in major aspects of reading (group testing).

> *California Achievement Tests, Reading*
> *Gates-MacGinitie Reading Tests*
> *Nelson-Denny Reading Test*

SPECIFIC DIAGNOSIS IN READING

Kaufman Test of Educational Achievement, Comprehensive Form—measures specific decoding and comprehension skills (individual testing).
Stanford Diagnostic Reading Test—measures auditory discrimination, phonetic analysis, structural analysis, auditory vocabulary, vocabulary, word parts, word reading comprehension, reading rate, scanning and skimming (group testing).
Test of Reading Comprehension, Revised—measures specific comprehension skills (individual testing).
Woodcock Reading Mastery Tests, Revised—measure visual auditory learning, letter identification, word identification, word attack, word comprehension, and passage comprehension (individual testing).

CHILD-STUDY DIAGNOSIS IN READING

Diagnostic Reading Scales—measure word-recognition, oral reading, silent reading, listening comprehension, and phonics skills (individual testing).
Durrell Analysis of Reading Difficulty—measures oral reading, silent reading, listening comprehension, listening vocabulary, word recognition/word analysis, spelling, auditory analysis of words and word elements, pronunciation of word elements, visual memory of words, prereading phonics abilities (individual testing).
Gates-McKillop-Horowitz Reading Diagnostic Tests—measure oral reading, reading sentences, words (flash and untimed), word attack, recognizing the visual form of sounds, auditory tests, and written expression (individual testing).

diagnostic test is based upon the detailed directions accompanying it. For further information see Buros (1985).

Diagnostic Reading Scales. Grades 1–7: Word Recognition Lists (word list 1, word list 2, word list 3); Reading Selections (two sets of graded paragraphs); Word Analysis and Phonics Tests (initial consonants, final consonants, consonant digraphs, consonant blends, initial consonant substitution, initial consonant sounds recognized auditorily, auditory discrimination, short and long vowel sounds, vowels with r, vowel diphthongs and digraphs, common syllables or phonograms, blending) (Spache, 1981).

Durrell Analysis of Reading Difficulty (3rd edition). Grades K–6: Oral Reading; Silent Reading; Listening Comprehension; Listening Vocabulary; Word Recognition/Word Analysis; Spelling; Auditory Analysis of Words and Word Elements; Pronunciation of Word Elements; Visual Memory of Words; Prereading Phonics Abilities (Durrell and Catterson, 1980).

Gates-McKillop-Horowitz Reading Diagnostic Tests. Grades 1–6: Oral Reading (omissions, additions, repetitions, directional errors, wrong beginning, wrong middle, wrong ending, wrong in several parts, and accent errors); Reading Sentences; Words (flash and untimed); Word Attack (syllabication, recognizing and blending common word parts, reading words, giving letter sounds, naming capital letters, and naming lower-case letters); Recognizing the Visual Form of Vowels; Auditory Tests (auditory blending and auditory discrimination); Written Expression (spelling and informal writing sample) (Gates, McKillop, and Horowitz, 1981).

INFORMAL DIAGNOSIS

The diagnosis of reading ability and deficiencies is best achieved through using standardized tests and procedures such as have just been described. In program planning for the child with reading difficulties, however, it is also wise to gather additional qualitative information by less formal procedures such as analysis of classroom reading and use of informal reading inventories.

Analysis of Classroom Reading

Classroom teachers have the opportunity to make extensive informal analyses of the reading achievement of their students. During the school day the teacher may note each child's overall performance on a variety of daily reading tasks. The child's response to reading instruction, proficiency in oral and silent reading, performance on worksheets and reading activities can be evaluated informally by the classroom teacher. The astute classroom teacher, through day-by-day observation, is able to judge when a child requires an adjustment in the difficulty level of material he is asked to read. She can evaluate, especially through a simple record keeping procedure, the nature of a given child's word recognition or comprehension difficulties. In addition, the classroom teacher may observe for extended periods of time on a daily basis each child's attitude toward reading, efficiency in extended reading, and skill in reading a wide variety of types of materials.

It is usually the classroom teacher who first recognizes that a child is experiencing reading difficulties. It is often the classroom teacher who makes, based solely on classroom diagnosis, special adaptations to assist a child in successfully overcoming minor reading problems. It is generally the classroom teacher who brings a child's emergent reading difficulties to the attention of the reading specialist and others who can provide remedial services. It is the classroom teacher who works with specialists in coordinating special reading programs with the ongoing classroom routine. The classroom teacher helps support the progress of children receiving special help by fostering their improving competence in applying reading skills in the classroom and by encouraging their more favorable attitudes toward reading.

Although reading specialists make the more time-consuming and thorough analyses of reading problems necessary to plan special instruction for the child with serious reading difficulties, classroom teachers use informal methods of diagnosis and instructional adaptation to promote optimal reading growth for all children in the classroom on a continuing basis.

Informal Reading Inventories

Use of informal reading inventories allows for instructional adjustments based on an estimate of the child's three reading levels—independent reading level, instructional level, and the reading level at which the child becomes frustrated. In addition, informal reading inventories allow teachers to make a qualitative evaluation of a child's word-recognition and comprehension strengths and weaknesses.

A variety of informal reading inventories have been produced for general reading evaluation. These inventories are well-constructed and convenient. A few examples of general informal reading inventories are listed next.

Basic Reading Inventory (3rd edition).   Grades Pre-Primer–8: Forms A, B, and C; Graded word lists and graded passages used to determine independent reading level, instructional reading level, frustration level, strengths and weaknesses in work attack (phonic analysis, context cues, and structural analysis), strengths and weaknesses in comprehension, and listening level (Johns, 1985).

Analytical Reading Inventory (3rd edition).   Grades Primer–9: Forms A, B, and C; Graded word lists (Primer–Grade 6) and graded passages (Primer–Grade 9) used to determine general level of word recognition; strengths and weaknesses in word recognition skills; performance in oral and/or silent reading; comprehension strategies; independent reading level; instructional reading level; frustration reading level; and reading capacity or listening level (Woods & Moe, 1985).

Ekwall Reading Inventory (2nd edition).   Grades Pre-Primer–9: Graded word list (the *San Diego Quick Assessment*) to check word knowledge and word analysis skills as well as rapid determination of student's independent, instructional, and frustration reading levels; graded reading passages (four passages at each level) measure oral and silent independent reading level, instructional reading level, frustration reading level, word analysis skills, comprehension, oral versus silent reading, sight vocabulary, oral reading errors, characteristics of the reader, rate of reading, semantic-syntactic abilities, and listening comprehension; phonics survey (the *El Paso Phonics Survey*) measures initial consonant sounds, ending consonant *x,* initial consonant clusters, vowels, vowel teams, and special letter combinations (Ekwall, 1986).

Preferable to published informal inventories are inventories constructed by reading specialists or teachers using materials available for instruction. These inventories are superior because they give information specifically useful for making instructional decisions for a given child.

Estimating reading levels. A child's reading level can be estimated by using carefully-graded materials similar to those available for instruction. These materials should not have been previously used with the child. Selections of from 100 to 150 words should be chosen from each successive difficulty level. A few questions involving both fact, inference, and vocabulary should be constructed for each selection. After the child, starting at a relatively easy level, has read each selection aloud to the teacher or specialist, he then answers the comprehension questions based upon its content. If the child has great difficulty with the first reading selection, he is moved back to an easier level. When the child reads with ease, he is then asked to read successively more difficult selections until his reading levels are determined. Betts (1957) has outlined reading levels as follows:

1. The child's *independent reading level* is ascertained from the book in which he can read with no more than one error in word recognition (pronunciation) in each 100 words and has a comprehension score of at least 90 percent. At this level the child must read aloud in a natural conversational tone. The reading should be rhythmical and well-phrased. At the same time the child is free from tension and has good reading posture. His silent reading will be faster than his oral reading and free from vocalizations. This is the level at which the child should do extensive supplementary reading for enjoyment or for information in line with his interests. At this *independent reading level,* the child has complete control of experience (concepts), vocabulary, construction, and organization. He has, therefore, maximum opportunity for doing the thinking that is required for a full understanding of what he is reading.

2. The *instructional reading level* is determined from the level of the book in which the child can read with no more than one word-recognition error in each 20 words and with a comprehension score of at least 75 percent. This is the level at which a pupil is able to make successful progress in reading under a *teacher's guidance.* In the classroom, oral reading after silent study is performed without tension, in a conversational tone, and with rhythm and proper phrasing. Silent reading is faster than oral, except at the beginning levels. The child is able to properly use word-recognition clues and techniques. When using challenging materials at this level and with purposeful reading directed by the teacher, the result should be maximum progress in acquiring reading abilities.

3. The *frustration reading level* is marked by the book in which the child "bogs down" when he tries to read. The child reads orally without rhythm and in an unnatural voice. Errors and refusals are numerous. Tensions are obvious. The child comprehends less than half of what he is trying to read. The test should be stopped as soon as it is clear that the child is at his frustration level.

No child should be asked to go on reading at the frustration level when being taught or in any other situation. The teacher, however, should recognize that such a level exists. Too frequently children are found to be working at their frustration levels in classes in which instruction is not satisfactorily adjusted to individual differences.

Informal diagnosis of word-recognition difficulties. Word-recognition difficulties are diagnosed effectively by evaluating oral reading behavior. Many of the standardized individual diagnostic tests described previously in this chapter have used quantitative measures of oral reading performance to find the strengths and weaknesses of the disabled reader. Often additional insights into the disabled reader's problems can be obtained by informal qualitative appraisals of the child's oral reading habits and errors.

After the child's reading levels have been determined, as just described, the specialist selects material more advanced than the child's instructional level, so as to get a good sample of reading errors, but still below the level of frustration, so that meaningful reading is possible. The child should read the selection aloud without any help. He should also be told to guess any of the words he does not know and that he will be asked to retell the story when he finishes it. Every error should be recorded so that it can be classified according to type. A tape recording of the oral reading sample might be helpful in making a careful study of the errors.

We have found that three types of classifications are necessary to obtain a complete understanding of disabled readers' word-recognition problems. First we classify the errors to indicate the child's phonic and structural decoding strengths and weaknesses. The error classifications we use are:

> *Vowel errors.* Mispronunciations that alter one or more vowel sounds, as *dig* read *dug*.
>
> *Consonant errors.* Alteration of one or more consonant sounds, as *send* read *sent*.
>
> *Addition of sounds.* Insertion of one or more sounds in a word, as *tack* read *track*.
>
> *Omission of sounds.* Mispronunciations that involve omission of one or more sounds in a word, as *blind* read *bind*.
>
> *Substitutions of words.* Substitution of a word unrelated in form or sound to the word to be read, as *lived* read *was*.
>
> *Repetition of words.* Words repeated, whether read correctly or incorrectly are counted as repetitions as, *"a boy a boy had a dog"* (one repetition).
>
> *Addition of words.* Insertion of words into the text, when *once there was* is read *once upon a time there was* (three word additions).
>
> *Omission of words.* Omissions of words from the text, as *a little pig* read *a pig*.
>
> *Refusals and words aided.* Refusal of a child to attempt a word or when a word is supplied by the specialist after a delay of 15 seconds.

Suggestions for helping children overcome such word-recognition problems are discussed in Chapters 11 and 12.

Next we study possible faulty perceptual habits such as a tendency to reverse letters or words. We also look for error patterns predominately involving specific parts of words such as wrong beginnings, wrong middles, wrong endings, or wrong in several parts. Suggestions for helping children overcome such perceptual errors are discussed in Chapters 11 and 12.

The third type of diagnosis of oral reading behavior deals with limitations in the use of meaning clues to word recognition. We have found helpful a somewhat modified use of the linguistic classification of oral reading miscues suggested by Goodman and Burke (1972). We are interested especially in word miscues that indicate (1) ineffective use of clues gained from the reader's background (for example, a child might quickly recognize a word, such as *rhinoceros,* if he were reading about a trip to the zoo); (2) miscues that indicate little use of syntactic aids derived from knowledge of language structure (for example, *"They all were happy,"* read as *"They all where happy"*); (3) miscues that indicate a lack of use of semantic aids gained from an ongoing understanding of the content presented (for example, "The boy was riding a horse," read as "The boy was riding a house").

We assess the reader's limitations in the use of meaning clues in anticipating the next word or words to be read. Skill in using meaning clues facilitates any perceptual skills. We also diagnose the disabled reader's difficulties in using meaning clues to check the accuracy of decoded, unknown words. These last two limitations are identified by the number of repetitions made, the compatibility of the errors made with the ongoing content, and the omissions or additions of words that alter the meaning of the passage being read.

A more complete analysis of miscues, developed by Goodman and Burke, involves classifying each miscue according to:

1. Graphic similarity; how similar does the miscue look compared to the correct word?
2. Sound similarity; how similar does the miscue sound compared to the correct word?
3. Grammatical function; is the grammatical function of the reader's oral response the same as that of the printed word?
4. Syntactic acceptability; how structurally acceptable is the miscue?
5. Semantic acceptability; how acceptable is the meaning of the miscue?
6. Meaning change; how much does the miscue change the meaning of the story?
7. Correction; how successful was any attempt to correct the miscue?

For further information the specialist should refer to the *Reading Miscue Inventory Manual* developed by Goodman and Burke (1972).

Having the child pronounce words from word lists provides additional information about word-recognition skills. The words should be selected to be at the child's instructional level. Errors are recorded and analyzed. Next we have the child again try to pronounce the missed or refused words to discover his identification patterns. After this the missed words are presented orally to the child for him to use in oral sentences to ascertain whether they are part of his meaning vocabulary.

The remedial methods suggested throughout this book emphasize the use of meaning clues, because all skills are taught in meaningful reading situations rather than in isolated drills. The remedial methods suggested in Chapter 10 are specifically designed to correct deficiencies in meaning clues to word recognition.

Construction of an informal reading inventory. Many reading specialists find it convenient to construct an informal, diagnostic booklet. This booklet can be made easily by using representative passages selected from various grade levels of a basic reading series. Oral reading passages should be affixed to the left-hand page of the booklet with a comparable selection for silent reading affixed to the right-hand page. On the next page, a list of five comprehension questions for each passage should be listed in the following order: first, a summary question should be used, followed by two factual questions, then an inferential question, and then a vocabulary question if possible. On the fourth page, a list of words selected from the back of the reader from which the oral and silent reading passages were taken, should be typed on the page for use as a vocabulary test, as previously described. The same four-page procedure is repeated at half-yearly intervals using selections from the same reading series. Grade-level tabs should be used for quick selection of passages. For more detailed suggestions the specialist should refer to *Informal Reading Inventories* (Johnson, Kress, and Pikulski, 1987).

Use of commercially-produced informal reading inventories save the time needed to make the booklet. Self-created informal inventories, however, can be constructed so that they are more ideal in any given diagnostic situation.

Suggestions for the Reading Specialist

A specialist collecting information from informal sources should follow certain procedures that will enable the data obtained to be as accurate as possible. These suggestions may be helpful for collecting evaluative data:

1. *Isolate specific outcomes or characteristics to be evaluated.* If, for example, information is needed on the method of attack a child uses on words in isolation when working orally, the observer should be alert to all of the approaches that might be used by the child.

2. *Define the observable results or characteristics in exact terms.* The specialist should have, for example, a checklist of possible methods that the child might use when orally solving a word-recognition problem.

3. *Plan the informal situation so that reading results or characteristics will be easily observable.* The child whose methods of word study are to be observed should be given a list of words of increasing difficulty, and should be requested to work out the unknown words aloud so that the specialist can note which word-recognition approaches the child is using.

4. *Classify information in uniform and useful ways.* The specialist studying word recognition may wish to classify the errors made by a child as to both location within the word (beginning, middle, ending, or reversal errors) and phonetic types (vowel, consonant blend, digraph, addition of sounds, omission of sounds, or transposition of sounds). The specialist should classify the analytical attack under categories such as spelling, letter-by-letter sounding, phonic, structural, syllabic, or a combination of these forms of attack on words. The specialist should also notice if the child tries to recognize each word as a sight word without any otherwise discernible form of attack.

5. *Make a record of the findings, with illustrative samples of the performance on which the judgments were made.* Using the methods of word study just described, the child might be found to be attempting a phonic approach to the problem, but his knowledge of word elements may be weak. Sample words should be listed to show (1) visual separation of the words, (2) elements miscalled, (3) any difficulty in synthesis that results, and (4) the final pronunciation of the word. In addition, a summary of the specialist's opinion at the time should be recorded.

6. *Evaluate the significance of the observed behavior or characteristic.* The specialist, in the example cited previously, should indicate the importance of the information to the understanding of the instructional needs of the child.

The usefulness of information from informal procedures depends on the experience of the observer, the number of observations, the degree to which the observations are unbiased, and the relevance of the information to the understanding of the child's reading difficulties. Many elements in reading diagnosis must be determined by informal procedures.

The information acquired by informal approaches should be gathered as systematically as possible, and it must be interpreted and used with caution. Misjudgments will occur if the personal biases of the specialist are allowed to influence diagnostic judgments, even on normative data. Misjudgments are even more prevalent when the data are collected informally. For example, a specialist may have a special interest in reversals. When a child makes a few, as many children do, they may be overemphasized by the specialist. As a result, remediation may dwell unnecessarily on reversals rather than on the child's true difficulty.

Informal procedures have merit when they allow the specialist to explore further some characteristic suspected from more standardized measurements. Many

FIGURE 8-2 Informal diagnostic inventory

Name_____ School_____ Grade_____ Age_____

Intelligence Test_____ I.Q._____ M.A._____ Date_____

Standardized Group Reading Tests: *Reading Expectancy Grade*_____

1. _____ R.G._____   2. _____ R.G._____

3. _____ R.G._____   4. _____ R.G._____

Reading Levels   *Average Reading Grade*_____

1. Independent_____   2. Instructional_____   3. Frustration_____

_____

*Oral Reading from Basic Reader at Grade Level*_____ *Basic Series*_____

1. Oral Reading Skill
    (a) Slow Rate_____   (b) Poor Comprehension_____
    (c) Over-fast Rate_____   (d) Inappropriate Phrasing_____
    (e) Faulty Enunciation_____   (f) Faulty Expression_____
    (g) Unusual Posture_____   (h) Pointing_____
    (i) Signs of Tension_____   (j) Word-by-word_____

2. Word Recognition Difficulties
    (a) Omissions_____   (b) Additions_____
    (c) Repetitions_____   (d) Reversals_____
    (e) Wrong Beginnings_____   (f) Wrong Middles_____
    (g) Wrong Endings_____   (h) Wrong in Several Parts_____
    (i) Refusals_____   (j) Limited Self-Correction_____
    (k) Semantic Miscues_____   (l) Syntactic Miscues_____
    (m) Limited Expectancy Clues_____ (n) Others_____

Silent Reading: continue in same book as above

1. Rate: Words per Minute_____ 2. Comprehension: % Correct_____
3. Lip Movements_____ 4. Audible Speech_____
5. Finger Pointing_____ 6. Head Movements_____
7. Signs of Tension_____ 8. Distractibility_____

Word Pronunciation: from _Word List_ in same basic reader

1. Technique Used
    (a)   Whole Word_____ (b) Structural_____
    (c)   Syllabic_____ (d) Phonics_____
    (e)   Letter-by-letter_____ (f) Spelling_____

2. Errors
    (a)   Faulty vowels_____ (b) Faulty Consonants_____
    (c)   Reversals_____ (d) Addition of Sounds_____
    (e)   Omission of Sounds_____ (f) Substitution of Words_____
    (g)   Faulty Visual Analysis_____ (h) Faulty Blending_____
    (i)   Words Refused_____ (j) Others_____

Other Relevant Data

 1. Hearing_____ 2. Vision_____
 3. Handedness_____ 4. Eyedness_____
 5. Speech_____ 6. Any Physical Difficulties_____
 7. Language Usage_____ 8. Fluency_____
 9. Ability to concentrate_____ 10. Persistence_____
11. Emotional reactions (confident, shy, over-aggressive, negative, cheerful, etc.) _____

12. Attitudes toward (school, teacher, reading) _____

13. Home environment _____
14. Other observations _____

Tentative diagnosis of case: 1. _____
2. etc. _____

Suggested appropriate remedial plan: 1. _____
2. etc. _____

(Permission for duplication and use of the *Informal Diagnostic Inventory* is hereby granted.)

times, when administering a standardized diagnostic reading test, the specialist notices a possible reading difficulty that should be studied further. The specialist will complete the test as designed so as not to invalidate it, but then may informally explore items to follow a "hunch." For example, the specialist may be giving a standardized list of isolated words to find out how well a child can work out the pronunciations in an untimed situation. The test is administered and scored properly. The specialist may have noted, however, that the child seemed to have trouble in visually separating the words into usable elements. The examiner then may wish to go back to some of the words missed, and by covering up parts of the words, show the child the correct way to analyze them. The specialist might then see whether the child could have recognized the words had his visual analysis been correct. This information would be recorded but would not enter into the application of the normative data. The *Informal Diagnostic Inventory* in Figure 8–2 has been organized to facilitate recording data obtained during informal diagnosis.

Informal observation of the child's oral reading when confronted with selections of increasing difficulty often provides insights into his reading problems. The specialist should especially note word-by-word reading, failure to use context clues, inability to group words into thought units or language patterns, limited sentence sense, or any other indication of a basic comprehension problem. Many of these basic abilities are most easily detected by the way in which a child reads aloud a passage that is somewhat difficult for him. Specific suggestions for correcting difficulties in these basic comprehension abilities will be given in Chapter 14.

USE OF STANDARDIZED READING DIAGNOSTIC TESTS IN COMBINATION WITH INFORMAL PROCEDURES

In clinical diagnosis at the child study level, a combination of standardized diagnostic tests and brief informal procedures can be used. In this way the specialist has the advantages of the impartial standardized procedures and the freedom to design his own reading and learning tasks using whatever materials seem most appropriate.

For example, after considering referral information, intelligence testing results, and results of standardized group reading tests, a clinician might choose to administer the word list and paragraph sections of the *Spache Diagnostic Reading Scales*. From such limited use of a standardized reading diagnostic test, the clinician would have adequate information to judge the student's relative strengths in reading comprehension, rate of comprehension, and general word recognition.

If word recognition and reading comprehension appeared to be strengths, but the rate of comprehension was noticeably slow, the clinician could proceed directly to refinement and verification of the diagnosis. Using materials at the reading level indicated by the diagnostic test just administered, the clinician could set specific purposes for rapid reading, to appraise whether the slow rate indicated inefficient word recognition, overconcern with detailed comprehension, or simply a habitual response to all reading tasks.

Similarly, in the area of comprehension, a child-study level, diagnostic finding could be sharpened. For example, a student who was not accurate in factual detail recall could be given a suitable selection and asked several questions requiring recall of factual detail. The specialist could then ask the student to explain how he arrived at his answers. In this way, misunderstandings of word meanings in context reading or insufficient attention to syntactic clues to precise understanding often are uncovered. The diagnostician should review *all* answers and should not indicate whether any answer is considered good or bad. It is diagnostically important to know how the child arrived at his answers and the exact nature of his understandings and misunderstandings. The child should also be directed to find where the relevant information is in the passage. It is important to determine how efficiently this is accomplished and whether, in the review process, the student is able to clear up spontaneously any of his own confusions.

Similar diagnostic procedures can be used in most areas of comprehension difficulty. It is important to assess how the child approaches comprehension tasks, the nature of his misunderstandings, and his ability to correct his own errors when his attention is specifically focused on a single aspect of reading comprehension.

When the diagnostic concern is centered on word recognition difficulties, the diagnostician must make, refine, and verify judgments about its various aspects. Using referral information and a child's performance on the word list and paragraph sections of the standardized diagnostic test, a clinician might decide the child's weakness included lack of instant recognition of common words he should know by sight at his level of reading development. This judgment could be verified and refined by additional testing, using word lists from the child's own reading series or from remedial instructional materials. A trial lesson might be taught by the clinician to determine whether any special methodologies, such as a word-tracing method, would enhance learning.

When word recognition difficulties appear to result from inadequate analytic techniques, diagnostic information obtained from word lists and paragraph sections of standardized diagnostic tests is often found to give insufficient information to enable the specialist to turn directly to informal diagnostic methods. For a standardized picture of word recognition techniques as used in silent reading, a diagnostic instrument such as the *Stanford Diagnostic Reading Test* should be used. From a comparison of results obtained from this instrument, along with diagnostic insights from referral information and oral word lists and paragraph reading, the specialist will be able to evaluate the relative strengths and weaknesses within the broader general area of word recognition. Informal procedures then can be used to refine and verify the diagnosis.

For example, if a student appeared to be ineffective in using meaning clues as an aid to word recognition, the specialist could have the student complete some simple, informal cloze passages to further analyze the nature of the difficulty. Some short paragraphs could be prepared or selected and the student could be asked to fill in the blanks. For diagnosis, a paragraph of the following form could be used:

Filling in blanks demands _____ background knowledge, language competence, and reading _____, to supply a meaningful _____ when all graphic clues are _____.

From the nature of the errors and from a discussion of errors with the student, the specialist will be able to refine and verify the diagnosis. Two cautions are important. First, the specialist should select or prepare cloze passages at a distinctly easy reading level for the student because all graphic cues to recognition of certain words have been eliminated. Second, the student should have developed sufficiently good reading and writing skills to be able to complete the task independently. For information on the use of the cloze procedure to judge readability see Bormuth (1967).

Similarly if the student demonstrated difficulty with word beginnings and with beginning sounds, the specialist might want to check more thoroughly the exact nature of the student's confusion by having him read aloud a list of common words beginning with the essential beginning blends and digraphs. A few sample exercises and activities might also be tried in order to help the clinician decide how the child might be helped most effectively to gain a functional knowledge of common word beginnings.

When the major diagnostic concern involves word-recognition techniques used in oral reading, the specialist should first obtain a complete, unified, standardized picture of oral word-recognition by means of an oral-reading diagnostic instrument such as the *Gates-McKillop-Horowitz Reading Diagnostic Tests*. When using this instrument, the following subtests should be administered: (1) oral reading, (2) words: flash, (3) words: untimed, and (4) knowledge of word parts: word attack (starting with syllabication, recognizing and blending common parts, or reading words—whichever seems most appropriate). Other information pertinent to the child-study can be obtained through judicious use of additional subtests useful to a more complete understanding of a child's word-recognition difficulties. Appropriate comparisons of results obtained from these subtests, together with referral information and other standardized and informal diagnostic assessment, will suggest weaknesses which can and should be understood even more completely through informal testing procedures.

For the child with a reading disability, standardized tests serve best to put into perspective major areas of reading competence or concern. Informal methods are best, once an area of concern has been established, to clarify what exactly should be taught and how learning can be enhanced.

SUMMARY

A classification of reading difficulties shows that both standardized and informal procedures are needed to diagnose the needs of disabled readers. The diagnosis is a series of screenings going as far as needed from general diagnosis to specific diagnosis, to child-study diagnosis, until all the information necessary to develop an appropriate individual plan of remediation is gathered. Representative standardized procedures appropriate for each level of diagnosis are presented.

Suggested informal procedures are described including classroom analysis and specialist-constructed informal reading inventories. Systematic informal data collection methods are presented. A sample *Informal Diagnostic Inventory* is offered.

Whenever detailed diagnosis of reading difficulty is called for, the most appropriate evaluative techniques must be chosen from both standardized and informal procedures. Skill in choosing the proper techniques in testing and in interpreting results comes from both effort and experience.

STUDY QUESTIONS

1. Differentiate between general, specific, and child-study diagnosis.
2. Why is analysis of a child's classroom reading an essential part of a complete reading assessment?
3. Describe the reading behavior of a child at the *independent, instructional,* and *frustration levels* of reading.
4. What three types of classifications are said to be necessary to obtain a complete understanding of a disabled reader's word recognition problems?
5. What is the diagnostic importance of understanding how a student has arrived at his answers?
6. What is meant by "using informal procedures to verify and refine the results of standardized testing"?

SELECTED READINGS

BARR, R. AND M. SADOW. *Reading Diagnosis for Teachers.* New York: Longman, Inc., 1985.

HARRIS, A. J., AND E. R. SIPAY. *How to Increase Reading Ability,* 8th ed., Chap. 7. New York: Longman, Inc., 1985.

MARZANO, R. J., P. J. HAGERTY, S. W. VALENCIA, AND P. P. DISTEFANO. *Reading Diagnosis and Instruction,* Chaps. 5, 6, and 7. Englewood Cliffs, NJ: Prentice-Hall, Inc., 1987.

ROSWELL, F. AND G. NATCHEZ. *Reading Disability: Diagnosis and Treatment,* 2nd ed., Chap. 2. New York: Basic Books, Inc., Publishers, 1971.

SPACHE, G. D. *Diagnosing and Correcting Reading Disabilities,* Chap. 7. Boston: Allyn & Bacon, Inc., 1976.

WILSON, R. M. AND C. J. CLELAND. *Diagnostic and Remedial Reading for Classroom and Clinic,* 5th ed., Chap. 4. Columbus, OH: Charles E. Merrill Publishing Company, 1985.

9

Planning Appropriate Remediation

The specialist or reading teacher studies the diagnostic findings and then arranges learning conditions in which the disabled reader can grow in reading at an accelerated rate. In making an *appropriate educational plan of remediation,* it is necessary to identify the specific limitations in the disabled reader's reading profile that are impeding reading growth. Methods, motivation, and materials are considered in formulating the educational plan most suited to the disabled reader's remedial program.

The remedial program must be based on more than an understanding of the child's reading needs. It must also be based on the child's characteristics. The child who is hearing-impaired needs an approach to reading different from that for his counterpart with normal hearing. The child with poor vision needs adjustment in methods and, if his limitation is severe enough, in materials also. The child who is a slow learner needs modified methods, and so does the one who is behaviorally disordered. The modifications of instruction for such children will be discussed in a later chapter.

As each case is different, there can be no "bag of tricks." Nor can there be a universal approach which will solve disabled readers' problems. Many times remedial training suited to one child would be detrimental to another. If, for example, a remedial program has been planned to develop more adequate phrasing, the child might be required to do considerable prepared oral reading in order to help him read in thought units. This same recommendation might be harmful to the disabled reader who is already overvocalizing in his silent reading. It could exaggerate the faulty habit he has acquired and increase his disability. To sum up, every remedial program must be planned on the basis of a thorough appraisal of the child's instructional needs, his strengths and weaknesses, and the environment in which correction is to take place.

The appropriate remedial plan should be in written form indicating in some detail what is to be recommended for each case. This must be done because it is too difficult to remember each child, his needs, the level of his attainments, and his limitations with the exactness that is necessary for an effective corrective program. The written case report should indicate the nature of the disability and the type of exercises recommended to correct it. It should identify the level of material to be used. The written plan should state any physical or sensory characteristics that need to be corrected or for which the program needs to be modified. Interests, hobbies, and attitudes should become part of the written record. Most important, it should include a description of the remedial program recommended and the types of material and exercises to be used.

The original individual plan of remedial work is not to be considered permanent. It needs to be modified from time to time as the child progresses in reading. Often a disabled reader changes rapidly in his instructional needs. The better the diagnosis and the more successful the remedial plan, the more rapidly his needs will change. One disabled reader, for example, may have failed to build analytical word-recognition techniques but depends on sight vocabulary and context clues to recognize new words. He would be given remedial work designed to teach him the analytical techniques. After a time, he may develop considerable skill in word study, but he may not make a corresponding gain in rate of reading. His problem would no longer be one of developing word analysis. In fact, emphasis on this phase of the program might become detrimental to his future reading growth. The use of larger word elements and other more rapid word-recognition techniques and further building of sight vocabulary would be advisable. As the problem changes, so must the plan of remediation in order to meet new reading needs.

Because the child's instructional needs change rapidly, it is unwise to put him into a remedial program that resembles a factory production line. Such a program assumes that once a given child's level of reading performance is identified, all that is needed is to put him through a set of exercises uniform for all children. The disabled reader whose needs change rapidly as his limitations are corrected is in dire need of a program that readily adjusts to every change in his reading pattern. To achieve success, a remedial program must be based on a continuous diagnosis, and the basic plan must be modified somewhat as the instructional needs change.

In some instances, the original plan of remediation does not result in improvement. When this occurs, a reevaluation of the diagnosis and perhaps additional appraisals should be made. A somewhat altered approach to instruction may be necessary for success.

Inasmuch as an *appropriate individual educational plan of remediation* is necessary for correcting each disabled reader's problem, the following elements should be considered:

1. Remedial plans must be individualized.
2. The remedial plan must encourage the disabled reader.
3. Materials and exercises must be appropriate.
4. The remedial plan must use effective teaching procedures.
5. The plan must enlist cooperative efforts.

REMEDIAL PLANS MUST BE INDIVIDUALIZED

The disabled reader is one who has failed to respond to reading programs designed to meet the instructional needs and characteristics of the majority of children. The onset of reading disability is usually gradual. The child who becomes a disabled reader gets into a moderate amount of difficulty, misses some instruction, or in some way falls behind or gets confused. The reading curriculum and the class itself go on, while the child is left behind. Soon the child finds himself hopelessly out of things. He can no longer read well enough to keep up with his group. He may develop an aversion to reading and is quite likely to develop poor reading habits. All of these things accumulate until it is apparent to the teacher that the child has become a disabled reader. He has not learned the skills and abilities essential to effective reading. Faulty habits of reading have become established. He is developing or has already developed a dislike of and antagonism toward reading and his sense of defeat mounts higher and higher.

A plan designed to treat reading disability is based on the assumption that children learn differently and need programs that meet their individual requirements. Such programs must be based on recognition of a particular child's physical and mental characteristics and must be individually designed to be efficient in overcoming his difficulties.

The Remedial Plan Should Be in Keeping with the Child's Characteristics

The expected results of instruction and the methods used will need to conform to the child's characteristics. If the child is lacking in general intelligence, he cannot be expected to reach the goals in reading for children of greater mental capability nor can he be expected to progress as rapidly. The remedial teacher would be wise to mofidy the goals of the program. The prognosis for rate of gain is usually directly proportional to the general intelligence of the child and the seriousness of his problem. In addition to being flexible in the results she expects, the remedial teacher would be wise to modify the methods of instruction to meet the slow-learning child's needs. Slow-learning children need more concrete experiences, more carefully given directions, and more repetition and drill than do children of higher intelligence.

If a child has poor vision or poor hearing, modifications in methods need to be made. Such limitations make learning to read more difficult but in no way preclude the child from achieving. Even children with serious visual and auditory impairments have been taught to read. The disabled reader with lesser sensory handicaps can be taught more efficiently if his limitations are known and modifications in methods of instruction are made. Adjustments in methods that have proved helpful will be discussed in Chapter 13.

Remedial Instruction Should Be Specific

The remedial teacher should focus instruction upon the child's specific reading needs. The diagnosis has usually indicated that there is something specifically wrong with the pattern of his reading performance. One child, for example, may have learned to read with speed but falls short of the accuracy required in certain situations. This child should read material with factual content and should read for purposes that demand exact recall of those facts. Another disabled reader may be so overconcerned with detail that he reads extremely slowly, looking for more facts than the author wrote. He becomes so concerned with detail that he cannot understand the author's overall intent. The teacher should endeavor to make him less compulsive, so that the rate of reading and its results can be compatible with the purposes of this particular reading.

The principle that remedial instruction should be specific and not general means that the remedial teacher should emphasize those phases of reading development that will correct the reading limitations. It does not mean that just one type of exercise should be used, nor does it mean that a specific skill or ability should be isolated and receive drill. For a disabled reader with an insufficient knowledge of the larger visual and structural elements used in word recognition, the teacher would be in error if she used a method that consisted exclusively of isolated drill on word elements. A better procedure would be to emphasize having the child read material at the proper level of difficulty.

He would read for several purposes, but when he encountered a word-recognition problem, the teacher would help him by emphasizing the larger elements in the word. When exercises for developing basic skills and abilities were studied, the remedial teacher would have him do those that gave him experience in using the larger visual and structural parts of words. The teacher could find or construct additional exercises and activities that would provide experiences with the larger elements in words he already knew, so that he could learn to use these larger word elements in recognizing new words.

The workbook exercises accompanying basic readers may also be used. The disabled reader may need to do only certain selected pages. This is because the child has an uneven profile, and he may have emphasized one phase of reading instruction to the detriment of another. The child who needs a greater knowledge of large visual and structural elements may have failed to develop them because he overemphasized letter-by-letter sounding in word recognition. Such a child should avoid exercises that teach the knowledge of letter sounds.

A Variety of Remedial Techniques Should Be Used

There is an unfortunate tendency, once remedial instruction has been prescribed, to stick to one specific type of exercise to overcome a known deficiency. Basing a remedial program on a diagnosis does not imply that a given exercise can be used until the child's reading disability is corrected. There are many ways to develop each of the skills and abilities in reading. An effective remedial plan includes a variety of teaching techniques and instructional procedures.

Many sources describing teaching techniques are available to the remedial teacher. Professional books on remedial instruction in reading give suggestions for correcting specific types of reading difficulties. Mueser (1981) has edited a group of remedial techniques. Manuals and workbooks accompanying basal reading programs are also sources of teaching techniques. The exercises suggested for teaching the skills and abilities when first introduced in such manuals and workbooks may prove beneficial to remedial programs. If, for example, a fifth-grade child has difficulty finding root words in affixed words, the teacher can find many and varied exercises in second- and third-grade manuals and workbooks to teach this skill. As she examines the teaching techniques suggested in various materials, the remedial teacher can accumulate a variety of exercises for each of the important types of disabilities listed in Chapter 8. She can keep the program dynamic and interesting to the child by using a variety of teaching techniques and at the same time be sure that the instruction emphasizes the skill development indicated in the *individual educational plan of remediation*.

In using a variety of teaching methods and techniques, care must be taken that the teaching approaches do not confuse the child. The directions should be simple, and the teaching techniques should not be changed too often. The exercises should be as nearly like reading as possible. The child should not have to spend time learning complicated procedures or directions. Enough variety should be introduced, however, to keep the program stimulating.

The Remedial Plan Should Assure Energetic Learning

Growth in reading presupposes an energetic learner. Of course the child must learn to read by reading. He must attack the printed page vigorously and often if he is to succeed. A fatigued child cannot be expected to make gains during the remedial period. Therefore the length of the period for remedial instruction should be such that concentrated work is possible. The disabled reader frequently finds it difficult to read for any considerable length of time. His lack of attention may be due to a variety of causes. It may be lack of physical stamina, it may be that he is not getting enough sleep at night, or it may be that his emotional reactions to reading diminish his vitality. His inattention or lack of vigor may be a reaction to an unsuccessful situation. Whatever the cause, most children, if properly motivated, can apply themselves to reading at least for a short period of time. Obviously, if lack of attention and vigor result from a condition that can be corrected, the correction should be made. In any case, the length of the remedial reading period should be adjusted so that an energetic attack can be maintained.

Frequently it is necessary to divide the remedial sessions into short periods. The child may work with the remedial teacher for a period of 45 minutes. At the start of remedial training, it may be necessary to have him read for only ten minutes for specific purposes and then have him use the results of his reading in some creative activity, such as drawing or constructing. Then he might work on some skill-development exercises which emphasize the training he needs. These exercises might entail rereading the material he read at the first part of the session or they may be word-recognition drill on new words from the material read. Finally, the child might be asked to tell about books he has been reading independently. As he gains in reading growth, the length of concentrated reading time should be increased. Soon the child who has no physical limitation will be reading longer without interruption. When this is so, creative activities can be used less frequently.

THE REMEDIAL PLAN MUST ENCOURAGE THE DISABLED READER

Most disabled readers are discouraged about their failure to learn to read. They frequently think that they cannot learn. This lack of confidence in their ability to learn is detrimental to possible reading growth. The effective learner is a confident and purposeful learner, one who has a desire to learn and finds pleasure in working toward this goal. In order that a disabled reader may go ahead rapidly in learning to read, it is necessary for him to know that he can learn and to see that he is progressing satisfactorily.

Frequently the disabled reader is tense or insecure. He has had no real opportunity to gain confidence in himself because most of the school day is spent reading. For some time he has been much less effective in school work than his intellectual level would indicate that he should be. This child may become submissive or demanding, aggressive or withdrawn, or show his basic insecurity in a variety of ways. He may develop attitudes of indifference, dislike, or rejection. He may resist help, display few interests, or be antagonistic toward reading instruction. Remedial reading programs must overcome these attitudes and related behavior problems.

One of the first responsibilities of the remedial teacher is to develop in the child a need for learning to read. The second is to gain his confidence to such a degree that he will know that she has taken a personal interest and that she will solve his reading problem. A direct attack on the reading problem by a businesslike, considerate adult will do much to overcome tensions and reading-avoidant attitudes. When a child recognizes that an interest is taken in him and his reading problem, it increases his sense of personal worth and confidence in himself.

The Plan Should Emphasize Success

In order that the remedial program be encouraging to the child, his success rather than his mistakes should be emphasized. Teachers have a tendency to point out errors to children rather than to make them feel that for the most part they are doing well. A disabled reader who is reminded continually of his errors may become overwhelmed by a sense of defeat. A wise teacher will start him in a remedial program that is somewhat easy for him so that his successful performance will be immediately apparent. As he gains confidence, the difficulty of the reading materials will be increased. The teacher should always be quick to recognize when the child has put forth a real effort and has done something well. Many times, particularly at the start, recognition will have to be given for activities related to the reading rather than the reading itself. Gradually the teacher will find more opportunities to give praise for actual reading that is well-done. At all times it should be remembered that the effectiveness of remedial instruction depends in no small measure upon the child's gain in confidence. This gain in confidence is brought about through successful experience with reading which in the past had caused him so much difficulty.

Emphasis upon success does not mean that errors are to be overlooked. A child's faulty reading, of course, must be brought to his attention. Errors in word recognition must be pointed out. Faulty habits in reading which limit his speed must be recognized by him before they can be corrected. Sometimes it is necessary to demand greater exactness in reading. While it is true that the teacher must point out his mistakes, she must at all times indicate that he is improving and that for the most part he really is doing well. If, for example, a child calls the word *house, horse* in the sentence ''The dog ran up to the house,'' the teacher should point out to him that he had the sentence nearly correct, but that in order to be exactly right he should have looked at the center part of the last word a little more carefully. As a matter of fact, the child did recognize most of the words in the sentence. He made an error that indicated that he was using the context well and that his error was a very slight one indeed. The words *house* and *horse* do look much alike.

In a comprehension lesson, the child may give the wrong answer to a question. Instead of saying that the answer is wrong, it would be far better for the teacher to say, ''Let's see what the book says about this'' and then find out why the child made his error. It will be frequently found that he did not understand the meaning of a word or that he failed to notice a key word such as *not,* or that he had not grouped the words into proper thought units. Whatever the cause, it should be found and the child should be shown the correct way to read the passage. The attitude of the teacher should be not one of pointing out errors but one of helping the child learn to read.

An effective remedial program must be one that satisfies the child, makes him feel that he is getting along well, and keeps at a minimum any anxiety which he feels about his reading progress. The teacher's responsibility in encouraging the child to read energetically is great. She should neither hurry him unduly nor allow him to dawdle; she should be sure he is working hard and yet avoid putting pressure on him. Practically all children can be expected to work intently in developing reading ability. This is especially true if the reading materials are at the right level, if the child is properly motivated, and if he is reading for purposes that are real to him. There should always be a friendly atmosphere but one that keeps uppermost the point of view that the child is there to learn to read.

Growth in Reading Should Be Demonstrated

The disabled reader needs to have his reading growth demonstrated to him. There are many ways to do this. The choice of method for demonstrating progress will depend on the nature of the child's reading problem. If, for example, the child is trying to develop a sight vocabulary, he could make a picture dictionary of the words he is trying to learn. As the dictionary becomes larger, he recognizes that he has increased his sight vocabulary. The child who is working on accuracy of comprehension could develop a chart (Figure 9-1) in which he indicates his percent of accuracy from week to week. If he fails to gain over the period of a week, the teacher simplifies the material or asks more general questions so that accuracy increases. Then as the child gains confidence, the difficulty of the material is again increased gradually. It is good for the child to go back, from time to time, and reread something that he has read previously. He will discover that material that was

FIGURE 9-1 An Accuracy Bar Chart

difficult for him a short while ago is now relatively easy for him to read. This will be especially true if the teacher takes time to prepare him to read it. Tape recordings of former and improved oral reading of the same passages are especially effective as the child clearly hears the improvement for himself.

Whatever the nature of the difficulty, it is important for the remedial program to be organized to demonstrate to the child that he is progressing toward his goal of better reading. The disabled reader who has been in difficulty for a long time needs whatever encouragement can be given. He needs not only to be in a comfortable learning situation but also to see that he is making effective advancement in reading.

Remedial Programs Should Not Be Substituted for Enjoyable Activities

The remedial teacher must organize periods of instruction so that children are not required to come for training at a time that competes with other activities of great importance to them. For example, it is sometimes a practice to give children extra help after school. This is a bad time for a child who enjoys outdoor sports with friends and who finds this the only time that outdoor games are played in his neighborhood. In scheduling summer reading programs, it is wise to delay their start until a week or so after school is out and the children have found they have time that they do not know what to do with. Even then, the better scheduling time for classes is probably in the morning, because the majority of things that the child likes to do, such as going swimming or playing baseball, are done in the afternoon.

The busy classroom teacher often finds it difficult to give a child the attention he needs when the class is in session. She may select recess time or the time in which other children have art or music activities for helping a child with his reading. Such a practice is understandable but is not good for the correction of a reading disability. A better time would be to work with the children needing reeducation while the rest of the class is busily engaged in studying or reading independently. Whatever time is used for giving remedial help, it is important that it not conflict with activities that are important to the child.

MATERIALS AND EXERCISES MUST BE APPROPRIATE

The selection of appropriate material for remedial work in reading is one of the main problems the remedial teacher has to solve. Some teachers feel that the most important element is that the material deal with a subject in which the child is interested. Others feel that the level of difficulty is of even greater importance. Still others believe that having material compatible with the nature of the remedial instruction is of paramount importance. There can be no doubt that all three of these elements enter into the selection. Without trying to decide among them, we may conclude that the more important considerations in selecting material are that the materials must be

1. Suitable in level of difficulty
2. Suitable in type
3. At the appropriate level of interest and format
4. Abundant

Materials Must Be Suitable in Level of Difficulty

The child grows in reading by reading; therefore the material that is used for remedial instruction should be of a difficulty level that enables him to read comfortably and with enjoyment. The diagnosis will have disclosed the level at which the disabled reader could be expected to read. The remedial teacher must pick out materials at that level to suit the child. The difficulty of material can be judged in many ways. Readability formulas, such as the Dale-Chall (1948) and the Spache (1953) formulas are useful in estimating reading level. Comprehensive book lists, which include information on level of difficulty, such as those provided by Spache (1975, 1978) and Zintz (1981, appendix B) are helpful. The extensive listing of easy-to-read, high interest, content area books offered by McCormick (1987, appendix D), which includes information on level of difficulty, should also be of value.

The books in most reading series are graded carefully and indicate the level of reading maturity necessary for their use. In general, readers of second-grade level are suitable to the child whose skills are of second-grade maturity. Third-grade books are suitable for the child whose skill development is approximately that of a third-grade child. The difficulty level of ungraded materials can be estimated by formula or by using a reading series as a difficulty-rating scale. The difficulty of an ungraded library book, for example, may be judged by comparing it with the various grade levels of a reading series. The book can be compared with a third-grade reader, and if it is judged to be harder, it then can be compared with a fourth-grade reader, and so forth until the approximate level of difficulty can be estimated. In making the judgment, the teacher should look at the number of unusual words it contains, the length of its sentences, the number of prepositional phrases, the number of unusual word orders, and the complexity of the ideas it includes. In judging level of difficulty, it is important that the remedial teacher remember that the results of standardized survey tests tend to overestimate the skill development of a reading-disabled child. Therefore it is usually wise to start remedial instruction with material that is somewhat lower than the child's general reading score as indicated by standardized tests.

The difficulty of the material appropriate for remedial instruction will vary somewhat with the nature of the disability. The teacher should modify the level of difficulty according to the goals of instruction to be achieved by the use of that material. For example, if the child's major problem is one of developing sight vocabulary, the material should be relatively easy, with few new words being introduced. Those that are introduced should be used often in the material. For this child, a relatively easy level would be desirable. For the child who needs training in analyzing words effectively, a higher concentration of new vocabulary would be desirable. The child could meet one new word in approximately every 20 running words. This would give him an opportunity to use the techniques of word analysis that he needs to develop, and at the same time it would enable him to maintain the thought of the passage so that meaning clues would be used as a means of checking the accuracy of his word recognition.

A child who is trying to increase his speed of comprehension should use material that is easy for him. This would have few if any word-recognition problems for him. But the child who is trying to increase his power of comprehension should use material which challenges him; but he must have a reasonable chance of successfully comprehending the material.

Materials Must Be Suitable in Type

It is said that any kind of material suitable for teaching reading in the first place is suitable for remedial instruction. While this is true, it is important to recognize that the material must be carefully selected to meet the disabled reader's instructional needs. The type of material that is suitable for one kind of disability is not necessarily appropriate for another. If the major problem is that of increasing speed of reading, the best material would be short stories with fast-moving plots. The material should not only be easy in reading difficulty, but the content should also be such that the child can read it to gain a general impression or the general significance. If the problem is one in the word recognition area, a reader, along with the exercises found in the manuals and workbooks related to the word-recognition problem, would be excellent reading material to use. If the problem is in the comprehension area and increased accuracy in reading is sought, science or social studies material with a lot of facts should be used. In every instance, the material should be at the appropriate level of difficulty, but it should also be conducive to the goals of reading expected.

Materials Must Be at the Appropriate Level of Interest and Format

A relatively mature and intelligent twelve-year-old will usually not find first- and second-grade material interesting, nor will he find the format very attractive. A child with second-grade reading ability must nevertheless use material that he can read. The problem facing the remedial teacher in this respect is very great. Second-grade books are designed for children seven or eight years of age. The pictures are of small children and the print looks large and juvenile. The topics are for a seven- or eight-year-old and not for a twelve-year-old. Many books that might be used for remedial reading instruction lose some of their value because they lack interest and have the wrong format. Nonetheless, there can be no compromise with using material that is at the appropriate level of difficulty. The problem is how to find material at a suitable level and as appealing as possible to a child of more mature age.

An increasingly large number of books for remedial work is being developed. Books designed primarily for the less-capable reader include *Action* and *Double Action Libraries* (Scholastic Book Services), the *Mystery Adventure Series* (Benefic Press), and the *Morgan Bay Mysteries* (Addison-Wesley Publishing Company).

Material designed for use with disabled readers who require selective skill development include the *Reading Comprehension Series* . (Bowmar/Noble Publishers), *Dolch First Reading Books* (DLM Teaching Resources), and the *Specific Skills Series* (Barnell Loft, Ltd.).

Phonetically consistent materials useful for readers who are weak in the phonic aspects of word recognition include series such as *Corrective Reading: Decoding* (Science Research Associates, Inc). These materials prove helpful when used according to individual student needs.

The skillbooks that accompany readers can also be used selectively to provide specific practice. Skillbooks often appear more mature than the readers they accompany. Drill exercises give no indication of the maturity level of the reader who is expected to use them.

Materials Must Be Abundant

In selecting material for remedial work, the first consideration is that it be at the correct level of difficulty. The second is that it be appropriate in type. The third is that it have the proper format and meet the interest level of the child. Another consideration in reading is that the materials be abundant. There should be a wide variety of material meeting many interests and at various levels of difficulty. For any one child, there should be ample material for him to read. There should be material for his remedial instruction and also for his independent reading. The independent reading for a remedial reading case should be considerably easier than that used in remedial instruction. The material for independent reading needs to be on many topics because the children will have a wide variety of interests. The material that the disabled reader is to read independently should fulfill an existing interest he already has, while the material that is used for instructional purposes must be such that he can be motivated to take an interest in reading it.

The use of computers.   Recently there has been increasing interest in the use of computers in remedial reading instruction. To assess the instructional value of computers, one must judge the value of the computer itself as a means of presenting reading materials and also evaluate the worth of the computer-based materials available. Computer programs as instructional materials should be evaluated by the same criteria as are applied to other materials used for reading improvement.

An advantage of computer use in remedial reading instruction is the eagerness of many reading-disabled children to work with computers even when these same children resist other forms of reading. Another advantage is the opportunity computers afford children to take risks, even make mistakes, in private with no other person looking on. Computers respond consistently, appropriately, and predictably when children work with them. They provide adequate feedback so that children know if they are right or wrong and they provide adequate repetition so that children learn completely. Computers invite children to learn actively and to respond frequently. They free the teacher to work with others. Disadvantages of computer use include cost and inadequate programs. Inadequate programs that are instructionally deficient or difficult for the child to operate should not be used.

An evaluation of computer programs as instructional materials finds many attractive computer programs available at *all levels of difficulty.* In fact, some programs with voice synthesizers make it possible for the child to receive all instructions through listening. Many types of programs are currently available including drill programs for various phases of word attack and comprehension, programs to teach students the mechanics of writing, programs for the development of vocabulary and comprehension using the cloze procedure, and programs with voice synthesizers that are being developed to allow the computer to work with the child using the neurological impress method. In addition, programs are available which provide students with simulations, interactive fiction, and problem-solving opportunities. For more information see Blanchard, Mason, and Daniel (1987) or Strickland, Feeley, and Wepner (1987).

Computer programs are *interesting* to many children and are available in a *variety of formats.* Computer programs can provide visual hints that help children attend to passages, words, or parts of words by illuminating these as appropriate or by providing selective color cuing. By using voice synthesis computers can simultaneously present words both visually and auditorily. The format of computer programs is usually inviting to children and does not appear immature to them. Educational programs are numerous and are becoming *increasingly more abundant.*

The use of computers for remedial reading instruction appeals to most students, serves to free teachers, and provides an abundance of specialized learning materials. At present, however, most computer materials are designed to provide drill and therefore do not relieve the teacher from the responsibility of introducing and teaching new skills. In addition, computer materials will not lead to improvement in reading unless they are specifically selected to match each student's learning needs. Computer materials add to the material resources of the teacher. They need to be managed with careful judgment.

THE REMEDIAL PLAN MUST USE EFFECTIVE TEACHING PROCEDURES

During the discussion of planning for the treatment of reading difficulties, it was implied that remedial instruction requires sound teaching procedures directed toward the specific needs of the child. The most essential difference between remedial instruction and developmental instruction is in the amount of individualization and in the extent of study of the disabled reader, rather than in the uniqueness of the methods or materials used in instruction. The authors consider the reading of context materials to be at the core of any remedial plan. The remedial plan for the disabled reader should include the reading of context selections, taught in much the same way as they are in a developmental reading program. In teaching a selection, there are a series of steps necessary to foster reading growth wherever taught. These steps are essential to good teaching of reading at any level. They form the lesson plan for teaching a selection step-by-step, as follows:

1. Building readiness
2. Introducing new or difficult words
3. Setting purposes for reading
4. Guiding silent reading
5. Discussing content read
6. Rereading if desirable
7. Developing specific skills and abilities
8. Extending to related supplementary material
9. Utilizing the results of reading

Unfortunately some of these steps in reading instruction are not always followed in remedial work. Readiness should be built carefully for every topic and every selection to be read by the disabled reader. This includes the creation of interest in, the development of background for, and the introduction of new words for each selection the disabled reader reads. The child who has difficulty in reading, just as the other children who do not, should understand the purposes for reading before it is done. Another step of teaching a selection that should never be neglected is developing specific skills and abilities. For remedial instruction, this step is of paramount importance. Having disabled readers merely read and discuss a selection does not itself develop the skills and abilities necessary for orderly growth in reading capability. The most important phases of instruction take place in the preparatory activities, during which background knowledge is provided, new vocabulary is introduced, purposes are set, and in follow-up skill exercises. A teacher demonstrates her teaching skill when she shows the disabled reader how to read and when she provides him with the experiences and drills necessary for establishing the specific skills and abilities that make for mature reading.

Many types of reading-disabled children need reinforcing exercises beyond those for students with normal reading growth. In the following chapters on remedial instructions for specific reading problems, sample types of supplementary reinforcing exercises are suggested.

The disabled reader should also use the results of his reading in a creative activity. If, for example, he has read a selection about flood control to find what techniques are used, it would be as important for him to make a diagram of a river bed illustrating what he had learned as it would be for children in the developmental reading program. Using the results of their reading is a good procedure for all children. It is essential practice, though often neglected for those who are disabled readers. The results of reading may be used in a discussion, a picture drawn, a chart made, or a map planned. There should be relatively little time given to these things, but above all, the creative work should be the child's own.

The remedial teacher will find it helpful to keep a cumulative account of the child's progress. The record should include the books read, the type of exercises used and the success of each, any charts used to show the child his progress, and the results of periodic tests. Any indications of interests and anecdotal accounts of the child's reactions to the remedial program should be included. By studying this record, the teacher can compare periods of rapid growth with the types of exercises used and books read. A study of past records will recall those approaches that were successful with other children with similar reading problems. The teacher can assemble a file of such folders, arranged according to the specific problem involved.

Reading Processes Must Be Made Meaningful to the Learner

One reason why the disabled reader is in difficulty is because he does not understand the process involved in being a good reader. The remedial teacher has responsibility not only for maintaining orderly sequences of skill development but also for making these steps understood by the child. The teacher should not only teach him to use context clues in word recognition but should also let him see how helpful this is in word recognition. The teacher should also show him how to organize the material he reads for effective retention. She should show him why it is effective. The child should understand the importance of reading certain material carefully with attention to detail, while other material can be read rapidly to understand its general ideas.

If the remedial teacher expects the child to retain knowledge of word elements, it is important for her to show him how much they will aid him in recognizing new words. For too long, many remedial teachers have felt that if the child is stimulated to read material at the correct level of difficulty he develops automatically the needed skills. This point of view can be questioned. A more reasonable assumption is that the child should be shown how to read and how much he can use each added reading accomplishment. Suppose a child, for example, has learned by rote to pronounce a list of isolated prefixes—how much better it would have been to point out to him the prefixes in words and show him how they change the meaning of the root words.

The remedial teacher will find that explaining the processes of reading to the learner helps to solve his reading confusions. Drill on isolated parts of words is not as effective as is a meaningful approach to reading. The remedial program should be concerned with explaining reading processes to the child. The day has long since passed when it was assumed that if we but interested the child in reading he would go ahead on his own to develop skills of which he was unaware.

Remedial Procedures Should Be as Nearly Like the Reading Act as Possible

Although there are available many devices and mechanical aids for remedial instruction, most reading growth comes from training allied with reading itself. Most expensive equipment is unnecessary and often wastes time that could be used for more productive reading activities. In establishing a reading center, priority should be given to obtaining varied reading materials. These include books, pamphlets, and skill-development materials of a wide range of reading difficulty. A typewriter, with primer-size type, is another desirable item to have. A computer and printer are also useful to the teacher in constructing materials to meet specific needs and vocabularies.

The exercises should not only be designed to develop specific skills but should also utilize these skills in meaningful reading content. For example, even in a simple exercise for developing rapid sight recognition of words, it is better to have the child read the word flashed before him, and at the same time tell whether it names an animal or is an action verb, than just identify the words without giving any thought to their meaning. In reading, the child must not only identify a word but must also associate meaning with it. Exercises that place skill development in context rather than in isolation are superior to those that do not. The remedial suggestions made in the following chapters illustrate this principle of remedial instruction.

The more that exercises used in building skills and abilities approximate real reading, the more likely they will be transferred to reading. For example, if a child uses phonics in recognizing words, he will be more likely to use phonics in identifying new words than if the same elements had been taught by use of isolated drills. Not only will he be more likely to transfer what he has learned to new situations, but he will also establish the habit of noting the phonetic patterns within troublesome words and discover many more useful aids to word recognition.

The Teacher Must Be Optimistic

A teacher helping a child overcome a reading disability should be a buoyant, energetic person. She must make the disabled reader sense her confidence in him. The problems in correcting a complex reading disability may seem to be almost insurmountable. Nevertheless, the teacher must show each disabled reader that she knows he will learn to read. This attitude comes from a thorough understanding of the child's instructional needs, a sound diagnosis, and a remedial program planned well enough in advance that it is clearly in mind. The teacher gains immediate confidence through knowing exactly what is going to be done during each remedial lesson. A well-prepared teacher who knows exactly where each session is going will instill confidence in the child. With preparation, there usually will be progress in reading.

The teacher can be optimistic because most reading disability cases do show immediate gains from remedial instruction. If the child's reading problem and his characteristics have been evaluated carefully, and if the program has been based upon an appropriate individual remedial plan, success is practically assured. Of course the teacher's confidence may sometimes be shaken. There are periods during the corrective treatment of practically every poor reader when there is little evidence of new growth. But all the same, confidence in the child's ultimate success must remain, even when things do not appear to be going well. Under some circumstances, the remedial plan should be restudied and the diagnosis reviewed, but all this need not diminish confidence in the child's ultimate success.

The Child Needs Group and Individual Work

The disabled reader needs to share experiences with other children just as much as, or even more than, the child whose growth in reading is normal. Not only should his classroom work be organized so that he can participate in some of the important activities of the class, but he should also see that other children have problems with reading. It is recommended that disabled readers work in groups whenever possible. Much can be gained by the disabled reader seeing other children around him with similar difficulties who are making progress in overcoming them. It is often assumed that remedial reading instruction is a formal procedure in which the child is separated from other children and drilled until his disability is corrected. Such instruction is unwise. It is a boost to the child to know that there are other children who are learning to read who are able to use their newly gained proficiencies in reading.

THE PLAN MUST ENLIST COOPERATIVE EFFORTS

Although implementation of the remedial plan may be the direct responsibility of the remedial reading teacher, many other people should be involved in formulating and helping to implement an *individual plan of remediation,* including outside consultants, classroom teachers, parents, and the remedial reader as well.

The Remedial Plan Should Involve Outside Consultants

It would be rather unusual for such professionals as the school principal, the school psychologist, the school social worker, a physician, a media expert, a speech pathologist, or the school nurse to be in any way involved in the direct remediation of a disabled reader. Nevertheless, the insights of one or more of these professionals may prove invaluable to the formulation of the appropriate individual remedial plans. Knowledge of a student's reading difficulties and a remedial plan help other professionals coordinate their efforts. Some children receive not only remedial reading services but also the services of other professionals such as a social worker or a speech pathologist. It is important for the remedial reading teacher and such other professionals to share information, insights, and concerns on a regular basis.

The Remedial Plan Should Involve Classroom Teachers

In most people's minds, including those of most reading-disabled children and their parents, success or failure in reading is measured not in the school reading center or resource room but in the regular classroom. That is where the child spends the greater part of his day and that is where he must establish social relationships with his peers. If a child is to really find success in school, he must find it in the classroom. For this reason, it is imperative for classroom teachers to be cooperatively and closely involved in initial planning and to maintain involvement in order to coordinate their efforts with those of the reading specialist. Direct observation of a student's classroom behavior by the remedial reading teacher and consultation with the classroom teacher enable the remedial reading teacher to plan activities that benefit the child directly in the classroom. For example, if students in the classroom have been told that they may make an optional, brief, oral report on a book that they think others in the class might enjoy, the remedial reading teacher could encourage an insecure, reading-disabled child to do so. The remedial reading teacher could aid the child in the selection of a book which he could read successfully but which would also appeal to his classmates, and she could give him an opportunity to practice his presentation privately in order to gain the confidence he needs to speak effectively to the class. In consultation with the remedial reading teacher, the classroom teacher can adapt and adjust classroom expectations to ensure that when the reading-disabled child exerts honest effort he will be successful. Although a student may be making real and rapid progress in reading in the reading center or resource room, he will be denied a true sense of accomplishment if the rest of his day is filled with reading demands which are far beyond him. He will lose the opportunity to practice his newly acquired reading skills in the regular classroom; he will lose the opportunity to view himself and have his classmates view him as a reader; he will lose the positive attitudes he may have acquired about reading; and he will lose that sense of confidence necessary to learning.

The Remedial Plan Should Involve the Parents

Parental cooperation is beneficial to successful remediation for two reasons. First, parents can make a unique contribution to a teacher's understanding of their child. Parents are concerned with their children's behavior in nonschool settings and for this reason are often aware of certain attributes which teachers are less likely to see. For example, it is often parents who alert teachers to signs of tension or frustration which a child hides when in school. It is the parent who is the first to sense that positive change of attitude which characterizes a child's response to successful remediation. The second reason parental cooperation is so beneficial is because parents are very important people in a child's life. When his parents understand the remedial plan and support it, a child receives a form of encouragement which helps him overcome his reading difficulty.

Furthermore, parents are concerned about their children's difficulties, sometimes extremely concerned. Complete understanding of the remedial plan and information about the program's outcome help to relieve the extreme anxiety some parents feel when their children have reading problems. Some parents of disabled readers become interested in directly aiding their children in reading. Parents can do much to help their children with reading, but their efforts are most beneficial when they receive guidance from the remedial reading teacher and when they enhance and support the remedial plan.

The Remedial Plan Should Involve the Child

The true focus of every successful remedial plan is the disabled reader himself. It is the child, after all, who has to learn. If the child is not enthusiastic about the plan or does not believe in it, the efforts of consultants, teachers and parents will have little effect. The child should aid as much as possible in formulating the plan; older students often have valuable insights into the nature of their reading problems. At the secondary level, many wise remedial reading teachers have found that enlisting students' cooperation in planning activities, choosing materials, and setting goals was a necessary first step in provoking interest in reading improvement. Discussing with a child his feelings and attitudes about reading and about plans for reading improvement is an essential beginning to help him develop more positive feelings and attitudes about reading, about learning, and even about himself. It is important for every one concerned, most of all the child, to understand the remedial program, to support it, and to cooperate with it.

SUMMARY

In making an *appropriate educational plan of remediation,* it is necessary to identify the specific limitations hindering reading growth. Although the remedial work for each disabled reader must be different in certain respects, there are some common elements among the corrective programs. The remedial program must be designed to emphasize the child's instructional needs as shown by the diagnosis, and therefore there can be no universal approach to all cases. The remedial program for each reading-disabled child must be planned carefully and written down. It is necessary to modify the program from time to time to keep abreast of the child's changing instructional needs. Even though the program is planned to emphasize overcoming a specific disability, a variety of remedial techniques should be used. The remedial teacher will find manuals and instruction booklets for commercial materials a good source of teaching techniques.

Remedial reading programs must be individualized and must be designed in keeping with the child's instructional needs and characteristics. It is necessary to modify the approaches to reading in order to adjust limitations such as poor hearing or poor vision. Remedial instruction should not drill on one specific skill or ability in isolation, but should provide new experience in whatever skills are needed in connection with purposeful reading. The length of remedial sessions should be planned so that the child will not become fatigued or inattentive.

Reading instruction for the disabled reader must be well-organized so that skills and abilities can be developed smoothly with no undue burden on the child, with little chance for overemphasis, and with no omission of essential learnings. The teacher should not only maintain an orderly sequence of skill development but should also make the steps understood by the child.

The remedial reading program must encourage the child, since much of his trouble was caused by loss of confidence in his ability to learn. The teacher should be optimistic, the child's successes should be emphasized, and his progress should be demonstrated to him. Materials must be geared to the child's reading abilities and instructional needs; they should be at the appropriate level of difficulty and consist of the proper content; they should be as near as possible to his interests; and they should look "mature" to the child. Computer materials provide attractive supplements to the remedial program with great appeal for many disabled readers. The materials used for remedial instruction must be of such difficulty that the child can read them and so interesting that he will be motivated to read them. There can be no compromise with the difficulty level of the material, because the child will not be interested in reading material he cannot read, no matter how attractive the subject matter. In all remedial work, sound teaching procedures should be used and artificial devices and isolated drill should be avoided.

Needed resource experts—the classroom teacher, the parents, and most of all, the disabled reader himself—should have an active part in formulating the *individual plan of remediation*.

STUDY QUESTIONS

1. Why must the remedial plan be based on more than an understanding of the child's reading needs?

2. Why is it necessary to give the student successful reading experiences? How can the teacher help a child see success?

3. What features would you include in an individual reading program for a fifth-grade student who tested at a beginning third-grade level on a standardized test? The student loves sports and outdoor activities. He hates to read. His word attack is extremely poor. He has frequently been embarrassed in oral reading situations in his classroom. Be sure to consider motivation and demonstration of progress, as well as levels and kinds of appropriate reading materials you would initially consider using with this student.

4. Why must a child be prepared for reading in remedial instruction by building readiness, developing background, introducing new words, and setting immediate purposes?

5. Is one-to-one instruction always best? Why or why not?

6. What are the advantages of child involvement in remedial planning? Should all students getting remedial help be involved to the same extent in planning?

SELECTED READINGS

EKWALL, E. E. *Teacher's Handbook on Diagnosis and Remediation in Reading,* 2nd ed., Chap. 2. Boston: Allyn & Bacon, Inc., 1986.

HARRIS, A. J., AND E. R. SIPAY. *How to Increase Reading Ability,* 8th ed., Chap. 11. New York: Longman, Inc., 1985.

McCORMICK, S. *Remedial and Clinical Reading Instruction,* Chap. 10. Columbus, OH: Charles E. Merrill Publishing Company, 1987.

SPACHE, G. D. *Diagnosing and Correcting Reading Disabilities,* Chap. 10. Boston: Allyn & Bacon, Inc. 1976.

ZINTZ, M. V. *Corrective Reading,* 4th ed., Chaps. 8 and 9, Appendix B. Dubuque, IA: William C. Brown Company, Publishers, 1981.

10

Correcting Deficiencies in Meaning Clues to Word Recognition

Skill in word recognition is a fundamental part of the proficiency of a capable reader at any level. As the child matures in reading, the materials and methods used in teaching him gradually demand more and more independent word recognition. The child who has failed to establish effective means of identifying and recognizing words for his level of advancement is handicapped in all other aspects of reading.

Modern approaches to teaching word recognition must be based upon integration of the unique nature of reading growth, as analyzed by reading research workers, and oral communication, as described by linguistic research workers. The first-grade reading studies sponsored by the United States Office of Education gave some insight into the development of word-recognition skills. The major conclusions reached by Bond and Dykstra (1967), resulting from their analyses of the combined data compiled from 27 individual studies, offer some definitive evidence of the importance of word-study skills to reading success. They found that regardless of the approach to reading instruction used in the first grade, word-recognition skills must be emphasized. A second-year follow-up study (1967) indicated that this was true for the second grade as well.

The combined analyses also showed that much of the variation in success in reading during the first two years of reading instruction could be accounted for by attributes the children brought to the learning situation. Capabilities such as auditory and visual discrimination and pre-first-grade familiarity with print are substantially related to success in learning to read, whatever approach to initial instruction is used. These attributes are considered by some authorities to have a direct relationship to the child's preschool interest in words and their printed symbols. These capabilities are readiness factors for the development of word-recognition skills.

The combined data from these extensive studies further show that combinations of methods including such components as basal readers, phonics and linguistic training, and language experiences, are superior to any of these approaches used alone. Those programs which were especially effective in developing word-recognition skills were not as productive in the comprehension areas. Conversely, those programs which emphasized meaning needed to be augmented by a more intensive word-recognition program.

These studies further indicated that initial reading programs should strive for a better balance between phonetically regular words, as emphasized by some linguists, and high-utility words, emphasized in many basal readers. The use of vocabularies selected largely on the basis of their frequency of use or utility can generate word-recognition problems. It was also evident that the sole use of words spelled in a phonetically regular way makes meaningful reading difficult to acquire.

The analyses also showed that encouraging children to write the words as they learned to read them and to associate words with sounds and meanings was helpful in developing word-recognition skills.

How to correct difficulties in the *word-perceptual* skills, necessary in recognizing the printed symbols of word meanings, will be the concern of the next two chapters. These skills must be taught so as to encourage a child to attempt *rapid recognition* of known or partially familiar words, so that he will be able to group them into thought units. At the same time, training in *word identification* must be given, so that the learner can develop skill in decoding the printed forms of words that these symbols represent when he first sees them in their written forms. These skills are not easily developed, and it is little wonder that some children run into difficulties before they acquire them. In fact most severely disabled readers have weaknesses in the word-recognition area.

Word study involves two types of goals. The first is expanding meaning vocabulary and teaching word-recognition techniques so that meanings accompany the identification of the symbols. The child must learn to associate meaning with printed symbols. His meaning must be clear and precise if he is to comprehend the material he is reading. He must also be able to select, among all the meanings of a word, the one that is correct for the particular context in which it is used. The word *run,* which is used in most preprimers, has 56 different definitions, even in a dictionary used in the elementary grades. The child must learn to use context as he recognizes the printed symbols to help him select the correct meaning. For example, the meaning of *run* can be derived from the content in the statements "He was tired after the long run," and "All will turn out well in the long run." Often the sentence alone will not give the meaning of a word; only the gist of the passage will. For example, the precise meaning of *run* cannot be derived from the sentence, "He was out of breath after he made the run." In order to understand the word *run,* the reader must know not only that the boy was playing baseball, but also that he scored rather than chased a fly ball. The development of word meaning will be discussed in detail in Chapter 14; but it is important to teach word-recognition techniques in such a way that words are rapidly recognized and the proper meanings associated with them.

The second goal of instruction in word study is the development of a set of flexible skills and knowledges that enable the child to recognize words he already knows and identify new words with speed and understanding. *Word identification* and *word recognition* are closely related features of word perception. First contact with a new word form calls for identification of the printed symbol in terms of its sound and meaning. Subsequent contacts develop recognition. In this text, the development of word recognition implies identification as the first step in the process. Until a printed symbol is grasped at a glance, until it has become what we term a *sight word,* recognition requires some degree of identification. Instruction in word recognition is designed to enable the child to perform three interrelated tasks. *First,* the child must be able to recognize known words rapidly with a minimum of analysis. For example, if he knows the word *think* as a sight word, he should not analyze it into *th-ink,* pronouncing each part and then blending it into the word *think.* Indeed, to do so again and again would be most detrimental to his reading. There are children who have difficulty in reading for just this reason. *Second,* the child should be skilled in recognizing partially known words with little analysis. If the child knows the word *think,* he should be adept at identifying it in all of its variant forms. Applying syntactic skills, he should need but a glance at the word to enable him to recognize and know the meaning of *think, thinks, thinking,* and as he gains maturity, *unthinkable.* In such words, the child should learn to identify the root word, recognize the modified form rapidly, and understand the changed meaning. *Third,* the child must develop a flexible set of skills that enable him to identify new words by himself. As he matures in reading, he must be able not only to pronounce the new words, but also to be so skilled that he can recognize them silently without interrupting the thought of the passage.

Instruction in word identification is complex indeed. It is understandable why reading instruction has progressed through a series of methods from a spelling approach to a whole-word approach, to phonetic emphasis systems, to sentence or context emphasis, to the modern composite methods using context, whole-word, phonics, and structural analysis as aids to word identification. The major problem in the modern approach is teaching the flexible set of skills needed so that none will be omitted or over- or underemphasized and so that the more analytical and time-consuming aids to recognition will be used only when needed. To teach the child the word-recognition techniques necessary for him to recognize known words and to identify new ones visually or phonetically, at least five sorts of "balance" must be maintained.

First, a balance between the establishment of *word-recognition techniques* and the development of *meaning vocabulary* is desirable for reading growth. If there is too much isolated drill on word parts, the child may become a capable word-caller, but he may not understand what he is reading. The child may be able to make a fairly accurate attempt at pronouncing new words, but unless what he pronounces has meaning accompanying it, the results may be erroneous. Even though the early lessons in reading use very common words, the teacher who neglects to introduce the words in context may encourage overemphasis on analytical techniques at the expense of word meaning. Conversely the teacher who neglects to teach identification skills may cause the child to make random attempts to say any word that comes to mind or may make the child too dependent on her. Word-recognition skills should be taught in context rather than in isolation. They should be taught by means of whole words rather than by use of isolated word elements. Word-recognition skills must be taught and learned as part of the coordinated reading program.

Second, a balance between the acquisition of *sight vocabulary*—words the child knows at a glance—and the establishment of *word-recognition skills* is essential. The child must learn to recognize at sight an ever-increasing number of words, because it is on these that his fluency as a reader depends. These words also provide much of his ability to derive meaning from printed matter. If the child is led to place too much emphasis on either one of these learnings at the expense of the other, the results will be serious. The teacher may place so much emphasis upon building sight vocabulary that the child fails to establish the needed word-recognition techniques. This child may seem to progress well at the start, but he will soon become a disabled reader. He will lack independence, since he has no way of identifying new words by himself. A reading program that stresses word-recognition skills and neglects to build sight vocabulary is encouraging the child to become a slow, laborious, and overanalytical reader. The child needs to build both an ever-increasing sight vocabulary and a more diversified set of word-recognition techniques. The child who underuses one in favor of the other will have serious trouble reading. This is one of the most difficult balances to achieve. As a result, there are many children who proceed to use analysis on words that they really know at sight, and there are other children who are at a loss to work out the pronunciation of new words independently because they are weak in the identifying skills.

Third, there must be a balance between the *meaning clues* and the *analytical aids* to word recognition. The child who depends too much on meaning clues to recognition will make many errors that have little relationship to the appearance of the word he miscalls. These errors are in substituting words that make sense though they are not the words of the author nor do they evoke his meaning. For example, this child might read the sentence "The ship sailed over the equator," as "The ship sailed over the seas." Such a reader is often inaccurate and misses out in comprehension. On the other hand, the child who depends too much upon analytical and blending aids to the exclusion of meaning also may be inaccurate. The errors might reflect reasonable letter-sound associations, but they make no real sense. For example, the sentence, "The Scottish girl's dress was plaid," might be read "The Scottish girl's dress was played." In either this case or the former, little or no understanding results. The child must develop both abilities, and when he has done so he can use them to reinforce one another. The child who lacks the analytical techniques is handicapped because exact recognition is often impossible from context alone. The child who depends too much upon word analysis is unable to use context to speed recognition and to check the accuracy of his recognition through the sense it makes.

Fourth, a balance between *phonic* and *structural* techniques must be maintained. If the teacher places too much emphasis on phonics training, the child may fail to develop the ability to use larger structural elements in the recognition of words. The result may be an element-by-element, sound-blending approach which is ineffective as a major means of word recognition. This emphasis may teach the child to separate words to such an extent that synthesis or blending of sounds into one word becomes impossible. But if the emphasis on larger structural and visual elements is too great, the child's skill in using smaller elements or letter sounds may not be sufficiently developed for him to recognize certain words such as unusual names that require sounding. Many children with reading disability have failed to establish this balance and hence have become either overanalytical or lack sufficient knowledge of phonics.

Fifth, there must be a balance between the emphasis placed on *knowledge of word parts* and the *orderly inspection of words* along the line of print from the left to right and from the beginning of the word to the end. If too much stress is placed, for example, on word families such as the *at* family in *cat, sat, fat, hat,* the child may neglect the beginning elements of words and thus make an unreasonable number of errors in them. Another child using this emphasis may develop reversal problems because he has the habit of looking at the end of words to pick up his clues to recognition. When a child makes an excessive number of errors in any specific location within words, it usually indicates that knowledge of word parts has been emphasized at the expense of orderly inspection from the beginning to end of each word he studies. In this respect, another balance is required in the orderly inspection of words, which is that the child must develop flexibility in his visual analysis of the word he is trying to recognize. For example, suppose the word is *frighten;* the child selects *fri* as the first element he recognizes. Unless he quickly rejects this result of his visual analysis, he will be unable to work out the rest of the word, because *ght* will not be very helpful to him. He may try to sound each letter, *g—h—t,* and then get into marked confusion. A child who was more flexible in the visual analysis of words would reject the first separation of the word and break it into more suitable parts, such as *fr—ight-en.* Then, applying his knowledge of the elements, he would be able to pronounce the word with little difficulty.

Word recognition is much more complex than is assumed in programs emphasizing a single set of skills or in instruction placing the child in a stimulating reading environment and expecting him to discover all the needed skills and to maintain the balances among them. Word recognition entails too many interrelated learnings to allow the program to be narrow or incidental.

The major source of word-recognition difficulty is in the child's failure to establish one or more of these basic learnings or in his overdependence on any of them. Word-recognition problems are often found to be at the root of the difficulty of those disabled readers who fall into the categories of *limiting* and *complex* reading disability. The more prevalent meaning-clue disabilities are listed following. Each will be discussed along with the methods of correction that have been found helpful.

1. Failure to associate meaning with printed symbols
2. Insufficient sight vocabulary
3. Failure to use meaning clues

FAILURE TO ASSOCIATE MEANING WITH PRINTED SYMBOLS

The real goal of all word recognition is to enable the child to identify words and associate the correct meanings with them. Often programs of word recognition emphasize oral word study and pronunciation so strongly that the child fails to establish the habit, or to sense the importance of, understanding the meaning of printed symbols. The child may give fairly close approximations to the pronunciation of the words he studies, but he may not have identified the word as one he knows in his listening or speaking vocabulary. Sometimes the teacher can detect mispronunciation that indicates that the word was almost, but not quite, recognized. At other times, it is necessary to ask the child what the word means in order to detect whether he is having this basic difficulty. Of course, a relatively low level of performance by a child on oral vocabulary or meaning vocabulary tests, when compared with his skill in word-recognition techniques, such as knowledge of word elements and visual analysis of words, indicates this type of difficulty.

Remedial work for such difficulties should emphasize the basic comprehension abilities and reading for meaning that will be described in Chapter 14. In all word-recognition exercises, the meanings of the words should be emphasized. Drill on isolated word elements should be rejected for this type of child. Whenever possible, word-identification exercises should be in contextual settings so that there is the need to recognize not only the word but also its meaning to successfully complete the tasks.

There are methods related to real reading which help the child develop the habit and ability of associating meanings with word symbols. For example, the child may be requested to draw illustrations for a story he is reading. To do so, it is necessary for him to attend to the meaning of descriptive words. If the child is expected to retell a story in his own words rather than to repeat the words in the book, he will learn to interpret the meaning of the word symbols. Any comprehension exercise which does not allow the child to merely repeat the words of the book encourages the association of meaning with the words read.

Besides emphasizing word meanings in all reading comprehension, the child always must develop his word-recognition techniques in relevant settings, if he is to be encouraged to associate precise ideas with the printed symbols. The child who is limited in this ability may profit from exercises of the following types:

1. Exercises to develop clear sensory impressions.
   a. What did you hear:
      when a stone hit the water?
      splash   crack
   b. An animal with stripes on it is a:
      elephant   horse   zebra
   c. Match the words with the phrase that tells the same thing.
      Put the number of the word before the phrase.
      1. lagged   _____flowed with force
      2. gushed   _____moved slowly
      3. gurgled   _____made a noise as it flowed
      4. rushed   _____moved rapidly along
   d. Put *J* before each word that would tell about a jolly person.
      _____merry   _____laughing   _____joyful
      _____beaming   _____bitter   _____dreary
2. Exercises to develop precise meanings.
   a. In each line, find two words that have an opposite meaning.
      good   tired   sad   bad
      right   bad   wrong   trouble
      wet   dry   damp   moist
   b. Find the words that have a similar meaning.
      glow   bright   shine   spark
      rushed   walked   ran   hurried
      replied   said   answered   wrote
   c. Complete the sentence with the best word from those listed following the sentence.
      When the boy saw the people far away, he _____ to them.
      said   shouted   whispered   muttered
3. Exercises to develop extensiveness of meaning.
   a. Tell the difference in the meaning of *roll* in the following sentences:
      (1) We ate a *roll* for lunch.
      (2) We watched the big waves *roll* along the beach.
      (3) Get a *roll* of paper.
      (4) Please *roll* the ball to Jim.
      (5) The dog could *roll* over.
      (6) The teacher called the *roll*.
      (7) We could see the *roll* of the hills.
      (8) We could hear the *roll* of the drums.
   b. Put the number of the right definition in front of each sentence.
      trunk   (1) The main stem of a tree   _____He picked up
                                                   the peanut with
                                                   his trunk.

(2) A box used to carry clothes   _____The trunk of the oak was rough.

(3) Part of an elephant   _____He put the trunk on the train.

Computer programs such as *Tiger's Tales* (Hermann, 1987) feature presentation of new words in association with pictures. When the child matches a word to a picture correctly, he is rewarded with a short animated reward sequence. If the child matches incorrectly, the wrong words are crossed out and disappear, leaving only the correct word and picture. Provisions are included in the program to insure ample review. Interactive, child-determined, stories emphasize the meanings of these words in a contextual setting.

Further suggestions, which will be made in Chapter 14, aid in building the habit of attending to word meanings and also develop skill in associating meaning with word symbols. Many times a child makes a close approximation to a word by the use of phonics and other word-recognition techniques, but unless he keeps the context in mind, the word remains unidentified. In addition to exercises, extensive reading, coupled with the habit of noticing expressive use of words, aids in encouraging the child to associate meaning with printed symbols.

When children listen carefully to their teacher's expressive reading of a well-written story they learn to associate meaning with print. The creation of language experience stories helps children associate their own words with printed symbols. Expressive writing, illustrating stories, dramatizing stories, creating puppet shows, and other such activities emphasize the meaning carried by words. Since the goal of all reading is to derive meaning from the printed page and since this goal must be achieved by recognizing printed symbols and their meanings, all word-recognition exercises should demand not only the identification of words but also an understanding of their meanings.

INSUFFICIENT SIGHT VOCABULARY

The importance of forming the habit of rapidly recognizing known words, rather than studying each word encountered as though it never had been seen before, cannot be emphasized too strongly. The child who fails to build a large sight vocabulary and who does not have the habit of recognizing these words at a glance cannot hope to become an able reader. He will be limited not only in his ability to group words into thought units, necessary for comprehension and fluency, but he will also be seriously handicapped in identifying new words. This latter limitation comes about in two ways. First, the child will be unable to use context clues effectively, because the vocabulary load of unknown words will be too great. Second, he will be inefficient in the more mature methods of word study. Affixed words, for example, will be difficult to recognize because the child does not know the root word, since for him it is not a sight word. Compound words will also present him with a tough problem, since he has not developed the habit of sight recognition of the two smaller words from which the compound is made. The child who does not have a substantial sight vocabulary, and who does not have the habit of recognizing those words as known units, will find learning to read a most confusing enterprise. For these reasons, modern instruction in reading emphasizes the building of a sight vocabulary from the start.

Children who rely too completely on working out words analytically may fail to acquire a sight vocabulary. In the early grades, the teacher may find it difficult to detect that these children are not building a sight vocabulary. Eventually, however, persistence in this practice will prove detrimental to reading growth. Detailed study of each word will have to be rejected and a sight vocabulary built or severe disability will occur.

In other children, a limited sight vocabulary is easily detected. They may be word-by-word readers, making phonetic errors with words they should know at sight or they may fail to phrase well in oral reading. Another indication is the tendency for the child to make about an equal number of errors regardless of the difficulty of the material he is reading. If a child, for example, makes about the same percentage of errors in reading a second-grade reader as he makes in a fourth-grade reader, he is likely to be limited in his development of a sight vocabulary. If he tends to make more mistakes on small common words than he does on polysyllabic words, he is probably limited in sight vocabulary.

The teacher can easily measure sight vocabulary by rapid-exposure techniques. She can flash words printed on cards for quick exposures. The child who cannot readily identify common words at a glance has failed to develop a sight vocabulary. When using flash cards, if the child makes a considerably greater number of errors than he does when looking at the same words for an unlimited time, he can be assumed to have an insufficient sight vocabulary. These indications of limited ability in recognizing words at a glance mandate remedial work in building a larger sight vocabulary.

Remedial training for increasing the sight vocabulary of a disabled reader is done best by using material at a level of difficulty that is somewhat easy for the child. Exercises that require rapid reading to locate a specific statement or to understand the general significance of the passage should be emphasized for a child who is trying to increase his sight vocabulary. He should be given exercises that require new vocabulary to be read as whole words, and those which require the analysis of words should be avoided. Exercises that emphasize rapid word recognition rather than analysis should be used. Extensive reading of easy material is desirable so that rapid recognition of words is encouraged.

The following illustrative types of exercises, using the basic vocabulary that is being developed, have proven effective as additional reinforcement of the habit of reading words at a glance.

1. Exercises in which the word is so much expected that recognition is rapid.

     In winter there is _____.
     snow   house   well

2. Exercises in which a child finds the correct word in a list on the chalkboard as the teacher gives the clue.

   Find the word in this list that tells us where we:

Clue	Words
buy food	farm
go swimming	table
find cows	store
eat dinner	beach

3. Exercises that require meaningful scanning of a list.
   See how fast you can draw a line around all the things that can run.

horse	house	girl	pig
tree	dog	road	man
cat	boy	store	window

4. Various word games that call for immediate responses and require sight recognition of words and their meanings.

   a. Cards with names of animals printed on them can be used. Two children can play together. One child can flash the cards and the other can respond. Words like the following can be used:

chicken	elephant	bird	goose
dog	duck	pony	donkey
horse	goat	wren	fish

   One child may tell the name of an animal with four feet as the cards are flashed. Then the other may tell which can fly.

   b. Another set of cards could be made of verbs and the child could tell which words on the cards tell movement. The types of words that might be used are:

afraid	listen	march	walk
jump	roll	sleep	feel
think	skip	ride	guess
flew	know	slide	was

   c. A fish-pond game is played in which words are attached to paper clips and the child uses a pole with a magnet on the end of the line. If the child can read at a glance the word that he fishes out of the pond, it is caught. If he has to study the word, that fish gets away, but he may be able to catch it another time. Any words that caused the child trouble in his reader could be used in this game, as well as other words that he knows well.

   d. A game similar to "authors" can be played with words. The words are grouped in sets of four similar things, such as clothes, animals, trees, time, food, toys, people, and colors. Four children may play together. Each child gets eight cards and the remaining cards are placed in a pile in the center. The children take turns drawing one card from the center pile and then discarding one. The child who first gets two complete sets of four similar words wins the game. The set of word cards for this game might be these:

Clothes	Animals	Trees	Time
coat	lion	oak	afternoon
hat	elephant	maple	spring
shoe	donkey	fir	tomorrow
dress	horse	willow	morning

Food	Toys	People	Colors
bread	doll	aunt	yellow
pudding	wagon	father	green
peanuts	football	uncle	blue
carrots	balloon	mother	brown

Furniture	Flowers	Places	Meals
chair	rose	farm	breakfast
table	tulip	beach	dinner
bed	daisy	city	lunch
desk	poppy	zoo	supper

e. Many other games such as Wordo (like Bingo), Old Maid, Spin the Wheel, Climb the Ladder, Dominoes with words, and Grab Bag can be played.

All of the preceding exercises and activities can be developed using phrases, too.

5. One of the best exercises involves the rapid recognition of groups of high-utility words. These words are typed on flash cards and are presented rapidly.

a. Directions. The child demonstrates understanding through action.

jump up	point to me
sit down	open the book
come here	look at the door
raise your hand	go to the window

b. Classification. The child demonstrates recognition by indicating whether the words tell about something one would find in a home or at a zoo.

table and chairs	barking seal
lion and tiger	iron cage
set of dishes	baby elephant
pretty picture	pots and pans
big red rug	little brown monkey

Computer programs such as *Trickster Coyote* (Prentice Associates, 1986), provide practice in reading words quickly and matching them with definitions. Presented in an exciting game format, this program can be played by up to four players. Students are given an opportunity to study any words they miss. Teachers may reprogram the game to include any words they choose. As is true for many computer games, some students will require teacher assistance in learning how to play the game at the onset.

Any exercises or activities used in building sight vocabulary should encourage the child to inspect the words rapidly rather than resort to detailed study of them. The words should be presented in contexts that require understanding of the word meanings.

The child should be reading material that introduces new words gradually and repeats them at well-spaced intervals. If the child is motivated to read a selection, if the new words are introduced before the selection is read, and if the purposes require rapid reading, the child should increase his sight vocabulary. When this instruction is reinforced with exercises like those previously described using the words being emphasized, the gains should be even greater. In all reading and drill, recognizing the meaning of the words should be required. What the child with an insufficient sight vocabulary needs is experience in recognizing the word and its meaning at a glance.

FAILURE TO USE MEANING CLUES

Meaning clues are among the most important aids to word recognition. The effective adult reader uses these clues in all word identification and recognition. Meaning clues enable the reader to anticipate new or unfamiliar words before he actually sees them. No matter what other aids to recognition are used, the proficient reader always uses some form of meaning clue to aid him, such as (1) anticipating words he might expect from prior knowledge of a given topic, or (2) use of context to (a) gain the meaning of a passage (*semantic clue*), or (b) sense the structure of a sentence (*syntactic clue*).

The authors of this book agree with Goodman (1973) that word recognition is, in a sense, "a psycholinguistic guessing game." In word recognition, the child anticipates the word through prior knowledge and context clues. He then applies word-recognition skills, such as perceptual skills, for instant recognition, or decoding skills for more intensive identification, if necessary. Simultaneously, he checks the correctness of his "guess" by the sense it makes in relation to the preceding content. He sometimes resorts to rereading if he doubts accuracy or if the "guess" does not satisfy the content immediately following.

Many disabled readers have failed to acquire this ability and they are ineffective in word recognition. The failure to use meaning clues precludes the acquisition of such mature reading skills as grouping words in thought units. It also limits the development of accuracy in using the other word-recognition techniques. The ineffective use of meaning clues forces the child to analyze carefully many words that should be identified with a minimum of inspection.

Meaning clues can be divided into two types. The first is prior knowledge, which enable the mature reader to anticipate the sorts of words and concepts that he is likely to encounter when reading about a given topic. If, for example, a mature reader is reading about soil conservation, he might expect to meet such words as *erosion, soil depletion, levee, irrigation, rotation,* and *drainage.* This anticipation would make the recognition or identification of the words more rapid than if they unexpectedly appeared in prose on some other subject. The second type of meaning clue is the context clue. The use of context clues is a rapid recognition technique in which a word or phrase is so completely anticipated from the meaning of the sentence or paragraph that the merest flick of a glance is all that is needed to confirm that it is that expected word or phrase. Even if the word symbol is unfamiliar, the context plus a minimum of inspection is all that is needed for its identification.

Weakness in Use of Prior Knowledge

The child who does not anticipate words that he is likely to meet when reading about a specific topic or within a specific field is to some degree handicapped in word recognition. There are many children and even some adult readers who fail to use their knowledge of a subject as an aid to word identification and recognition. There are many adult readers, for example, who skip the graphic presentation of the facts discussed in the running comment. A brief study of the table, chart, or graph would enable them to anticipate the context and the words within the passage. The reader who uses the pictorial aids effectively becomes a more fluent and understanding reader of a passage, partly because he is prepared for those words. He can identify them with ease and devote himself to the meaning of what is read rather than to the mere recognition of words. For the younger reader, picture clues operate in much the same way. A well-illustrated book builds prior knowledge, which helps a child succeed with the text. The child, however, must be taught to use such pictures effectively. Many reading materials use pictures as a means of building the habit of anticipating words and concepts. There is, unfortunately, a possibility of danger in the overuse of pictures. If the picture tells too much of the story or if all the concepts are illustrated, there is little for the child to discover by reading. The preparatory activities preceding reading on a topic, which include planning, development of background, and introduction to new words, are a form of building prior knowledge for the youngsters. These activities are necessary in both the regular classroom and the resource room. Teaching that neglects such essentials of reading instruction predispose the child to be weak in using the prior knowledge he has and in gaining the prior knowledge he needs.

The ineffective use of prior knowledge in word recognition can be detected by noting unusual difficulty in recognizing the words specifically related to a topic. It can also be suspected of the child who is always weak in telling words he might expect to find in a passage about some given topic. If, for example, a child is asked to tell what words might be used in a story about a rabbit and if he could not mention some such words as *jump, carrot, run, hop, long ears, cottontail,* and *burrow,* he is probably weak in using prior knowledge.

The remedial work for this child would be, for the most part, to place greater emphasis on the readiness development which precedes the reading of a topic and on each selection within the topic. The child who is weak in using prior knowledge needs more attention given to the introductions of units and selections, more picture study before reading, more opportunity for vocabulary development on a particular topic or selection to be read, and more careful planning of the results expected. Thoughtful reading rather than just recall should be emphasized. Suggestions for the introduction and building of readiness can be found in most manuals that accompany basal readers.

Activities and exercises to develop effective use of prior knowledge include:

1. Prereading instruction using pictures to build prior knowledge. For example, for material to be read about various types of animals in the zoo, a study of several pictures would enable the children to anticipate the names of the animals. Then, before each selection is read, a review of the names of the animals in the selection can be made. The picture clues become a great aid to recognition of such difficult words as *baboon, kangaroo, hippopotamus, elephant, orangutan, zebra, panther,* and *crocodile.*

2. Exercises using knowledge of the topic to build prior knowledge clues.

   a. Mark the words you would expect to read about in a farm story, F. Mark those in a city story, C.

__stores	__cattle	__tractor	__streets
__chickens	__bus	__escalator	__traffic
__crowds	__hay stack	__silo	__meadow

   b. Which of the following phrases would you expect an old seafaring man to say? Put S before them.

   _____a square-rigged ship
   _____pretty autumn leaves
   _____over the bulwarks
   _____the larboard boats
   _____the well-filled silo
   _____port the helm
   _____a ship of the desert

Failure to Use Context Clues

The child who has failed to develop ability in using context clues as an aid to word recognition is indeed in difficulty. This ability is one of the most important means of word recognition. It is a rapid technique which enables the reader to identify a word immediately. For example, in the sentence "The man put his hat on his _____," it is not difficult for the child to know from the context that the missing word is *head.* At least the meaning of the sentence enables the child to anticipate the few words it could possibly be, rather than one of the 800,000 it might be if it were just any word without regard to context. In addition, the use of context clues makes the selection of the correct meaning of the word possible. In the sentence used in the preceding example, the word *head* could only have been a part of the man; it could not have been the *head of a stream* nor a *head of steam*.

The reader who uses contextual aids is more likely to recognize a new word correctly than if he were using no such aid. He can often make an approximation of the pronunciation of a word from his analytical techniques. The context clues enable him to identify the word even though he picked up only an approximation of the actual word from his analysis. Context clues usually work in combination with other word-recognition techniques. These meaning clues make the application of analytical techniques much more rapid and accurate.

An equally, if not more, important use of context clues is that they act as a check on the application of all the other recognition techniques. Just as in subtraction it pays to add afterward so as to check the answer, so in reading it pays to check the meaning of the sentence to see if the problem in word recognition has been solved correctly. When the child has figured out a word, he must be aware of whether it makes sense in the context in which it is found. If it does, he has probably found the correct solution. If it does not, he should reinspect the word because he undoubtedly has made a mistake. Without at least a fair degree of skill in the use of context clues, the child will be slow and inaccurate in word recognition. With this skill, he can be a good reader if he also has other well-developed word-recognition techniques. A child who depends on contextual clues alone also will be inaccurate. It is important to know that many children who are thought to be in difficulty in reading because of limited skill in analytical techniques or because they have insufficient knowledge of phonetic, structural, or visual elements are really in difficulty because they are not using context clues well.

The child who is limited in the use of context clues is spotted easily. If he makes as many errors when reading words in context as he does when he is reading a list of words, then he is not making sufficient use of the meaning of sentences or paragraphs as an aid to recognition. If the child's errors do not fit the meaning of the sentences and tend to be far afield, he is not using context clues. If, for example, the child reads the word *cat* as *sat* in the sentence "The dog ran after the cat," he is not using context because *sat* makes no sense at all. If, however, he reads *cat* as *car,* he is probably using context because *car* would make sense.

Remedial training in the use of context clues should have the child read materials at a level of difficulty in which he encounters about one new word in every forty running words. He should be reading for purposes that demand thorough understanding of the content. In the more severe cases of this type, a separate and immediate purpose for each paragraph or sentence should be stated. This emphasizes reading for meaning and enables the child to recognize known words at a glance and use context clues as an aid to other techniques in the identification of unfamiliar words. The teacher may need to ask the child from time to time what he thinks the word might be or, more generally, "Does that make sense?" On occasion the child may use the context plus the initial sound to help him solve a difficult word.

In addition to the preceding suggestions, the following more formal exercises encourage the child to use context clues:

1. Exercises in which the meaning of the sentence indicates the word to be recognized.
    a. The boys rode over the snow on it. What was it?
       boat   store   sled
    b. Mother put a candle on the cake for Bob's _____.
       football   birthday   bedroom
2. Exercises in which the child reads a paragraph, filling in the missing words, using the initial elements given. He does not need to write them but reads the sentences to himself. Comprehension questions can be asked.
    Billy caught the ball.
    Then he th_____ the ball to his father.
    Father c_____ the ball, too.
    Billy and his father were pl_____ catch.
    A dog came to play.
    He j_____ up and got the ball.
    Then he ran a_____ with it.
3. Exercises in which context plus initial elements are used as aids to word recognition.
    a. We will get some apples at the st_____.
       store   steep   farm
    b. The car went down the str_____.
       strong   road   street
4. Riddles in which the context gives the answer.
    It lives in a zoo.
    It hops about.
    It carries a baby in its pouch.
    It is a_____.
    elephant   crocodile   kangaroo
5. Closure-type exercises using syntax clues and initial-element clues.
    a. They went sw_____ at the beach.
    b. Tom l_____ candy.
    c. Mary likes h_____ new doll.
    d. The boys w_____ to play, but they d_____ not have a ball.
6. Pure Cloze exercises in which the student must fill in the blank from sentence and paragraph meaning.
    Mary and John went to the_____to buy some candy.
    On their way home they meet their_____Tom.
    Tom was riding his_____bicycle.

In this type of exercise it is imperative that the reading be at an easy level for the student. For this use of the Cloze technique, any word which fits the meaning and the structure of the sentence will do.

7. Deletions of nonsense additions. Exercises in which the child reads a paragraph and deletes the words which do not belong because they do not make sense.

    Mary and John went dog to the store to barn buy some candy. On their zoo way home they met their friend Tom. Tom was kangaroo riding his new bicycle.

CASE STUDY OF A PRIMARY GRADE STUDENT WITH DIFFICULTY RELATING MEANING TO PRINTED SYMBOLS

Steven, a third-grade student, was referred to the school reading center by his classroom teacher toward the middle of the school year. She was concerned because he did not seem to understand what he read, did not participate in class discussions relating to materials read, and although his oral reading was accurate in terms of word pronunciation, his phrasing was poor and he ignored punctuation.

School history.   Steven had attended the same school all of his primary school years. There was no record of previous academic problems in school and he had not previously received special help in reading.

School behavior.   During his third-grade year Steven became increasingly reticent about participating in classroom discussion and activities. He had difficulty completing independent work. However when his classroom teacher worked individually with Steven, he paid attention to what was expected and tried hard.

Abilities.   According to the *Wechsler Intelligence Scale for Children, Revised,* his ability to learn was low average, with a full-scale I.Q. of 90. His performance I.Q. was 96 and his verbal I.Q. was 85. This would place his reading expectancy at the 3.3 level, based on his full-scale I.Q.

Reading achievement testing.   In the fall of Steven's third-grade year he was given the *Metropolitan Achievement Test* along with the rest of the third grade. His grade scores and percentile ranks in reading and spelling were

NAME OF SUBTEST	GRADE EQUIVALENT	PERCENTILE RANK
Word Knowledge	2.7	36
Word Analysis	3.2	56
Reading Comprehension	2.7	34
(Total Reading)	(2.7)	(36)
Spelling	3.0	44

In order to determine the exact nature and severity of Steven's reading problem, the reading center diagnostician administered the *Woodcock Reading Mastery Tests, Revised.* Steven's scores were

NAME OF SUBTEST	GRADE EQUIVALENT	PERCENTILE RANK	STANDARD SCORE
Word Identification	3.7	52	101
Word Attack	4.2	56	102
Basic Skills	3.8	57	103
Word Comprehension	1.9	3	72
Passage Comprehension	2.6	14	84
Comprehension Skill	2.2	6	77
Total Reading	2.9	20	90

Steven was also given the *Diagnostic Reading Scales*. On the Word Recognition subtest he achieved at a satisfactory level for his grade. His pronunciations were phonetically very close to the correct word (e.g., "triumpant" for "triumphant" and "standidize" for "standardize"). During oral reading, he pronounced most words correctly but often accented the wrong syllable of multisyllabic words, and he failed to note punctuation. Errors in comprehension indicated poor understanding of what he read. Silent reading comprehension was poor. Steven's reading rate was slow. His reading potential, as measured by listening to selections read aloud to him and answering questions about them, was satisfactory for his grade level.

Observation of behavior.   Steven was cooperative during individual testing. His responses were slow and careful; he spoke with a soft voice and put his head on the desk at times. He often complained that the tests were too long and that he was tired.

Interpretation of test results.   Steven is a third-grade child of low average ability to learn. General, specific, and child-study diagnostic testing revealed that Steven is making adequate general progress in reading at his grade level. However all measures suggest that word-identification skills surpass word-knowledge and comprehension skills. His performance suggested that Steven has difficulty working flexibly with word meanings. Case study testing revealed that he had great difficulty understanding the meaning of selections he read aloud and greater difficulty with selections he read silently. However, when listening, Steven was able to understand material at a reasonable level of difficulty for a third-grade child.

Informal testing was conducted during which Steven pronounced difficult words and told what they meant, then listened to the diagnostician pronounce them and then told what they meant. Although Steven's ability to pronounce the words was good (18/20), his ability to define words or use them in a sentence was much poorer (12/20). After hearing the diagnostician pronounce the words, Steven was able to define or use 16 of the 20 words correctly.

In the child-study meeting, it was decided that although Steven's progress in reading was generally satisfactory for his grade level and mental ability, he was having a specific problem associating meaning with printed words. Word-pronunciation was a strength for Steven and his ability to associate meaning with spoken words was satisfactory. It was decided that Steven should have small group work with the reading specialist for a limited amount of time for direct assistance with his problem. Difficulties with nonparticipation, incomplete assignments, and fatigue were judged to be a result of his specific reading problems, not a cause.

It is also useful, in considering remediation for Steven, to answer the diagnostic questions posed in Chapter seven.

1. *Is Steven correctly classified as a disabled reader?* Steven is an example of a child with a limiting reading disability. Although his word-pronunciation skills are satisfactorily advanced for his grade placement, he has unusual difficulty associating printed words with their meanings.

2. *What is the nature of the training needed?* The remedial plan for Steven included (1) a variety of highly interesting children's books on a wide range of topics; (2) specific vocabulary development drills; (3) oral reading of plays, poems, and exercises designed for expressive reading; (4) tape-recording of oral reading so that he could monitor his expression and note progress; (5) games used to stress multiple word meanings and precise word meanings, and (6) developing a word bank of words he wanted to save from his favorite stories. Since Steven was remediated in a small group setting, many of his oral reading activities and word-meaning games were participated in by the entire group.

3. *Who can most effectively give the remedial work?* Steven received three months of small group instruction on a daily basis. Although he could have received corrective instruction in his classroom, it was felt best to remediate him for a limited time in the reading center because of his reticence to speak. In the reading center, he would be able to use techniques involving a great deal of oral reading and taping. At the beginning of his fourth-grade year, Steven returned to the regular classroom on a full-time basis.

4. *How can improvement be made most efficiently?* Since oral reading and listening were relative strengths for Steven, they were emphasized in developing associations between printed words and meanings. Enjoyable activities were chosen for Steven; the reading selections were often humorous. Not only formal methods were used, but also less structured group activities which seemed to help Steven express himself more freely.

5. *Does the child have any limiting conditions that must be considered?* In the regular classroom, Steven had given little evidence of interest and participation in class activities. Although he worked hard on assignments given by his teacher, he had difficulty completing them and rarely joined spontaneously with the other children in less structured activities. In a small group situation, with much adult encouragement, and use of materials handpicked to delight him, Steven developed the need to know what the words meant and responded with increasing enthusiasm.

6. *Are there any environmental conditions that might interfere with progress in reading?* Both the parents and the classroom teacher supported Steven's reading program entirely.

Results.   In the beginning of the fourth-grade year Steven returned full-time to the regular classroom. He seemed enthusiastic and confident in the classroom and appeared to adequately understand what he read. When group standardized tests were administered during his fourth-grade year, gains in word and passage comprehension were evident.

SUMMARY

It is important for all readers to develop skills in word recognition. Word study involves two major goals. The first of these involves developing a word-meaning vocabulary and developing word-recognition techniques in such a way that the identification of symbols is accompanied by meaning. The second major goal is to develop flexibility in applying word-recognition techniques. It is necessary to maintain five balances among word-recognition techniques: 1) balance between the establishment of word-recognition techniques and meaning vocabulary; 2) development of word-recognition skills must be balanced with sight vocabulary development; 3) development of meaning clues in word recognition must be balanced with the use of analytical aids; 4) use of phonic techniques must be balanced with use of structural techniques; and 5) balance between the emphasis placed on knowledge of word parts and the orderly left-to-right inspection of words.

Meaning clues are helpful to word recognition in three ways. *First,* they enable the reader to anticipate the words he is to read. This makes the recognition of known words rapid and accurate and allows the reader to work out the identification of unfamiliar words with a minimum of study. *Second,* the use of these clues is essential as a check on the accuracy of his recognition. If the word recognized does not make sense, it should be his habit to study further the word missed. *Third,* the application of other word-recognition techniques frequently gives the child only an approximation of the word; then the meaning clues enable him to recognize the word correctly.

Reading behaviors suggestive of failure to associate meaning with printed symbols, insufficient sight vocabulary, and ineffective use of meaning clues were presented. Suggested techniques and sample exercises demonstrated the type of learning activities which could aid a child in overcoming each of these specific reading problems.

STUDY QUESTIONS

1. Why is the development of reading skills alone not enough? Why must a reasonable balance of skills be maintained?
2. What clues should alert a teacher that a child is not associating meaning (or correct meaning) with words read?
3. List three characteristics of good exercises, games, or activities designed to increase sight recognition of common words.
4. How may expectancy clues be built for a youngster who has little, or no, prior knowledge of the general topic to be covered in a reading selection?
5. Why is the successful use of context clues considered more essential than some of the other skills in word recognition?

SELECTED READINGS

EKWALL, E. E. *Teacher's Handbook on Diagnosis and Remediation in Reading,* 2nd ed., Chaps. 3 and 4. Boston: Allyn & Bacon, Inc. 1986.

HARRIS, A. J. AND E. R. SIPAY. *How to Increase Reading Ability,* 8th ed., Chap. 12. New York: Longman, Inc., 1985.

McCORMICK, S. *Remedial and Clinical Reading Instruction,* Chaps. 12 and 14. Columbus, OH: Charles E. Merrill Publishing Company, 1987.

MILLER, W. H. *Reading Correction Kit,* 2nd ed., Chap. 3. West Nyack, NY: The Center for Applied Research in Education, Inc., 1982.

RUPLEY, W. H. AND T. R. BLAIR. *Reading Diagnosis and Remediation: Classroom and Clinic,* 2nd ed., Chap. 8. Boston: Houghton Mifflin Company, 1983.

11

Correcting Faulty Perceptual and Decoding Skills in Word Recognition

Proficiency in both the use of meaning clues and the application of analytical word-recognition techniques is required if the reader is to associate the correct concept with the printed symbol. Meaning clues alone are not enough for good reading at any level. They must be accompanied by the use of a flexible set of word-recognition skills. It is through the interaction of all the word-study skills that a competent reader improves reading proficiency.

The set of skills needed to reinforce the meaning clues to word recognition can be grouped under three types of interrelated learnings; (1) flexible visual perceptual habits, (2) knowledge of phonics and structural word elements, and (3) fluent oral and visual synthesis of word parts. Weakness in any one, or any combination, of these types of achievements precludes adequate growth in reading. Disabled readers, deficient in word-recognition skills, are classified as having a limiting or complex disability. This chapter will discuss the basic problems of faulty word-study skills under the following headings:

1. General suggestions for correcting word-recognition difficulties
2. Ineffective visual perceptual habits
3. Limited knowledge of word elements
4. Lack of fluent oral and visual synthesis

GENERAL SUGGESTIONS FOR CORRECTING
WORD-RECOGNITION DIFFICULTIES

To correct limitations in word-study skills, the instructional procedures must be carefully planned according to the findings of a thorough diagnosis. There are certain general suggestions that aid in making the remedial teaching effective. These suggestions, suitable to any type of word-skill deficiencies, are

1. Teach word recognition in material that is at the disabled reader's instructional level. Any material that is used for reading is helpful in teaching word recognition. There are certain precautions that must be observed, however. The material should not have too many new words. Obviously if the disabled reader is to use the meaning of the printed page and context clues to aid him in word recognition, he must know a sufficient number of sight words so that the meaning will not become lost. In the initial lessons, it is especially important that new words should not be too numerous.

2. Teach word recognition when it is important to the disabled reader to recognize the word. If the purpose of reading is real to the disabled reader and if he has accepted it, he will make a more vigorous attack on difficult words that prevent him from reaching his goal. This will help him persist in recognizing the words even though it entails careful analysis.

3. Always teach word recognition in meaningful material. Because the objective of all word-recognition techniques is to recognize words, it is better to develop the techniques in the content in which they are going to be used, meaningful content. This allows the disabled reader to use not only the analytical techniques but also the various meaning clues. It teaches him to interpret a word in the context in which he finds it. Word recognition is not word calling but the recognition of the correct meaning of a word in a given situation. Teaching word recognition in context encourages a balance between the development of meaning vocabulary and the word-recognition techniques.

4. Undertake the more analytical types of word recognition techniques only after the disabled reader is aware of the meaningful nature of reading, has established the habit of recognizing words as whole words, and has built a supportive sight vocabulary. This enables the disabled reader to use meaning clues, and it also encourages him to use more rapid recognition techniques.

5. Be sure that the disabled reader knows the meaning of the words he is trying to identify or has the background necessary to derive their meaning. It is obvious that the disabled reader should have, or be able to secure, the meaning of the word he is attempting to recognize. It is difficult enough for him to use identification clues when meaning is present. But if meaning is absent, he may not know whether he has studied the word adequately.

6. Teach the disabled reader to analyze the word visually before he attempts to sound it out. Visual analysis must always precede sounding, because it is through visual analysis that the reader isolates usable word elements to be sounded. A large part of the ability to decode words effectively is the ability to locate usable elements. Flexible study of words is essential, because a faulty start will have to be rejected quickly if words are to be recognized by analytical means.

7. Teach the disabled reader to develop the habit of noticing similarities and differences among words. Through many comparisons, most of which he himself will make, the disabled reader can establish this habit—one that encourages careful and rapid inspection of words and helps to develop many of the word-recognition techniques. The

disabled reader can use this procedure, for instance, to build his own families of words and to notice similarities in meaning and configurations of words with the same roots. This habit encourages building large sight-recognition vocabularies and discourages overanalysis.

8. Teach the ability to locate a new word-recognition element in known words before applying that element to identification of new words. The disabled reader is led to discover, for example, the initial-letter sound in the known words *run, ride,* and *rat* before he uses this knowledge in identifying the new word *rabbit.*

9. Build the reader's habit of inspecting words rapidly, thoroughly, and systematically from left to right. Many of the difficulties in word recognition result from failure to study the whole word systematically, starting at the left and looking completely through the word from left to right. The disabled reader who fails to inspect words from left to right may recognize a word like *stop* as *pots* at one time, and *tops* at another. Although the parts are recognized adequately, the order of those parts is confused, causing difficulty. Reversal problems may be caused by failure to establish a systematic left-to-right inspection of words. The neglect of any part of the word during inspection can cause difficulty.

10. Adjust instruction in word-recognition techniques to the individual. In developing word-recognition techniques, it should be kept in mind that there are some disabled readers who do not profit from certain types of instruction. For example, for a disabled reader with auditory deficiency, it is unfortunate to emphasize phonics approaches. Sometimes phonics approaches may have to be omitted entirely. In developing independence in word recognition for a disabled reader with faulty vision, more dependence should be placed on large word elements, such as syllables, than would be necessary for the child with normal vision.

11. Avoid drill on isolated word elements or use of artificial teaching devices. Whenever possible, the disabled reader should recognize and remember words as sight words. Drill on isolated elements tends to cause the disabled reader to analyze words that he otherwise might have recognized quite easily at sight. Excessive analysis, if transferred to actual reading, may interfere with reading fluency and with the understanding of meaning.

12. Discuss with the disabled reader exactly what his problem is and let him aid in formulating his individual remedial plan. The disabled reader will be more motivated to participate actively in remediation if he is working toward known goals. Knowledge and awareness of the problem and the plan allows the disabled reader to be a more effective learner and enables him to assist his teacher in making some instructional decisions. The child will feel a greater sense of accomplishment when he achieves reading goals that have become his own, not just his teacher's.

INEFFECTIVE VISUAL-PERCEPTUAL HABITS

The ability to read depends upon a group of visual-perceptual skills and habits essential to decoding the printed symbols. These skills must be highly coordinated and flexible if a reader is to read in thought units at speeds that far exceed the rate at which he can listen. The thought units are made up of words that are so quickly perceived that they can be grouped together and recognized at a single glance. The disabled reader is often in major difficulty because his reading perceptual habits preclude such rapid recognition of words. His problem may be in any one, or in any combination, of the following interrelated perceptual defects:

1. Faulty visual analysis of words
2. Excessive word-perception errors
3. Overanalytical habits

Faulty Visual Analysis of Words

Visual analysis of an unfamiliar word must always precede the application of knowledge of word parts. Both of these come before the final synthesis of the parts into recognition of a word. For example, a child unfamiliar with the word *something* might visually separate the word into *so—met—hing*. He would then apply his knowledge of the parts, pronouncing each in turn. Then he would try to blend the parts and find that he had failed in his attempt because his original visual separation of the word was wrong. He would have to reject his first visual analysis and make another one. This time he might see the first of the two small words from which the word *something* is made and separate the word into *some—th—ing*. Then applying his knowledge of the parts and synthesizing them, he would be able to recognize the word. Of course this approach to recognizing the word *something* would have been rather immature. A more advanced reader would have visually analyzed the word into the largest known elements, *some* and *thing*. He would visually recognize these parts and then synthesize them. Aided by the context clues, the separate parts would not have to be spoken and blended, but the whole word *something* would have been recognized at a glance. Nonetheless, the word would have been visually analyzed, knowledges applied and then synthesized, all with great rapidity.

The visual analysis of words must be flexible and diversified if the child is to become an able reader. To do so, the child must develop great skill in the visual analysis of words. He must, at a glance, be able to separate the word into elements useful in recognizing it. An element useful in one word may not be so in another. For example, the element *on* in the word *upon* is useful, but separating *on* out of the word *portion* would be detrimental to recognizing the whole word. The child must be flexible, so that when one method does not work, he can quickly reexamine the word and reanalyze it visually. He must analyze a word only when he does not know it as a sight word, and even then he should select the largest usable elements in the word rather than resort to piecemeal analysis.

The child who is disabled in the visual analysis of words can be identified by the classroom teacher in two ways. *First,* when pronouncing words verbally he selects inappropriate elements to sound out and often he tries again and again to use the same analysis even when it does not work. *Second,* when the examiner shows him how to analyze the word by covering up parts of it, if the child is able to recognize it, then at least one of his problems in word recognition is faulty visual analysis.

Remedial training for a child with this kind of disability must focus on two results. *First,* it should give the child help in finding the most useful structural, visual, and phonic elements in words. *Second,* it must develop flexibility in the visual attack on words, teaching the child to use the larger elements first but to change quickly from an analysis that does not work to one that does.

The most effective remedial measures are similar to those used by the teacher when first developing this ability. In introducing unfamiliar words during the preparatory phase of teaching a selection, the teacher should work carefully in showing such a disabled reader how to visually analyze the new words. In the follow-up phases of teaching a selection, the visual analysis skill should be emphasized. Such training as finding similarities in known words like *fight* and *sight* or *three* and *throw* gives the child experience in visual analysis. The material for such training should be at the instructional level of difficulty so that the child needs to analyze words visually. Help in finding parts of compound words or in isolating root words in affixed words is excellent experience in visual analysis. Syllabifying words is also useful. Reinforcing exercises like the following, first using known words and then having the child find similar elements in unknown words, should be used liberally with a child seriously deficient in visual analysis of words:

1. Exercises in finding the root word in words with variant ending forms.
   a. Find the root words from which these words are made.
      (1) looks   looking   looked
      (2) worker   worked   working
   b. Find the root words in words having variant endings, such as: *want* in *wanting; wait* in *waited; swim* in *swimming.*
2. Exercises having the child use syntax clues in choosing between variant forms, such as:

             wanting
   a. The bear   the honey.
             wanted

             talk
   b. The man was talking to them.
             talked
3. Exercises that require finding similar blends.
   a. You see the picture of the clown, say clown. Look at the words here and circle the ones that begin like clown and that tell something we can do.
      clap   clean   clocks
      come   clothes   play
      climb   cook   clam
4. Exercises that emphasize seeing similar word parts.
   a. Fill in the right word.
      (1) She wanted to _____ for joy.
          sing   shout   shoe
      (2) String is not as _____ as rope.
          street   big   strong

   b. Draw a line under the right word.
     (1) The sun cannot be seen at _____.
       fight   night   right   sight
     (2) The train runs on a _____.
       sack   black   track   tack

5. Exercises that teach syllabication.
   a. Say the words below and decide how many parts you hear. These parts are syllables. Write the number of syllables after each word.

about____	surprise____	something____
rabbit____	together____	thermometer____
cat____	wonderful____	banana____

   b. Mark the syllables in these words, as: dif/fer/ent.

ahead	forgotten	furniture
yellow	interested	tomorrow
after	moment	electricity

6. Exercises that emphasize seeing both parts of compound words.
   a. Find the two small words in each compound word and tell how they help us know what it means.

fireplace	baseball	sailboat
fireside	football	rowboat
firefly	basketball	ferryboat

   b. Take one of the two words from each compound word below the sentence and make a new compound word to fill in the blank.
     (1) We were seated by the _____ to get warm.
       firehouse   inside
     (2) The wind makes the _____ go fast.
       sailfish   steamboat

7. Exercises that develop skill in analyzing affixed words.
   a. Draw a line around the part of the word that means *again.*

relive	remake	retell
rework	replay	relearn

   b. Draw a line around the root word, the word from which the larger word is made. Tell how the prefix and suffix change the meaning of the root word.

unfriendly	unthankful	distrustful
unkindly	unlikely	dishonestly
disagreeable	repayable	unkindness

The experience that the child gains from exercises to improve his visual analysis of words must be used in meaningful settings. The child should be asked to put these words in sentences immediately or tell the derived meanings. This sort of drill should not be used in isolation but as a part of a broader program of word recognition. The words in these exercises should be familiar to the child or be words that will soon be introduced in the basic reading program.

Flexibility and the habit of dividing words into the largest usable elements should be stressed. The program should teach the child to avoid faulty approaches to word recognition, such as letter-by-letter spelling or sounding. Sounding of individual letters, for example, may help a child to recognize a small word, such as *cat*, but it would be extremely confusing in recognizing longer or more complicated words, such as *telephone* or *impatient*. Yet some children do this letter-by-letter sounding of all unfamiliar words.

Many children have difficulty in word recognition because they are too dependent on one technique or because they do not use the most efficient ones. For example, they may have the habit of searching for known little words in larger words. This technique is helpful in identifying compound words or affixed words, but it is detrimental to recognizing many other words. Finding *ear* in *bear* is of doubtful help, as is finding *to—get—her* in the word *together*. The exercises must encourage a diversified and flexible attack on words. They must also emphasize orderly progression through the word from its beginning element to its end.

Excessive Word-Perception Errors

Some children's word perceptual difficulties are different from those just discussed. Their mispronunciations tend to form a consistent pattern that can be readily diagnosed. These errors are classified in many ways by different workers in the reading field. They are best thought of as word-perception errors. In general the classifications are based on where the errors are located in the words in which they occur. For example, a child may make an excessive number of errors in the initial part of words, such as calling *house, mouse*. Another child might cluster his errors around the middle of words. He might call *house, horse*. A third child may make an unusually high percentage of errors at the end of words. He might call *house, hour*.

For a certain child, these errors tend to be most frequent in a specific part of the word because his word perception consistently neglects that part of the word. Roughly, these perceptual errors can be classified as Initial Errors, Middle Errors, and Ending Errors. The child can also confuse the order of word parts and make Orientation Errors.

Locational errors can be diagnosed by classifying a sample of errors made in word pronunciation. This method is used in the *Gates-McKillop-Horowitz Reading Diagnostic Tests*. The diagnostician may also collect a sample of errors to classify informally. The disadvantage of this is that he cannot know the number of possibilities present in the sample he takes, nor can he judge how frequently a certain type of error typically occurs.

Initial errors indicate that the child, as he inspects words, neglects to notice the beginnings of words closely enough. He makes errors such as calling *his, this* or *the, he*. Another type of initial error is calling the word *tall, fall* or *when, then*.

The remedial procedures used for correcting initial errors are similar to those for better visual analysis of words and knowledge of initial elements. The difference is emphasis. For the child who makes an undue number of errors in the initial part of words, even though he knows initial elements, the exercises focus his attention more directly and systematically on the beginning of words. Building a picture dictionary causes the child to look systematically at the words. Exercises in alphabetizing words help him pay greater attention to word beginnings. Sorting labeled pictures for filing also helps. The child should be shown the nature of his errors and the difference between the word he pronounced and the way it actually appeared in print. For example, if he calls *cat, eat,* he should be shown that he got the word almost right, but that he must pay closer attention to the beginning of the word. This sort of encouragement should be maintained. All exercises on initial consonant blends and digraphs help to overcome a child's tendency to neglect the beginnings of words. The following exercises are also good:

1. Multiple-choice questions in which the child is asked to differentiate among initial elements.

    boat.
    The man put on his goat.
    coat.

2. Classification exercises that emphasize initial sounds and word meanings.

    Find every word that starts like *crack* and is something we can eat.

crab	candy	cranberries
apple	crown	cradle
cracker	bread	crumbs

3. Multiple-choice exercises in which the initial blend is given.

    The car went down the str_____.   strange   road   street

Middle errors result from two major causes. First, the child may hurry his inspection of unfamiliar words to such an extent that he neglects the middles of words. Second, he may have limited knowledge of vowel sounds. Exercises that teach the sounds of vowels are helpful. Methods that encourage the child to inspect words in an orderly fashion help correct any tendency to neglect the middle of the word. Copying some of the words that cause difficulty may help, as does tracing the words. Using context as a check on accuracy encourages the child to reinspect the words missed. A child using context clues, for example, could not very well call *cat, cot* in the sentence, "The cat climbed the tree," without rereading to find out what was wrong. He should be told why he needs to make a closer inspection of the middles of words and what the difference is between the error made and the printed word. Multiple-choice exercises are helpful in correcting this difficulty because the child must differentiate the middle parts of words.

pen.
1. The pig was in the pan.
pin.

children.
2. The egg was laid by the citizen.
chicken.

Ending errors are made frequently. Even good readers, when they do make errors, tend to make ending errors more frequently than other locational errors. An overemphasis on word endings can cause neglect of the very important initial elements, and it may also cause reversals and other orientational confusions. The mature reader starts at the beginning of an unfamiliar word and works systematically along it from left to right until it is completely inspected. All exercises designed to increase knowledge of variant endings, word families, and suffixes help to eliminate errors in the final elements of words. If the exercises are in contextual settings, the child must differentiate both beginnings and endings of words. These exercises are helpful in calling attention to the final element while maintaining a systematic inspection of the word. One exercise frequently used by teachers may be harmful. Finding words in a list that belong to a *word family,* such as the *at* family or the *ay* family, without using meaning as a check could be detrimental if the child selects the words by endings alone without recognizing what the words are. This could result in neglect of the important initial element of words and disruption of the orderly left-to-right inspection of each word. Another precaution is to avoid overreacting to ending errors in oral reading by children who have perfect understanding but whose mispronunciations simply reflect dialectal differences.

Here are some exercises that may be used safely.

1. Finish the word. It should rhyme with *call.*
    The boy was playing with a b_____.
    tall   back   ball
2. Find the word that ends like *coat* which you would like to play with.
    goat   doll   float
    gloat   boat   clock

Orientation confusions are among the most troublesome perceptual errors made by disabled readers. Orientation problems will be discussed in the next chapter, which deals with the extremely disabled reader.

Overanalytical Habits

The overanalytical reader is the child who either fails to build an adequate sight vocabulary and must attack many words he meets or acquires the habit of analyzing all words, even those he knows at sight.

Habitual overanalysis takes two forms. The child may analyze words he knows at sight. This is not only slow and impedes thoughtful reading, but it also can lead the child to make unnecessary errors in word recognition. Some children have so thoroughly established the habit of analyzing known words that they make more errors when allowed unlimited time to pronounce a list of words than they do when the same list of words is flashed before them by a tachistoscope, forcing them to read the words at sight. It should be remembered that word-recognition techniques should be so ingrained that the child will identify known words without detailed study, and that he will rapidly recognize the words he knows in any of their variant forms. He will resort to time-consuming, analytical procedures only when he is working out words he has not met previously. A good reader inspects a word in only as much detail as is required for its recognition. The overanalytical reader reverses this process. He approaches most words as unfamiliar. He studies them in detail, isolates elements within them, applies his knowledge of word elements, and then synthesizes the elements back into a word, only to find that it is familiar. This pattern is harmful both to reading fluency and to comprehension. The child is so concerned with analyzing known words that he has no time to understand content. It takes him so long to recognize each word that he cannot group them into thought units. Both his comprehension and his speed of reading of connected material suffer.

The second type of overanalytical reader is the one who breaks words into too many parts. Instead of using large elements known to him, he resorts too early and too often to a study of individual letter sounds. This habit of recognizing words is extremely inefficient and often confusing. For many words, letter-by-letter sounding precludes recognition. Take the words in the previous sentence, for example, and try to sound each letter in the words and then blend them into the words. Not all of the words could be recognized in this way, and even for those that could, it would be a time-consuming and inefficient method. It is foolish, for example, for a child who knows the word *talk* to resort to a letter-by-letter sounding of the word *talking*. Yet many overanalytical readers do this. It would be equally foolish and totally ineffective for the child who knew *tion* in *action* to try a letter-by-letter sounding of that element. Care must be taken to maintain proper balances in word recognition.

Some children who are overanalytical go to the extreme of a "spelling attack" on words. They try to remember each new word by spelling it out. For example, they encounter the unknown word *donkey,* and try to learn it by naming each letter. It is impossible for a child to remember all of the words he is expected to learn by trying to recall the sequence of letters through spelling. There are children who, when asked to work out an unknown word aloud, name each letter in turn and sometimes, after calling the letters, can say the word. For example, a child will see the word *horse,* which he doesn't identify. When asked to try to pronounce it, he will say, "*h—o—r—s—e, horse.*" This type of word recognition is detrimental to reading growth.

The overanalytical reader can be detected by studying his relative effectiveness on timed and untimed word-recognition tests. He can also be identified by asking him to work on words orally when he gets into difficulty. A third way of detecting this type of difficulty is to note children who rank relatively high on tests of word elements but who are low on tests of word recognition. They also tend to be slow readers with poor comprehension.

The remedial treatment for children who tend to analyze words that are already known as sight words is to give more training with exercises suitable for increasing sight vocabulary, associating words with meanings, and using context clues effectively. Flash techniques such as a tachistoscope or an overhead projector are helpful. Rapid exposure of word cards is useful too. All these exercises should be used just to reinforce the emphases that should be applied to the child's other reading experiences. Reading material with few if any word difficulties, for purposes that require rapid reading, such as reading to get the general significance of a paragraph, scanning to find a specific bit of information, or reading to predict outcomes, helps overcome overanalytical tendencies.

The overanalytical reader who breaks words up into too many parts is corrected by emphasizing structural analysis and knowledge of the larger elements. Stress on syllabication rather than on sounding each letter is desirable. Noting root words, prefixes, suffixes, and variant endings gives the child the habit of analyzing words into larger elements. Instruction in word recognition should encourage him to select as large elements as he can when he is working out the recognition of words not known at sight. In remedial work, weight should be put on exercises for developing effective visual analysis that teach the child to isolate the larger structural and visual elements within words. In addition, it should be stressed that wide reading of relatively easy material helps the child who tends to resort to piecemeal observation of words.

LIMITED KNOWLEDGE OF WORD ELEMENTS

The child who is to become a capable, fluent, and independent reader must develop an extensive knowledge of word elements. There is no point for the child to be skillful in visually analyzing words unless he knows what the parts say. It does not help, for example, for the child to separate visually the word *spring* into *spr—ing* unless he knows how the initial blend *spr* and the ending *ing* sound. The child needs to learn a vast number of word parts. The larger the elements he can use in recognizing words, the more fluent and meaningful his reading will be. The more he uses context and meaning clues, the less he needs to analyze the words. It is often necessary for a child to break a word into small parts in order to recognize it. This does not aid him if he does not know the small elements. The child must master the knowledge of many phonic, structural, and visual elements in words.

The diagnostician has several ways of detecting limited knowledge of word parts. Most diagnostic reading tests sample the more useful phonic, structural, and visual elements. Any weakness on these tests in comparison with the child's general reading capability indicates that he may be limited in the number of elements with which he is familiar. Another means of spotting this weakness is difficulty in associating sounds with word elements when the child is working out the pronunciation of words orally. If the child uses reasonable visual analysis of a word but does not know letter sounds, common phonograms, or visual elements, he is limited in his knowledge of word parts. If he seems to be able to break a word into syllables but cannot pronounce many of them, he is limited in his knowledge of important word parts and should be given remedial training to increase his phonic, structural, and visual knowledges.

When the teacher or remedial worker points out to a child the similarity between a new word and other words he knows, he is receiving instruction in word-element knowledge. Manuals accompanying basic reading programs offer many suggestions for introducing new vocabulary to the child before he reads a selection. In presenting the new words, the teacher is supposed not only to make the meaning clear but also to show the child the most efficient visual analysis of each word and compare it, when necessary, with known words which contain the element which might cause the child difficulty. If, for example, the new word is *trouble,* the teacher might say that it begins like *train* and ends like *double.* The three words should be written on the chalkboard. The teacher might also say it is something we would rather not have. The teacher would have given some instruction in the knowledge of how *tr* and *ouble* sound.

Manuals of most reading series give suggestions for instructing children in knowledge of word parts. Reading series, used at an appropriate level of difficulty, can provide good material for children who need extra instruction and practice in knowledge of word parts because of the systematic introduction of word parts and the vocabulary control maintained by the authors. An emphasis on the introduction of new vocabulary and on word study is essential. Word-recognition exercises in skill books accompanying the readers should also be used.

If other materials are used, the remedial teacher should use words that might cause trouble or that illustrate an important word element. These words should be introduced as new words, as suggested in *teaching a selection,* described in Chapter 9.

Some remedial teachers report success in using a linguistically regular approach, as described by Fries (1963) and Bloomfield and Barnhart (1961). Programmed materials with a linguistically regular vocabulary, such as *The Programmed Reading Series* (Sullivan Associates, 1973), have proved effective in training children seriously confused in distinguishing the phonemic and print signal relationships described by linguists.

All the exercises suggested in the preceding section for improving visual analysis of words aid in teaching knowledge of visual, structural, and phonic elements. Additional exercises like the following are beneficial to the child limited in his knowledge of word parts. The words used should be familiar or should be words soon to be learned.

1. Exercises to teach initial consonant sounds.
    a. Say the words *can* and *come.* Put C before all the words that start like *can* and *come* and that also name an animal.

    _____cat _____cookies _____chicken
    _____duck _____elephant _____cake
    _____eel _____calf _____cub

    b. Write the first part of the word in the space. It starts like one of the words below the sentence.
       (1) The dog ran __ome.
           son   hope   cone
       (2) The cat wanted some __ilk.
           pig   like   mill

2. Exercises to teach initial blend sounds.
   a. Write in the blank the word that begins with the same blend as the word underlined.
      (1) The <u>branch</u> soon_____.
         bring   fell   broke
      (2) The <u>block</u> was painted_____.
         brown   blue   green
   b. Draw a line under the right word. It must start with the same blend as the key word.
      (1) *clown*   (2) *smile*
                feet.   brown.
         The cat has   claws.   The puppy was   small.
                close.   smoke.

The disabled reader, limited in this area, may be taught other important blends, such as: *cr, dr, fl, gl, pl, scr, sk, sl, sn, sp,* and *st,* in exercises such as those just presented.

3. Exercises to reinforce knowledge of digraph sounds.
   a. Finish the words. They begin like one of the words below the sentences. The first one is done for you.
      (1) <u>Th</u>at cat can run.
         Boy   This   Sing
      (2) ___ere will we go?
         What   Hear   Play
      (3) The ___est was full of gold.
         toy   boy   chair
      (4) We get wool from ___eep.
         ducks   ships   sleds
      (5) His brother was only ___ee.
         where   thread   see
   b. Draw a line around the right word. It must start with the same digraph as the key word.
      (1) *church*
                   chimney.
         We make butter in a   pail.
                   churn.
      (2) *ship*
                   coat.
         She put on her new   shoes.
                   sharp.

4. Exercise to teach vowel sounds.
   a. The vowels *a, e, i, o, u* say their names in many words. This is their long sound. Write the vowel that is long following each word. Then use the word in a sentence.

      age_____   dine_____   vase_____
      like_____   cave_____   use_____
      alone_____   home_____   rope_____

Call attention to the fact that each word has one consonant between the vowel and the final *e;* that usually makes the first vowel have a *long* sound. Some exceptions may be given, as:

give   love   come   where
some   live   whose   were

b. Write the vowel that is *long* following each word. Then use the word in a sentence.

peach____   snail____   heel____
reach____   road____   keep____
tease____   bead____   leaf____
plains____   boat____   mean____

Call attention to the fact that many times when two vowels come together the first vowel takes the long sound and the second vowel is silent. Some exceptions may be given, as:

bread   heavy   meant
break   great   house
chief   head   piece

c. Put in the right word. It must have a short vowel.

The boy ran after the____

boat   game   cat

Other exercises using context clues can be used, because context clues can help the child tell whether a vowel is long or short in an unknown word.

5. Exercises to teach hard and soft consonant sounds.

a. When C has the sound of *S* it has a soft sound. When it sounds like *K* it has a hard sound. Put *S* following the sentences in which *C* is soft and *H* when it is hard. The first one is done for you.

(1) We went to the camp. H
(2) I saw his face.____
(3) We rode on a camel.____
(4) It sold for ten cents.____
(5) The calf was brown.____

b. Similar exercises can be used to teach the other hard and soft consonant sounds.

6. Exercises using syntactical clues to teach variant endings.

a. Draw a line under the right word.

            drink
(1) The cat   her milk.
        drinks.
            wanted
(2) Now she   to run away.
        wanting

7. Exercises using context clues to teach common word elements.

a. Put in the right word. It must end like the key word.

(1) *talk*
    We had a brisk ____.
    chalk   walk   run

(2) *light*
It was a dark _____.
right   room   night

b. See how many words you can make that rhyme with the following words. Use each of them in a sentence.
bat   street   bright
ball   rake   sand

The exercises designed to increase knowledge of visual, structural, and phonic elements as often as possible should be put in contextual settings. This is desirable because many times the true sound of an element can be known only from its use in context. For example, the vowel sound in *read* cannot be known out of context. Context also stimulates more rapid recognition of the parts being taught, and it offers an immediate and independent check on the accuracy of the association of the printed symbols with the pronunciation. There are certain drill devices used to increase the disabled reader's knowledge of word parts. They should be used sparingly, and the words drilled should be read in context so that the elements learned have a reasonable chance of being transferred into actual reading. These devices include word wheels, word slips, word tachistoscopes, and certain computer programs.

Word wheels are constructed by cutting two disks. One should be about five inches in diameter and the other slightly smaller. On the larger disk, words are printed with the initial element missing. These words should all start at the same distance from the center (about one inch) and progress toward the outer edge like the spokes of a wheel. Only words that begin with the same word element should be used on one disk. The initial element should be omitted. For example, if the initial blend *str* is to be taught, words such as *strap, strong, straw, string, strip, stream,* and *strange* could be used. The word endings only are printed on the larger disk (see

FIGURE 11-1   "str" word wheel

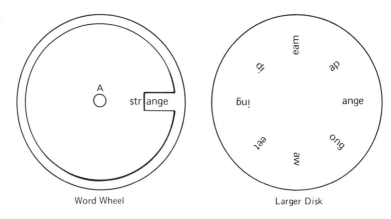

Word Wheel   Larger Disk

Figure 11-1). In the smaller disk, a radial slit of the proper size and position is cut to expose one word ending at a time. The initial blend *str* is printed just to the left of the slit (see Figure 11-1). The two disks are fastened together at the center with a paper fastener (A), with the smaller disk on top. As the lower disk is rotated, the *str* on the smaller disk makes a word as it combines with each ending on the larger disk.

Other word parts can be taught this way. With word endings, such as *ing, ake,* or *alk,* the word wheel needs to be changed so that the ending is printed at the right of the slit cut in the smaller disk and the word beginnings are printed on the larger disk (See figure 11-2).

Word slips can be constructed to practice the various word parts. They have an advantage over word wheels because they are easier to make. A manila folder can be used to make the removable faces and slips. Figure 11-3 illustrates the use of a word slip. The removable faces and slips can be varied to drill on any particular word part. The word slips and faces are made by typing the word part to be drilled at the appropriate place on the face (see Figure 11-3, faces, 1, 2, and 3). The remaining parts of the words can be typed or printed at intervals on the slip. A permanent poster-board back can be used for all exercises, since the face is removable.

Word beginnings that could be typed on word slips to use with the *ing* ending on removable face 2 are *th, s, br, r, str, wr,* and *k.* The following words could also be used with this face: *walk, talk, sing, jump, build, play, say, feed, hear,* etc.

Slips and faces, such as face 1, could be made for all the important initial consonants, blends, and digraphs. Number 2 faces and slips could be made for all the important variant endings and phonograms. Number 3 faces and slips could be made to teach long and short vowels and vowel combinations. The words used in these exercises should be those taught in the basal readers or taken from lists of common words as compiled by Dolch (1960) and Harris and Jacobson (1972).

The word-slip devices can be used as a tachistoscope by moving a small card up and down to expose quickly each new word to be studied. This is sometimes advisable for the child who has a tendency to dawdle or to break words into too

FIGURE 11-2 "ing" word wheel

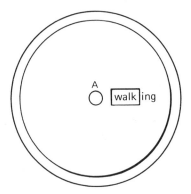

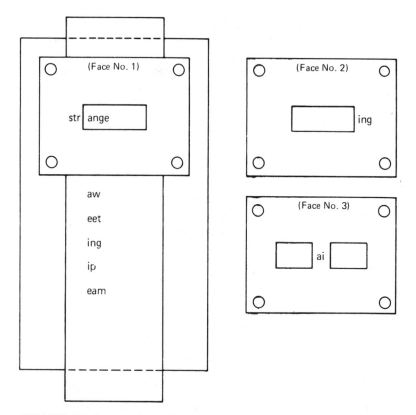

FIGURE 11-3 Word slip device

many parts. The word-slip device can also be used for drill on sight words if another face, with just an exposure slit without any letters, is made. In this case, the words on the typed slip should be spaced further apart with a heavy black line between them. The teacher shows the black line, says "ready," exposes the word for an instant, and then moves the word slip to the next black line while the child responds.

Computer programs such as *Word Munchers* (Minnesota Educational Computing Corporation, 1985) also provide review of phonic elements in words using a motivational game-like format. These computer programs are useful for review only. They serve to supplement, rather than to replace, systematic teacher-directed instruction.

A more detailed way of teaching the child to relate word elements to sounds will be discussed in the next chapter, on extremely disabled readers. These methods are individual and time-consuming, but they do help the child severely limited in knowledge of word parts. Sound-tracing methods will also be discussed in the next chapter.

LACK OF FLUENT ORAL AND VISUAL SYNTHESIS

The child must be able to reassemble a word after he has visually separated it into parts and recognized them. Effective and rapid synthesis of the parts into the whole word is essential to word recognition. Many children have difficulty with their reading because they lack ability in word synthesis. This ability is called auditory blending. In actual reading, the word parts are neither thoroughly sounded nor auditorily blended. It is relatively infrequent that a mature reader resorts to auditory blending. He usually perceives the larger elements within a word visually and then synthesizes it visually without resorting to oral pronunciation at all. In the word *anytime,* for example, the able reader sees the words *any* and *time* in the larger word. He does not pronounce these parts nor does he pronounce the word as a whole, but he immediately sees that it is a compound word made up of two well-known words. The mature reader identifies the word *anytime* by visually synthesizing the known parts and knows the meaning of the compound word. This form of visual analysis, perception, and synthesis takes place so rapidly that the mature reader is rarely aware of such perceptual acts. He immediately senses the meaning of the printed symbol without reflecting on the symbol itself.

The mature reader, while reading silently, does not even sound out the parts of a broken word at the end of a line of print. He just looks at the part of the word on the upper line and then quickly glances down to the remainder of the word on the next line. He immediately identifies the word and its meaning. No oral pronunciation or auditory blending takes place.

The child who is beginning to learn to read or the child who is disabled in word synthesis cannot so readily synthesize words visually. Indeed, he often finds it difficult to blend a word auditorily once he has pronounced it part by part. In his early reading instruction, the child is often required to sound out words part by part and then blend the sound elements together. Sometimes he makes too great a separation of the parts when orally studying the word, and he cannot auditorily reassemble it.

Some children have difficulty with word synthesis because they lack the capacity to blend sounds orally. They are, for example, unable to tell what word an examiner is saying when he pronounces the word part by part. If he says the word *drink* as *dr—ink,* with about a second of time between the parts, the child cannot tell what the word is. In some cases, the child cannot even tell that the examiner is saying *drink* if he pronounces it normally a second time after he has dissociated it. Bond (1935) has shown that a child who is limited in this ability is much more likely to become a disabled reader when taught by methods requiring him to use auditory blending than he would be if visual recognition and synthesis were emphasized.

Many children have difficulty in blending because the word parts were learned in isolation rather than in words, or they were taught too often in drill exercises rather than in contextual settings. In such situations, the child learns to lean too heavily on oral pronunciation and auditory blending of word parts. Often the oral pronunciation of words, part by part, leads the child to pause between each part, making blending difficult if not impossible. Frequently, the child who resorts to letter-by-letter sounding has forgotten the beginning of the word before he has completed the parts. This does not necessarily indicate that the child has a synthesis difficulty, but rather, it suggests an erroneous technique of word recognition which should be corrected.

The diagnosis of inability to synthesize words is somewhat complex. Three judgments must be made: (1) Is the child's problem really one of poor synthesis or is it the result of ineffective analytical techniques? (2) Is the child's problem one of poor auditory blending or is it poor visual synthesis? (3) Is the child's difficulty the result of faulty learning or is he auditorily handicapped? These questions can be decided by studying the results of reading diagnostic tests. In the *Gates-McKillop-Horowitz Reading Diagnostic Tests* (described in Chapter 8), the results of the tests of Syllabication, Recognizing and Blending Common Word Parts, and Auditory Blending will indicate whether the child has a real deficiency in visual or auditory synthesis.

The diagnostician can also observe the child's ability to reassemble words that have been correctly analyzed and pronounced, part by part. If the child is unable to blend words analyzed, he lacks ability in auditory blending. The specialist can pronounce some words, part by part, to determine whether the child can blend the sounds he hears. If the child is able to blend words and recognize them similarly to other children of his age and grade, the diagnostician can be sure that the child's difficulty is not due to an auditory handicap.

The remedial work that should be given to a child poor in the visual synthesis of words is to have him recognize words presented to him by rapid-exposure techniques. A spaced slip of words correctly analyzed into syllables could be exposed in the word-slip tachistoscope and the child could tell some fact about each word. For example, the following list could be used and the child could tell if the word named an animal or a food:

ba	boon		chip	munk	
but	ter		don	key	
buf	fa	lo	choc	o	late
ce	re	al	cook	ies	
bum	ble	bee	lem	on	ade
car	rot		let	tuce	
mon	key		rob	in	

Any of the word-slip exercises, developed for teaching the child with limited knowledge of word elements, can also be used for rapid exposure exercises to sharpen visual synthesis. This tachistoscopic type of rapid exposure is also helpful in overcoming the overanalytical reader's problems. It is useful as a quick-exposure technique for developing quick recognition of sight words, as just described.

Typed exercises with many words broken at the ends of the lines read under timed conditions help in developing rapid visual synthesis of words.

For the child who lacks ability in auditory blending, any sounding out of words should be done in a smooth rather than interrupted fashion. He should have much experience in blending two-syllable words, and he should have oral blending training. The teacher could pronounce words with the syllables only slightly separated, and the child could say the parts and blend. It would be best to start with two-syllable words and gradually build up to longer words. Then single syllable words could be separated and blended. For children with difficulty in blending, because they have learned to separate the words so distinctly that they are unable to synthesize them, there should be more exercises for developing sight vocabulary, for associating meanings with words, and for using context clues. Children with this type of difficulty should also read a lot of relatively easy material.

CASE STUDY OF AN UPPER ELEMENTARY GRADE STUDENT WITH DIFFICULTY IN WORD RECOGNITION

When Andy was referred to the Psycho-Educational Clinic for study, he was an attractive boy from a fourth-grade classroom. He was large for a boy ten years and six months of age. His teacher was concerned about Andy's reading progress. She described his discussions in class and his expression of his ideas as very good. In certain class activities he was an eager participant, while in others he tended to withdraw. His teacher was well-aware that there was a relationship between Andy's tendency to lose interest in an activity and the amount of reading involved in it. She also noticed that he had to gather most of his information from class discussions, but once he had sufficient information, his reasoning and judgment about what he had just learned were mature. She had watched the difficulties he experienced whenever he was asked to read aloud. She knew that Andy was a disabled reader.

From an examination of Andy's cumulative records and recent test scores, his teacher had made the general diagnosis that his reading disability called for more detailed study. These records showed that Andy had a reading score of 2.5. His arithmetic grade score was 3.5 for problem solving and 5.2 for computation. His score on a group intelligence test indicated that he had an I.Q. of 98. His previous school records showed that Andy had repeated the third grade and that during the second year in that grade, less reading growth took place than in the previous year.

Andy's teacher did not think that the 98 I.Q. represented his true intelligence, even though it was in keeping with the level of his general school achievement. She based this judgment on the quality of his discussions of a topic he knew something about and on his score in the computation section of the arithmetic test. She had also noticed that when problems were read to him, his arithmetical reasoning seemed competent. From all of this information, she felt that a thorough study of Andy's educational problem was required.

At the clinic, a more specific diagnosis was made, as the first step in studying Andy's problem. This phase of the diagnosis consisted of giving the *Wechsler Intelligence Scale for Children, Revised* and the *Stanford Diagnostic Reading Test, Green Level*. The intelligence test indicated that Andy had a Full Scale I.Q. of 124; a Verbal I.Q. of 126 and a Performance I.Q. of 123 and that he should be expected to read at $(4.2 \times 1.24) + 1.0$, or at about the sixth-grade level. (The grade expectancy was computed by the formula explained in Chapter 3.) A comparison between the scores obtained thus far showed that Andy was a bright boy who should be reading at about the sixth-grade level of difficulty. His arithmetic scores of 3.5 for problem solving (written problems) and 5.2 for computation (no reading involved) showed that he was doing reasonably well in an area not directly related to reading. The *Stanford Diagnostic Reading Test, Green Level (Fall Norms)* scores showed the following:

Auditory Vocabulary	5.8
Auditory Discrimination	3.6
Phonetic Analysis	3.2
Structural Analysis	1.3
Reading Comprehension	
Literal	2.7
Inferential	2.5
Total Reading Comprehension	2.5
TOTAL READING	2.7

Andy's average reading achievement of only 2.7 showed that he was seriously disabled in reading. His auditory abilities and skill in phonetic analysis appeared to be strengths in comparison to his ability to recognize words and to answer literal and inferential questions about passages he read. His skill in structural analysis seemed to be a major weakness. The pattern of scores in the areas of reading measured, indicated that his problem was a basic one. A study of the comprehension subtest revealed accurate performance on the items he attempted, but such slow speed that he completed only about two-thirds of the test, even though the time limits are ample for the ordinary child.

Andy was also tested using an informal reading inventory constructed by the reading specialist. It was found that he could comfortably read material no higher than beginning second-grade level, and that he was frustrated by material beyond halfway through the second-grade level. An analysis of his errors revealed that when he was asked to read material that was difficult for him, he started to leave out words and his frequency of errors increased as he continued to read. Although his use of context appeared to be adequate when he read easy material, when reading became difficult for him, he started to leave out words and his frequency of errors increased as he continued to read. Although his use of context appeared to be adequate when he read easy material, when reading became difficult for him, he was not able to use context effectively to predict words, to correct errors, or to anticipate sentence structure. Andy tended to make errors involving word beginnings. Although his knowledge of letter sound associations appeared to be good, he had difficulty identifying larger word parts such as phonograms, syllables, prefixes, and suffixes. When large word parts were isolated for him, he had difficulty pronouncing them. He read slowly both silently and orally.

It was felt, from the information thus far obtained, that Andy should be classified as a child with a *limiting disability in reading* and that his area of difficulty was in word recognition. A thorough case study was made.

We must now answer the questions raised in Chapter 7.

1. Is Andy correctly classified as a disabled reader? The case study showed that he was indeed a disabled reader, and that there was no indication of any physical, mental, or neurological condition to alter his classification to anything other than disability in reading. Even when Andy was tense and nonfluent when reading aloud, there was no evidence of any basic emotional problem. There seemed, however, to be an emotional involvement with respect to his reading and some accompanying avoidance of reading activities.

2. What is the training needed? This is the essential question in reeducating a child who has been classified correctly as a disabled reader. Andy's performance on the *Stanford Diagnostic Reading Test* and on the informal reading inventory showed his pattern of reading limitations. He could not be expected to become a good reader until his basic word-recognition problems were corrected. Andy's pattern of responses suggested that the remedial emphasis should be placed on:

   a. Word recognition skills: (1) attention to word beginnings, (2) visual analysis of large word parts, and (3) recognition of large word parts.
   b. Use of context: (1) to predict words, (2) to correct errors, and (3) to anticipate sentence structure.
   c. Reading fluency.

Parts of the *Gates-McKillop-Horowitz Reading Diagnostic Tests* were also given to Andy. A study of the tabulated results of his responses indicated that this test verified some of the conclusions obtained from previous testing. Specifically, Andy made a disproportionate number of errors in the beginnings of words, his knowledge of large word parts was inadequate for his general reading level, and he was ineffective in the use of context as an aid to word recognition. It added the information that Andy had a relatively good sight vocabulary compared to his overall functioning in reading, and also that when he was given more time to study words his performance deteriorated.

3. Who can give most effective remedial work? From recommendations made after the diagnosis was completed, it was decided that Andy could be remediated best in the school reading center, since his limiting disability needed only focused instruction and minor emotional support.

4. How can improvement be made most efficiently? Andy was given remedial work in the school reading center for an hour each day in material at the

beginning second-grade level of difficulty. Exercises and activities designed to improve visual awareness of beginning elements, analysis and recognition of large word parts, and use of context were emphasized. Games, word wheels, and computer programs suitable for practicing these skills were also used for review and because Andy enjoyed them. Short selections were used for practice in rapid reading.

5. Does the child have any limiting conditions that must be considered? Andy had no visual or hearing difficulties, and no other limiting condition was identified.

6. Are there any environmental conditions that might interfere with progress in reading? Andy's parents were very concerned about his reading, as well they might be. His mother had tried to help him at home, but didn't feel that he was making any progress, and so she discontinued working with him. His mother thought there was something wrong with Andy's memory, because the words they worked on one day were forgotten the next. She was eager to cooperate and accepted the suggestion of helping him by showing approval of his reading, discussing it with him in a relaxed manner, and telling him words he didn't know. The technical teaching was left to the reading specialist.

Andy's classroom teacher was also informed of the results of his reading assessment. She already knew that he was a slow reader and an ineffective one. She was interested in the findings of the complete diagnosis and was pleased to make adjustments to his level of reading in the regular classroom.

At the end of six months of instruction in the reading center, Andy was measured again. His reading achievement, as tested by the *Stanford Diagnostic Reading Test, Green Level (Spring Norms),* showed gratifying results.

Auditory Vocabulary	5.9
Auditory Discrimination	3.9
Phonetic Analysis	4.5
Structural Analysis	3.6
Reading Comprehension	
Literal	3.8
Inferential	3.5
Total Reading Comprehension	3.3
TOTAL READING	4.6

Andy continued to work in the reading center for the remainder of his fourth-grade year. At the beginning of his fifth-grade year he discontinued work in the reading center. He was still disabled in reading, but he had overcome much of his basic difficulty. His cooperative fifth-grade classroom teacher was able to give him the additional instruction and experience he needed.

SUMMARY

Word recognition is difficult and complex to learn. It requires a highly integrated and flexible set of skills and abilities. To avoid some of the more serious types of word-recognition difficulties, well-organized instruction must be given at all levels.

The child must be started by teaching him the habit of trying to recognize words as words. Early training includes the use of context clues, picture clues, and teacher's questions. Then the child is taught to note similarities in initial elements and gradually to acquire the whole hierarchy of word-recognition techniques. These skills and knowledges fall roughly into five types: (1) ability to recognize many words at sight and to associate meanings with printed symbols; (2) skill in using context clues and other meaning aids to anticipate the words to be recognized and to check on their accuracy; (3) skill in using flexible and efficient perceptual techniques in visually analyzing words into usable recognition elements; (4) knowledge of a wide variety of visual, structural, and phonic elements; (5) skill in both auditory blending and visual synthesis of word parts into word entities.

The major sources of difficulty in word recognition involve failure to establish these basic learnings and failure to maintain a balance among them. The best method for correcting difficulties in word recognition is to have the disabled reader develop these skills and knowledges in the course of reading meaningful material in a reading program. The remedial teacher should take great care in the methods she uses to introduce new words, so that the child's strengths can be utilized and any limitations in recognition can be corrected while the proper balances are maintained. Exercises stressing the skills needed by the child should be emphasized.

Workbook exercises that accompany basic readers are one source of materials for developing word-recognition skills and knowledges. Besides these, the remedial teacher needs to use supplementary exercises. Various types of exercises helpful in correcting limitations in word recognition have been described in this chapter. They should be used with caution and be recognized as drill devices rather than as a complete solution to the disabled reader's word-recognition problems. The disabled reader needs more than the usual amount of practice in those areas in which he has failed to learn sufficiently to maintain a balance among the word-recognition skills.

STUDY QUESTIONS

1. What is visual analysis? Why does it precede the application of knowledge of word parts? How can a teacher identify faulty visual analysis using informal techniques?

2. What is the danger of informal analysis compared with standardized test analysis of locational errors? Why is it more difficult to construct useful exercises for ending errors than for beginning errors?

3. How can overanalytical readers who tend to analyze words they already know and those who tend to analyze unknown words into too many parts be helped?

4. When should drill be used to enhance knowledge of word elements? Why must exercises designed to increase knowledge of visual, structural, and phonic elements be put in contextual settings?

5. What diagnostic judgments should be made when a child appears to have unusual difficulty synthesizing words?

SELECTED READINGS

EKWALL, E. E. *Teacher's Handbook on Diagnosis and Remediation in Reading,* 2nd ed., Chaps. 4 and 5. Boston: Allyn & Bacon, Inc., 1986.

McCORMICK, S. *Remedial and Clinical Reading Instruction,* Chap. 13. Columbus, OH: Charles E. Merrill Publishing Company, 1987.

RUPLEY, W. H., AND T. R. BLAIR. *Reading Diagnosis and Remediation: Classroom and Clinic,* 2nd ed., Chap. 9. Boston: Houghton Mifflin Company, 1983.

SPACHE, G. D. *Diagnosing and Correcting Reading Disabilities,* Chap. 8. Boston: Allyn & Bacon, Inc., 1976.

WILSON, R. M. AND C. J. CLELAND. *Diagnostic and Remedial Reading for Classroom and Clinic,* 5th ed., Chap. 8. Columbus, OH: Charles E. Merrill Publishing Company, 1985.

12

Treating the Extremely Disabled Reader

Reading disability varies in degree. Some disabled readers have learned practically nothing; others read poorly, but at a level barely below what is reasonable to expect of them based on their reading expectancy. Disability in reading between these extremes can be graded in very small steps. Extreme disability cases, sometimes called nonreaders, dyslexics, or symbol association dysfunction cases are simply at the low end of the range. They are the most stubborn cases of disability, who have failed to learn even after fairly extended instruction. They are not all alike. Extremely disabled readers differ in backgrounds, attitudes, perceptual competencies, special difficulties, and other respects. It is necessary to recognize individual differences among extremely disabled readers in organizing effective remedial instruction. No single method or formula of remediation can possibly work for all extremely disabled readers.

METHODS OF TREATMENT

Teaching skill is very important for helping these extreme cases. Besides understanding the reading process, the teacher should be familiar with a variety of diagnostic and remedial procedures. She must be versatile in adapting these both to accurate diagnosis of difficulties and to planning appropriate instruction for each particular case. Patience, sympathetic understanding of the pupil's difficulties, and skillful guidance and encouragement throughout the instructional program are important for aiding these extreme cases.

Certain methods of remedial instruction have been notably successful in teaching extremely disabled readers to read. Three of these general approaches are outlined briefly in the following sections.

Kinesthetic-Auditory Visual Emphasis Methods

The Fernald method, described in detail by Fernald (1971), was originally designed for and used successfully with extremely disabled readers. The features of the technique are to teach the child to write words correctly, to motivate him to do this, to have him read the printed copy of what he has written, and to move on eventually to extensive reading of materials other than his own. The program consists of four stages which are modified and summarized here.

Stage 1: The child learns by tracing words. The essence of this first stage is to have the child learn words through finger tracing of written copy while pronouncing each part of the word. This is repeated until the child *can write the word without looking at the copy.* Clinical experience shows it is best if the words are written in large letters. They may be written for the child with crayon on paper or with chalk on the chalkboard. Some teachers even have the child trace in the air with his eyes closed after having traced on paper or chalkboard. Cursive writing is preferred, but many teachers feel that it is best to use manuscript writing with young children. Words learned through tracing may be used in stories a child wishes to write and may be filed according to alphabetical order. Points stressed in this first stage are that finger contact is important in tracing, pronunciation must coincide with tracing, words must be written without looking at the copy, words should always be written as units, and words should always be used in context. This means that the child must use the words in meaningful groups in sentences.

Duration of tracing period. The length of the tracing period varies greatly from child to child depending on individual need for tracing to retain the word. Usually the tracing period continues for about one or two months.

Material used. In the Fernald method, materials are not simplified in either vocabulary or subject matter. Any word or sentence the child is capable of using properly in oral language can be learned so that it can be written and read. Clinical experience shows that when children learn using tracing methods, longer words are often retained better than are shorter ones.

Stage 2. This is similar to stage 1 except that the child no longer needs to trace. Rather, he is able to learn a new word by looking at it, saying to himself as he looks at it, and then writing it without looking at the copy. With multisyllabic words he says each part of the word as he writes it, stressing the syllables. Using new words for writing activities and filing them is continued. In all activities, pronouncing words as whole, unbroken units is emphasized.

Stage 3.   This stage dispenses with the use of specially prepared copy. The child now learns directly from standard printed words. He must still look at a printed word, say it to himself, and then write it. He may read from ordinary books, with the teacher telling him words he does not know. Upon the conclusion of reading, the aided words are learned by the child, following the look-say-write method described previously. Many teachers choose to select the books children read in this stage so as to minimize the number of unknown words a child will encounter.

Stage 4.   The child is able to recognize some new words from their resemblance to words or word parts he remembers and on the basis of context clues. As in the previous stage, the teacher tells the child all words he cannot recognize. Difficult words are looked at, said, and then written from memory. Retention of words learned in this way is reported to be 80% to 95%.

During remedial instruction the child is not required to sound out any word when he is reading, nor is any word sounded out for him by the teacher. Nevertheless children taught by this method do acquire phonics skills through the tracing-sounding and writing-sounding training. Although Fernald's children were weak in phonics at the beginning of instruction and were given no formal training in phonics, they were able at the end of instruction to pass phonics tests at their age level. For a much more complete description of the Fernald method, consult Fernald (1971, Chapter 5).

Many teachers have reported great success in having children trace troublesome words in the air with their eyes closed while pronouncing the words. This modification emphasizes kinesthetic and auditory clues to word recognition while reducing the role of vision. For some children with severe visual-perceptual problems, tracing in the air with closed eyes seems to enable them to acquire an organized percept of the word which eludes them when vision is involved.

When teaching a group of children, a kinesthetic-auditory-visual emphasis can be achieved to some extent by inviting the children to listen carefully to the word pronounced, to look carefully at the word in print, to softly say the word, and to write the word.

Evaluation.   When used by experienced clinicians, the Fernald method is undoubtedly successful. In the early stages it tends to be time-consuming. In an extreme case, the tracing may continue for eight months, although the average is only two months. But other methods also require long periods of instruction when dealing with extreme disabilities. So the time factor can hardly be termed a drawback. When the instruction is given properly, the pupils can be as well-motivated as by any other method.

It is worthwhile inquiring into why this method is successful. Fernald considers the *kinesthesis,* coupled with enthusiastic and efficient teaching, the key to its success. It should be noted that in addition to kinesthesis, other important features are included in proper teaching of the method: (1) The child learns effectively the left-to-right sequences of perception by his simultaneous tracing-sounding and writing-sounding of words. (2) The visual structure of the word is associated with sounding the pronounceable units of the word. (3) Skill in phonics is learned without being taught formally. As part of this sounding, the child learns what is equivalent to consonant substitution in recognition of new words. After recognizing a familiar element in a word, the child attaches the proper beginning or ending sound. Meanings supplied by the verbal context are used to choose the proper ending or beginning to recognize the new word. In the sentence "Mary *took* the kitten home," the element *ook* may be associated with or recognized as part of the familiar word *book* or *look.* The context then helps to give the proper word *took.* Also through tracing-writing-sounding, many initial and final elements become familiar to the child so that he makes the substitution readily. (4) The very nature of the program leads to skill in syllabication. The Fernald method teaches left-to-right direction of word perception, the visual form of words, skill in phonics (including syllabication and the equivalent of consonant substitution), and use of context clues for identification and recognition of words. (5) Added to all this is the fact that the child is strongly motivated by working with materials interesting to him. Although the kinesthetic aspects of this method may be very important for certain visually handicapped and neurologically impaired children, and for certain children with visual-perceptual or visual-processing difficulties, it should be noted that the emphasis on left-to-right perception, visual structure of words, skill in phonics, skill in syllabication, and use of context are inherent to the method when properly taught. It is doubtful that kinesthesis alone is responsible for the success of the method, but rather kinesthesis in combination with a sound, well-balanced program for teaching word perception in remedial instruction. Besides word recognition, the Fernald method stresses vocabulary and concept development and comprehension.

Auditory (Sound-Blending)-Emphasis Methods

A strong phonics approach has been incorporated into a number of remedial procedures. Comprehensive programs which have been successful in teaching excessively disabled readers are those developed by Monroe (1932) and by Gillingham and Stillman (1960). To use any phonics-based remedial approach, it is imperative that the teacher be familiar with the details of the program. Teachers using these approaches should be familiar with *Children Who Cannot Read* by Monroe or *Remedial Training for Children with Specific Disability in Reading, Spelling, and Penmanship* by Gillingham and Stillman.

Successful phonics-based techniques emphasize patient, repetitive, drill work, but include sufficient variety to retain the learner's interest without sacrificing the fundamental purposes of the drill. Such remedial programs must be prescribed by the teacher for each reading-disabled child. Known phonics elements should be passed over very lightly and unknown elements should receive heavy emphasis in order to ensure maximum benefit to each child.

Monroe's method.   In extreme cases, faulty vowels and consonants are major sources of difficulty. Although exact remedial needs differ from child to child, many who are severely disabled need instruction in discriminating specific speech sounds, in associating visual symbols with letter sounds, and in coordinating the temporal sequence of sounds with the left-to-right sequence of letters in a word.

One of the first steps is to strengthen the ability to discriminate speech sounds. Pictures of several objects beginning with the same consonant, or containing the same vowel, are mounted on cards. The pictures may be obtained from magazines or old books. Examples of typical initial consonants used are

> *b* as in boy, book   *m* as in man, moon
> *c* as in coat, cat   *t* as in tiger, table, etc.

As far as possible, words which contain a vowel immediately after the initial consonant are chosen for this early drill. Single consonant sounds are learned more readily than consonant blends. Thus the *s* sound is learned more easily in *seed* than in *store*.

Cards with pictures are arranged similarly for the vowels, such as

> *a* as in man, cat   *o* as in box, top
> *e* as in pen, hen   *i* as in fire, kite, etc.

To develop discrimination, the instruction is started with unlike sounds, as *m* compared with *s*. The cards for *m* and *s* are arranged in a row in mixed order.

> men   soap   moon   seed

The child is instructed to sound the *m* and then name the object in the picture. After he succeeds with unlike sounds, the more difficult discriminations are taught, as *s* and *sh* in *seed* and *shell*. These drills are varied by asking the child to give words beginning with a certain sound. A similar procedure is followed in the drills on vowels.

The next step is associating the letters with their most frequent sounds. Tracing is introduced as a reinforcement when necessary. The child traces a letter written by the teacher. He sounds it as he traces. This is repeated until he can look at the letter and sound it correctly without tracing. Ordinarily, five or six consonant sounds can be learned at one sitting. After learning several consonant and vowel sounds, the child is taught blending letter sounds into words. The sounding-tracing method is an important aid in this. The sounding becomes a slow distinct articulation of the word as a unit while being traced. Recall is tested by presenting the words printed on cards. With this the child is encouraged to articulate the separate letter sounds and blend them. The phonics skills the child acquires give him a feeling of mastery in word recognition.

The child next progresses to reading specially prepared phonetic stories. He is soon able to handle stories in ordinary primers and first readers. Nonphonetic words are learned by tracing-sounding. As the child gains in vocabulary and reading ability, the nonphonetic words are identified from context.

Monroe found it necessary to give the child a definite motor cue to the correct direction for left-to-right sequence in perceiving words. This is accomplished by tracing-sounding similar to that practiced by Fernald.

Failure to discriminate consonant blends and failure to discriminate word forms accurately frequently leads to adding sounds. The sounds more frequently added are *r* and *l*. When this tendency persists, drills are given on lists of words which are alike except for th presence of *r* or *l*. Examples include *fog* and *frog, pan* and *plan*.

Errors of omission, addition, substitution, or repetition are usually the result of the lack of accurate word recognition or overemphasis on speed. Reading aloud by the teacher and child together helps, as does more emphasis on developing better word-analysis skills and going back to easier reading materials. If any of these errors remain, the teacher should call them to the attention of the disabled reader so that he may try to avoid them. A tape recorder can be useful as a check on accuracy. Emphasis on context clues is also helpful.

The Gillingham-Stillman Method.   Another phonics approach, advanced by Gillingham and Stillman, has been widely used with children experiencing serious reading difficulties. In contrast to methods generally advocated in this text, which deal with letters and sounds found in words, the Gillingham-Stillman method teaches the sounds of the letters and then builds these letters into words. Letter-sound correspondence is established by forming close associations between visual, auditory, and kinesthetic elements.

First the child is taught the name of each letter. This is done by showing a letter card and teaching the child to say the name. Second, sounds are taught. If the child's production of sounds is faulty, the teacher produces the sound and the child imitates it. Such drill is given only when needed and for no longer than necessary.

Third, a practice drill is given. The teacher says the names of various letters and the child responds with the related sound he has learned. Fourth, practice is given as necessary in tracing, copying, and writing from memory to dictation. In all instances the child says the name of each letter as he writes it.

The procedure progresses through the teaching of letters, elements, and syllables, to work with words. Lessons are highly structured, and reading, spelling, and handwriting are all taught in a unified program. Special materials with a high degree of phonics consistency are employed. The student learning by this method is required to do no reading or spelling except with the remedial teacher.

Evaluation. Both auditory-emphasis methods are definite, rigid, drill programs requiring much time. They progress from letter sounds to words in sentences. Both methods use kinesthesis as an aid to associating letters with their sounds. They delay reading of words longer than the Fernald method. However, the teaching of reading to extremely disabled readers takes time whatever the method used. When successful, the Monroe technique enables the child to use reading skills in a variety of ordinary reading materials more quickly than does the Gillingham-Stillman method, which stresses keeping the child in a restricted set of reading materials during his training. The view taken in this book is that although these techniques are necessary for some severely retarded readers, generally other methods achieve quicker results. The Gillingham-Stillman method in particular is exceptionally rigid and restrictive and is only recommended for the most severe cases of reading disability who have failed to establish fundamental phonics knowledge.

Visual-Structural Emphasis Methods

These approaches are similar to those used in good classroom teaching, but they consist of an enriched program. The approach to word study emphasizes visual-structural inspection and widely uses work sheet exercises. The child is encouraged to recognize words as entities, and in word study, to inspect the word carefully part by part from left to right. At the same time, the child notes similarities and differences, including minimal differences in words, with early emphasis on word beginnings and then on the overall structure of the words. In this way, the child establishes a knowledge of word elements in the actual process of contextual reading. Knowledge of phonic, structural, and phonemic elements is not neglected, but is taught so closely with actual reading that the transfer of the skills into total word-recognition capabilities is accomplished. When successful, this method helps to make fluent, thoughtful readers. It is true that some children need more diversified programs, with added intensive drill on the word elements themselves.

Remedial instruction for extremely disabled readers is like that for normal pupils except that the program of instruction is managed more carefully. Its adjustment to individual needs and individual instruction is emphasized. The teacher has to spend more time and exercise more care in demonstrating and explaining the techniques. Additional explanations and suggestions are given as needed. She is careful that the pupil moves ahead at the proper pace. When a method does not appear to help, the teacher shifts to some other form of help.

If the more individualized teaching of the commonly used procedures is not successful, the teacher may resort to some of the techniques ordinarily used only with severely disabled readers. First, the customary methods of observing words, using context clues, visual and auditory analysis, and development of appropriate left-to-right orientation in word perception are given a fair trial. If the child's responses then reveal inadequate progress in learning to read, the teacher may resort to tracing and writing techniques. Even in this case, the tracing and writing is not continued for weeks and months. It is used merely as a means of getting the child started, so he will consistently maintain the left-to-right progression in reading words. Once the child has begun to make headway in the tracing-writing technique, he should be shifted back to a program that covers the full range of reading activities for a normal reader.

Evaluation. Visual-structural emphasis methods have certain advantages. (1) They tend to be flexible. Provisions are made for shifting temporarily to more specialized techniques when needed, such as tracing-writing approaches or phonic drills. (2) Many, but not all, severely disabled readers achieve overall reading improvement sooner with visual-structural methods than with the more specialized techniques. (3) Often it is desirable to start the severely disabled reader with a visual-structural program. If after a fair trial, progress is not satisfactory, the teacher can turn to one of the other techniques. Tracing-writing approaches seem to benefit most the child who has difficulty forming an organized percept of whole words, and auditory (sound-blending) methods seem to help most the child who is notably stronger in auditory than in other learning abilities. After some progress is made with highly specialized, fixed procedures, a gradual transition can be made toward the broader and less mechanical instruction used with typical readers.

General statement. Almost any competent remedial teacher can teach many of her extremely disabled children to read by use of any one of the methods discussed here. To be really expert, the teacher should be able to use each of the methods effectively and, after a thorough analysis of a child's reading needs, apply the method most suitable in that particular case. There is no single, "sure-fire" method for teaching every extremely disabled reader; the same is true for less extreme cases.

Probably the reason for the success of highly specialized methods used with extremely disabled readers is that a high percentage of the most seriously disabled readers have basic problems with word-recognition, which is the aspect of reading these methods stress. It should be also noted that although these methods are successful in general, they can prove very detrimental to a specific individual. In the opinion of the authors of this book, the best approach to extreme reading disability appears to lie in making an exact diagnosis and then applying the indicated remedial work, which in some instances might well be a tracing-writing or a phonics drill program. In most cases, however, a more balanced approach, such as described in Chapters 10 and 11 should be used.

TREATING ORIENTATIONAL DIFFICULTIES

Word-orientation confusions are among the most troublesome errors made by extremely disabled readers. The problems of full reversals, part reversals, axial rotations of letters, and other orientational confusions in word recognition interfere with successful reading development. Any child who makes an extreme number of such errors has a limiting condition which must be corrected before continued growth in reading can be expected.

The term "reversals" is used to describe different kinds of errors in orientation. These errors are in observing letters in reverse orientation, as *d* for *b* when reading *dig* for *big*, or perceiving letters in reverse order or partial reverse order. Examples of complete reversals are reading *saw* for *was*, or *no* for *on*. Partial reversals are illustrated by reading *own* for *now*, or *ate* for *tea*. Also there may be reversals of the order of words in a sentence, as "The rat caught a cat" for "The cat caught a rat."

During the preschool years, the child has learned to recognize people, landscapes, animals, and objects, both from firsthand visual experience and from viewing pictures and diagrams. In all this, the direction of the perceptual sequences, as revealed by eye movements, is neither orderly nor oriented to a specific direction. Rather, they are a series of brief glances while the eyes move in an irregular pattern of fixations over the object or picture. The direction of the movements is just as likely to be from right to left as left to right, or upward as downward, or obliquely in any direction. As the child looks over an object, noting points of interest or searching for familiar items, the direction of the eye movements is not only irregular but also unpredictable to a large degree. These habits of perception are established before entering school. Unless systematic instruction is given by the time the child begins to read words and sentences, he is likely to continue the habit of examining objects with irregular directional sequences in viewing words. To be efficient, the child must read words in a sentence, one after another from left to right. Unless a word is recognized at a glance, he must proceed along the word from left to right to identify it correctly.

Development of proper directional habits in reading requires two related instructional tasks. The first is acquisition of the left-to-right sequence of eye movements along a line of print. This is a somewhat gross orientation which nonetheless must be learned. The second task is establishment of the left-to-right direction of attack required for proficient word identification and recognition. This is a more precise and difficult skill. Contrary to one's first impression, these two aspects of sequential orientation in reading are related only roughly. It is true that both involve beginning at the left and progressing toward the right. But a child may have learned to begin at the left end of a line of print and, in general, move his eyes toward the right without having mastered proper directional orientation within particular words. Extensive and continuing training is needed for the latter.

Word Perception

As noted in the preceding section, the wrong orientation in perceiving words results in reversal errors. Both diagnosis and remedial instruction for reversals are necessarily more elaborate than for directional habits in reading lines of print. The most satisfactory diagnosis of reversal tendencies is obtained through the use of standardized tests such as the Gates-McKillop-Horowitz described in Chapter 8.

It has already been noted that it is normal for beginners to make some reversals and that these are gradually eliminated by most children as they progress in reading. For each pupil with a reading problem, therefore, it must be seen whether reversals are common enough to cause trouble rather than being merely occasional incidents in ordinarily adequate reading. In other words, it is necessary to decide whether the frequency of reversals is merely a sign of immature reading or is a genuine reading handicap.

As soon as children begin to read words and lines of print, proper directional orientation must be stressed. Effective reading is achieved only when perceptual sequences, largely guided by eye movements, move from left to right. Except for sight words, those which are recognized at a glance, the children must be instructed to examine a word from left to right in working out its recognition. It is necessary for the teacher to demonstrate repeatedly the proper directional orientation in perceiving words. She should be sure, before using these terms, that all pupils have learned through preliminary and partly incidental training, the meaning of left and right.

The left-to-right habit is by no means confined to beginning instruction in reading. The training is continued, more or less, throughout instruction for development of the word-recognition techniques. Such training is constructive only when done correctly and systematically. Working out word identification through attention to initial consonants, consonant substitution, phonetic analysis, structural analysis, syllabication, and use of the dictionary requires constant attention to left-to-right orientation. Many pupils with proper directional habits in the early stages of reading drop the habit at later stages unless additional instruction is given.

Remedial Procedures

In general, significant degrees of reversing the order of letters in words occur more frequently among the more severely retarded readers (deHirsh, Jansky and Langford, 1966). This is not surprising when one refers back to the causes of reversals in word perception discussed previously. The child who has severe eye defects, who has received inadequate training in left-to-right orientation, who has been taught to emphasize word endings rather than beginnings, or who has been exposed to an improper program of phonics training, not only develops reversals but also seldom progresses far in learning to read. Any analysis of the methods successfully used to instruct nonreaders or severely retarded readers reveals that much emphasis is given to orderly, left-to-right inspection of words, with stress on developing an adequate apprehension of words as entities and with instruction in the proper blending of letter sounds into word units.

The remedial teacher must not assume that correction of reversal tendencies is the entire instruction program for any reversal case. Ordinarily other difficulties are present and must be remedied. But when reversals exist in significant numbers, as is found in about ten percent of disability cases, they are very important and require carefully organized and sometimes prolonged treatment.

At first, the teacher explains the necessity of viewing words from left to right. She accompanies this explanation with a demonstration. After writing a word on the chalkboard or on paper, she moves a pointer or her finger along the word as she pronounces it slowly. To emphasize the procedure when a restudy is needed, she then quickly moves her finger back to the very beginning of the word and progresses to the right again as she reads it a second time. This time, the teacher should stress the desirability of grasping the word as a unit after the difficult part is worked out. Next, the method of recognizing an unfamiliar word found in the context of a sentence is explained and demonstrated in a similar manner. The finger underlines the words as they are read. After a slight pause on reaching the unfamiliar word, the teacher moves her finger slowly along the word, pronouncing it as she did with the isolated word. The explanations and demonstrations are repeated as often as necessary while the pupil is practicing the left-to-right orientation in perceiving words. It is desirable for the pupil to practice with words in sentence context as soon as possible so that he may use context clues as much as possible in word recognition. In practicing sentences he will become accustomed to using the left-to-right progression along lines of print and to identifying unknown words in actual reading situations. Guided practice is transferred to sentences and paragraphs in book materials as soon as possible. It is important for the teacher to make sure that skill in proper perceptual orientation in reading isolated words and words in isolated sentences does transfer to book reading. For some children, this transfer is difficult and they need much directed practice.

Although a child may be encouraged at first to use his finger or a manila marker to guide his perception along the lines of print and along the successive letters in an unknown word, certain precautions are necessary. This is definitely a crutch and should gradually be eliminated when no longer needed. Some teachers feel that use of a marker is better because it is easier to eliminate than is finger pointing. Whether the child uses his finger or a marker, the teacher should instruct the pupil so that the perceptual aid is used properly, that is, the child should not point at one word after another with stops, but should use a consistent and *continuous* sliding movement from left to right to guide sequences of perception. Otherwise the finger or marker may be used only to keep the place rather than to promote left-to-right progression. It accomplishes nothing if the finger or marker is moved forward and backward along a line or a word, or if it is held in one place while the reader examines a word in random order. Using the finger or marker as a pointer produces proper directional movements in reading and corrects reversal tendencies only when carefully supervised by the teacher.

Other Motor Aids

Use of the tracing-sounding-writing approach, described in detail earlier in this chapter, is one of the most useful procedures with persistent reversal cases. A modification of phonics emphasis and sounding-tracing is also effective. The procedure is illustrated by the following example. The word *man* is written in large, cursive writing on a piece of paper. Attention is directed to the word and its pronunciation. The child is asked to say *man* as slowly as possible, as demonstrated by the teacher. He then traces over the word while saying *man* slowly. He is encouraged to trace quickly and speak slowly, so as to come out even. The aim of this is to pronounce the word distinctly and slowly enough that its sequence of sounds becomes evident. Further training teaches the knack of sliding the voice from one sound to the next so that the word is pronounced as a unit.

A sound-dictation method has been substituted as a variation of the tracing method. Here the child writes the words as the teacher dictates their sounds slowly, first having told the child he would hear the separate sounds and having asked him to say them slowly as he writes the letters for each sound. Thus she pronounces *man,* first having asked the child both to say and to write whatever word she says. For *man,* the child is told that the *a* is short by hearing the teacher sound it that way. In this method, the child must have learned the letters that correspond to the letter sounds and know how to write them. Children with second- and third-grade achievement usually do well on such drills. According to Monroe (1935) writing from dictation with these directions is as helpful as tracing, and some children prefer to write. Both the tracing-sounding and the writing-sounding techniques encourage discrimination of sound sequences in words and the coordination of these with visual sequences.

Writing words.   Many children with reversal problems have already had some experience in writing. The remedial teacher can make good use of writing to promote correct orientation in dealing with words. When writing, it is necessary to begin at the left and move to the right. So when it is used to develop left-to-right orientation, it should be free writing rather than copying material from a chalkboard, a chart, or a book. The latter tends to become a piecemeal operation rather than a continuous sequence. The training can be started with simple words and sentences. Some polysyllabic words should be used as soon as the child can handle them. He should be encouraged to observe and pronounce aloud to himself each word as he writes it. This calls attention to the sequence of the word elements needed for correct perception. To become effective in correcting reversals, the child must observe the correct order of letters and letter sounds in the words he is writing. Whether the writing used is cursive or manuscript, the same precautions should be given to the child.

If there is any tendency to use mirror writing, which can occur in writing from right to left, it will immediately be obvious. Ordinarily, this reverse writing can be corrected by explaining to the child the need to move from left to right and by having him start writing words at the extreme left of the paper or chalkboard. He will then move readily in the only direction possible, which is to the right. In extreme cases, the child may be told when writing sentences to write the separate words underneath each other, each word starting at the left margin of the paper. Or the teacher may make a short vertical line at which the first letter of each succeeding word in a sentence is to begin. This special procedure can be eliminated after some practice.

Typing.   Typing has been suggested as a technique for developing correct orientation in word perception. Presumably, the child is forced to observe the proper sequence of letters in words as he types them. It is true that he will get some practice in noting the beginning of words on the copy as he types the first letter, then the second, then the third, and so on through the word. But if he is just learning to type, he is merely typing series of letters that happen to be in groups. He will be so engrossed in selecting and pressing each key that he is unable to use the correct techniques of word perception either on the copy or in what he types. Studies of typewriting reveal that words are typed as units only after a typist becomes fairly skilled. This certainly would not be the case with most young children. Furthermore, if it is beginning typing, there likely is little understanding of what is being typed. The beginner's attention is devoted to the mechanics of typing letters, not to word units and meanings. Moreover, it is possible to type words and not recognize them. Left-to-right progression along a word must be combined with identification of the word in order to be effective in developing correct orientation in word perception. The teacher will find it very difficult to teach proper orientation for word perception through typing. Other methods are better and less cumbersome.

Other Procedures

There are several other procedures for teaching the correct directional orientation in perceiving words. Of primary concern is developing the habit of initial attention to beginnings of words. Familiarity with and proper *use of initial consonants and consonant blends* as explained in the previous chapter are extremely important. Many children with reversal problems do not have this knowledge. While deficiencies in knowledge of initial consonants are being remedied, there are a variety of exercises for teaching the child to notice word beginnings first of all. The following are examples.

1. To direct attention to the initial sound of words and at the same time ensure that the whole word is read, sentences are arranged with one word missing. The child is instructed to read each sentence, to notice the beginning sound that is underlined in one word of the sentences, and then to draw a circle around the word below the sentence that begins with the same sound and makes sense in the sentence. To choose correctly, the child must note both the beginning sound and the meaning of the right word.

John <u>w</u>et his feet in the _____.

wall   lake   water

<u>M</u>ary's kitten likes to drink _____.

milk   make   cream

2. Training in consonant substitution may be used to teach the child to notice word beginnings. Two samples are given next.

a. For contextual meaning, first show the child a sentence such as, "He came to see the new game." Ask him to read the sentence and find two words that look alike except for the first letter. Pronounce *came* and have the child point to the letter that stands for the first sound. Do the same for *game*. Then write the letters *t, s, n, g, c,* and have him give the sounds of the letters. Then write the word *came*. After the beginning letter is located correctly, erase *c* and substitute *t*. Pronounce the new word. Continue with the word *game*. Interchange initial consonants *s, n,* and *c* again, emphasizing the role of the initial letter and its sound in pronouncing the words.

b. Present to the child a word such as *may* or *last* or *pig*. Then ask him to tell you a word that looks and sounds like *may* except at the beginning. When he mentions a word like *day,* erase the *m* in *may* while he watches and substitute the initial consonant of the word mentioned. Ask the child to pronounce the new word and to note how changing just the first letter makes a new word.

When using consonant substitution to accustom a child to notice word beginnings, it should be remembered always to stress initial letters and sounds. For example, if working with consonants *y* and *w,* say, "Which of the two words below the sentence should be used in the blank?"

Jane likes to _____ in the snow.
talk   walk

3. Various games may be played for informal training in using initial consonants to direct attention to word beginnings. *Consonant Lotto* and the first part of *Group Sounding Game* in the Dolch materials (The Garrard Press, Champaign, Illinois) are designed for this purpose.

Word wheels and the other devices described in the previous chapter may be made for drill on initial consonants in emphasizing word beginnings. In using a word wheel, words having the same ending are used, like *throat, coat, goat, boat, float, gloat*. On the bottom disk, only the word beginnings are typed or printed, and they are placed so that they show through an opening in the top disk, on which the ending *-oat,* is printed to the right of the opening. The two disks may be rotated so that the child can see that by changing the initial elements new words are made. This causes the child to pay attention to the word beginnings in order to recognize the words shown.

In a similar manner, a column of initial elements of words having the same ending can be typed or printed, using triple spacing, on a slip cut from a manila folder. Then an exposure card can be made by cutting a slit in a piece of manila folder. The word ending should be typed or printed just to the right of the slit. (See the word-slip device in Chapter 11.) When the slip is moved into position, the various initial elements are exposed, one after another, for the child to use in making the words. He will notice the changing elements, since they determine what the words will be.

In all this work, the teacher should present the exercise so that the child always sees the initial consonant as the word is exposed. This is done by going at a leisurely pace, by pointing to the initial consonant, and by having the child sound the consonant and blend it with the word ending. If this is not done, the child may remember the initial sound and look first at the ending. The purpose is to teach the child always to notice first the beginning of the word. Noticing the beginning of a word first must become an ingrained habit.

4. It has been suggested that a demonstration of reversal errors is valuable in discussing directional orientation in word perception. The purpose of this is to show a child what happens when he starts reading at the end or the middle of a word rather than at the beginning. For instance, the teacher writes *war* and *raw* one above the other. She then points out that the same letters are in both words, but they are different words so that he should always start at the left end of a word in reading it. Similarly she calls attention to *left* and *felt* or other partial or complete reversals.

5. Alphabetizing and dictionary exercises promote left-to-right orientation in perceiving words. For early practice in alphabetizing, the child should have a file box or folder with the alphabet marked on the dividing cards. A single word that has been learned is written on a slip of paper. The word is then filed by its initial letter. When the order of the alphabet has been learned, several words beginning with the same letter can be filed according to the sequence of letters within the word. All this develops the habit of looking first at the beginnings of words, and then progressing from left to right. Exercises for developing skills in alphabetizing and using the dictionary are given in teachers' manuals and workbooks accompanying basic reader series.

A picture dictionary can be made for a relatively immature reading level. This teaches a child the alphabet as used for classification. Also, when he is writing a word for his dictionary, it gives him practice in going through a word from left to right.

Preventing Reversals

It is desirable to teach elementary reading so that severe reversal tendencies are not created. From the start, proper orientation in word study should be stressed, as discussed in the early parts of this chapter and in the previous chapter. This becomes particularly important in teaching the various aspects of word analysis such as initial consonants, phonograms, and blending letter sounds into proper sequences. The first letter or letter group in a word should be sounded first, followed by an orderly progression to the right. A well-organized program of teaching word analysis (see preceding chapter), with attention to individual needs, should help to establish the normal left-to-right progression needed to prevent regressions.

SUMMARY

The extremely disabled reader is the child who has learned little or no reading during several or more years in school. Three types of remedial methods have proved to be especially successful in teaching these children to read. A tracing-sounding-writing method, such as was suggested originally by Fernald has been effective in developing left-to-right orientation in word perception, in directing attention to the visual characteristics of words, in developing skill in phonics and syllabication, and in the use of context in recognizing words. Such teaching also emphasizes developing vocabulary, concepts, and comprehension, but it is detailed and time-consuming and must be done on an individual basis. The method is often successful with extremely disabled readers, but it requires an unusually great amount of teacher time.

Phonics (sound-blending) methods, such as those developed by Monroe and by Gillingham and Stillman, have been successful with certain cases of extreme disability. These methods are phonics-based and emphasize the patient repetition of the necessary drill. Tracing-sounding is employed when necessary. Phonics methods are very useful for many children, though they should not be used with those who are already overanalytical.

Another method is one which embodies all the procedures and techniques taught to typical children in good classroom programs. This method works when children receive intensive instruction based on an accurate understanding of their needs.

The expert remedial teacher should be familiar with all these methods so that she will use the right procedure in each case. The writers suggest that a careful diagnosis can usually specify the area of difficulty and indicate the type of remedial instruction needed. Such a diagnosis shows which approach or combination of approaches would be best.

A special problem which most beginning readers experience and soon eliminate, but which remains a genuine reading handicap for a few, is difficulty with left-to-right word perception.

Many methods to eliminate reversal tendencies in word perception have been described. The more important include (1) explanation and demonstration of the left-to-right progression in studying unknown words, (2) the Fernald tracing-sounding-writing method, (3) the combined phonic and sounding-tracing method, (4) writing words, (5) training in use of initial consonants and consonant substitution, and (6) alphabetizing and dictionary exercises.

Remedial instruction includes methods which direct the pupil's attention to the beginning of a word and which lead to a consistent left-to-right progression in studying a word. These encourage the habit of noticing the beginnings of words and then a visual left-to-right survey of word elements followed by sounding and blending of these elements into word entities. The particular methods used will depend upon the nature and severity of the difficulties as revealed by diagnosis.

STUDY QUESTIONS

1. Describe the stages used in teaching a student to read new words with the Fernald approach. What cautions are indicated when using this method?

2. What essential similarities and differences were there between the two phonics approaches discussed in this chapter?
3. What can teachers do to help students with orientational difficulties?

SELECTED READINGS

FERNALD, G. M. *Remedial Techniques in Basic School Subjects.* New York: McGraw-Hill Book Company, 1971.

GILLINGHAM, A., AND B. W. STILLMAN. *Remedial Training for Children with Specific Disability in Reading, Spelling, and Penmanship.* Cambridge, Mass.: Educators Publishing Service, Inc., 1960.

KIRK, S. A., J. M. KLIEBHAN, AND J. W. LERNER. *Teaching Reading to Slow and Disabled Learners,* Chap. 6. Boston: Houghton Mifflin Company, 1978.

MONROE, M. *Children Who Cannot Read.* Chicago: University of Chicago Press, 1932.

MYERS, P. I., AND D. D. HAMMILL. *Methods for Learning Disorders,* 3rd ed., Chap. 9. New York: John Wiley & Sons, Inc., 1976.

ROSWELL, F., AND G. NATCHEZ. *Reading Disability: Diagnosis and Treatment,* 2nd ed., Chap. 5. New York: Basic Books, Inc., Publishers, 1971.

13

Adapting Instruction to the Handicapped Child

Teachers must be aware that some children with reading difficulties also have special learning handicaps. Complex disability cases not only need expert remedial reading instruction but must also have instruction modified according to the characteristics of their specific handicapping conditions.

Many atypical children find complex learning, such as reading, confusing and frustrating. Others with similar and equal handicaps learn to read exceedingly well despite the handicaps. For example, many mildly hearing-impaired children derive great satisfaction from reading. If their reading skills become well-developed, these children may become such avid readers that they eventually demonstrate better-than-average reading achievement. But if an atypical child becomes a disabled reader, his remedial problem becomes complex. Atypical conditions which may contribute to and complicate the correction of reading difficulties include poor eyesight, defective hearing, speech defects, emotional problems, neurological limitations, and the like. The diagnostic and remedial methods described in previous chapters are, by themselves, insufficient to solve the learning problems of handicapped children.

In some instances the educational program for any specific group of handicapped children may be conducted in special classes using methods and equipment designed to meet their particular instructional needs. In other instances, these children are taught in the regular classroom and perhaps in the resource room with procedures adapted as needed to enable handicapped children to progress effectively. Appropriate educational adjustments are treated well in books dealing with the psychology and education of exceptional children and youth. In this chapter, we discuss the special modifications of remedial procedures needed for dealing with the added complications a handicapping condition causes in coexistence with reading difficulties.

Throughout this book, the emphasis has been on adapting instruction to the requirements of the individual as ascertained by a careful diagnosis. When dealing with disabled readers, complicated by handicaps, there is need for even more individualized treatment. For the best results, there must be a more careful and thorough probing of each individual's needs, and a more continuous and usually prolonged application of individualized remedial instruction. The fundamental principles of remedial instruction needed for the specially handicapped do not differ basically from those discussed earlier. However, much depends upon skillful guidance. The fullest measure of success is achieved when an alert teacher senses every aspect of a pupil's difficulty and has at her command just the right procedures, demonstrations, materials, and instructional techniques to overcome or at least alleviate the discovered difficulty. She must know just what materials and procedures to select for a particular difficulty, and when to shift from one procedure to another in order to help the student continue to improve in reading. In other words, the teacher must be flexible in organizing her remedial programs, in beginning at the right point, and in introducing new materials and techniques to promote continuous progress toward learning to read better.

Especially relevant is the personality of the teacher, who must be willing to work patiently to gain and to maintain good rapport with the child. For success, the child must like his teacher and expect that she is going to help him. Only when there are close personal relations between pupil and teacher is it possible for the teacher to provide the incentives which will maintain the level of motivation necessary to achieve lasting improvement in reading. Besides being well-trained, the teacher must like children and be enthusiastic about her work. It is not too much to say that success in teaching handicapped children depends largely upon the teacher.

It is inconceivable that any single, narrow, or limited approach to reading will be found adequate for helping complex reading disability cases become effective readers. The very nature of the learning adjustments atypical children must make in order to learn to read successfully varies from one type of handicap to another. The programs for these children have to be devised to foster the adjustments in learning that the children must make in order to be effective learners.

Handicapped children with reading difficulties especially need to feel successful in the remedial venture. Teachers must be flexible in their methods in order to sustain positive attitudes. They must remember that the basic task in teaching a reading-disabled handicapped child is to modify the teaching procedures used to correct the diagnosed reading problem in light of the unique adjustments that must be made to overcome the additional learning problems raised by the nature of the child's handicap.

The categories of handicapped children for whom the teacher must modify remedial methods include:

1. The visually-impaired child
2. The auditorily-impaired child
3. The neurologically-impaired child
4. The emotionally maladjusted child
5. The mentally handicapped child
6. The speech-impaired child

THE VISUALLY-IMPAIRED CHILD

Many visual defects such as ordinary myopia, hyperopia, astigmatism, and muscular imbalance can be remedied by properly fitted glasses or other medical means. Children with fully corrected vision suffer no visual handicap when they learn to read.

Every child should have visual screening and, adequate follow-up when needed before he receives any instruction in reading. Any necessary treatment or correction must be provided. There should be periodic visual examinations throughout the school years to identify and correct any significant defects which may develop. Methods for diagnosing visual impairments were discussed in Chapter 4.

A small number of children have visual impairments which cannot be corrected completely by glasses. Accompanied by consultation with a competent eye specialist, educational adaptations are necessary for children with low visual acuity. In teaching children with low visual acuity, lesson length, typography, and illumination must be considered. Reading periods should be brief and the conditions of reading should make the visual task as effortless as possible. There is ample evidence that both normal and visually deficient readers find that words in large type sizes are easier to perceive correctly. Elementary age children express a preference for large type, as do children with low visual acuity (Weiss 1982). It is also advisable to use material printed in a line length of about 24 to 27 picas (four to four and one-half inches) with ample leading or space between lines for children with visual acuity problems. Supplementary material can be prepared for these children, using typewriters with primer-sized type. Visually handicapped children should have an ample amount and variety of reading material.

The visually-impaired child needs abundant illumination. This means at least 50-foot candles of light in any area where visually demanding activities such as reading, art and craft work, chalkboard work, or writing are performed. Felt-tipped pens and pencils which produce thick black lines should be used.

Reading should be coordinated with other means of learning. Learning through listening and discussing should be emphasized, and creative activities such as creative dramatics are beneficial. The teacher must assume responsibility for encouraging learning through listening and doing. This entails much teacher discussion, reading aloud, story telling, guidance of student discussion, and supervision of creative activities. Audiovisual instruction, such as audio tapes, sound motion pictures, tape-slide presentations, video tapes, and television, are all beneficial.

Visually handicapped children are usually not at a disadvantage in the auditory discrimination of words. Phonics emphasis in beginning reading instruction is helpful for many visually deficient children. However, care must be taken that letter-sound associations are not overemphasized and, as soon as possible, the children's attention must be directed to whole-word recognition and to perceiving the larger pronounceable units of words such as syllables, word roots, prefixes, and suffixes. This enhances effective visual perception and minimizes the need for minute examination of letter detail in working out words. Context clues should be stressed as an aid to word recognition and to recognition of words in thought units. Any procedure which leads to perceiving groups of words, whole words, and larger parts of words in word attack helps reduce the detailed visual work in reading.

Many children suffer from a mild degree of visual impairment, making their handicap less serious. These children can participate in the regular reading program. The teacher should select recreational reading materials with good print, see that there is adequate illumination in the classroom, and encourage these students to rest their eyes frequently. Some children benefit greatly from being taught to use paper or tagboard markers to isolate the line of print they are reading and thus to minimize visual distraction. Speed of reading should be deemphasized, and accurate word recognition and close attention to meaning should be stressed. As with the more serious cases of visual impairment, these children should be taught to recognize words by the use of phonics, combining this with attention to larger units and relying heavily on content.

THE AUDITORILY IMPAIRED CHILD

Adaptations for the auditorily limited child differ, since hearing impairments occur in varying degrees. The deaf are those whose hearing loss is so severe and is acquired so young that it precludes the normal development of spoken language. Other children are classified as partially hearing. They are able to use spoken language, but their auditory handicap limits their language learning and use of language. Auditory limitations range from slight to profound.

The sooner the hearing loss is detected the better, because appropriate help in the early years enables children to use their hearing as effectively as possible and to acquire language as fully as possible. All children should be given an adequate hearing screening before entering school. The measurement of hearing has been discussed in Chapter 4.

Slight hearing impairment. Moderate educational adaptations help the child with a slight hearing impairment to succeed in the regular classroom. Such a pupil should be given a favorable seat close to where the teacher usually talks to the class. Speech should always be enunciated clearly whenever the hearing-handicapped child is involved. He will be able to follow oral discussions more accurately if he watches the lips of the person speaking. Some training in speech reading is helpful. To avoid embarrassing the hearing-impaired child, discussion groups should be arranged so that he can watch the lips of each speaker without obviously turning his head. Seating the children in a semicircle or around a table does this nicely.

The child with a hearing impairment is likely to have some degree of difficulty in auditory discrimination. Because of this, the teaching of word perception should emphasize a visual approach to word identification and word recognition rather than phonics. This does not imply that word sounds should not be taught. The auditorily limited child needs a great deal of emphasis on auditory discrimination as an aid to speech and as an aid to reading. However, depending upon the specific nature of the auditory handicap, the child will not be able to use phonics as an aid to word recognition as successfully as a child with normal hearing. For this reason, more attention than usual should be paid to the visual characteristics of words and to the use of visual analysis along with context clues for recognizing words previously met and for identifying unfamiliar words. The extent of the emphasis on visual and lack of emphasis on auditory identification and recognition techniques depends upon how much difficulty the child has with auditory discrimination. If the teacher is sensitive to the child's auditory limitations, the child with a relatively slight hearing defect should be able to make normal progress in learning to read.

Mild and marked hearing impairment.   Mildly hearing-impaired children are under a severe handicap in learning to read in classes in which oral reading and phonics are stressed. They need more emphasis upon silent reading and a visual approach to word perception. It is important that they be given many opportunities to show what they know through action. Much reliance on work-sheet activities is important. Language difficulties may preclude a clear understanding of words read unless the teacher provides many opportunities for the hearing-impaired child to demonstrate understanding. These children should receive special speech-reading and language instruction.

The hearing-impaired child may experience adjustment difficulties unless special care is taken. Such a child can easily feel alienated from his peers. Every effort should be made to make the child feel that he belongs to the group in his classwork and play activities.

Severe and extreme hearing impairment.   There is great difficulty teaching reaching to children with severe and extreme hearing impairments, especially those children who have not developed language concepts. Visual materials are used for these children. Words are introduced in a variety of ways, usually using actual objects, and by actions and demonstration. Extensive use is made of pictures in association with words and of picture dictionary material. Mastery of each step is required before going on to the next. Progress from words to phrases to sentences to paragraphs is achieved by successful learners.

Teaching children with serious auditory impairments to read is a highly specialized task which the ordinary remedial teacher will not encounter. Those who teach these children should consult such references as Hart (1976).

THE NEUROLOGICALLY IMPAIRED CHILD

There are a limited number of reading disability children who, after carefully planned and thoroughly implemented programs of reeducation, fail to show the desired progress. Some of these children may be handicapped by neurological impairment. This conclusion should never be assumed unless supported by expert medical evidence. Whatever can be done medically to improve the learning ability of these children should precede or accompany any attempt at reading-improvement programs.

Remedial-reading programs for children who have a neurological problem should take into account the behavioral characteristics of each child. Response patterns which suggest neurological impairment include visual perception and synthesis problems, auditory discrimination and blending difficulties, symbol-sound or symbol-meaning association problems, and motor-coordination limitations. These anomalies necessitate two types of adaptations in remedial reading instruction. *First,* training to improve the child's visual, auditory, associative, or motor skills is indicated. *Second,* adaptations must be made in the methods of remedial instruction so as to use the child's strengths and avoid his weakness in direct application to reading tasks.

Visual perception and synthesis problems. The abilities to perceive differences in word configurations and to note the fine distinctions within the printed symbols are necessary for effectiveness in word recognition and for success in learning to read. The child who cannot visually distinguish rapidly between word patterns such as *fall* and *fell, learn* and *lean,* or *stop* and *tops* will have trouble in acquiring even the beginning reading skills. Many children start learning to read with just such limitations. For the neurologically impaired, these problems of visual perception may be even more troublesome. Direct training in noting likenesses and differences may be given in much the same way that they are developed in reading-readiness materials. The teacher dealing with a child with such neurological impairment will find the materials developed for typical prereading children who are immature in visual perception and synthesis to be effective in teaching the handicapped child. For all but the most severely handicapped, the exercises which deal with actual similarities and differences in printed symbols are more useful than those using geometric designs. Matching exercises involving individual stimulus cards prompt close visual attention and reduce distractability. Tracing exercises greatly benefit some neurologically impaired children, especially if they are encouraged to trace large figures or symbols. During the school day, these children should be encouraged to participate fully in appropriate art, craft, and physical education activities. Children with poor visual perception often have difficulty with these activities; yet with sensible adaptations, such pursuits help strengthen visual perceptual abilities. In dealing with the disabled reader who has such a visual-neurological impairment, the paramount remedial reading task is to teach him to attend to word patterns as effectively as his limited perceptual capacity will allow.

Reading-readiness books contain exercises which are carefully scaled in difficulty. These exercises are designed to develop the perceptual skills needed in reading and to give varied experience and practice in visual perception and synthesis. The remedial teacher can use such exercises as models for making additional exercises, since the neurologically limited child requires considerably more training to develop perceptual skills. Caution should be exercised in the length of the practice periods used for such training. These periods should not be extended to the point of fatigue. It should also be pointed out that this training can continue along with regular remedial teaching designed to improve word-recognition skills. Much of the ability in visual discrimination, as applied to words, is developed in the actual process of learning word-recognition techniques.

In teaching the child with limited visual perception, the remedial program should lean more heavily upon methods that emphasize auditory sound-blending approaches to reading. For children who still do not make progress, kinesthetic-auditory-visual training may be needed. The periods of visual perceptual activity should be of short duration and well spaced. Sometimes it is necessary to break the reading material into single sentences or short paragraphs. These are read and discussed one at a time, thus giving the child frequent intervals of visual relaxation. As he matures in reading and perceptual skills, the segments of reading can be lengthened. Even then the child should be encouraged to look up from the print to relax and to think about the content he has read. The use of context clues should be developed as an aid to recognition.

Auditory discrimination and blending difficulties.   Children who cannot detect the differences in spoken words that sound somewhat alike, who are not able to select which of two words completes a rhyme, or who cannot discriminate well enough to select which of a group of words starts with the same sound as a given spoken word do not have the auditory capabilities necessary to learn to read by certain methods of instruction. Such word-discrimination skills must exist in order to profit from oral word study and phonics training. The ability to blend letter sounds or phonemes into whole words when given orally is required for oral-phonetic training methods to succeed.

Auditory skills can be developed by having the child learn to listen more carefully to word sound patterns. Materials for instruction are as extensive as the rhymes and words found in children's literature and in the spoken language of the children being taught. As with visual skills, the remedial teacher can find many excellent suggestions in prereading materials and oral games used in kindergarten. Each of these sources will provide the teacher with models of exercises that she can develop. The neurologically limited child who has auditory discrimination and blending deficiencies needs a more extensive program of training than does the usual child. The auditory training might well start with distinguishing between gross sounds such as crumpling paper, running water, shutting doors, and typewriting. Then it might progress to noting which of two out of four orally presented words sound the same; first using words that have markedly contrasting patterns, such as *make, want, make, have;* and then progressing to finer discriminations, as *roam, room, ram, roam.* The child should be able to make these auditory discriminations with his eyes closed or when his teacher is not in view, to ensure that he has heard the differences rather than read his teacher's lips. Auditory training periods should be short to ensure attention and because such training tends to be tiring. Picture cards may be used for the child to perform such activities as naming the pictures and then sorting the cards according to the beginning sounds of the picture names. These children like visual clues, occasionally need practice in recalling the names of common objects pictured, and should be able to distinguish clearly sounds in words based on their own as well as on other people's pronunciations. To specifically enhance sound-blending skills, the teacher can ask the child to hand her the picture of the c--ar or of the b--oa--t. Many exercises designed to develop auditory skills are included in reading-readiness materials.

Symbol association problems.   The abilities needed to make instant and accurate associations between printed symbols and spoken sounds, and between printed symbols and meaningful words, are necessary for effective reading. The child who cannot make these associations instantly will be a faltering reader, and the child who cannot make them accurately will be unable to make much progress at all. For most children, these difficulties signal that the pace of reading instruction has been too fast and that they have have not been given enough opportunity for review. For the neurologically impaired, symbol association problems may be much more severe.

Direct training in symbol-sound and symbol-meaning associations may have to be given in a manner similar to that used in beginning reading instruction. Some neurologically impaired children require so much practice that the remedial reading teacher may have to find or design many supplementary materials to maintain interest. Gamelike activities can make repetitive practice seem more enjoyable. Sorting word cards into categories by meaning gives good practice in symbol-meaning associations. The teacher of such children must be able to judge when to practice further and when to move on. Enough practice is essential, but too much only causes the child to fall farther behind. The issue is complicated further by the great variability in associative abilities which some neurologically impaired children demonstrate from one day to the next. The willingness to make appropriate instructional adjustments and to emphasize at all times what the child has done well, maximizes instructional effectiveness for the neurologically impaired child.

Motor coordination limitations.   The major area of limited motor coordination related to reading is oculomotor coordination. The child with an oculomotor control problem has difficulty focusing on the printed page and coordinating the two eyes during the reading act. He also has trouble following the line of print rhythmically as he progresses along the line. Kephart (1971) gives suggestions for improving such oculomotor coordination.

It is enough to state here that methods using markers as aids to maintaining line location, sweeping below the line of print with a marker, and emphasizing left-to-right progression are helpful. The section dealing with orientational problems in word recognition, discussed in Chapter 12, discusses methods that should help the child overcome oculomotor problems in reading. Kinesthetic methods are often suggested to supplement adequate oculomotor control in reading. Clinical workers giving remedial training to severely handicapped children may find the methods suggested by Fernald (1971) helpful.

Correcting the reading disabilities of the neurologically impaired child is difficult and usually time-consuming. But if training and adjustments are made, even these children can develop reading capability. Additional suggestions for teaching children with learning disorders associated with neurological impairment are described by Cruickshank (1971), Kephart (1971), and Myers and Hammill (1976).

Teachers and clinicians working with reading disability cases should be aware that many symptoms of neurological impairment are shown by the typical reading disability case, and a child should not be assumed to have a neurological problem unless it is confirmed by a medical examination.

Normal children with perceptual and motor problems should have training similar to that just described in this section. The training need not be as intensified and progress could be expected to be more rapid than it is in the case of the neurologically-impaired child.

THE EMOTIONALLY MALADJUSTED CHILD

The role of emotional maladjustment in reading disability was discussed in Chapter 6. There it was noted that most reading-disabled students show some emotional maladjustment. Some children are maladjusted when they first arrive at school. Others develop emotional reactions when frustrated in their attempts to learn to read. Whatever the roots of the trouble, it is certain that some degree of emotional maladjustment is a concern for many of the students remedial teachers instruct.

Reading-disabled children are often characterized by a variety of behaviors ranging from lack of persistence, inattentiveness, anxiety, and submissiveness to overdemanding behavior, anger, and hostility. These behaviors also range from just noticeable to very obvious.

Gentile and McMillan (1987) believe that some of these behaviors can be understood as flight or fight reactions to the stress associated with reading difficulty. If a student's behavior is understood as a flight reaction, the teacher should focus on interaction with the student and drawing the student out. The student should be moved toward participation in the reading task and toward a meaningful relationship with the teacher. The teacher should attempt to build motivation and should provide helpful prompting as necessary.

If a student's behavior is understood as a fight reaction, the teacher must severely limit interaction with the student, especially confrontational interaction, and move the student back to the reading task. The teacher must be concise and consistent and should keep verbal interaction to an absolute minimum. The teacher should avoid prompting and should attempt to redirect the student's confrontational motivation to the task at hand.

Hewett and Taylor (1980) have stressed the importance of helping children with adjustment and learning problems to behave as learners. This is necessary because certain specific behaviors interfere with reading progress. These behaviors include inattention to reading tasks, lack of active response to reading, and inability to complete work.

To help children attend to reading, the teacher first of all should consider the physical environment. It should be free from distraction. Many children can attend to their reading better when allowed to work in a carrel or study booth. For others it is helpful to remove all unnecessary materials from work surfaces, as these materials are often distracting. Short, definite units of work are an aid to the child who has difficulty attending to his reading. Tokens for paying attention such as those made of plastic, colorful stickers, or simple check marks can be awarded to a child for attentive behavior. Charts or other records of progress in paying attention to reading often help children learn to increase their attention to reading.

In the clinic, teachers have noticed that jewelry such as dangling beads or brightly colored pins distract certain students. Teachers have also observed that a soft voice and short, simple, direct instructions help children who have difficulty attending. Gamelike supplementary reading activities often help children attend to reading tasks, because of the added incentive of wanting to win. Very few children will attend to reading when they have no purpose for reading, when the reading seems uninteresting to them, or when it is too difficult .

Clinical cases of complex disability are seen who refuse to read at all or respond only minimally to reading tasks. These are children who read orally so slowly and hesitantly and in such a muffled tone that they cannot be heard, or they stop at every difficult word and refuse to try, or they rush rapidly through all reading with little thought of the meaning, thinking only of finishing. It is also easy to find children who spend their reading time trying to converse with the teacher about any conceivable subject rather than proceeding with their reading, and those who are perpetually late and frequently absent. To help such children respond to reading, teachers can reduce the level and amount of reading the child must do until he can see that it can be accomplished easily. Instructions for reading should be specific, not vague and open-ended, because vague and open-ended reading tasks appear to these children to be without end. The teacher should guarantee the child success by having him compete against himself, not against others. As an example, she might have him see if he could do better today than he did yesterday. Charts of the child's work are helpful for comparison. Reading selections closely tied to the child's interests help to kindle enthusiasm for reading.

Children having difficulty completing their work can be helped if the teacher carefully prepares and organizes their work. Often teachers find that they must plan in stages what must be done to finish a work sheet or reading selection and then help the student by these same stages finish the work. Often children who have difficulty completing their work are not aware of time. Therefore it is essential to give them ample time to complete their reading and they must be given time reminders. It is also important to reward and praise them for completing their reading.

When reading remediation is successful, the usual result is that as the child gains power in reading his stress is reduced, his confusions diminish, his interest expands, and he appears to be a happier, better-adjusted person. His confidence has been reestablished. Other evidences of personal and social well-being become apparent. Care must be taken to ensure continuing success, but from time to time the child must be given material difficult enough to challenge his growing capability.

THE MENTALLY HANDICAPPED CHILD

Children with below-average intelligence are commonly classified into the following groups according to Kirk, Kliebhan, and Lerner (1978): (1) slow learners (I.Q. 68–85), (2) mildly mentally retarded (I.Q. 52–67), (3) moderately mentally retarded (I.Q. 36–51), (4) severely mentally retarded (I.Q. 20–35), and (5) profoundly mentally retarded (I.Q. 19 and below). People with I.Q.s in the moderately mentally retarded range can learn to read on a word-by-word basis when given intensive instruction and massive review. For those with I.Q.s of about 50 to about 70, progress in reading is extremely slow. With superior extended reading instruction, the expected reading grade of a child with an I.Q. of 70 is 5.2 at age sixteen (Brueckner and Bond, 1955). Ordinarily children with I.Q.s of about 50 to 70 receive reading instruction in a special education class or resource room. Children with I.Q.s above 70 are usually able to achieve more, and if given excellent instruction, may be expected to achieve reading grades at the 6.0 to 7.5 grade level by the age of sixteen. It is the reading instruction of the children with I.Q.s between 68 and 85, who are taught in regular classes, that we will consider in our disucssion of slow learners. In general, slow learners can, with proper instruction, make progress up to the grade level corresponding to their mental age. The consensus of educators is that mentally retarded children should be started on a systematic reading program only when they reach a mental age of at least six years. As noted by Kirk, Kliebhan, and Lerner (1978), slow learners differ from normal children in learning to read because they cannot be expected to begin learning to read at the chronological age of six, and even thereafter they naturally learn at a slower rate. They become discouraged in regular classrooms because of continued failure. This and their usually somewhat impoverished environmental and experiential background are reflected in poor language usage.

The slow learners need a prolonged prereading and reading readiness period.

On entering school, they are more retarded than the normal child in the abilities and skills which form the basis for success in beginning reading. According to Savage and Mooney (1979), the readiness program for slow learners should be more intense and prolonged than normal, so as to reduce the difficulty of the new learnings required when the pupil actually begins to read. The general aspects of reading readiness have been discussed in earlier chapters. Details of such programs may be found in Durkin (1976), Lapp and Flood (1978), and Tinker and McCullough (1975).

During the prereading training and when the child's mental age is between five and six, he is able to learn to recognize his name and a few words used as labels and signs. Before reaching at least six years mental age, systematic reading instruction as is ordinarily given results only in a tremendous waste of time and energy on the part of the teacher, because so little is learned from it. Nevertheless, if special instructional methods (described later) are employed, these children can be given profitable reading instruction before six years mental age. Otherwise some of them would not begin to read until they are eight or nine years old.

The mentally retarded child differs from the normal one in his reading progress, mainly by being a slower learner. He is ready to begin formal lessons at a somewhat later chronological age and he progresses at a slower rate. This means that at each succeeding level in the developmental program, he should have more materials and more individualized guidance than the normal child. The slow learner needs many repetitions of a word in the context of basic reading materials before he can learn it. This is in addition to his encounters with such words in appropriate supplementary reading. The reading materials used are the same as those which have proved satisfactory with regular pupils. But there is more of the material, and the instruction is more individualized and more intensive. Repetition, explanation, demonstrations, provision of experience units, and amount of recreational reading should be extensive.

Reading Disability

When classroom reading instruction and materials are not adjusted to the slow learner, he may become reading disabled. That is, his reading achievement may come to be less than what is reasonable to expect for him. According to evidence cited by Kirk (1940) between five and ten percent of mentally retarded children are reading-disabled and should profit from remedial instruction. Coincidentally, this is about the frequency of reading disabilities found among children with average and above average intelligence. Precise diagnosis of the extent and nature of reading disability among mentally handicapped children rests on the use of techniques described in earlier chapters.

Remedial Instruction

Results cited by Kirk (1940) and by Featherstone (1951) demonstrate that slow learners who become reading disabled profit significantly from remedial instruction. For instance, in a group of 10 children, with mean C.A. of 12-9 and mean I.Q. of 75, an average gain of 1.2 school grades was achieved by 68 standard lessons, each 30 minutes long, over a period of about 5 months. This rate of progress was 5 times that of 100 unselected children of similar mental ability. Furthermore, 5 months after the remedial training ceased, these children continued to progress in the regular classroom situation at a rate twice that of the 100 children who had not had the remedial instruction. Most of the 10 remedial cases also showed better general adjustment and improved attitudes and behavior as they became more proficient in reading. Other data cited revealed similar gains. It was concluded that significant and satisfying results can be obtained from remedial instruction with slow-learning children who are disabled in reading.

The Hegge-Kirk remedial method was devised primarily for mentally retarded children. The details of this method are given in *Remedial Reading Drills,* by Hegge, Kirk, and Kirk (1945). The method in its initial stage is primarily a phonic method. It is more complete than most phonic systems. There is much drill and an emphasis on certain principles of learning, such as the concrete associative aids used to help the child learn a new sound. Retention is aided by having the child say the sound, write it, and then blend the sounds into words. Sentence reading, story reading, and teaching words as entities are introduced at the appropriate places as the child progresses. Any teacher who plans to use the method should consult Kirk (1940).

The following suggestions, adapted from Brueckner and Bond (1955, pp. 188–90) provide procedures for teaching slow-learning children to read:

1. Instruction in reading should begin later than for normal children. Due to limited intelligence, slow-learning children have not acquired the experience necessary for initial instruction in reading by the age of six years or six years and six months. Although it is not wise to wait for a mental age of six years and six months, initial instruction should be deferred as long as is required to make progress in the prerequisite learnings.

2. Slow-learning children develop reading ability in much the same ways as normal children, but at a somewhat slower pace. This is true for their capability in word recognition, vocabulary readiness, and the setting of purposes. Any necessary modifications in instruction are more in a changed emphasis than in a drastically different program.

3. A large amount of carefully controlled material must be used with slow learners. To make new words a permanent part of the child's sight vocabulary, they must be introduced more slowly. That is, vocabulary development is more gradual.

4. Slow-learners require more review of basic words. This is achieved by use and reuse of workbook material, by rereading a selection several times for different purposes, and by reading much additional material with the same vocabulary.

5. The slow-learning child has to be given more detailed and simplified explanations and simpler techniques. Frequently he finds directions in workbooks or in informal exercises difficult to grasp. The teacher must be sure that each child understands what is expected in all reading assignments.

6. More concrete illustrations of the things about which he is reading are needed. In contrast with the average child, the slow learner is handicapped in generalizing and in thinking abstractly about what he is reading. He should be given every opportunity, therefore, to come into direct contact with the things about which he is studying.

7. Reading goals should be relatively short-range, that is, reached rather quickly. The slow learner cannot work effectively upon projects of long duration.

8. The slow learner requires more rereading before he can grasp the different purposes of what he reads. For example, if he is to read about a buffalo hunt, the first reading may be only to find out that the Indian boy shot a buffalo, the second reading to discover how the tribe prepared for the hunt, the third time to find out how the hunt actually was conducted, and so on. Although the brighter child could achieve most of the purposes listed by just one reading, the slow learner cannot. Furthermore, the latter does not mind rereading because each new time helps him get a fuller understanding of the story.

9. There should be more experience and more guidance in exploring the visual and auditory characteristics of words. For word-recognition skills to operate effectively, they must be applicable to a wide variety of words. These skills are difficult for slow learners to acquire. They profit from additional drill in analyzing words and in learning the sounds of different word elements. Since rapid reading is not important to slow learners, a moderate degree of overanalysis is of little consequence provided it does not interfere with comprehension.

10. It is advisable to use more oral reading and oral prestudy in instructing slow-learning children. Many of them need to vocalize what they are reading before they can comprehend it well. The fact that vocalization slows the reading rate is of little significance for these children.

11. Slow-learning children should do more building of models, cutting out of pictures, and the like in connection with their reading than other children do.

12. Finally, slow-learning children profit from being in the same classroom with average children, provided the instruction is adjusted somewhat to their special needs. Although the slow learner is not able to read much above his mental level, in many other respects his learning experiences may be similar to those of other children.

THE SPEECH-IMPAIRED CHILD

Occasionally, reading-disabled children also have speech impairments. The role of such impairments in reading difficulties was reviewed in Chapter 4. Difficulty with clear enunciation of words, a speech impairment, is often associated with inadequate auditory discrimination. In this case, some difficulty with word recognition is probable. Children who have difficulty with clear enunciation of words because of inadequate auditory discrimination, benefit less from the use of phonics as a major aid to word recognition than do children who discriminate sounds well. They progress better when emphasis is placed on study of the visual characteristics of words, especially during beginning reading. Also, silent rather than oral reading should be stressed.

Some children with speech defects are embarrassed when asked to read aloud or take part in discussion. In consideration of the child's sensitivities, the teacher should be sympathetic and tactful. But it is not wise to excuse the child altogether from oral work. The problem of balancing oral and silent work is delicate.

A first step is to give the child proper speech training with a speech therapist. As the child progresses toward smoother and more fluent speech, he gains self-confidence. One way of correcting speech difficulties is reading aloud. At first, the pupil should read some well-prepared selection aloud to his teacher in private. As the speech difficulty is overcome, the child will be ready and perhaps eager to do some oral reading in class. The teacher should encourage but not force the child to do this. At the same time, as the child becomes more sure of himself, remedial measures for correcting specific reading difficulties may be undertaken.

CASE STUDY OF AN UPPER ELEMENTARY STUDENT WITH A BASIC WORD RECOGNITION PROBLEM AND AN AUDITORY LIMITATION

Paul, a fifth-grade student, was referred to the Achievement Center for help in reading during an eight-week summer period. He came from the Achievement Center service area, where he had attended school during the previous school year. Before that he had attended a school in a district approximately 100 miles away.

School history.   When Paul was admitted to the center, he was eleven years and five months old. His school referral form showed that he had had a slight hearing impairment which was first diagnosed in the first grade. The child had received no type of special services before his fifth-grade year. He was referred for resource room services by his fifth-grade teacher, who also requested Achievement Center Services because of her concern for the child's reading difficulties.

School behavior.   According to the referral information, Paul was described as having an excellent attitude toward school, peers, and teachers. His classroom behavior was characterized by his fifth-grade classroom teacher as normal in all ways, except that he "always seemed unusually attentive." The classroom teacher's interpretation was that the child was straining to listen due to his auditory impairment.

Abilities.   According to the *Wechsler Intelligence Scale for Children (Revised),* his ability to learn was above average, with a full-scale I.Q. of 114. The difference between his verbal I.Q. and performance I.Q., however, was large. His verbal I.Q. was found to be 98 and his performance I.Q., 130. This would place his reading expectancy at 6.6. However, in view of the 32-point discrepancy between verbal and performance I.Q., the clinician noted that had his reading expectancy been based on his verbal I.Q. alone it would have been 4.8, and had it been based on his performance I.Q. alone, it would have been 7.4. The clinician felt that under the circumstances, it was difficult to conclude definitely what was reasonable to expect of this child in reading, but chose 6.6 as the best of the three alternatives.

Paul was given the *Peabody Individual Achievement Test.* His grade scores were:

NAME OF SUBTEST	GRADE EQUIVALENT	STANDARD SCORE
Mathematics	6.4	103
Reading Recognition	3.9	85
Reading Comprehension	5.3	97
Spelling	4.2	89
General Information	5.8	100
Total Test	5.0	97

Observation of behavior during testing.   Paul was cooperative during testing. He showed some signs of nervousness on the reading subtests. He ran his fingers through his hair and glanced around the room frequently.

Interpretation of test results.   Paul scored below his estimated potential in all areas tested except mathematics. Mathematics vocabulary and reasoning appeared to be adequate.

The clinician decided to test him further in reading and spelling to determine his strengths and weaknesses in those academic subjects, but noted that mathematical computation was not adequately screened by the diagnostic instrument. The clinician noted that Paul's spelling was at a 4.2-grade level on a test which required him to pick the correctly spelled word from four visual presentations. To prevent a superficial diagnosis, the clinician administered the spelling subtest of the *Wide Range Achievement Test.* Paul achieved a grade equivalent of 2.9, with a standard score of 77, and a percentile rank of 6. The discrepancy was sufficient to cause suspicion that the difference was due to the different tasks that the child was expected to perform. Although the *Peabody Individual Achievement Test* required a highly visual form of spelling, the *Wide Range Achievement Test* required Paul to spell words from dictation.

Diagnostic Achievement Tests.

Durrell Analysis of Reading Difficulty   (selected sections)

NAME OF SUBTEST	GRADE EQUIVALENT	COMPREHENSION
Oral Reading	4L	Good
Silent Reading	4L	Fair
Listening Comprehension	3	—
Flash Words	3H	—
Word Analysis	4H	—

Observation of behavior.   Paul appeared to be nervous during testing. He moved a great deal in his chair and ran his fingers through his hair. He appeared to be trying very hard to do well.

Interpretation of test results.   On this test, the oral and silent reading were at the same grade level and well below his estimated reading potential. The low scores appeared to be due to slow reading time. Comprehension was better in oral reading, when compared with silent reading. Both flash words and word analysis scores were below his estimated level, with flash words being significantly lower. From the results of these four subtests, it appeared that Paul had difficulty in immediate recognition of words, which seemed to result in accurate but slow and inefficient reading at a fourth-grade level. Paul's score on the listening comprehension subtest showed this skill to be one of significant weakness for him. This very important skill necessary for school success required remediation.

Silent Reading Diagnostic Test.

NAME OF SUBTEST	GRADE EQUIVALENT
Word Recognition Skills	
Total Right	3.6
Words in Isolation	3.8
Words in Context	3.1
Recognition Techniques	
Total Right	6.2
Visual Structural Analysis	6.8
Syllabication	6.0
Word Synthesis	4.5
Phonic Knowledge	
Total Right	3.9
Beginning Sounds	4.0
Ending Sounds	4.0
Vowel and Consonant Sounds	3.0

Observation of behavior.   Paul appeared to try very hard. He showed some signs of nervousness: tapping his pencil on the table, running his fingers through his hair, and asking when the test would be over.

Interpretations of test results.   Paul's weaknesses on the *Silent Reading Diagnostic Test* were in the areas of Word Recognition Skills and Phonic Knowledge. He showed strength in the Recognition Techniques, mostly in visual analysis, and weakness in his knowledge of phonics, especially in isolated single-letter sounds. His error pattern showed strength in proper left-to-right visual inspection of words, free from reversals or orientation difficulties.

Further informal testing in phonics knowledge revealed secure knowledge of CVC words and common vowel teams in reading, insecurity in application of phonics knowledge to spelling, and great difficulty in giving the sounds of isolated letters, especially short vowel sounds and *r*-controlled vowel sounds.

The answers to the chapter 7 diagnostic questions are

1. Is Paul correctly classified as a disabled reader? Yes, although he possessed some well-developed skills in visual analysis of words, his overall level of functioning in reading was well below what was reasonable to expect of him. He had a limiting condition complicated by a slight hearing impairment.

2. What is the nature of the training needed? The remedial plan for Paul included five items. (1) Phonics work-sheet activities stressing visual associations among word elements, larger word parts, and their sounds, which Paul completed silently. (2) Games using word and phrase cards designed to exemplify various phonics generalizations to which Paul was required to respond orally. (3) He was also taught to make visual-mental pictures to aid himself with certain difficult sounds. For example, he chose to think of a view of a city to help himself with the

soft sound of ''c.'' (4) Paul was encouraged to read during reading instruction time and especially at home from several high-interest, easy-reading level books which were chosen to be at a recreational reading level. He also did some prepared oral reading. (5) There were exercises in which Paul listened to short, simple stories about subjects interesting to him and then paraphrased the stories, answered questions about them, or drew illustrations of them. He also followed increasingly complex oral directions.

3. Who can most effectively give the remedial work? Paul received 40 hours of direct one-to-one instruction during the summer and returned to his school in the fall, where he received daily, small-group instruction. Diagnostic findings were shared with the concerned teacher.

4. How can improvement be made most efficiently? Aside from encouraging Paul to do a lot of recreational reading, the rest of the educational program emphasized overcoming auditory difficulties by using visual means and emphasizing work-sheet activities and games. Although much of his work was done silently, he did respond orally in gamelike situations, in prepared reading situations, and in response to short stories read to him.

5. Does the child have any limiting conditions that must be considered? Paul was a friendly, likable, well-mannered boy. But because he was hearing-impaired, he was uneasy and insecure in situations in which he had to listen carefully. It seemed to be important in teaching him to use visual examples and to help him see what was wanted. Once he knew what was expected, he worked well. He enjoyed activities in which he could express himself through drawing and he was able to draw fairly well.

6. Are there any environmental conditions that might interfere with progress in reading? The parents were completely supportive of Paul and of the reading program. They were interested in the books he brought home for reading and showed obvious delight in his progress.

Results.   After the summer instruction period, Paul demonstrated mastery of all letter sounds in reading. His silent and oral reading speed became more typical of a fifth than of a fourth-grade student. His listening improved to the point where he could obey a series of five complex commands with 100 percent accuracy. As Paul progressed in the program, it was noted that he became less tense when he read. His mother also remarked that at home she noticed he was beginning to enjoy reading. Paul continued to make gains in subsequent small-group instruction during his sixth-grade year. Then the instructional emphasis was changed and letter-sound associations were no longer stressed. Rather, instruction was directed toward helping Paul develop his knowledge of word meanings, increase his fund of sight words, utilize context clues, and rely heavily on his visual abilities in reading. Although during his sixth-grade year Paul had not as yet reached his expectancy level in reading, his classroom work reflected improvement in reading and was comparable to that of his classmates.

SUMMARY

In this chapter, we have considered the modifications of remedial instruction that are necessary for correcting reading disabilities made more complex because of limiting conditions within the child. Children who have reading problems and who are also learning under other handicaps are encountered by every remedial teacher. Frequently the overall education of these children is directed by specialists who have been trained to teach children with the various handicaps discussed in this chapter. The remedial reading teacher can obtain many helpful suggestions and insights into the particular adjustments needed for a specific child by discussing the child's problems with the special-education teacher. The responsibility of the remedial teacher is to diagnose the reading problem, locate the nature of the confusions in reading, and suggest modifications in reading methods needed for correcting the disability. The classroom teacher, working cooperatively with the remedial reading teacher, should be aware of the child's reading program, so that other phases of his education may be coordinated with the reading-improvement program. What these children need most is an adequate diagnosis of the nature of their reading disabilities and a well-planned program of remedial instruction, modified to take into account their learning handicaps.

Among the children with complex reading disabilities are those who are visually-impaired, auditorily-impaired, neurologically-impaired, emotionally maladjusted, mentally handicapped, or speech-impaired. Individualized treatment is necessary for any child with a complex reading disability. The teacher is especially important in working with handicapped children. She must be patient and understanding. It is essential that she be skilled and versatile in remedial reading because one approach will not fit all.

Children with moderate visual impairments should be taught by methods that emphasize auditory approaches. Those with more severe visual handicaps require, in addition, bright light, large print, and short reading periods. Learning activities that do not require close visual work should be stressed.

Children with mild hearing impairment get along well in normal classroom activities that emphasize visual approaches to reading. Overreliance on phonics should be avoided in teaching hearing-impaired children. For them, visual techniques of word recognition should be stressed even more than for children with milder hearing impairments. Children with severe and extreme hearing impairments should be taught to read by specialists in deaf education. Emphasis should be upon sight words, the visual characteristics of words, and silent reading.

The few disabled readers who also have neurological impairments constitute some of the most complex remedial cases. These children require carefully arranged training programs, designed to develop their impaired perceptual and motor skills to the fullest extent possible. They also require remedial reading instruction that is modified to use their areas of strength and to avoid their weak perceptual and motor skills.

Most children with reading disabilities show some symptoms of emotional maladjustment or behavioral disorder. A variety of behaviors are common. Certain students need to be drawn out while others need to be instructed with a minimum of teacher interaction. Children experiencing behavioral disorders benefit from close managment coupled with reasonable goals.

Mentally handicapped children can also be reading disabled. The proportion of reading disabilities in this group is about the same as among children with average and above-average intelligence. With proper instruction, the mentally handicapped can learn to read and to maintain their reading competence at a reasonable level. A modified phonics approach stressing drill has been used successfully in remedial work with slow-learning children. The Hegge-Kirk method, which provides gradual introduction of skills, much repetition, and involves a great deal of phonics drill, represents a method that has worked well with many educable children. A broader method, similar to good developmental reading instruction, but highly individualized, seems appropriate for nonremedial, mentally handicapped children in the regular classroom.

Children with speech difficulties should have corrective work in speech by a specialist. As their speech becomes better and more fluent, they may be reintroduced to regular methods of remedial instruction.

STUDY QUESTIONS

1. What educational adaptations should be considered for low vision children?
2. How do educational adaptations for the child with slight hearing impairment, with mild and marked hearing impairment, and with severe and extreme hearing impairment differ?
3. Why do teachers of the neurologically-limited child have to adjust instruction on a daily basis for some of their students?
4. How can children be helped to attend to their reading, to work actively, and to complete their work?
5. What simple educational adaptations most benefit slow learners?

SELECTED READINGS

GENTILE, L. M., AND M. M. McMILLAN. *Stress and Reading Difficulties.* Newark, DE: International Reading Association, Inc, 1987.

HART, B. O. *Teaching Reading to Deaf Children.* New York: Alexander Graham Bell Association for the Deaf, 1976.

HEWETT, F. M., AND F. D. TAYLOR. *The Emotionally Disturbed Child in the Classroom: The Orchestration of Success,* 2nd ed., Chaps. 6, 8, and 9. Boston: Allyn & Bacon, Inc., 1980.

KIRK, S. A. AND J. J. GALLAGHER. *Educating Exceptional Children,* 5th ed., Chaps. 4–9. Boston: Houghton Mifflin Company, 1986.

McCORMICK, S. *Remedial and Clinical Reading Instruction,* Chap. 20. Columbus, OH: Charles E. Merrill Publishing Company, 1987.

MOORES, D. F. *Educating the Deaf: Psychology, Principles, and Practices,* 2nd ed., Chap. 13. Boston: Houghton Mifflin Company, 1982.

MYERS, P. E., AND D. D. HAMMILL. *Methods for Learning Disorders,* 3rd ed., Chap. 7. New York: John Wiley & Sons, Inc., 1976.

SAVAGE, J. F., AND J. F. MOONEY. *Teaching Reading to Children with Special Needs,* Chaps. 4–7. Boston: Allyn & Bacon, Inc., 1979.

TELFORD, C. W. AND J. M. SAWREY. *The Exceptional Individual,* 4th ed., Chaps. 10, 11, 13, and 14. Englewood Cliffs, NJ: Prentice-Hall, Inc., 1981.

14

Correcting Basic Comprehension Deficiencies

At all grade levels reading instruction should serve to develop comprehension. The fundamental goal in seeking to produce effective readers is to enable them to comprehend whatever printed materials will serve their purpose, no matter how difficult these materials may be. The acquisition of a sight vocabulary, skill in recognizing words, and verbal facility in general, are all aimed at achieving adequate understanding and interpretation of the meanings embodied in printed symbols. The extent to which these meanings are clearly and accurately understood and interpreted by the reader represents the degree to which he has become a good reader.

Comprehension depends on the background the reader brings to the reading, his vocabulary development, and his ability to interpret the author's words into concepts. Through constant attention to words and their use the child builds a meaning vocabulary. He attends to words, phrases, and sentence structure because he finds them useful in getting along in his environment. There is a wide variety in the vocabulary, the use of sentence structure clues (*syntax clues*), and the use of significant meaning clues (*semantic clues*) that children bring to reading. They possess various language components because of the differences in the preschool learning environments they have experienced. Even their language patterns may be quite different one from another.

It has been emphasized that true reading is reading with understanding or comprehension. Comprehension depends on facility in using concepts or meanings evolved through experience. To be of use in reading, the concepts acquired through experience must be attached to words or groups of words as symbols of their meanings. These words become a part of one's understanding and speaking vocabulary. Then, when a reader recognizes a word or group of words, perception of the printed symbol stimulates recollection or construction of meanings for which the symbol stands. Obviously, the meanings recalled are those possessed by the reader and necessarily must have evolved through prior experience. The meaning may be derived directly from those prior experiences, or it may consist of a newly constructed meaning which results from combining and reorganizing meanings already possessed by the reader. The author brings known ideas together in such a way that the reader senses a new relationship and therefore gains a new idea, concept, or sensory impression. Take for instance, the meanings aroused when a fourth-grade city child reads the sentence ''The tired rider drooped in his saddle as his spotted horse walked along the mountain trail.'' Since the reader has not seen such a rider, he may organize the meaning of the sentence from a variety of remembered visual experiences as (1) his father napping with his head bent forward as he rests in an easy chair, (2) a bridle path through the park, (3) a mounted policeman sitting erect on his black horse, (4) a spotted black and white dog, and (5) the scenery during an auto trip through hilly country. By combining these concepts, the child may achieve an approximation of the meaning intended by the writer of the sentence. So one reads primarily with his experiences, which are based upon sensory impressions such as hearing, seeing, tasting, smelling, and touching. Also involved is one's behavior in adjusting to all kinds of situations, including the accompanying emotional reactions and imagination.

The development of concepts which carry meanings begins early in a child's life. Activities at home, hearing the talk of parents and other children and adults, listening to radio and viewing television, trips around the neighborhood, and sometimes more extended travel are all involved in developing a hearing-meaning vocabulary. Concepts are acquired. The child begins to use words and, later, sentences correctly. Using oral language forms precisely is acquired gradually. For use in reading, a meaning must be attached to a word, for it is only by the use of words that meanings can be recalled. If the recalled meanings are to be precise, the words which stand for those meanings have been in the usage vocabulary of the reader. The degree to which he is able to use a word in his language and thinking determines to a large extent how effectively he will be able to use it in reading.

In normal development, a child's experiences lead him to use sentences for verbal communication. Sentences are groups of words organized into meaningful relationships. Nearly all reading matter is in the form of sentences. How well a reader understands sentences and how skillful he is in using sentence forms determines how well he will be able to read print organized into sentences. The precise meanings of certain words in a sentence are comprehended from the context of the sentence.

The comprehension of sentences is facilitated when reading is done by thought units. A thought unit is a group of words which make up a meaningful sequence in a sentence. For instance, in the sentence "One of the men / saw the bricks / start to fall," there are three thought units as the spacings indicate. Verbal facility in oral communication leads to phrasing into thought units. Growth in reading sentences by thought units, however, is relatively slow. It is dependent on increased efficiency in the recognition of single words. Only when the child has developed an adequate sight vocabulary, can he group words into thought units. Some grouping (two-word units) occurs during the latter part of grade one. Progress is more rapid from the third grade on. The average reader is fairly proficient in reading by thought units by the time he reaches the sixth grade.

The child with good verbal facility is able to organize his ideas into thought units, which are reflected in his spoken sentences. A similar trend is found in reading. The child who is a word-by-word reader seldom grasps the meaning of a sentence as a whole. But when a child is reading by thought units, the resulting organization of the material aids comprehension. Proficiency in perceiving words in thought units is usually accompanied by understanding of the material being read.

Attention must also be directed to comprehension of paragraphs and larger units. To comprehend the material in a paragraph requires an understanding of the relations between the sentences in that paragraph. This involves identifying the topical sentence containing the key idea and understanding its relation to the explanatory or amplifying sentences.

We must also note the relation between paragraphs in longer selections. In a well-written story or article, the paragraphs are arranged in an orderly manner. The introductory paragraph or paragraphs usually briefly present the plan, central theme, or purpose of the story or article. Succeeding paragraphs, arranged in logical sequence, carry the story through its principal points and on to the ending. In expository material, the paragraphs follow one another in orderly sequence, providing the details to explain the event, process, or activity outlined in the introduction. For comprehension of larger units, the pupil needs to understand this relation between the introductory and subsequent paragraphs.

Essentially the same processes are involved in comprehending printed material and in understanding spoken words. In both, perception of words provokes meanings which lead to comprehension. The meanings provoked by the perceived words depend mainly on two factors: (1) the learner's or the reader's entire background of experience, and (2) his facility in language usage for purposes of communication. Children show marked differences in the length and complexity of a selection which they can comprehend.

During the primary grades, when pupils are in the process of mastering the mechanics of reading, listening comprehension tends to be reading comprehension. It must be kept in mind that when a child begins grade one, there is a six-year lag between reading comprehension and listening comprehension. From birth on, the child has been developing listening comprehension. Furthermore, at the first-grade level, a child normally would hear more running words in two days than he reads in the entire first-grade program. Word repetition and vocabulary control in first-grade materials are advantageous to rapid development in reading comprehension.

As soon as there is progress in mastering the mechanics of reading, occurring sooner for the more able child, the two modes of comprehension become equal. Then, as greater proficiency and maturity are reached, reading comprehension may become more proficient than listening comprehension. In the primary grades, considerable time must be devoted to developing word-recognition techniques and to building a sight vocabulary. As these skills improve, there is greater opportunity for the pupil to concentrate on comprehension. Then, with a richer background of reading and other experiences, with increasing maturity and improved reading proficiency through the upper grades, reading comprehension becomes superior to listening comprehension. This is because the reader can stop and reflect, evaluate or debate, or reread parts of the material.

The implication of these trends for instruction to improve reading comprehension seems clear. Though word-recognition techniques and other mechanics should be emphasized in the early grades, so that they may become as automatic as possible, comprehension should not be neglected. With mastery of the mechanics, the major portion of the pupil's attention during reading can be devoted to comprehension. With the teacher's guidance, this will become more and more proficient. Thus, the well-balanced program of instruction through the grades is dominant in developing reading comprehension to a level that is as good as or better than listening comprehension. This balanced program will also, of course, give appropriate emphasis to oral language and usage, which play an important role in improving reading.

This development of reading comprehension to a high level of proficiency should be stressed through the grades. As the child progresses, his acquisition of information depends more and more upon what he reads. It is desirable, therefore, for reading comprehension to become as good as or better than listening comprehension.

Essential to mature reading comprehension is the development of the child's metacognition or awareness and control of his own thought processes. Examples of metacognitive abilities include setting one's own reading goals, determining one's own methods for reaching them, deciding for oneself what strategies to pursue if difficulties are encountered, and confirming for oneself when reading goals are attained. There is also a distinct need for improving the ability to comprehend a wide variety of materials for many purposes. Different abilities are used when one is reading to decide which of two items is a ''best buy'' as compared with reading to enjoy a book of poetry.

Overcoming specific comprehension defects will be discussed in the next chapter. The disabled reader who is low in all types of comprehension is limited in either suitable word-recognition skills, discussed in Chapters 10 and 11, or in one or more of the basic comprehension abilities. This chapter will be devoted to a discussion of remedial teaching of the basic comprehension abilities, under the following headings:

1. Limited meaning vocabulary
2. Ineffective use of sentence sense
3. Insufficient comprehension of longer units

LIMITED MEANING VOCABULARY

The acquisition of word meanings is fundamental to all comprehension in reading. When word meanings are ample, precise, and rich, and when semantic variations are understood, there are adequate concepts for the pupils to draw upon to do effective reading. Without satisfactory word meanings, comprehension of either spoken or printed language is impossible. Comprehension of sentences and paragraphs naturally requires an understanding of their words.

There are four classifications of vocabulary: listening, speaking, reading, and writing. When a child enters school, his listening vocabulary far exceeds the other three. While estimates of the size of the listening vocabularies of first-grade children vary considerably, the consensus is that the average is nearly 20,000 words. Whatever the actual number, authorities agree that the listening vocabularies of first-grade children are extensive, and that the size has increased in recent years because of television, motion pictures, travel, and more reading aloud to children by their parents.

Entering first-grade children's average speaking vocabularies are about 6,000 words. Their reading and writing vocabularies are little more than their own names. Within a few years, the typical child's reading vocabulary exceeds his speaking vocabulary, and for some, their reading vocabulary surpasses the listening vocabulary.

Some children will not have developed meaning vocabularies large enough to read and understand materials above the third-grade level. These children should be classified as disabled in one of the basic comprehension abilities, namely, limited in meaning vocabulary (see case study in Chapter 10). There are two tasks in remediation. First, the meaning vocabulary must be increased, and second, the habit of paying attention to words and their meanings must be established.

It must be recognized that word meaning has several aspects which are not discrete but overlap both in their importance and development. The teaching of vocabulary entails more than merely teaching the child to recognize words. It comprises, in addition to recognition, enriching new words and extending their meanings.

The nature and accuracy of the meaning depends upon several factors.

1. The extensiveness of meaning depends upon the number and kinds of situations in which the word is met.

2. The accuracy depends upon the skill with which the reader relates the new understanding to previous backgrounds.
3. The vividness depends upon the emotion, interest, acceptance, and purposefulness of the reader.
4. Retention depends upon the usefulness of the word to the reader.

General Remedial Approaches to Limited Meaning Vocabulary

There are general approaches to vocabulary development, used by the classroom teacher from the first grade on, that should be emphasized further for the disabled reader who has shown limited growth in learning word meanings and who has failed to establish the habit of attending to their meanings. These approaches include the use of firsthand experiences, wide reading, and audiovisual aids.

Firsthand experiences offer many opportunities for building understanding of words and for acquiring the habit of learning their meanings. Reading-disabled children are frequently deficient in those experiences which furnish a supply of word meanings sufficient to ensure reading with understanding. The remedial teacher should provide the needed experiences as much as possible. The procedures are essentially the same as in any good instructional program. The only difference is that the instruction is more individualized. Part of the time the teacher will be concerned with a single child. At other times she may deal with a small group of children with similar deficiencies. Furnishing the desired experiences should be integrated with the rest of a well-coordinated program of remedial instruction.

Although teachers often plan field trips to provide firsthand experiences, many valuable firsthand experiences do not necessarily involve elaborate field trips. McCormick (1987) suggests taking students outside to examine details of the school building or walking to nearby sites. Highlights of the trip can be filmed for later use in language development. A second alternative is to make use of real experiences that students have had outside of school. For example, an athletic event a student has attended can be the basis of vocabulary building activities. Firsthand experiences within the classroom, such as, when a child brings in a model airplane to show the class, when science experiments are performed, or when a presentation is made by a parent or member of the community, can form the basis for vocabulary development for a small group of remedial readers. Reutzel (1985) has suggested that, on occasion, enrichment activities suggested as the last part of a basal reader lesson, can be introduced first, to build experiential background and introduce essential vocabulary.

To gain the most from an experience, careful planning is necessary. As noted by Dolch (1951), experience alone does not educate. Since the meanings a child learns from reading are determined by the nature and clearness of his concepts, these experiences should yield as varied and accurate meanings as possible. Acquiring experiences should be a purposeful activity. Children should be prepared beforehand so that they may look for and understand as many features as possible. They should know what to look for and what questions they would like to have answered.

If experiences are to be profitable, the child must think about them, seek out their meaning, and use them in subsequent speaking, listening, and reading. For motivation toward this end, there must be an opportunity both before and after an experience for discussion guided by the teacher. During this exchange of ideas and answering of questions, there will be opportunity to define purposes, extend information, clear up misconceptions, and clarify and enrich meanings. This preparation for experience and the discussion following it tends to be highly profitable whatever the nature of the experience. Development of word meanings and concepts is also promoted by the exchange of experiences in informal discussion. In all this planning and discussion, children should be encouraged to seek meaning in everything they encounter and to ask for additional explanations and further clarification of whatever they do not understand.

Growth in word meanings comes with use. Having acquired new "labels" or words through experience, children should be provided the opportunity for prompt use of the new vocabulary in speaking, listening, writing, and reading.

Wide reading is another way in which word meanings and the habit of attending to them is built. Many remedial teachers select a book highly interesting to a disabled reader and read it aloud to him as a motivating device. They show the child some of the rewards that come from being able to read. These remedial teachers also use the content of the book to teach word meanings and the habit of studying them. The teacher discusses the story with the child, pointing out the well-chosen words and picturesque connotations the author used. She also shows the disabled reader ways in which the content defines the meaning of words and how the author defines words for the reader. Both the teacher and the disabled reader are aware that his problem is one of building vocabulary. A disabled reader should be shown how a mature reader uses these aids for vocabulary development. This is applicable to the intermediate-grade child, and even more to the high school and adult disabled reader. It is at these levels that lack of vocabulary growth becomes most evident.

The disabled reader should be encouraged to note by himself words that are attractive to him, that have unusual meanings, or that are especially descriptive. In this way, the habit of attending to word meanings is developed and vocabulary-building skills are gained. The disabled reader who is limited in vocabulary should also do extensive independent reading both during reading sessions and at home.

Remedial teachers can have interesting easy-to-read materials available for students and can ask them to check these out for home reading. Parents can provide a short block of time in the home, free of distractions, when children are expected to read. Classroom teachers can encourage all children, including remedial readers, to read more widely by providing short blocks of class time for children to read materials of their own choosing.

The extension and enrichment of word meanings are aided by wide reading of interesting and relatively easy materials. For such reading, not more than one unfamiliar word should appear in 100 to 200 running words. Ordinarily each new book, story, or article that is read introduces new words to the reader and repeats words previously encountered. The use of old words in a variety of contexts broadens and clarifies their meanings. The more important new words are seen enough to acquire more and more meaning. It is unrealistic to expect that a clear meaning for every new word will be learned right away. This does not mean that unfamiliar words should be ignored. It is particularly important that the reader pay attention to any unfamiliar words he meets in context. Eventually many of these words become familiar. Motivation is maintained by guiding children to material which catches their interest and has just the right amount of difficulty, so that the context will yield the most intelligible clues to the meaning of any new words.

In any wide reading program, the proper use of clues from their contexts is essential if the concepts or meanings of the new words are to be learned satisfactorily. The remedial teacher, therefore, needs to test the child's skill in the use of various context clues and structural aids and to give whatever instruction is necessary, using methods described later. For best results, this checking and training in the use of clues must be a continuing program with each disabled reader, since this skill is ordinarily slow to develop.

The disabled reader should be encouraged to discuss his independent reading with his remedial teacher. The discussion should include new words he has found useful, and it should include using them in his own speech. He should also report on the aids to meaning he used in enlarging his vocabulary. This can be done because the disabled reader helped in formulating the *plan of his remedial program.*

Audiovisual aids can be used to build clear, precise, and extensive meanings of words. It is not feasible, and frequently not possible, to develop word meanings by direct experience alone. Much worthwhile experience can be provided pupils through secondary media. Among these are such visual and auditory aids as models and construction projects, dramatization, pictures, exhibits of materials related to a new topic, motion pictures, filmstrips, chalkboard sketches, charts, maps, slides, recordings, radio and television programs, and educational talks by outsiders.

In using these vicarious aids to build word meanings, the remedial teacher should recognize that vocabularies are built to the extent that these aids are used properly. It is inefficient merely to present such experiences without first preparing the students for them and without following the presentation with discussion. The preparatory work should set purposes for viewing or listening. These purposes should include the idea that vocabulary growth is one outcome of the experience. The preparatory work should indicate the way in which the audiovisual material may best be studied. During the discussion following the presentation, the students should be encouraged to use the new vocabulary and even to explain the meanings of the terms used. The fundamental steps in teaching a reading selection, discussed in Chapter 9 could well be used in teaching audiovisual material. It is obvious that the teacher should preview the material in order to prepare for using it in the classroom.

Formal Methods of Enriching Word Meanings

The teaching of word meaning is valuable only when it is done properly. We have emphasized that direct, systematic, well-planned drill on words in context increases knowledge of vocabulary, but that teaching of words in isolation is usually wasteful and ineffective. The correct meaning of a word frequently depends on its context. Often, familiar words are used in an unfamiliar sense. Teaching these new meanings of old words and the relation of the particular meaning to context is a considerable part of vocabulary training. (The teaching of word meanings for technical terms found in the content fields is a topic to be taken up in the next chapter.)

In the present discussion, the authors, defend the view that word study can be profitable in developing meanings only to the degree that it consists of using each word in various contexts, of associating it with concrete experiences, of giving it a sufficient number of oral and written repetitions in a varied program of wide reading. First of all, word study should deal with new words met in context. Learning a word's meaning then fulfills the child's immediate need, his present desire to understand the passage. This should be followed by using the word in discussion and in oral and written activities. Finally, he should read several materials in which the word occurs frequently.

Since many words have several meanings or shades of meaning, the initial contact with a new word in context can provide it with only a limited meaning. To extend and enrich the meaning of a new word, the word should also be presented in various contexts selected to bring out and emphasize different shades of meaning or different meanings. Exercises of this kind may be followed by discussions and other exercises designed to point up the different shades of meaning. It is also helpful for the remedial teacher to introduce activities which apply meanings of the word to such concrete situations as demonstration and use of equipment, giving titles to pictures or drawings, and writing letters. These concrete activities are useful techniques for extending and enriching the meaning of a word through association with doing something that is not strictly limited to talking and reading. Besides these, more formal reinforcing exercises are helpful in overcoming limited vocabulary difficulties. These will be discussed under the following headings:

1. Role of the basic sight vocabulary
2. Use of context clues and authors' definitions
3. Use of structural aids
4. Use of the dictionary

Role of the basic sight vocabulary.   As already implied, the child can make little progress in reading without a basic sight vocabulary. This becomes especially important for the disabled reader. The Dolch basic sight vocabulary (1945) of 220 service words contains about 65 percent of all the words in the reading material of the primary grades and nearly 60 percent of those in intermediate grades. With normal progress, the child will have mastered these 220 service words during his third year in school.

Many disabled readers are particularly deficient in recognizing and understanding the proper use of these words. When recognition of these words is being taught, emphasis should be on developing an understanding of their meaning in context. One way to do this is to organize exercises like the following:

Directions: Read the sentence on the left and then underline the word at the right that gives the idea or meaning of the word underlined in the sentence.

1. He sat *under* the tree.   (*a*) when   (*b*) where   (*c*) how   (*d*) why
2. He left *on* July 6.   (*a*) when   (*b*) where   (*c*) how   (*d*) why
3. He ran *because* he was late.   (*a*) when   (*b*) where   (*c*) how   (*d*) why
4. Jack has a *brown* coat.   (*a*) color   (*b*) wood   (*c*) cloth   (*d*) straw
5. Ann has the *right* box.   (*a*) odd   (*b*) wooden   (*c*) correct   (*d*) small

The meanings of some of these service words can be taught best in terms of usage in context rather than as defining words. For instance:

When John and Bill reached home, mother gave them some cookies.

Children are taught that *them* means the persons, animals, or things talked or written about.

A variety of sentences to illustrate this meaning should be presented to the disabled reader. Similar treatment should be given to the meanings of such words as *they, could,* and *what.*

Many of the basic sight words are particularly difficult for disabled readers to learn and retain. It is a cardinal principle that those words which carry the most meaning are remembered best. Without the teacher's guidance, such words as *where, their, by, myself,* and *which* do not have much meaning to many disabled readers.

Use of context clues and authors' definitions. The meaning of a new word can frequently be derived from its context. To do this, the child needs to comprehend the rest of the words in the sentence or passage. Many disabled readers make little or no use of context in trying to discover the meanings of unfamiliar words. They should be taught to read the rest of the sentence or passage and then look back and try to decide what the unknown word probably means. For instance, note the sentence:

The Indians in the canoe were from a reservation, the land set aside for Indians who still lived in the northern part of the state.

The word *reservation* acquires meaning from the context which follows in the rest of the sentence. Take another example:

Although Mary was surprised when Jack <u>glared</u> at her, she was not disturbed by his angry look.

If a sentence is part of a story, other sentences may amplify and clarify the meaning. Although some "meanings" may be wrong, this training usually builds considerable skill in deriving meaning from context.

Context clues to word meanings frequently come from the author's definitions. Such a definition may be the explanation given in the rest of the sentence or it may come from another word or phrase in the sentence. Sometimes it is in a separate sentence. A few examples follow:

1. When Mother did not like the <u>retort</u> Harry made, she asked him to <u>answer</u> her more politely.
2. The boys were delighted with the summer <u>cruise—a voyage by steamship</u> on the Great Lakes.
3. Just after we got on the train the <u>conductor</u> gave the engineer the signal to start. In addition to <u>directing the trainmen</u>, the conductor also <u>collects the passengers' tickets</u>.

Another difficulty which disabled readers have is in choosing the correct meaning of a word that has several meanings. For instance, the correct meaning of *paid* in the following sentence depends on the context of the complete sentence: "Jack paid dearly for his mistake." In fact, the correct meaning for such words is sensed *only* in terms of the context.

Use of structural aids.   Direct, systematic, well-organized drill on words is valuable for the disabled reader in developing word meanings when this drill is on words in context or is related to the usage of words in context. When the remedial teacher produces sufficient motivation to lead to a general interest in words, she will find it profitable to devote some study to the meanings suggested by common prefixes, suffixes, and word roots, and to synonyms and antonyms. This approach to word study should be used when a word that lends itself to analysis is met in context. A few examples will illustrate.

1. The sailors <u>aboard</u> the ship (prefix and word root).
2. He has a <u>kingly</u> appearance (word root and suffix).
3. The army was <u>undefeated</u> (prefix, root, suffix).

In addition to identifying the root word and prefix or suffix with their meanings, the teacher can explore the possibility of making other words by adding other prefixes or suffixes at appropriate times. The meanings of the more common word roots, prefixes, and suffixes may be worked out in this manner. The disabled reader will be helped by such reinforcement training in identifying and understanding word roots, prefixes, and suffixes as used in the following types of exercises:

1. Draw a line under the root word in each of the following and tell what the root word means:

   worker   untie   kindly

2. Draw a line under the prefix in each of the following and tell how the prefix changes the meaning of the root word:

   unlike   return   displace

3. Draw a line under the suffix in each of the following and tell how the suffix changes the meaning of the root word:

   slowly   kindness   doubtful

After roots, prefixes, and suffixes have been identified, their uses in developing meanings should be brought out through discussion and supplementary exercises. One way of doing this is to rewrite sentences. The disabled reader is given a sentence containing words with prefixes. He is asked to identify the word with a prefix and then told to rewrite the sentence with a new word or phrase that will replace it without changing the meaning of the sentence. Example:

Your bicycle is unlike mine.
Your bicycle is different from mine.

Training in structural aids to meaning should be given in context, as illustrated in the following exercises:

The prefix *un* can mean (a) not, (b) opposite action, or (c) something was removed. Show which meaning is implied by putting the appropriate letter before each sentence.

_____1. The boy untied the horse.

_____2. The man was unkind to the horse.

_____3. The rider was unhorsed.

Complete the following sentences:

1. A snowball is a ball made of _____.
2. A steamboat is a boat run by _____.
3. A flowerpot is a pot for a _____.
4. A fireplace is a place to have a _____.

Use of the dictionary. Proper use of a good dictionary can be an important aid to the disabled reader in developing word meanings. Few children acquire the dictionary habit or know the wealth of fascinating information that can be found in a dictionary. Development of the dictionary habit depends upon a well-organized program of instruction carried out by a skilled and enthusiastic remedial teacher. No child will enjoy using a dictionary to get word meanings until he has become skillful in finding a desired word quickly. After finding a word, the child must know how to select from the several meanings listed the one that fits the context from which the word came. This means that he must have a grasp of the meaning of the rest of the sentence or paragraph in which the unknown word occurs. Considerable training is required to develop skill in choosing correct dictionary meanings. Exercises such as those found in workbooks are easily constructed. An example follows:

Directions: Several numbered definitions are given for the word in heavy black type. Read the word and its definitions. Next read the sentences below the definitions. Write the number of the definition in front of the sentence in which the meaning of the word is used.

grate (1) grind off in small pieces (2) rub with a harsh sound (3) have an annoying or unpleasant effect

_____Please grate the cheese to put on the salad.

_____Mary's manners always grate on me.

In addition to developing skill in using the dictionary to find word meanings, this type of exercise provides further training in deriving meanings from context clues and in noting different meanings for the same word.

Experience with synonyms and antonyms enriches word meanings when the words are in context. Some dictionaries for children give synonyms for certain words but not antonyms. Ordinarily exercises like those just given or like those to follow are used for choosing words of like or opposite meanings.

Directions (synonyms): Read each sentence and note the underlined word in it. Select from the list of words below the sentences the word that means the same or nearly the same as the underlined word. Write the word selected on the line after the sentence.

Father had no reason to doubt Jim. _____
The automobile repairman needs many implements. _____
trucks   tools   avoid   mistrust

In a similar way, exploring synonyms (words of like meaning) and antonyms (opposites) of words in context enriches the meaning of words. Supplementary exercises like the following may be used:

1. Underline the word that means the same as beautiful:
    pale   pretty   lonely   thoughtful
2. Underline the word that means the opposite of noisy:
    boastful   tiny   quiet   rosy

Informal Methods of Enriching Vocabulary

There are many creative approaches to enriching and expanding the vocabularies of disabled readers. These approaches also develop the word-study habits necessary for continuing growth in the reading vocabularies of intermediate, high school, and adult readers. The following activities are merely suggestions from many possible ones. The Cloze technique, often used in testing comprehension, can be used as an imaginative use of word meanings.

As the horse approached his stable, he _____ ahead, but his rider _____ _____ in the saddle.

The student is to think of as many groups of words as he can to complete the sentence in order to change the picture the sentence paints. The student might think of groups such as

> galloped, slumped over
> trudged, sat erect
> walked, felt insecure
> stumbled, sat confidently

The disabled reader might help his remedial teacher by writing exercises for younger readers. Multiple-choice exercises using antonyms, synonyms, or semantic variations could be constructed. A dictionary could be used to find the choices. This would be both a creative and a useful dictionary activity.

Another dictionary exercise which would be both instructive and motivating would be for the disabled reader to make his own dictionary of new words that he found interesting. He would see his list of interesting words grow, and he would discover new meanings for many of them.

Encouraging the disabled reader to write stories about events for his parents to read is another good activity. He should use the new words he has found interesting. Experience charts are an especially effective and creative activity in building vocabulary when groups of disabled readers work together. The group should discuss the choice of words while making the experience chart and decide why one word expresses an idea better than another.

INEFFECTIVE USE OF SENTENCE SENSE

Besides the meanings of words, there are many other basic comprehension skills needed to understand sentences. The ones needed in sentence comprehension are reading in thought units, using punctuation as an aid to meaning, interpreting connectives, identifying pronoun-antecedent relationships, and adjusting to varied sentence structures. To comprehend the increasingly more complex sentences the student will meet in intermediate grades, high school, and adult reading, he must be able to understand the relationships among the various parts of sentences. These skills must continue to develop for complete comprehension. The disabled reader who is weak in one or more of these basic skills will be discussed under the following headings:

1. Inability to group words into thought units
2. Ineffective use of punctuation
3. Limited skill in interpreting connectives
4. Confusion in identifying pronoun-antecedent relationships
5. Ineffective use of syntax
6. Inability to adjust to varied sentence structures

Inability to group words into thought units.   It has already been noted that reading by thought units promotes comprehension of sentences. Many disabled readers are either word-by-word readers or they tend to group words inappropriately, so that clear comprehension of the sentence as a whole is impossible. At the start of instruction in reading, the child must recognize each word separately. In the beginning, he is required by his immaturity to study each word closely in order to identify it at all, so there is little likelihood that he will be able to group several together for recognition as a thought unit. As the child becomes more adept at word identification and as he builds a stock of words that he can recognize at sight, he is able to group some together.

The first grouping by thought units rather than by individual words is in two-word combinations, as "the cat," "Daddy said," or "to ride." Such grouping of words takes place only after the child is very familiar with each of the words and only when they are set off together by the typography. For example, in the sentence "Daddy said, 'We can stop,'" the punctuation makes the grouping of "Daddy said" a natural and easy thing to understand. Later, at the primer level, when two-line sentences begin to appear, additional help is given to the child to help him learn to read in thought units. A sentence would be printed like the following:

> Judy said, "Put the duck
> in the water."

The child would almost be forced by the format to read by thought units. Still later, he is expected to be able to analyze a sentence into thought units rapidly as he progresses along the line of print. This is a mature sort of reading that must be predicated on recognizing the words and phrases at sight.

Inability to read in thought units can be diagnosed in several ways. The simplest method is to listen to the disabled reader read easy material orally. If he reads in a word-by-word manner or if he clusters words in meaningless groups, he is probably ineffective in recognizing thought units in his silent reading, and he is certainly not reading orally by thought units. Another method of diagnosing this ability is to flash phrases before the child for recognition. If he reads the phrases significantly less well than does the usual child of equal general reading ability, it is safe to assume that he has limited ability in recognizing thought units in isolation. It is then probable that he cannot pick out and recognize thought units in a sentence.

Remedial methods for the child who has been diagnosed as disabled in reading thought units must be based on the premise that ultimately he will have to learn to recognize meaningful groups of words as he silently reads consecutive printed matter. He will be reading sentences, not isolated thought units. Skill in reading by groups of words is dependent in part on the ability to analyze the sentences into reasonable units. It is also necessary for the disabled reader to encompass the group of words he separates into single ideas. The remedial work must teach the child to rapidly recognize thought units of several words and also to spot such groups of words in the sentences he reads. Many disabled readers are able to recognize isolated thought units flashed before them, but they are incapable of reading silently or aloud by thought units. Since they cannot readily divide a sentence into proper clusters of words, they must read each word separately.

Remedial instruction designed to enable a child to read in thought units should be done in context or the phrases learned in isolation should be read immediately in complete sentences. The following exercises will give instruction and experience in reading by thought units:

1. Whenever the remedial teacher introduces new words in a selection, it is desirable to have them read in the phrases in which the child will see them.
2. After the selection has been read, the child can reread to locate certain expressive phrases suggested by the teacher.
3. Preparing material to read orally provides excellent experience in reading by thought units.
4. Multiple-choice exercises in which phrases are used as answers and distractors may be used.
   a. Draw a line under the correct phrase to complete the sentence.
                      over the fence.
      (1) The ball sailed down the hole.
                      under the water.

                  flew away.
      (2) The dog talked softly.
                  ran fast.
   b. Quickly find the phrases on the pages given to answer these questions.

Question	Phrase
Where was the rooster?	(near the barn)
Who was happy?	(the white bear)
When did the boys swim?	(one summer day)

   c. Mark off the thought units in the following sentences and tell the *who, or what, did what, where, why* questions they answer.
1. The large truck went slowly down the street.
2. Billy and Frank quickly made a snow fort to hid behind.

   d. Draw a line from the phrase to the word that has a similar meaning.

a big meal	stroke
to rub softly	feast
to cut down	chop

   e. Find these phrases in your book on the page I give, and tell what they mean.

answer the knock	with a splash
bright as stars	cry for help
break the horse	fine fishing country

   f. On the pages I tell you, find a phrase that makes you:

hear something	(the screaming gulls)
feel something	(the cool breeze)
see something	(colored autumn leaves)
smell something	(sweet-scented flowers)
taste something	(a sour apple)

5. The use of rapid exposure techniques described in Chapter 11, will aid in teaching disabled readers to recognize a phrase or thought unit with one eye fixation. For group work, an opaque projector can be used. A piece of cardboard is placed before the lens and moved up and down to expose thought units for about one-half a second. The phrases for this work should be in the form of sentences, such as the following:

A brown beaver
was at work
near the island.
He was making
a tunnel
at the bottom
of the pond.

6. Sentences may be separated into thought units to be read by the children:

The old man   with the angry face   was happy now.
He had found   the one thing   he liked.

Ineffective use of punctuation.   Inadequately interpreting punctuation or ignoring it altogether may also hinder sentence comprehension. Possibly the most common difficulty with punctuation among disabled readers is the failure to learn the more common uses of the comma, that is, to separate words and groups of words written as a series in a sentence, to set off an appositive, or to set off a parenthetical expression in a sentence.

Informal procedures must be used to find out if a child is using punctuation properly. For instance, commas properly used should aid in grouping words into thought units. Much is learned about commas by having the pupil read sentences aloud. If commas are not used to guide inflection and emphasis in phrasing, it is likely that the child does not understand the function of the punctuation marks in what he reads. Under these conditions, he will have difficulty in comprehending the full meaning of a sentence. Test sentences like the following may be taken from reading textbooks and used to illustrate the use of commas:

1.   Deer, too, were there.
2.   They stood still, heads up, listening.
3.   Mary said, "Now we can go home."
4.   After dark, when all was quiet, he slowly walked down the street.

A few children will need supervision to recognize that a capital letter is a clue to the beginning of a sentence and that a period or question mark signals the end of a sentence.

Remedial training in the use of punctuation to facilitate comprehension involves at least two things: (1) by discussion, attention of the pupil is directed to the punctuation within a sentence as indicating the relation between what has just been read and what follows; and (2) the pupil is given ample practice with sentences from the context of his reading. The training should start with relatively simple sentences and gradually progress to more complex ones. In all cases, the sentences should be made of words the child knows and can pronounce. In general, simple explanations and supervised practice lead to improvement.

In a similar manner, as the child progresses in his reading, he may need help in the interpretation of semicolons, colons, and dashes. This training is necessary for sentence comprehension and for oral reading. In fact, interpretive oral reading helps to develop these skills.

Limited skill in interpreting connectives.   The disabled reader who is weak in sentence comprehension must be taught how a sentence is unified. Remedial teaching should begin with direct sentences whose parts are easily found. Then more complex sentences should be introduced. Finally, the disabled reader should be taught the importance of learning connectives. He should be shown that they can change the anticipated flow of the thought or qualify it in some way. This is a problem often found in social studies material. Teaching the role of connectives should start with relatively simple illustrations and then provide some examples, taken from one of the student's social studies textbooks. A sentence like the following might be used:

We were going swimming, but a thunderstorm began, so we decided to watch television instead.

After the sentence is read, the disabled reader can be asked if the people went swimming, what words show that they did not go, and why they changed their minds.

Confusion in identifying pronoun-antecedent relationships. Sometimes difficulties arise when the thing or person referred to by a pronoun is not readily grasped. Disabled readers often have this kind of difficulty. The following type of exercise may be used for remedial instruction:

Directions: In the following sentences, the underlined word is used in place of the name of a person or thing already mentioned. Draw a circle around the word or words that tell who or what is meant by the underlined word.

1. After <u>he</u> arrived home from school, Jack shoveled the snow off the walk.
2. As the horses were freed, <u>they</u> galloped across the field.
3. Bill looked on with interest as <u>his</u> sister, Jane, rode toward <u>him</u> on <u>her</u> new bicycle.

Ineffective use of syntax.   Understanding word order within a sentence is vital to sentence comprehension. For example, the sentence, *Only Tom went to the store,* has a meaning different from *Tom went to the only store.* The disabled reader who cannot use syntax to grasp meaning while reading often will not comprehend what is read. The child should practice reading exercises which reinforce his knowledge of sentence relationships, such as: the actor, the action, and the object of the action. Exercises designed to bring together knowledge of spoken language and reading comprehension are helpful.

1. Read this sentence:
   The big gray elephants at the zoo wanted more roasted peanuts.
   a. Put "C" before the three most important words in the sentence.
      _____ zoo roasted peanuts
      _____ peanuts wanted elephants
      _____ elephants wanted peanuts
   b. Put "C" before the words that show the elephants had already had some peanuts.
      _____ wanted zoo peanuts   _____ wanted more peanuts
      _____ wanted roasted peanuts   _____ elephants roasted peanuts
2. Read this sentence:
   The boys ran to the circus to see the clowns do funny tricks.
   a. Who did tricks?
      _____ the boys   _____ the clowns   _____ the circus
   b. Why did the boys run to the circus?
      _____ to see the clowns   _____ to do some tricks
   c. Where did the boys run?
      _____ to see the clowns   _____ to the circus

d. What was funny?

_____ the tricks   _____ the boys   _____ the circus

Inability to adjust to varied sentence structures. The inability of disabled readers to sort out and properly relate the meanings in different parts of a sentence is sometimes complicated by sentence structure. For instance, difficulties may arise when the subject is last or between two parts of the predicate rather than at the beginning. Informal exercises for diagnosing such difficulties and for remedial instruction are similar to those described above for developing sentence comprehension. For example, what word answers the question "who" in each of the following sentences? "Hearing the low, rumbling sound again, Jack suddenly remembered something." "Then into the cool water went John."

Writers themselves are to blame for hindering sentence comprehension. Too frequently, sentences are excessively long and too complex for clear understanding. Sometimes they are just poorly written, but the reader must learn to make the adjustment if he wishes to read these materials.

The following types of exercises may be helpful in developing flexibility in adjusting to sentence structure:

Directions: Read each sentence. Then decide whether the underlined part tells when, why, how, what, or where. Draw a line under the right one of the words which follow the sentence.

1. *The large farm* belongs to father.   when   why   how   what
                                            where

2. *Because John was ill,* he did not go to school.   when   why   how
                                                        what   where

3. Mary's train will arrive at *six o'clock.*   when   why   how   what
                                                  where

A variation of the preceding example is to find and copy the word or words that answer the question, "who" or "where." After the pupil is informed that the sentences answer the questions "who" and "where," he is directed to write below the sentences the word or words that answer the questions.

1. The boy went to the chalkboard to write the word.
2. From school to the park is only one-half mile, explained the teacher.

	Words that tell	
Sentence Number	<u>Who?</u>	<u>Where?</u>
1	_____	_____
2	_____	_____

The responses may be made by having the child draw a line under the words that answer the question, "where," and the like.

In a similar manner, exercises may be constructed that answer the questions "when" and "what," or "why" and "how." They may be varied by using sentences or unusual structural patterns. The sentences may be taken directly from books or made from words in the reading vocabulary. Sample items may be found in Reading Aids through the Grades (Mueser, 1981).

INSUFFICIENT COMPREHENSION OF LONGER UNITS

Frequently disabled readers are unable to understand the meaning of a paragraph. These children tend to consider each sentence as a separate unit unrelated to the other sentences in the paragraph. It is possible for them to read and understand words, thought units, and sentences and yet not comprehend fully the connected material in a paragraph. Similarly some pupils are unable to sense the relation between paragraphs in stories and various expository materials. Comprehension of paragraphs and development of story sense will be considered in this section. The next chapter will cover specific comprehension defects.

Limited knowledge of paragraph organization. Comprehension of a paragraph requires an understanding of the relationships between sentences in that paragraph. Many readers, disabled in all types of comprehension, need guidance in identifying the topic sentence containing the key idea and in interpreting its relationship to explanatory or amplifying sentences.

Remedial teaching of paragraph organization centers on understanding the interrelationships among sentences. Exercises requiring the disabled reader to find which one of several statements best represents the general meaning of a given paragraph are helpful. Calling attention to various types of paragraph organization is even more important in increasing paragraph comprehension. This instruction should start with the simplest type, that in which the topic sentence is the first presented and the following sentences expand the main idea. The second type of paragraph presents a series of related facts and concepts, and the topic sentence comes last in the form of a generalization. This type of paragraph is used frequently in scientific writing. Finally, the disabled reader should be taught to recognize a third type of paragraph organization, the one in which introductory concepts are presented initially, followed by a summary topic sentence, and then concluded with sentences which modify or limit the general idea. This type of paragraph is often found in social studies materials.

To develop skill in finding the topic sentence, the child is given illustrations and explanations. After the examples and explanations, he is asked to find and underline the topic sentence in other paragraphs. Besides finding the topic sentence, the pupil should learn how the other sentences in the paragraph develop the idea presented in the topic sentence—by details, by emphasis, by explanations, by contrast, and by repetition of the same idea in other words. One technique of doing this is to number the sentences in a paragraph. Then through questions and analysis, the role of each sentence in relation to the others is discussed.

A well-written paragraph is concerned with one central idea. Training to grasp this idea may be carried out in various ways. A paragraph is given, followed by three phrases, one of which is the headline or title that best expresses the topic of the material in the paragraph. The disabled reader indicates which one is best. He may be asked to write a headline (topic) for the paragraph or to write a sentence expressing the topic; he may be given a topic sentence and asked to write a short paragraph with supporting and amplifying sentences. Another device is to give him a paragraph which is correct except for one sentence. The child is asked to underline the topic sentence and then to cross out the sentence which does not belong.

Although the comprehension of paragraphs is important in all reading, it is absolutely essential for clear understanding as the disabled reader moves into reading the content subjects. Some training for understanding paragraph unity is usually introduced when third-grade reading ability is reached. More formal training to develop paragraph comprehension becomes a regular part of reading instruction at the intermediate grade levels.

Inability to interrelate the parts of a total selection.   For full comprehension of longer units, the child should be taught to sense the relation between the paragraphs which make up the entire text (Hoskins, 1986). In good expository writing, the introductory paragraphs usually state the reason for the piece or what is to be described or explained. The following paragraphs give the details of the explanation in logical sequence. The final one or two paragraphs ordinarily state the outcome or conclusion, or they summarize what has been said.

In well-written narratives, text is organized by story grammar, which represents the important elements in a story and the relationships among these (Templeton and Mowery, 1985). For example, stories commonly comprise three parts: (1) the beginning, which gives either the time or the place of the story, or both, and sometimes also the characters; (2) the body of the story, which tells what happens, and (3) the final paragraphs, which usually relate the conclusion of events. Kent (1984) cautions that teachers need to be aware of the differences between expository and narrative text structure in order to teach useful strategies for comprehending each.

The remedial teacher aids in developing story sense by teaching text structure so that the disabled reader better understands the relation between paragraphs and is able to identify the main parts of stories and expository materials. Idol (1987) emphasizes the importance of explicit teacher demonstration and modeling of correct responses.

In teaching text structure a teacher might try one of the following. (1) Explain the three main parts of a story. Model finding these parts using an example. Ask questions about each part designed to show it's content. (2) Discuss the transitional expressions that often start a paragraph. Model, from an example, that these expressions precede the main idea or topic of many of the paragraphs from a selection. Such phrases as (a) *But something else has happened. . . .* (b) *Then he turned to John. . . .* (c) *When this was done, he began. . . .* (3) Have the child write one sentence to express the main idea in each paragraph of a story or an article. Then have him join these sentences together in a coordinated pattern of thought, using transitional words or phrases as needed. With expository materials, it is helpful to have the student try to make an outline of the main and subordinate ideas.

According to research by Smith and Friend (1986) direct instruction in text structure improves comprehension even for older students who are experiencing severe difficulty in reading comprehension.

SUMMARY

To read means to read with understanding. To accomplish this, there must be comprehension of words, thought units, sentences, paragraphs, and longer units. Instruction for developing comprehension coordinates all these into an integrated sequential program.

Listening comprehension develops ahead of reading comprehension in the early grades. As the mechanics of reading mature, reading comprehension catches up with and soon equals listening comprehension. With still further progress in reading, reading comprehension becomes superior.

Comprehension depends upon a group of concepts or meanings evolved through experience. Deficiencies discovered should be remedied as much as possible in the school. Firsthand experience is best, supplemented by vicarious, or secondhand, experience. The aim of such experiences is to form concepts tied to words, which can be used by the disabled reader in thinking, speaking, listening, writing, and reading.

Instruction techniques for teaching word meanings include pointing out the use of context clues, ensuring wide reading, encouraging the attitude of demanding understanding of words read and noting authors' definitions, studying words systematically, and using the dictionary. To be effective, all word study must use each word in context.

To comprehend sentences, the child must understand the words and the relations between these words and groups of words. He must also be able to read by thought units, interpret punctuation, and understand figures of speech, symbolic expressions, and semantic variations. Remedial instruction for sentence comprehension is based on informal exercises.

Paragraph comprehension depends on comprehension of the sentences and on understanding the relation between these sentences. Similarly, the comprehension of larger units is based upon paragraph comprehension and understanding the relations between the paragraphs involved.

STUDY QUESTIONS

1. For the successful reader, what is the relationship between listening comprehension and reading comprehension through the grades? What part do the mechanics of reading play in this relationship?

2. If experience alone does not educate, what can a teacher do to ensure that experiences do educate?

3. Why do some students, who have adequate word recognition in reading, experience difficulty in comprehending sentences?

4. What are some specific techniques to help a child who can read and understand words and sentences, but who is unable to understand the meaning of a paragraph?

SELECTED READINGS

BROWN D. A. *Reading Diagnosis and Remediation,* Chap. 13. Englewood Cliffs, NJ: Prentice-Hall, Inc., 1982.

DECHANT, E. *Diagnosis and Remediation of Reading Disabilities,* Chap. 11. Englewood Cliffs, NJ: Prentice-Hall, Inc., 1981.

DURKIN, D. *Teaching Young Children to Read,* 4th ed., Chap. 13. Boston: Allyn & Bacon, 1987.

HARRIS, A. J., AND E. R. SIPAY. *How to Increase Reading Ability,* 8th ed., Chap. 13. New York: Longman, Inc., 1985.

McCORMICK, S. *Remedial and Clinical Reading Instruction,* Chaps. 15 and 16. Columbus, OH: Charles E. Merrill Publishing Company, 1987.

McGINNIS, D. J., AND D. E. SMITH. *Analyzing and Treating Reading Problems,* Chap. 14. New York: Macmillan, Inc., 1982.

MUESER, A. M. *Reading Aids through the Grades; 4th ed., Section four. New York: Teachers College Press, 1981.*

SPACHE, G. D. AND E. B. SPACHE. *Reading in the Elementary School,* 5th ed., Chap. 14. Boston: Allyn & Bacon, Inc., 1986.

WILSON, R. M., AND C. J. CLELAND. *Diagnostic and Remedial Reading for Classroom and Clinic,* 5th ed., Chap. 9. Columbus, OH: Charles E. Merrill Publishing Company, 1985.

ZINTZ, M. V. *Corrective Reading,* 4th ed., Chap. 11. Dubuque, IA: William C. Brown Company, Publishers, 1981.

15

Overcoming Specific Comprehension Limitations

The preceding chapters of this book have considered the limitations in reading abilities affecting the disabled reader's entire reading achievement. Deficiencies in basic comprehension and in word recognition prevent effective reading of all types of materials and, unless corrected, preclude future reading growth. The disabled readers so far discussed are those classified as having *limiting* or *complex disabilities*. They often have difficulties in reading so severe or so complicated by various handicaps that they require extensive remedial adjustments.

This and the following chapters will consider students who are experiencing reading difficulties because of a *specific immaturity*. They need corrections in reading patterns that must be made if maturity in reading and satisfactory communication between author and reader are to be achieved. The readers to be discussed are basically competent readers, but they have specific problems that must be corrected if full realization of their reading potential is to be achieved. The reader with a specific immaturity can and should receive corrective training in the classroom or school reading center.

Remedial teaching, discussed in the remaining chapters, is of special importance in the intermediate grades, high school, and adult educational programs. Students with difficulties in these types of reading growth are often unable to progress in their entire education as well as they should because of a readily correctable reading problem.

Remedial teaching, discussed in the remaining chapters, is of special importance in the intermediate grades, high school, and adult educational programs. Students with difficulties in these types of reading growth are often unable to progress in their entire education as well as they should because of a readily correctable reading problem.

Among the more frequent areas of specific difficulties in comprehension abilities, basic study skills, and reading materials of the content fields are the following, which will be discussed in this chapter:

1. Limitations in specific comprehension abilities
   a. Inability to locate and retain information read
   b. Inadequate sense of organization of material
   c. Limited ability in evaluating what is read
   d. Immaturity in ability to interpret content
   e. Lack of appreciative abilities
2. Insufficient development of basic study skills
   a. Lack of skills needed to locate sources of information
   b. Inefficiency in using basic references
   c. Limited skills in interpreting pictorial and tabular materials
3. Deficiencies in reading content materials
   a. Social Studies
   b. Science
   c. Mathematics
   d. Literature

LIMITATIONS IN SPECIFIC COMPREHENSION ABILITIES

Comprehension is made of a number of basic abilities, including skill in recognizing words and their meanings, grouping words into thought units, and giving the proper emphasis to the thought units so that the sentences can be understood. Moreover, it is the ability to ascertain the relationship between the sentences that enables the reader to understand the paragraph. When the relationship between paragraphs is understood, the reader arrives at the meaning of the total passage.

Although these basic comprehension abilities underlie the communicative act of reading, they alone are not sufficient. The reader needs a group of diversified comprehension abilities with flexibility in their use. Unfortunately there are many adults for whom the reading program did not develop flexibility in the use of specific comprehension abilities. Some people read all material as though each illustrative detail were to be retained forever. They have not developed such higher-order comprehension abilities as the ability to organize facts so that generalizations can be made, the ability to evaluate, or the ability to reflect. Other people read primarily for appreciation and retain little of the content in material that should be read for more specific purposes.

Inability to Locate and Retain Information Read

This category of specific comprehension abilities requires exact, careful reading. The various comprehension abilities included are recalling specific items of information, noting the details within a passage, retaining fundamental concepts, using facts to answer specific questions, and finding statements to prove a point or to answer a question. These specific comprehension abilities begin their development in the child's early reading assignments and are continued as goals of instruction as long as systematic training is given. Many children, however, fail to establish a high degree of accuracy in the various ways of locating and retaining factual information. On the other hand, numerous other children are found to be overly exacting. These latter should be encouraged to read relatively easy material for the purpose of enjoyment, for predicting what is going to happen next, or to get the general gist of a story or passage.

Children who are not exacting enough in their reading or who cannot remember details within the passage when this is what is demanded by the purposes for reading should be given reading that requires the collection of factual information with close attention to detail, and then requires that this factual information be used. The material for children with a limited capacity for locating and retaining specific items of information should have considerable factual content. For this, science material is better than narrative; something from social studies is good provided it is designed to give information rather than an overall impression. In other words, the material that will be found most useful in developing ability to read for informational purposes will be material that contains plenty of facts.

A chart should be kept showing the disabled reader's percentage of correct responses. Children at all levels of general reading competency may be inexperienced or ineffective in this type of reading comprehension. The exercises and materials in which the disabled reader is expected to get practice in attending to specific details should be at a level somewhat below his general reading capability, but it does not have to be as simple as indicated by his measured score in this type of reading. By this we mean that if a disabled reader of fifth-grade age and mental ability has a general reading capability of 4.0 and measures 2.5 in reading to recall items of specific information, the remedial work ordinarily would not need to use material of 2.5 level of difficulty, though it ought to be somewhat easier than 4.0 in difficulty.

Here are a few samples of reading purposes that give experience in reading to locate and retain factual information.

1. Read the selection to find all the things a beaver uses in making his home.
2. Reread the selection to find additional facts to add to your list about the animals discussed.
3. Find and read sentences to prove or disprove these statements.
   a. A big sea lion weighs about six-hundred pounds.
   b. A big elephant may be eight feet high.

c. A baby kangaroo sleeps in its mother's pouch.
d. A full-grown kangaroo weighs more than a sea lion.
e. Baboons like to swim.

Inadequate Sense of Organization of Material

The specific types of comprehension included in this category have as their major distinguishing characteristic the ability to sense order or relationship among the facts read. They include abilities such as classifying and listing facts in a sensible manner, establishing a sequence of events, following a series of related directions, sensing relationships, and distinguishing between the major ideas and the related facts. These are exacting sorts of reading, but they are important. Reading to organize information begins in children's prereading exercises when they classify pictures of animals, for example, into those they would see on a farm and those they would see in a forest; or when they arrange a series of pictures in an orderly sequence of events. Some fail to develop the ability to sense the organization and relationship among the ideas they are reading, and this is a severe handicap in using printed material. These children need remedial work to become proficient in this area of comprehension abilities.

Material for developing the ability to organize and sense relationships among facts must naturally contain plenty of facts to organize and relate one to the other. Science and social studies materials at the proper level of difficulty can be used to develop these abilities. The remedial teacher must use reasons for reading which require the child to organize, and she should check on the child's effectiveness in carrying these out. Here are some specific purposes that help to teach sensing the organization of ideas and information.

1. Read about animals to make a summary chart showing where they live, what they eat, how to recognize them, how they protect themselves, who their enemies are, how they get ready for winter.
2. Read to make a list of (*a*) the kinds of damage done by floods, and (*b*) means that are used to prevent damage.
3. Read to summarize the information given about petroleum under the following headings: how petroleum was formed, how oil wells are located, how oil is obtained from below the ground, uses of petroleum, how we can conserve our petroleum resources.
4. Read to find and list in order the steps taken by Charles Hall in his experiments to find a quick and inexpensive way of changing alumina into aluminum.
5. Read to find out in what ways the life of a child who lives by the sea in Brittany is the same and how it is different from that of a child who lives in Bora Bora.

Limited Ability in Evaluating What Is Read

This group of comprehension abilities involves not only reading and understanding what the author said, but reflecting on it so that critical judgments can be made. It includes such specific types of comprehending as differentiating between fancy, fact, and opinion; judging the reasonableness and relevancy of ideas presented; sensing implied meanings; establishing cause-and-effect relationships; making comparisons; judging the authenticity of materials read; and critically appraising the validity of the author's presentation. Like all other comprehension abilities, these have their start in early reading lessons and develop as long as growth in reading continues. The time at which a child is asked if a fanciful tale really could have happened is the start of such instruction. Reading to evaluate includes some of the most important types of reading. The person who is taught to read, but not to reflect on what is read, frequently is in danger of coming to faulty conclusions. The child who is unable to read critically and to judge the reasonableness of material at his level of advancement should be given remedial instruction to overcome this deficiency. Reading to evaluate what is read is gradual in development and should not be left to chance learning.

The best material for learning how to evaluate is that written to influence people's opinions. Often ideas are implied rather than directly stated. Frequently there are cause-and-effect relationships, even in first-grade material, and often statements of fact and opinion can be compared. Any material that is at the child's general reading level may be used to increase his ability to evaluate what is read. Comprehension exercises found in basal readers often have the child reread material in order to evaluate it in a variety of ways. Exercises that teach the child to judge, reflect on, and evaluate are illustrated by the following:

1. Have the child, after reading a somewhat fanciful story about animals, reread it to distinguish between the realistic and the fanciful statements.
2. Have the child decide from the titles of stories whether they are likely to be real or fanciful.
3. Have the children discuss whether a story read could have happened and give their reasons for their opinions.
4. Have the child find and read aloud just the part that proves a point and no more.
5. Have the child find facts that are relevant to a topic.
6. Have the children read to find statements which characters make that they know to be true and those that are their opinions.

Immaturity in Ability to Interpret Content

This category of comprehension abilities is composed of types of reading that project the understanding of the selection beyond the statements of the author. It differs from organizing what is read in that it requires a child to derive new ideas from what he reads. Reading to interpret includes understanding the significance of a selection read, drawing an inference or conclusion not expressly stated, predicting the outcome of given events, forming one's own opinions, and inferring time and measurement relationships. These comprehension abilities require the reorganization of information and ideas expressed so that new relationships can be understood.

Some children with good general reading ability find it difficult to interpret what is read. This type of reading ability is best developed in material that requires careful, considered judgments. It is also developed by setting purposes for reading that necessitate reflecting upon what is read. The child must learn to take the facts and ideas presented, reorganize them, and recognize relationships among them that he did not find on the surface. Social studies and science lend themselves to these sorts of reasoning, but well-written narrative material and essays are also useful in developing the ability to interpret.

The main requirement of remedial instruction for the disabled reader who is otherwise a capable reader is to have him read for purposes that cause him to reflect upon what he reads. The following purposes illustrate the nature of reading assignments that encourage interpretive reading:

1. Have the children anticipate the ending of the story.
2. Have the children read to find out why the signing of the Magna Carta is important to them.
3. Have the children form conclusions about how climatic conditions have affected the ways in which people live.

Lack of Appreciative Abilities

This set of comprehension abilities is somewhat different from the others. The four types of specific limitations discussed previously dealt with noting and retaining factual information, organizing information, judging the authenticity of information, and interpreting it. Appreciation abilities deal more with the aesthetic qualities of reading. Reading abilities such as understanding the feeling expressed by the author; recognizing the plot, humor, and action; forming various sensory impressions; and understanding the personal qualities of the characters are essential for appreciating what is read. The basic reading program and the program of guided literature reading are designed to build these capabilities.

The child who cannot visualize the scene described, or sense the feeling of aloneness experienced by an early explorer, or appreciate the humor of an absurd situation is in reading difficulty, although the child may be able to do all of the factual types of reading. The best materials for developing reading to appreciate are literature, short stories, and anthologies. The child must read for reasons that encourage appreciation. It would be unfortunate to force the factual types of reading, required for other comprehension abilities, on the child when he is reading material that should be read for personal development, appreciation, or its own beauty.

To cultivate appreciation, the teacher first must find material that the child in difficulty can read and that will be interesting to the child. The child can be taught the abilities necessary for appreciation, using material that is suitable to one of his age and in accordance with his interests. The child is not limited in reading in general and has no basic defects in his skills and abilities. If he were so limited, these basic defects would be his primary problem and would receive first attention.

Although guiding children to read quality materials is essential in improving reading to appreciate, there are certain other things that can be done to encourage it.

The following illustrations indicate the kinds of experiences that improve appreciation:

1. Read a story to participate in a creative dramatic representation of one of the characters.
2. Read several stories to select one that would make a good play.
3. Have the child discuss how he thinks someone in the story felt.
4. Locate some descriptive words within a story.
5. Read for the enjoyment of a good story.

INSUFFICIENT DEVELOPMENT OF BASIC STUDY SKILLS

A child can be an excellent reader in general but at the same time be unable to (1) locate sources of information, (2) use basic references, or (3) interpret pictorial and tabular materials. A child who is limited in any of these skills has a specific difficulty in reading which should be corrected if he is to use the printed page effectively.

Each of the categories of basic study skills listed here is composed of many parts. The teacher must know just where a child's difficulty lies if remedial treatment is to be effective and not waste time on elements already mastered. It would be wasteful to spend time teaching a child who is weak in locating sources of information to alphabetize if he already knows how to alphabetize. It would be equally undesirable to spend time and effort teaching him key words, when his real difficulty is that he does not know in which type of book he can find the information he wants.

It is essential to study the disabled reader as he works in the area of his weakness. This requires sampling his performance in that area. For example, if he is weak in the use of basic references, it may be that he does not know whether the types of information he desires can be found in an encyclopedia, a dictionary, an atlas, an almanac, a telephone book, a standard text, or just where. By studying the selections he makes when answering questions such as; "Where would you be likely to find information about the time of the monsoons in India, the definition of a word, the address of another school, the population of a town, or the location of a country?" the specialist can narrow the problem.

A study of the disabled reader's efficiency in using the basic study skill in question is also needed. He may know which reference to use, under which heading to look for the information he wishes to find, and how to estimate pages within the reference, but still he may be slow and inefficient in using what he knows. The work sample will also give this necessary information.

Which remedial methods are proper is usually obvious when the nature of the difficulty is thoroughly diagnosed. The teacher needs to teach the child to do the things in which he is limited. If he does not know how to alphabetize, it is relatively easy to teach him the order of the letters and the fact that words are arranged in lists in this order by their first letters, then by the second letters, and so on, and that it is always done in this way. This is a different and much simpler type of learning than is, for example, word recognition, in which few such rules apply.

Lack of Skills Needed to Locate Sources of Information

Skill in finding sources of information is helpful to most study activities. The child who knows how and when to use the table of contents, the index, and the card catalog is better equipped for independent study than is the one who does not think of doing these things or is not as skillful at them. Among the most frequent limitations in this skill are (1) inability to decide which books contain the information wanted; (2) not knowing how to use such tools as the index, the table of contents, the card catalog, the reader's guide, and the like; (3) limited skill in estimating the probable key words under which the information is classified or inflexibility in selecting other references when the first one does not contain the information wanted; (4) inefficiency in finding words in an alphabetical listing, especially in those lists with major and subordinate subdivisions; (5) inability to find pages in a book; (6) little skimming ability, making it hard to find exact information.

The teacher must establish in which of these skills the child is behind and then give him reading assignments requiring their use in finding the information for a definite purpose. If he shows poor judgment as to which book might contain the information that he desires, the teacher can teach him how to choose a good source by asking him questions. If his weakness is in not knowing whether to use the table of contents or the index, she can explain the use of each and give him experience in using them. If use of key words is the difficulty, several topics can be chosen to show how they are listed, from general to specific, from common to unusual, from major to related headings.

If the child's weakness is in finding words in an alphabetical list, he must be drilled on the alphabet, on estimating how far through the alphabet one of the letters is, and on placing words in alphabetical order. The child who has insufficient skimming ability can be given many exercises that require the rapid location of specific facts within a page or a few pages on which the fact is known to be discussed. It might be well to start such exercises with the location of a date, since numbers on a page of print can readily be found.

Inefficiency in Using Basic References

The child who is capable of finding information in general may find using basic reference material confusing. His difficulty usually is not knowing what kind of information each reference contains. He does not know to which book he should refer for the kind of information he desires. The teacher should find out which of the references the child is unfamiliar with and give him experience in using them. Many adults, for example, do not know all of the types of information that can be most readily found in the telephone book. The child is often uncertain about the difference between an encyclopedia and a dictionary and which should be used to get a specific bit of information. He may be equally confused about what can be obtained from other reference books. After the teacher pinpoints the nature of the problem, an explanation of the contents of the different basic references and some experience in using each will usually correct the difficulty. At times it is necessary to have the child tell in which of the common reference books he would look to find such things as the facts about Columbus, the meaning of the word *Tory,* the amount of wheat grown in Kansas last year—each time checking the accuracy of his answer by looking up that topic.

Limited Skills in Interpreting Pictorial and Tabular Materials

Skill in reading maps, graphs, charts, and tables is becoming increasingly important to understand printed material. The child who fails to develop such skills will be handicapped in his reading in the content fields during his school years and also as an adult. If he is weak in this group of skills, the teacher should identify which kinds of pictorial and tabular aids are causing him difficulty and determine the exact nature of his trouble.

Again, as in most of the study skills, once the nature of the difficulty is known, the remedial work to be undertaken is definite. The child who has a disability in map reading, for example, may be in difficulty for a variety of reasons. He may be unaware that different maps use different scales. A map of his city may, for example, be larger than a map of his state, so he is troubled about distances and comparative sizes. He may get erroneous notions because he does not know that a flat map of a vast area must distort some things in order to show others. Many maps of the United States show Maine closer to the top than the state of Minnesota. Therefore many people think that Maine extends farther north than Minnesota, but in reality it does not. Because wall maps always have north at the top, many children think rivers flow downhill to the south and so they are surprised to learn that some rivers flow north and empty into Hudson Bay. There are many such faulty concepts established in trying to read maps.

In reading other types of pictorial and tabular materials, there are also many kinds of confusion. The specialist should first find the source of the difficulties and then give the child systematic instruction and purposeful experiences in order to overcome the weakness. The corrective work is best accomplished in the science and social studies units of those basic readers which systematically teach the study skills. They contain specific exercises to develop skill in interpretation of pictorial and tabular presentations. The principles these illustrate can be reinforced by the reading assignments in science and social studies classes. It must be realized that these skills begin to form early in the child's reading experience. Map reading may be started by interpreting a map which the teacher has made to show the children safe ways to go home from school. A chart showing daily temperatures at noon is often one of the child's early school experiences.

Remedial instruction for those children who are weak in these skills must progress from simple illustrative maps, graphs, charts, and tables to more complex ones. It will prove helpful to progress from representations of things that the child has experienced to more remote illustrative materials.

DEFICIENCIES IN READING CONTENT MATERIALS

In the intermediate grades and at more advanced educational levels, some students lack the flexibility necessary to adjust reading procedures and abilities to the distinct purposes and materials of each content field. By *content field,* we mean any field that uses a specific type of material which requires unique language structures, vocabularies, or purposes; for example, shop manuals, scientific or arithmetical materials, poetry, or even cookbooks. The adjustments are numerous and often subtle. Nonetheless when the specific problem or problems are pinpointed, direct instruction focused on the problems corrects the lack of proficiency in a given field. Diagnoses of poor reading within a content field are accomplished best by informal procedures and on-the-job observation. Once the problem is located, the remedial work is done best by the teacher of the specific content field, with supportive help by the reading center when needed.

The curricular materials of every field the child meets impose their own specific and unique demands upon his reading capabilities. Each field has unique reading problems. A fourth-grade child, for example, who has been reading stories for most of his three years of reading experience is confronted suddenly with a geography book. He has always read a story uninterrupted from the top of the first page on through several pages. In the geography book, he starts at the top of the page in the customary manner. He reads about ten lines and then is told to look at Figure 1 on page 12. He looks at Figure 1 on page 12, and returning to the page he had just left, starts at the top of the page again. He has always done this. He reads ten lines that seem familiar and is asked to look at Figure 1 on page 12. He says to himself that he has already looked at Figure 1 on page 12, so he goes on reading down the page. Somewhat later he reads, "You noticed in Figure 1 that. . . ." He had noticed no such things. No one had told him to look for them and he was unfamiliar with the ways of the geographer. These episodes are, of course, minor misunderstandings, but many reading disability cases are caused by an accumulation of such misunderstandings or faulty learnings, each small in itself.

The first indication that a student is having trouble in reading the materials in a specific subject usually comes from the teacher's observation of his classroom performance. She should check to see that the problem is not due to general reading disability but is limited to difficulty in reading the materials of the specific content area.

Some of the major difficulties encountered by the disabled reader are described in the sections that follow. The teacher should study the student's performance and determine which of these stumbling blocks is at the root of the problem. Then, working cooperatively with the disabled reader, she should formulate a plan for correcting the problem. The specific content fields to be discussed are social studies, science, mathematics, and literature. These fields give a sampling of the diversified types of reading to which a student must be able to adjust.

Social Studies

The content area of social studies can present severe reading problems to certain students. Students' understanding of historic, civic, economic, and geographic realities is often limited to what they gain through reading, because their direct experience in these areas tends to be restricted. The variety and amount of reading required is great.

Some of this reading may be done rapidly for the main idea. Other materials and purposes demand slow, careful reading with attention to closely packed, sometimes intricate, details. The degree of precision required for satisfactory results from much of the reading falls between these two extremes.

Special vocabulary. Commonly encountered stumbling blocks in reading social studies material are the specialized terms and their accompanying concepts. These include unique words such as *cuneiform, plateau,* and *integration,* as well as proper names of people, places, and events. There are also words with specialized meanings when they occur in certain contexts. These include *mouth, cape, run, court,* and *balance.* Especially difficult are abstract terms such as *democracy, culture,* and *civilization.* Although a student may be able to pronounce some of these words without help, many of the meanings are learned only gradually and with the teacher's aid.

Complex concepts. The concept gives meaning to an item of vocabulary. Consequently, the development of vocabulary meanings and the development of concepts progress hand in hand. In the social studies, many concepts, and consequently the word meanings, are very complex and difficult to learn. Extensive reading of appropriate materials helps this, but the number of topics to be covered should be restricted.

Selection, evaluation, and organization. The wide and extensive reading to achieve satisfactory progress in the social studies requires application of various kinds of comprehension and study skills. The student must be acquainted with source materials and their use in selecting pertinent information, be able to read critically and evaluate the selected materials, and be skillful in organizing the information to use in reports or discussions.

Readability.   The style of writing used in social studies textbooks frequently puts many obstacles before the reader. One instance of this is the many facts and ideas which are packed into a relatively small space without enough organizational clues in the form of headings, subheadings, and boldface or italic type to bring out clearly the relative importance of the different facts and ideas. Hence, there is little or no indication of which are most important to learn. Yet to memorize all the details is neither possible nor desirable. Under such conditions, the student is inclined to stumble along, learning indiscriminately some facts and ideas, or even learn nothing at all.

Content and skills.   Is it the teacher's responsibility to teach content or skills in social studies? It is assumed that the teacher will provide practice in the skills needed along with instruction in social studies content. Too frequently this does not happen. A survey by Austin and Morrison (1963) showed that teachers reported that they did not have time to teach everything and that they felt it was more important to cover subject matter than to teach the reading skills needed in the content areas. Herber (1965) points out that this dichotomy of either content or skills is not necessary if the skills are taught as they are needed to read the assigned selections in the required textbook, and "if the skills are taught functionally *as* students read the required text, using the text as the vehicle for skills development," (p. 95). If this is done, content and skills are taught simultaneously. Skills should not be pulled out of context and taught separately.

History.   Certain reading problems in the social studies are particularly apparent in the field of history. Three are of prime importance. *First,* the materials in history usually do not consider that the temporal order of events is not sensed readily by many pupils. *Second,* writers do not seem to appreciate that pupils tend to interpret everything in terms of present-day conditions. Consequently, it is difficult for pupils to see historical events in relation to the period when or the place where they occurred. This happens most frequently with the treatment of the historical predecessors of modern methods of communication, transportation, science, or living conditions in general. Good instruction requires that the pupils be furnished with as adequate a background as possible for interpreting past events in relation to the time and conditions in which they occurred. *Third,* the reading and interpretation of pictures, charts, maps, and related materials are specialized kinds of reading which develop relevant word meanings and concepts as well as provide information. Details for developing these skills were given earlier in this chapter.

Geography.   The reading problems common to the social studies also occur in geography. Others more specifically related to reading geographical materials should be noted briefly. *First,* to understand geographical material requires appreciation of such human conditions as housing, clothing, food, occupations, and traditions; of such material conditions as the physical features of landscapes, climate, and vegetation; and of the relation between the two sets of conditions.

Second, it is necessary for a pupil to maintain his geographic set in absorbing the contents, in verbal or quantitative form, which are relevant to a geographical unit. This set is made through preparation of the unit and definition of its purposes. *Third,* there is a problem in teaching the child to think concretely in terms of geographical location as he reads about different places and what goes on in them— such as methods of housing, transportation, and industry. *Fourth,* there is the problem of interrupted reading, as a geography text is organized so that it refers the child to material on other pages. *Fifth,* the child must be able to comprehend material projected in the form of a map and integrate this information with explanatory text material.

Science

For the child to understand the world in which he lives, he must learn some science. The variety of purposes for which science is read ranges from reading to gain general impressions and grasp relationships to reading to learn in detail the consecutive steps in an experiment, or to evaluate the conclusions arrived at in a class discussion. Many of the difficulties of reading science are due to the inherent difficulty of this material. Many of the problems encountered in reading science are similar to those met in social studies. Others are unique to science material, such as its purposes and emphases. Because of this, somewhat different reading abilities, skills, and techniques are required.

Vocabulary.   The language of science is precise and specific. Each branch of science—chemistry, biology or physics, and so on—uses its own vocabulary terms as well as the basic vocabulary used in more general reading. Since the terms embody scientific concepts, it is necessary for the student to learn the essentials of scientific vocabulary in any area if he is to comprehend the material. Examples of rather highly specialized scientific terms are *electromagnet, molecule, gravity,* and *lever.* The student must also learn specialized meanings of general words used in a scientific context. Examples from physics are *scale, charge,* and the verb *conduct.*

Concepts.   Even the elementary concepts in science are sometimes complex and difficult to understand. Two examples are the concepts represented by the terms *magnetism* and *photosynthesis.* The degree to which concepts in science are grasped depends upon the capabilities of the individual students, the clarity of the context in which the unfamiliar items of vocabulary occur, and the skill of the teacher in demonstrating and explaining them. Many reasonably concrete scientific concepts are readily demonstrated, explained, and understood, such as *electromagnetism* and *surface tension.* Many other scientific concepts are not subject to direct demonstration and therefore must be handled by means of verbal description and abstract explanation. These are difficult for the pupil to understand. Diagrams and similies are sometimes helpful in explaining or clarifying such concepts.

Pictures and diagrams.   The reading and interpretation of pictures and diagrams in science tends to be inadequate without some form of systematic instruction. Ordinarily an explanation of these pictures and diagrams is supplied in the accompanying legend as well as in the textual discussion of the facts and principles. Some children fail to relate this verbal discussion properly to the diagram or pictures. Abstract schematic diagrams themselves are still more difficult to read and interpret.

Following directions.   The directions to be followed in carrying out experiments in science are specific. Both children and adults seem to have great difficulty in following these printed directions. Yet the successful performance of the experiment requires that they be followed very carefully. This reading should therefore be done slowly, meticulously, and thoughtfully so that the sequential order of the steps described can be followed. Ordinarily, difficulty does not arise because the student cannot read and understand the words and sentences but rather because he does not follow them correctly, omits steps, or does them in the wrong order.

Comprehension abilities and study skills.   Remembering facts encountered is, on the whole, a minor aspect of reading science materials. More important is the recognition of relationships and the formulation of generalizations. The higher levels of comprehension in reading science materials can be achieved only when the student has learned to perceive the proper relationships among the pertinent facts. When this has been acquired, the student can then proceed to formulate his own statement of these relationships, in other words, to make a generalization. To achieve these ends, it is particularly important that the child learn to think while reading scientific materials. Skill in doing this is developed relatively slowly.

The abilities needed for comprehension and study are more or less constantly used in reading science materials. The particular skills employed depend upon the nature of the material and the purpose for the reading. The student must be prepared to vary his procedures for the most effective reading. For instance, when working on a topical unit in science, he must read to select, evaluate, and organize, and this he cannot do unless he can grasp relationships and make generalizations.

Mathematics

Reading mathematical material presents a variety of problems, some of them highly specific. Frequently there are more reading problems per page in mathematics than in any other subject. As noted for science, mathematics, too, has its own technical vocabulary (*numerator, quotient,* and so on). It also uses common words with a special meaning (*product, divided, power*), employs complex concepts, and involves the study of relationships and the making of generalizations. Pictures and diagrams must be read and interpreted. Much of this reading is concerned with exposition of processes and procedures, solving illustrative problems, and receiving directions for assignments.

Meaning of symbols. In arithmetic and other forms of mathematics, pupils must learn to attach meanings to highly abbreviated symbols such as $+$, $-$, $\div$, $=$, $\times$, and $\sqrt{}$. At first, reading dealt with words as symbols; now they are condensed to "shorthand" signs. Thus "is equal to" is represented by the symbol $=$. Also pupils need to learn to recognize promptly many specialized abbreviations such as *lb., ft., yd., cm., min.,* to mention only a few. Meanings must also be assigned both to numbers encountered in verbal contexts and to those same numbers isolated in columns (problems in addition, subtraction, and multiplication). In this the pupil must comprehend the place value of numbers such as 429, the significance of 0 in such numbers as 30 and 0.4, and the meaning of common and decimal fractions. One prerequisite for a student to solve a mathematical problem is that he have as accurate a command of all the technical symbols it uses as if these concepts were expressed uneconomically in words. Without systematic instruction, many students make slow progress in acquiring sufficient skill to understand and properly manipulate these symbols, abbreviations, and numerals.

Verbal problems. The statement of a verbal mathematical problem is ordinarily extremely compact and divorced from concrete text, and it involves complex relationships. Satisfactory reading of such a problem is achieved by slow, careful, precise progress, together with rereading and thinking. Besides having a clear understanding of words and phrases, the student must be able to select relevant facts and relationships between the pertinent words and phrases. Reading verbal mathematical problems is one of the most difficult reading tasks encountered in the content areas. There is little success without intensive concentration. The teacher should realize fully the reading difficulties the child faces. A good method for handling verbal problems is to encourage the students to adopt a pattern of procedure. The problem should be read to determine its nature and what processes should be used to solve it. Then it should be reread to select the relevant information and the processes to be used. The problem then should be solved and the answer checked for accuracy. To use this study procedure successfully the students must understand the number system and know the basic arithmetic facts discussed above. He must also possess a vocabulary foundation for quantitative reasoning and clues for the use of mathematical processes.

Literature

Unlike such areas as science, mathematics, and social studies, literature lacks a regular methodical sequence of content. Literary materials can be stories about men and women as well as animals, or they can be historical novels, poetry, plays, or essays. To a considerable degree, the primary concern of teaching literature has been the development of reading interests and tastes.

Ability to read literary materials profitably depends upon proficiency in many reading abilities. A major function of teaching literature is to develop the reading skills necessary for intelligent interpretation of an author's meaning, for sharing the moods he wishes his readers to feel, and for entering imaginatively into whatever experience he creates. These capabilities are usually those emphasized in the basic developmental reading program. They are refined, expanded, and perhaps supplemented with the teacher's guidance while reading literary materials. The better a student's proficiency in general reading comprehension and the larger his vocabulary, the more success he will have in reading literary materials. This is because both the texts and the books previously read have been primarily narrative, and literature is primarily narrative material.

Basic reading abilities.   In a way, general comprehension and vocabulary knowledge are products of progress in the reading abilities developed in the basic reading program. As the program unfolds, students progress in acquiring word-recognition techniques, reading by thought units, and techniques for increasing word knowledge, basic comprehension abilities, and special comprehension abilities. To read literary materials well at any grade level, the student should have made normal progress in acquiring these fundamental reading abilities taught in the basic course. In other words, the student will be able to read literary material satisfactorily at the reading level he has reached in the basic abilities, but not much higher.

Enrichment of meanings.   The profit gained from reading literary materials is in great part dependent upon the enrichment of meanings it brings. Important ways of enriching meanings are to be found almost anywhere in literature. One of these is a full appreciation of descriptive words, especially words associated with sensory impressions, with sights, sounds, taste, touch, and smell. Meanings are also enhanced through skill in interpreting figures of speech and symbolic expressions. The reader may need to draw upon his previous experience to interpret an illusion and to gain deeper insight into what is presented. Frequently the effects of writing depend on the reader's imaginative penetration into mere hints and suggestions.

General comment.   The foundations for successful reading of literature consist of the basic reading abilities and comprehension abilities presented in a broad developmental reading program. These are refined, expanded, and supplemented in reading literary materials.

In addition to the general level of reading ability, there are specific types of comprehension closely related to continued growth in reading literature. The two specific comprehension abilities, discussed earlier in this chapter, essential to success in reading the various types of materials in literature are *reading to interpret* and *reading to appreciate*. The teacher must check these two specific types of comprehension when diagnosing the student with difficulty in reading and enjoying literature. These two types of comprehension are needed to read poetry, narratives, drama, or essays. The authors suggest that the readers of this book review the suggestions for correcting weaknesses in these two comprehension abilities.

No other field has as big a problem in diversifying approaches to reading its materials as does literature. The skills needed for reading a drama are different from those needed for reading poetry, although both include sensory impressions, mood, and imagination. Both are related to proficiency in oral reading. Neither drama nor poetry should be read at a constant or rapid rate. For example, in the phrase, "the murmuring pines and the hemlocks," the reader should pause and let his imagination take over. He should sense the movement of the trees, smell the aroma, feel the rug of needles underfoot, hear the gentle wind, see the sunlight breaking through the branches, and see the pattern of shadows on the ground.

The next two chapters will deal with specific reading difficulties directly related to problems faced by literature teachers. One of these is a deficiency in the general rate of comprehension and the flexibility of rate needed. Another problem especially related to drama and poetry is deficiency in oral reading. The third deals with the student who does not have lasting interest in reading or who is a reluctant reader. These three reading disabilities must be corrected if reading literature is to become a permanent accomplishment for personal development and enjoyment.

SUMMARY

Three major groups of specific remedial problems are discussed in this chapter: the disabled reader who is limited in one or more types of comprehension, the one who has failed to develop some of the basic study skills, and the one who is an ineffective reader of content materials but who is in all other respects a competent reader. Each of these disabled readers needs remedial help to overcome a specific defect.

The usual method of correcting a specific type of comprehension difficulty is to have the disabled reader read material in a well-graded, basic reader at the appropriate level of difficulty. The purposes for reading the material should be such that the ability in which he is limited is stressed. The reasons for reading should be understood by the child before the reading is done, and there should be checks on the accuracy of the reading at the end. These check questions should reflect the specific comprehension ability being emphasized. The specific comprehension abilities discussed here were reading to retain factual information, to sense the organization of information, to judge the authenticity and relevance of information, to interpret the information given, and to appreciate.

The methods suggested for correcting limitations in basic study skills were to find exactly the skill in which the disabled reader was ineffective and then to teach that skill and give him enough practice to make it permanent. The basic study skills discussed were location of sources of information, use of basic references, interpretation of pictorial and tabular materials, and methods of organizing information.

Reading skills and abilities need to be adjusted to each subject-matter field. The comprehension abilities employed and the rate of reading depend on the nature and organization of the material, its difficulty, and the purpose for which the reading is to be done.

Social studies, science, mathematics, and literature are the four content fields considered. They involve a wide range of materials to be read, and somewhat different reading abilities are required in each field. Problems that arise in each were considered briefly.

STUDY QUESTIONS

1. Why is it that some readers have difficulty locating and retaining information read?

2. Do you agree or disagree that it is important for disabled readers to develop the ability to appreciate the aesthetic qualities of reading? Support your point of view.

3. How can a teacher help students who are unable to locate sources of information or are inefficient in using basic references?

4. How do the essential reading skills required for success in social studies, science, mathematics, and literature vary from one content field to another?

SELECTED READINGS

DeChant, E. *Diagnosis and Remediation of Reading Disabilities*, Chap. 12. Englewood Cliffs, NJ: Prentice-Hall, Inc., 1981.

Earle, R. A. *Teaching Reading and Mathematics*. Newark, DE: International Reading Association, 1976.

Harker, W. J. *Classroom Strategies for Secondary Reading*, 2nd ed. Newark, DE: International Reading Association, 1985.

Herber, H. L. *Teaching Reading in Content Areas*, 2nd ed., Englewood Cliffs, NJ: Prentice-Hall, Inc., 1978.

Kaluger, H., and C. J. Kolson. *Reading and Learning Disabilities*, 2nd ed., Chaps. 13 and 14. Columbus, OH: Charles E. Merrill Publishing Company, 1978.

Lunstrum, J. P., and B. L. Taylor. *Teaching Reading in the Social Studies*. Newark, DE: International Reading Association, 1978.

McCormick S. *Remedial and Clinical Reading Instruction*, Chap. 18. Columbus, OH: Charles E. Merrill Publishing Company, 1987.

Rupley, W. H., and T. R. Blair. *Reading Diagnosis and Remediation: A Primer for Classroom and Clinic*, Chaps. 11 and 12. Chicago: Rand McNally & Company, 1979.

Thelen, J. N. *Improving Reading in Science*, 2nd ed. Newark, DE: International Reading Association, 1984.

Tonjes, M. J., and M. V. Zintz. *Teaching Reading Thinking Study Skills in Content Classrooms*, 2nd ed., Chap. 8. Dubuque, IA: Wm. C. Brown Publishers, 1987.

16

Correcting Reading Rates and Oral Reading Difficulties

Two reading difficulties related to reading comprehension concern many people. Adults and students alike wonder how fast they can or should read. There are also many adults and students who feel uncomfortable in oral reading situations and often rightly so, in view of their lack of skill. Both of these reading difficulties often persist, even though the reader so disabled is mature in all other aspects of reading growth. Of course no one can be a rapid reader or an effective oral reader if he does not have the basic word-recognition skills and the basic comprehension abilities. Correcting inefficient rates of comprehension and overcoming ineffective oral reading are discussed in this chapter.

CORRECTING INEFFICIENT RATES OF COMPREHENSION

In recent years, much attention has been devoted to rapid reading in magazine articles and newspapers and on radio and television programs. The unsophisticated individual gains the impression that all he has to do to improve his reading is to read faster. Thus speed reading courses have become profitable business. Such courses are advertised widely in newspapers, magazines, and television and radio commercials. Concern for rate of reading is also reflected in the writings of professional educators. Public interest is heightened by enticing promises to teach people to read 1,000 or even up to 20,000 words per minute with good comprehension.

Since there is so much to read today and so much pressure to keep informed, the ability to read rapidly is a valuable asset. Increasing one's reading speed by 25 percent to 50 percent will save much time. Some readers can improve their rate by 50 percent to 100 percent.

Most people read unnecessarily slowly. It is best to read any material, whether a novel, business report, medical journal, textbook, or other material, as rapidly as possible with understanding. As we shall see shortly, it is possible to increase one's rate of reading by a considerable degree without loss of comprehension, but not from 12,000 to 20,000 words per minute. These claims are unrealistic. The question, "How fast should I read," can have no single answer. But it is safe to say that most of us should read much faster than we presently do. We will discuss what is involved in becoming a rapid reader.

Certain writers seem to believe that speed of reading is a valid measure of reading performance in itself, even when it is divorced from comprehension. The fact is that a measure of the rate at which words are recognized as words, with no reference to apprehending their meanings and relationships, yields a score of little or no significance in real life. Put plainly, "reading" without comprehension is not reading. The only practical and adequate definition of rate of reading is as the *rate of comprehension* of printed and written material. This is the definition followed in this book. To measure speed of reading, therefore, one must measure the rate with which material is comprehended. We must also bear in mind that comprehension itself is always to be considered in relation to the purpose for which the reading is done. In practice, it becomes important to know the rate at which a particular student grasps the general ideas in a story, or the rate at which he comprehends an exposition of history or science material, or the like. In tests, rate of reading is rate of comprehending as measured in the particular test. In consequence, standardized tests for speed of reading have certain limitations. One limitation is that the speed of reading attained is based on unnaturally short passages compared to the length of passages the student is usually expected to read. A second, even more serious, limitation is that the materials in such tests provide inadequate samples of all the different materials students must read; the speed of reading is measured for one only.

In some discussions it is assumed that speed of reading is a general ability that somehow transfers readily to the reading of a wide variety of materials. There is no such general speed of reading ability. Even for the proficient reader, the rate of reading is fairly specific to a particular reading situation.

Every teacher must realize that rapid reading in itself does not produce better understanding. A fast rate of comprehension is possible only if the pupil possesses the abilities necessary for clear and rapid understanding.

An uninformed person is likely to believe that a fast reader is inaccurate and poor in comprehension while a slow reader is accurate and comprehends better. Research on this question emphatically fails to substantiate this belief. There is the contrasting opinion that fast reading is good reading and that slowness makes for poor reading. Although some fast readers do comprehend better than slow readers, there are many exceptions: Fast readers are not always good readers.

In evaluating the data on rate related to comprehension, one should keep in mind that there is no general speed of reading skill nor any one comprehension skill. These skills are specific, varying with the kind of material and the purpose of reading (Spache 1976). Improvement in rate in one type of reading is not likely to transfer to any significant extent to all reading. It probably operates only in the particular type of material employed for the training. For example, improvement in rate of reading literature does not necessarily transfer appreciably and automatically to reading science.

The teacher should realize that neither slow nor fast reading by itself produces proper understanding. Accelerating reading in itself does not improve comprehension. For some pupils it may even decrease it. The best rate for a particular child to read a specific set of materials is pretty much an individual matter to be determined by individual diagnosis. Although the faster readers among mature readers usually comprehend better, there are exceptions. The best indications are that a program to improve speed of reading would be advantageous to most pupils who are advanced in the basic reading abilities, provided speed is not pushed to where adequate comprehension is impossible. Any general program for accelerating speed of reading for all pupils in a class is inadvisable. Finally, the true relationship may be that the child who has the necessary skills and abilities to comprehend well also has those necessary to read faster. So drill on speed of reading per se cannot be expected to be worthwhile. There are students, however, who have habits in silent reading that prevent them from adjusting their rate to the purpose and difficulty of the material. They always read at an undesirably slow rate.

Diagnosing Inefficient Rates of Comprehension

Taking into account what has been said above makes it appear hazardous to specify average rates of comprehension for the different grade levels. In a given grade, the average rate may be 290 words per minute for reading in one situation and only 140 words in another. It should be remembered that when average rates are given, they are for reading a specific kind of material for a set purpose. The published averages are usually for relatively easy materials from a reading test. They are not to be interpreted as norms for all kinds of material read for different purposes. Although standardized tests with norms give some information, most of the diagnosis must be gained from informal appraisals.

Standardized tests.   Standardized tests designed for measuring reading ability in the primary grades are ordinarily not concerned with speed. In fact it is unwise to stress speed of reading during the first three years in school. The emphasis should be on developing such things as sight vocabulary, word-recognition techniques, reading by thought units, vocabulary knowledge, and comprehension. Any attempt to measure speed at these levels might lead to misplaced pressure on speeded reading, before acquisition of the basic techniques upon which smooth, rapid reading depends.

Most standardized tests are designed to measure speed of reading of relatively short easy materials for a set purpose. The vocabulary concepts and sentence structures are simple. These tests should provide an opportunity for pupils to show their maximum speed of reading *specific, easy materials.*

Measures of speed of reading on standardized tests have limitations. As previously noted, the tests use very simple specific materials, and the purpose for which the reading is done is limited. Earlier discussion has indicated that speed on such tests is not closely related to speed in reading other kinds of materials. These tests are useful, therefore, only to gain some preliminary information about speed of reading. They are not appropriate for finding out the speed at which material in basic or supplementary tests will be read. Informal tests are needed for this.

Informal diagnosis.   For the most part, informal tests of reading rate are more useful for diagnostic purposes than standardized tests. When the test results are used to guide instruction, the teacher will want to know the rate at which a pupil can read material in the basic text or in units on history, or science, or geography, or another field. She will also want to know how versatile the pupil is in adapting his speed to changes in difficulty and to the varying purposes for the reading. These objectives can be reached only through informal tests.

Informal rate-of-reading tests are constructed easily. The teacher merely selects from a text, supplementary reader, or book employed in a unit, a series of consecutive paragraphs of the difficulty and complexity desired. The length of the test will vary with the type of material, the child's reading level, and the difficulty of the material. Ordinarily, the selection will contain from about 400 to 800 words. The longer selections may be used for more mature readers and for less exacting reading tasks.

There should be a set of comprehension questions for the child to answer when the reading is completed. These questions could be modeled from those in workbooks. The nature and number of the questions should be determined by the purpose for the reading. When reading is to get the main idea, the pupil may be asked to check the correct answer out of five listed. When reading to answer specific questions, there may be six or eight questions. If the purpose is to note important details, there may be ten or twelve questions. Unless comprehension is checked, a child may skip through the material to make a good record and not understand it adequately.

The purpose for the reading should be understood by the pupil before starting to read a selection. If individual testing is done, the child may read directly from a book. The number of words read per minute for two or three minutes of reading is computed.

If an entire class is to be tested at the same time, the selection should be mimeographed. A definite time limit, short enough so that the fast readers cannot quite finish, is set. Each pupil marks where he is when time is called and then counts the words read. Or all the pupils may be allowed to finish the selection. Each student copies down the last number, indicating elapsed time, that the teacher has listed on the chalkboard. The teacher changes the figure on the board at the end of every ten seconds. This method of timing is preferred, since the questions to be answered cover the entire selection.

Interpretations of diagnosis.   Grade or percentile norms are usually given for standardized tests. By consulting these, the teacher is able to discover whether the pupil is reading unduly slowly for the type of material used and for the purpose set by the test. The scores identify pupils who are fast and accurate, fast and inaccurate, slow and accurate, and slow and inaccurate.

In using the informal rate tests, the teacher can also take into account both rate and degree of comprehension. After testing several children, both good and poor readers, the teacher will have data to show whether a particular child reads relatively slowly or fast in a specific reading situation. For the scores on comprehension she will also be able to note accuracy of comprehension. Good comprehension is represented by about 85 percent accuracy; average comprehension by about 70 percent; and poor comprehension by about 50 percent or less.

Diagnosis should always consider comprehension along with rate. If the rate is high and comprehension low, or both rate and comprehension are low, exercises to increase rate are *not indicated*. But when rate is average or low and comprehension high, the pupil will undoubtedly profit from a program to increase his speed of reading.

As already indicated, the proficient reader adjusts his rate to the difficulty of the material, to the nature of the material, and to the purpose of the reading. The pupil who uses only one rate encounters many difficulties. If the habitual rate is fast, it is not suitable for reading difficult materials in content areas; if it is a slow, plodding rate, it is not suitable for story reading and other easy materials. Similarly, when the purpose is to grasp the main idea, the rate should be faster than when it is to note the important details.

Degree of versatility in adjusting rate may be ascertained as follows: (1) by use of informal tests, as previously described, the rates for reading materials at several levels of difficulty and complexity may be determined; (2) the rates for reading a single selection for different purposes may be measured. First, have the pupil read it for the general idea, then reread it to find the answers to certain questions, then read it again to note the important details. If roughly the same rate, either fast or slow, is used in all reading, remedial instruction is indicated to develop the ability to adjust speed of reading to fit the situation.

General Remediation for Inefficient Rates of Comprehension

To be effective, a program for increasing speed of reading must be organized carefully and must temporarily be the major instructional objective. The program should be confined to those pupils who show prospects of improving. Attempts to increase the reading speed of mentally handicapped children or those with a limiting or complex disability will most likely lead to confusion and discouragement rather than to more efficient reading.

Materials.   Relatively easy materials should be used, particularly in the early stages of the program. It should contain *very few,* if any, unfamiliar words. The difficulty level of the material should be one or two grades below the average reading grade level of the student. In general, the material should be selected from books other than basic texts. Only when there is considerable improvement in speed of reading the easy materials should the teacher *gradually* introduce the more difficult types of reading. It is essential, however, to make this transition so that the student will transfer appropriately rapid reading rates to regular classroom materials. The transition should be made under the teacher's observation and guidance, otherwise it may be only partial or nonexistent. It is possible for a child to learn to read easy material rapidly but not transfer this to other instructional materials.

In the early stages of the speeded program, there should be little emphasis on comprehension checks. The comprehension exercises should not be such that they delay rapid perception or interrupt the flow of ideas. It is enough in the early stages of the program merely to ask the student what a story is about. When rapid recognition of words and smooth phrasing become habitual, comprehension will improve. It will then be important to place more emphasis on comprehension checks. Rapid reading with adequate comprehension is, of course, the goal sought.

Motivation.   In any program for increasing speed of reading a variety of incentives is necessary if the pupil is to be motivated. Without motivation, a pupil does not feel any urgency to read faster and is not likely to do so. Proper incentives include the following. (1) The reading material used should be interesting *to the student.* An interested child is a motivated one. Other things being equal, he will be anxious to reach quickly the end of an interesting story to find out what happened. (2) A daily record of results should be kept. The teacher should greet any evidence of improvement with enthusiasm. Gains that are seen and appreciated motivate the child to even greater effort. (3) Avoid fatigue and boredom. All materials should be introduced with zest and in such a manner that the child will hope and expect to improve. If a child shows signs that he is tired or annoyed, pressure to read faster should be temporarily discontinued until he shows a more positive attitude. (4) The teacher's cheerful and sympathetic guidance will help maintain motivation. At times, this will mean working alone with a student to provide just the help and encouragement he needs. This is particularly important during the periods when no discernible gains can be observed, and the child becomes discouraged. (5) Allowing the child to participate with the teacher in organizing his remedial program will aid his motivation. The benefits he will enjoy when he can read faster should be discussed with him. His special difficulties should be talked over, and plans for improvement should be worked out jointly by the teacher and student. As obstacles arise or old habits crop up, procedures for eliminating them are also worked out together. The more clearly the student understands his difficulties and the more he participates in the remedial planning, the better his motivation will be for overcoming the handicaps. (6) The purpose for each exercise should be understood. Reading without a purpose—and this means a clearly understood purpose—cannot be well-motivated reading. Sometimes students may be reading with more attention to details than is necessary. A talk about this with the student will show what he is doing wrong and how to correct it. (7) When improved speed has been acquired through special exercises, incentives should be provided to motivate a transfer of the faster reading to leisure reading and to school subjects. All sorts of encouragement should be used; for example, praise for the number of stories or books read for enjoyment, discussion of the benefits of fast reading, and emphasis on doing class assignments speedily. The carry-over of the new habits to all types of reading will be promoted by training in flexibility. (8) After the special instruction for increasing rate of reading is completed, the teacher must be alert to relapses to the old slower rates. Motivation to maintain fast reading can be provided by special speed tests at periodic intervals, together with class discussion on the importance of adjusting speed to purposes and materials.

Working against time.   Practically everyone can read faster if he is inclined to or if he has an incentive to do so. As already noted, most students coast along at a comfortable rate in their reading. With the proper setting, which encourages a student to step up his speed of reading, and with well-organized practice day by day, real progress can be achieved.

An effective and much-used technique for increasing speed of reading is to work against time. Relatively easy material, a grade or so in difficulty below the pupil's grade placement, for example, is selected for the beginning exercises. These early exercises should be about 350 to 400 words in length. They may be mimeographed on one page. When the teacher is working with a single student, his reading may be done directly from a book or magazine. Five or six comprehensive questions are arranged on a separate sheet. These questions should be relatively easy, dealing with the general ideas in the story. After the story is finished, the material is taken away and the questions are answered. Comprehension may suffer during the early exercises but will improve as time goes on.

Each exercise should be introduced under as favorable conditions as possible. The purpose of the reading is made clear to the student. The setting should be such that the student will be eager to read as fast as possible with understanding. He should expect to improve over previous exercises. The teacher times the reading and computes the number of words per minute as his score. The student should be shown how to plot his scores on a simple graph so that he will see his gains. When little or no gain is achieved for a time, the teacher should be sympathetic and encouraging.

Two exercises per day provide enough pressure for this kind of work, and they should be separated by an hour or so. This *spaced learning* is more effective than several exercises, one after another. After the first few exercises, comprehension should be adequate. As the program gets well under way, no student should be pushed to read faster than he can comprehend.

Mechanical devices.   A number of mechanical devices have been developed and promoted for increasing speed of reading. Special motion pictures, pacers, short exposure devices, and computer programs have been used to give children practice in reading faster. Each of these methods presents phrases, lines of print, or words at speeds which may be varied by the teacher. Teacher-constructed flash cards can also be used for rapid presentation of words or phrases.

Although the use of machines is highly motivational for some students, children taught by regular methods make as great gains as those taught by machines. There is, however, always a possibility that a given child will improve with machine training but not by ordinary methods, though this remains unproven.

In general it seems that programs for improving speed of reading can be just as satisfactory without use of elaborate machines. This assumes that the materials are carefully selected, the program of training properly organized, and the instruction effectively carried out. If the teacher is able to provide incentives which will motivate the student, machines or other gadgets are not necessary to achieve satisfactory gains in speed of reading. In other words, use of certain machines does increase speed of reading, but their use is not necessary to get equivalent gains.

There are two other drawbacks to mechanical gadgets to increase speed of reading: (1) the machines are expensive, and (2) the use of machines too often becomes a ritual and overemphasizes the mechanical aspects of speeded reading over the more important processes of comprehension and thinking that result from reading.

Remediation for Specific Types of Inefficient Rates

Disabled readers deficient in the basic word-recognition skills and basic comprehension abilities are classified as having limiting or complex disabilities. These basic problems, which preclude all types of further reading growth, must be corrected before using any exercises to increase rate of reading. The remedial training needed for *basic word-recognition difficulties* is discussed in Chapters 10 and 11. The correction of *basic comprehension deficiencies* is discussed in Chapter 14.

There are two basic problems included in the discussion of remediation of specific types of rate problems, the overanalytical reader and the word-by-word reader. Both profit from programs to increase rate, and therefore the correction of these two types of disabilities and improvement in rate can be done concurrently. The remediation of these disabilities includes rapid-exposure techniques and rapid-reading exercises. For this reason, these disabilities are included in the following list of specific types of inefficient rates of reading to be discussed:

1.   The overanalytical reader
2.   The word-by-word reader

3. The reader with faulty habits
4. The reader with faulty eye movements
5. The reader with excessive vocalization
6. The inflexible reader

The overanalytical reader. Overanalysis takes two forms. One is the tendency to analyze words already known as sight words. The other is the tendency to break words into too many parts. The second type of overanalytical reader, for example, may fail to recognize the largest known parts within a word he is trying to identify. The remedial procedure for both types of overanalytical problems should be the training given in the section on treating *overanalytical habits* in Chapter 11 and also the *general remediation for inefficient rates of comprehension* given in this chapter. For this type of slow reader rapid-exposure devices are useful.

The word-by-word reader. The word-by-word reader is one who has failed to learn to read in thought units. He may not be able to recognize a group of three or four words at a glance. If so, rapid-recognition training with rapid-exposure techniques is useful. But he may not be able to group the words into thought units as he reads connected material. In this case, he should be given the training suggested under the heading, *thought units,* in Chapter 14. He should also be given the training suggested under the heading, *general remediation for inefficient rates of comprehension,* in this chapter. It should be noted that in Chapt 14, the use of rapid-exposure techniques is recommended for reading in thought units.

The reader with faulty habits. Some children have the habit of moving the finger or pointer along the line of print to guide their reading. Although justified with some children in early stages of learning or remedial work, the practice should be discarded as soon as feasible. The best way to break this habit is to discuss the problem with the student and then require him to hold the book with both hands. Continuing to point, while holding the book with both hands will be awkward for him, and to move his fingers along the print will remind him that he is pointing again.

Another faulty habit is head movements. Instead of sweeping along the line of print with appropriate eye movements, the student moves his head from left to right. This is stopped by explaining the problem to the student and then asking him to rest his chin on one hand as he attempts to read more rapidly. This practice will warn him if he moves his head again.

Many children develop a congenial, meandering way of reading that is considerably below the rate at which they might read with both understanding and pleasure. When this becomes habitual, as frequently happens, it is a handicap to proficient reading. This easy going dawdling permits attention to wander and fosters daydreaming. In addition, the child covers an inadequate amount of material in an allotted time. When unduly slow reading is really dawdling, exercises to promote an appropriate faster rate should be provided. In any reading, the correct rate is the fastest for the situation which produces proper comprehension. The general approaches to increasing rate of comprehension will usually overcome habitual dawdling.

The reader with faulty eye movements.   Much concern has been devoted to the relation of eye-movement patterns to speed of reading. Because rapid reading is accompanied by few fixations and few regressions per line of print, techniques to train eye movements have been developed for the purpose of increasing reading speed. A more appropriate procedure would be to promote reading efficiency. Whereas exercises in training eye movements tend to be mechanical and emphasize speed of reading, improvement in basic comprehension and rate of comprehension, following the procedures described in this book, will automatically result in better eye-movement sequences and faster reading.

The reader with excessive vocalization.   In the early stages of silent reading in the primary grades, many children tend to articulate words. At this level, vocalization does not slow down speed of silent reading, for the child can read no faster than he can talk. Later, as reading skill develops, vocalization becomes a handicap to improving speed of silent reading. With some children, the habit of pronouncing each word is so strong that it persists to adulthood if not corrected. The words may be whispered, or the lips and vocal organs may form the words without any sound. Whatever form the articulation takes, it is time-consuming. As long as the habit persists, silent reading can be no faster than the words can be articulated. Until vocalizing is eliminated at least in part, there can be little improvement in speed of reading. For most rapid reading, the vocalization must be either greatly reduced or eliminated.

A good technique for eliminating vocalization is to give the child reading material which is very easy and extremely interesting with practically no unfamiliar words. If the material is interesting and exciting, there will be motivation for rapid reading. The motivation should be such that the child will want to read the story rapidly to find out what happens. He is urged to do this. Particularly at first, books with short stories or mysteries should be used. These materials are valuable in the early stages of using fast reading to overcome vocalization. When a satisfactory rate of reading becomes habitual, the child can be guided to more diversified materials.

A rapid reader cannot vocalize, since it takes too long to articulate the words. When a child gets a good start in reading these easy stories, he should be encouraged in every way to race through them as rapidly as possible. For a while he may get little meaning, but at this stage this can be expected. With the rapid reading, vocalization will diminish. When vocalization has been reduced to a minimum, better comprehension will return.

The inflexible reader.   It has already been noted that *relatively* rapid reading is desired in any area of reading. That is, the reading should be at as fast a rate as the material can be comprehended. Although a properly fast rate of reading mathematical materials is relatively very slow, some students still read such materials at an undesirably slow rate. The same is true for areas such as science and social studies. Whatever the material and purpose, there can be unnecessarily slow or fast rates of reading. A rapid rate of reading in itself has no particular value. The proficient reader has several speeds, each of which can be used as the occasion demands. An essential part of the instructional program is to see that students acquire these speeds and gain skill in using them appropriately. The emphasis should be on making students adaptable, versatile readers who are able to adjust their rates to the nature and difficulty of the material and to the purpose of the reading. The goal is to *comprehend* at as fast a rate as possible. The best way to teach a child to comprehend at an appropriate rate is to furnish him with the skills and concepts to understand properly what he is to read. When this is done, he will learn to understand rapidly what he reads. Several aspects of this problem need attention.

For effective reading, rate must be appropriate to the nature and the difficulty of the material. The nature of materials varies widely. At one time the student may be reading a fast-moving story or an item of general interest in a newspaper. Here the appropriate rate of reading is relatively rapid. A short time later, the student may be reading geographic material concerned with the concept of erosion by wind and water. In this, a relatively slow rate of reading is necessary to grasp the ideas and relationships. Still later he may be reading the procedures for solving a mathematical or scientific problem, which requires a very slow, analytical procedure and often rereading. The student needs to exercise discrimination in sizing up the nature of the materials so that he may adopt a rate appropriate for understanding a particular kind of material.

Adjusting to variations in difficulty is similar. Variation in difficulty arises in many ways. Materials in some content areas have more facts than others, for example, science or mathematics compared with literature. At times, there is marked variation in difficulty within the same unit in a single area. These difficulties may occur when unfamiliar vocabulary terms and concepts, complex sentences and paragraphs, or any unusual constructions are encountered. Increased attention to content necessitates slower reading for adequate understanding. The student should read just as slowly as is needed to grasp what is presented. Any student who attempts to read all materials at the same rate, despite their content or difficulty, will be in trouble. To read with understanding and at an effective rate, he must be able to modify his rate to fit both. Easy material should be read faster than difficult material, and familiar material should be read faster than unfamiliar material.

Perhaps most important of all is the adjustment of rate of reading to the purpose for which the reading is done. This has been stressed in earlier discussions. If the student needs to get only a general impression or idea, or if he merely needs to look up a given item on a page, the speed should be relatively rapid. But if he needs to grasp the concepts in a given selection thoroughly, his pace should be relatively slow. This emphasizes the importance of purposeful reading. Before reading any unit, the child should be clear as to the purpose for reading. The most satisfactory purpose is one stated by the student himself. When he cannot do this the teacher's guidance should help provide him with a purpose *acceptable* to him. To be a really good reader, however, he must have learned to set his own purpose. This requires discrimination and flexibility. The student must be able to size up the materials and clearly understand the purpose for reading them. Then he must be flexible in choosing the appropriate rate for him to read with understanding. In other words, *the proficient reader is the adaptable, versatile reader.*

To gain flexibility in rate of reading, the child must learn to choose the particular speed for a particular situation and to read at that rate with understanding. This requires the teacher's guidance because every student reads many kinds of materials for many purposes. The development of flexibility in speed of reading tends to be difficult to learn.

Opportunities for guidance in adjusting speed of reading to the kinds of materials are abundant in teaching units in the content areas. Preparation for every unit should include discussion of the right reading procedures.

Another strategy is to have students read the same material several times, each time for a different specific purpose such as (1) to grasp the main idea, (2) to note the important details, (3) to answer questions given in advance, and (4) to evaluate what is read. Witty (1953) presents a useful outline of examples of reading purposes, reading materials, and reading methods. One column lists ''why you are reading;'' another, ''what you are reading;'' and a third, ''how you should read.''

There is always opportunity to guide the development of flexibility when teaching the specific comprehension abilities and study skills described in the previous chapter. Any instruction designed to develop comprehension in reading necessarily involves guiding the students to discover the most effective rate at which to read a specific set of material.

Gains to Be Expected

In the primary grades, while the mechanics of reading are being mastered and where much of the reading is oral, the rates of silent and oral reading are about the same. But in the fourth grade, children are ready to learn to read silently faster than they can possibly read orally. Spache (1970) states, ''If given proper instruction, children show proportionately more growth in speed of reading at about the fourth grade than during any other period in their schooling,'' (p. 247).

As noted earlier, the first step in organizing a speed of reading program in a school is to reduce to a minimum any habits that may hinder or obstruct gains in speed. When this is done, a teacher can expect practically all her students to increase their rate with training. There will be individual differences in the amount of gain achieved. There is ample evidence that training produces greater gains among the more fluent readers than among the less able ones.

In a properly conceived and executed program for a group at any school level, a few children achieve relatively small gains, many make moderate gains, and a few achieve large gains. An occasional child will make really exceptional improvement.

Ordinarily students are given special practice periods of ten to thirty minutes each. The program usually extends over several weeks with a total of 15 to 18 hours of training. Representative average gains for groups vary greatly. Harris and Sipay (1975), reported gains of 39 percent. With an intensive nine-week program of training high school students, Engelhardt (1965) obtained average group gains of 45 percent to 110 percent. If a school training program extends over two months or so, the teacher can expect an average gain of 40 percent to 50 percent. There is little evidence concerning transfer of rate to other reading materials or the degree to which the gains are maintained after the training stops.

In most programs to improve rate, comprehension is maintained at an adequate level (75 percent or higher). However, if speed alone is emphasized, comprehension may decrease. No student should be pushed to this stage.

How fast can a person be expected to read? Since many factors affect rate of reading, no single answer to this question can be given. The available data are usually for reading fairly easy material. With such material, 400 words per minute is very high for a seventh-grade student; 600 words per minute is very high and 850 exceedingly rare for college students. It is not uncommon for some well-educated adults to attain rates of 500 to 600 words per minute. These rates are for superior readers. There is, however, a physiological limit beyond which rate of reading cannot go. Spache (1970) points out that this limit is around 800 to 900 words per minute when one reads most of the words on a page. If we find reports of rates between 1200 and 1500 or more words per minute, they refer to partial reading, or skimming. Any claim that a person can be taught to read 10,000 or even 20,000 words per minute is unrealistic. Words simply cannot be seen at that rate.

As mentioned, there should be no stress in the primary grades upon improving rate of reading. For a majority of students up through about the fifth grade, a satisfactory rate can be expected as a result of a good developmental program. But some pupils in the intermediate grades can profit by a program to improve their rate of reading. These include the dawdlers and those who persist in their habits of slow reading after the major causal factors (vocalization, poor recognition of words, small sight vocabulary and so on) have been reduced or eliminated. Flexibility in reading rate should also be taught in the intermediate grades and beyond. In general, although sometimes attention is given to improving rates in the early intermediate grades, provisions for developing appropriate rates of reading seem desirable from the beginning of the sixth grade through high school and into the college years.

OVERCOMING INEFFECTIVE ORAL READING

The ultimate aim of oral reading instruction is to enable the reader to interpret a passage for others. The effective oral reader learns to interpret printed material in a relaxed and fluent manner to an audience. At the start, all oral reading should be prepared oral reading, but as the child matures in both silent and oral reading ability, he will become more adept at reading orally at sight. There are, then, sight and prepared oral reading, both of which can be interpretive. The amount of preparation needed for oral reading depends on the circumstances and the maturity of the reader. The parent who reads a story to his child is probably reading it at sight. Sharing a book by reading it aloud is also done at sight. In most other instances, oral reading is prepared, interpretive reading rather than sight reading. Both types of oral presentation should be outcomes of a reading program.

There are many adults who dislike to read orally. This probably is because of unhappy, early reading experiences and failure to develop oral reading ability. A good deal of instructional time spent having children read selections orally on sight, while the rest of the group follows silently each in his own book, is destructive to poor oral readers. As the better readers read ahead silently or supply words to their unfortunate classmate, the poor oral reader stumbles along with each of his errors apparent to all.

It should be noted that there are some children who are good silent readers and who have developed all the basic reading proficiencies but are seriously disabled in oral reading ability. These children constitute a group having a specific disability. If their poor oral reading is the result of some basic inadequacy, the major problem is correcting that difficulty. When there is no such underlying difficulty and the child is an ineffective oral reader, his problem should be diagnosed. The child who is poor in oral reading, but is otherwise an able reader for his general reading level, may suffer from one of the following difficulties: (1) he may have an inappropriate eye-voice span, (2) he may lack proper phrasing in oral reading, (3) his rate and timing in oral reading may be inappropriate, or (4) he may become frustrated while reading aloud.

Inappropriate Eye-Voice Span

Many children who are disabled in oral reading are in difficulty because their eye-voice span is inappropriate. They may be focusing their attention exclusively on the word they are speaking or they may be trying to maintain an eye-voice span that is too great for their general reading maturity. If it is the former, the child reads aloud in a halting and stumbling fashion with little expression and many pauses. He cannot anticipate the meaning of what he is reading and therefore cannot express it with his voice. He may very likely read in a monotone. Each word that he does not recognize at sight causes him to halt to inspect it, whereas with a longer eye-voice span, he would have time to identify words before pronouncing them.

If the child is trying to maintain too great an eye-voice span in oral reading, then he probably is an able silent reader who is transferring to oral reading his silent reading habits. He is racing ahead silently, perhaps at the rate of 300 to 400 words a minute, but he can pronounce words orally at only 140 words a minute. Such a child may try to maintain an eye-voice span of 8 to 10 words. If he does this in his oral reading, he will likely omit many words or read so rapidly that he can give but little expression to what he is reading aloud.

The diagnosis of eye-voice span is easy for the specialist to make. The child is given a book at the right level of difficulty for oral reading—a level at which he will encounter few word difficulties. He is given time to prepare the material and then he is asked to read it aloud to the examiner, who is at the child's right. As the child reads aloud, the examiner reads along silently with him. At intervals, the examiner covers the child's page with a three-by-five card in order to find out how many words the child is able to say after he can no longer see the print. This should be done three or four times before the examiner starts keeping the actual record. The examiner should cover the rest of the line of print when the child is pronouncing a word that comes about one-third of the way through it. This testing should also be done with unprepared or sight oral reading. In this way, the examiner obtains information on the eye-voice span of a child in both prepared and sight oral reading. Children in the early grades, with first- or second-grade reading ability, cannot maintain an eye-voice span of more than a word or two in unprepared oral reading. In sight oral reading, they can be expected to be little more than oral word-callers. Instruction in sight oral reading should be delayed until they have greater compentency in reading. They will, however, tend to have a longer eye-voice span when reading aloud material that they have prepared for oral reading and therefore can be expected to interpret more effectively.

Remedial instruction for the child with narrow eye-voice span should always be done in the prepared oral reading situation. The child should not do sight oral reading. Conversational passages are best for developing fluent oral reading for such a child. The material should be easy, with few if any unfamiliar words. The child should be encouraged to try to look ahead. Special attention should be given to phrasing. In certain cases, it works well to use the method of testing eye-voice span as a device for teaching the child to lengthen his span. The purpose for his oral reading should be real, such as preparing to read something aloud that he knows he is going to read to others. He should rehearse until he is satisfied that he is ready for the oral reading.

The child who is trying to maintain too long an eye-voice span needs to be taught to use one that is more appropriate to the oral reading situation. At the start of remedial training he should be given an opportunity to read prepared material before an audience. His oral reading should be recorded with a tape recorder so that he can develop awareness of his oral reading pattern and think about how to improve it. He should be taught how to pause from time to time while reading aloud, and he should be encouraged to look at his audience frequently. The problem of teaching the child who has too long an eye-voice span is in getting him to use his superior reading ability effectively in oral reading.

Lack of Proper Phrasing Ability

A pupil who is a poor oral reader may lack proper phrasing ability and tend to read aloud, either word by word or by clustering words into groups, disregarding the thought units involved. In either circumstance, attention to the meaning of what is read is neglected. The word-by-word reader can be detected immediately as he reads orally. Each word is pronounced as an unrelated entity. The words are read much in the manner that a mature reader might read a grocery list. When a child reads in this way, he may be directing his attention to the meaning of each word, but he is paying little attention to the interrelationships among them. The child who clusters words without regard to the real thought units is more difficult to detect when listening to his oral reading. What he reads may seem rather fluent, but it does not seem to make sense. This kind of oral reading sounds as though someone were trying to read a grocery list four words at a time and putting in expression not warranted by the dissociated content.

The remedial training for children who lack proper phrasing in oral reading is the same for both types. Word-by-word reading is often brought about in the first place by having children read material which is too difficult for them or which repeats words in a mechanical and more or less senseless way. Early books should introduce words at a slow rate. Words should be used frequently in meaningful content, without needless repetition. Beginning reading books that say, "Make, make, make it, John," or "See, see, oh, see," or "Look, look, oh look," are giving what is probably the best possible training in word-by-word reading.

The material used to correct the tendency to use inappropriate phrasing in oral reading should be easy for the child, avoid inane repetition, and include a considerable amount of conversation. Dramatic readings, tape recordings, dummy or live microphone readings, and other such activities encourage proper phrasing. No sight oral reading should be attempted until growth in phrasing is well established.

Inappropriate Rate and Poor Timing in Oral Reading

Many children who lack ability in oral reading attempt to read too rapidly or have a poor sense of timing. They may start out reading at a reasonable rate but go continually faster until little of what is read can be understood. The good oral reader at any level reads at a rate that is relatively slow. He has a moderate degree of flexibility in his rate so that he may express different moods by altering his rate of reading. He learns to use pauses effectively to hold the attention of his audience and also to emphasize important points.

One of the most helpful means of aiding the poor oral reader is to devote attention to his rate and timing. The child will profit from listening to good oral readers on the radio or on television and trying to emulate their performances. Tape recordings of the child's own reading will demonstrate his present pattern to him. Oral reading situations best suited to the child's needs are those in which he shares findings related to class enterprises. Having him be the news commentator during sharing periods is excellent because the news is made of short paragraphs giving accounts of different unrelated events. Each one is read, and then the child pauses before going on to the next. The pauses are short enough that he does not accelerate his reading. Reading long selections from a story should be avoided until the child has his speed and timing under control.

Frustration in Oral Reading

Some children who have had frequent unfortunate experiences in oral reading become insecure or even frightened in such situations. The child who is experiencing frustration during his oral reading can be detected by noting changes in the pitch of his voice while he reads. If his voice gets increasingly higher as he reads, he is becoming more and more frustrated. His errors may increase as he reads. Few situations are more highly emotionally charged than is oral reading for the poor reader. Everything that can be done to relieve his stress in oral reading situations should be done. To help the easily frustrated oral reader, have him read material that is free from difficulties, which he has prepared so well that he can feel confident. Another aid is to have the teacher near at hand and ready to prompt him if he gets into difficulty. Having the child read out of sight of his audience seems to lessen some of his tension and helps him establish confidence. Reading offstage as a narrator in a play or reading behind the screen for a puppet show often helps. A microphone placed in another room over which an announcement or a news report is read offers a good opportunity for the child to read, free from self-consciousness. If, under these conditions, the reading is well-prepared and the material is relatively easy to read, great progress can be expected. As soon as possible, the child should discard these devices and learn to read before his audience.

In working with an easily frustrated oral reader, certain precautions should be taken. His early oral reading experiences should grow out of a desire to share a story with others. He should be encouraged to tell the major part of the story in his own words and read orally only a small section; a paragraph or two is enough. He should select the part that he would like to read and prepare it in advance, even rehearsing it aloud with the teacher. Then when he does read it aloud to the group, if he gets into difficulty with a word, the teacher should supply it immediately. If, while reading, the child uses a high pitched or strained voice, reads at an unusually rapid rate, or shows any other sign of stress, he should finish by telling the rest of the story. Gradually he can increase the length of the selection he prepares for oral reading. Only after he becomes confident in situations to which he comes prepared to read orally to the group should he attempt to read aloud at sight. In all oral reading, the material should be relatively easy and free from words that the child is likely to find difficult.

General Methods for Developing Oral Reading Fluency in Young Readers

Much practice in appropriate materials is necessary to develop oral reading fluency in nonfluent young readers. Henk, Helfeldt, and Platt (1986) describe several useful methods for improving fluency. One technique is imitative reading, in which the teacher reads a portion of the text aloud, as the child reads it silently, followed by the child reading that portion aloud. Another method is radio reading, in which each student reads from a separate script while the teacher monitors from a master script. Repeated readings can also be used. In this method children reread a selection many times as they chart decreases in the time they require and in the errors they commit. An individual method can be used where teacher and student read aloud together or a choral reading method can be employed where the children read together aloud to promote fluent reading. Children should be urged to read practiced material, "Just like you would say it."

Self-Improvement of Oral Reading

As soon as children are old enough to recognize that they have problems in oral reading, they can be guided to want to improve their own oral reading abilities. For self-improvement of oral reading, children can use a checklist of questions. Each child checks his progress in the phase of oral reading upon which he is working. One may be working on his rate of reading, another may be working on phrasing, and a third on accuracy. The children may, under proper circumstances, judge the oral reading of one another. When this is done, they should tell what they liked, how well they think a child did in respect to what he was working on, and any ways in which they think he might do still better. Such a list as the following will prove helpful:

1. Did he select material that is of interest to his listeners?
2. Was he well enough prepared?
3. Did he read loud enough for all to hear?
4. Did he read as though he were telling the story?
5. Was he reading at a pleasant rate?
6. Did he express the meaning well?
7. Was he relaxed and did he have good posture?
8. Did he use the punctuation marks to help him?
9. Did he make us feel he wanted to read his story to us?

When oral reading is taught properly, not only is interpretive reading enhanced, but also oral language patterns are improved and better silent reading results. The child who is accustomed to reading aloud with pleasure will use some of the expressions he likes in his spoken language. He will gain feelings of confidence before groups and will sense the importance of adequate preparation. His silent reading will improve because, in his preparation for oral reading, he will be concerned with the meaning, the characterizations, and the action which he is to interpret to others. His concern with thought units in oral reading will teach him to cluster words together properly in his silent reading. Modern programs of oral reading appear to be vastly superior to the "round-the-room" reading of bygone days which produced the many insecure oral readers among the adults of today.

CASE STUDY OF A HIGH SCHOOL STUDENT WITH A BASIC COMPREHENSION LIMITATION AND POOR RATE OF READING

John, a ninth-grade student, was referred to a university clinic for work in reading during a ten-week summer period. He came from a distant state and stayed with his grandparents during his remedial work. He also registered in a summer reading improvement class. He had attended a school system in one of the mountain states during his elementary and junior high school years.

School history.   At the time John was admitted to the clinic, he was sixteen years, five months old. His school record showed that he had repeated the second grade because of an illness which kept him out of school for the last two months of the school year. John's work up until that time seemed to be progressing well, except for a notation that he was having some difficulty in oral reading.

The rest of the elementary-grade years of the record showed that he was progressing with somewhat below-average success in social studies and reading, but maintained good achievement in arithmetic and science. John was known to be a bright, cooperative boy, although his teachers noted that he was somewhat shy and withdrawn. His teachers had made a special effort to get him to participate in class activities. During his junior high school years, John continued to do reasonably well in mathematics courses, somewhat poorly in science, and very poorly in social studies and English.

As a result of a conference with John, it was found that he had received instruction at a reading center during the preceding year to increase his speed of reading. He said that he had improved a little, but try as he would, he could not seem to read fast enough to keep up with his assignments. John indicated that he took his books home and read his regular texts with great care, but could not find the time to do the extra reading required in the English and social studies courses. He found the mathematics and science courses easier to cover. He also said that he did not like to participate in class discussions.

Physical status.   John's physical status was excellent and there was no indication of any sensory limitation. He liked to go hiking in the mountains and was very fond of skiing, which he did often. His shyness seemed to be limited to the classroom, since he participated in skiing, swimming, and tennis with his friends.

Abilities.   John was found to be an intellectually able boy. He was measured on the *Wechsler-Adult Intelligence Scale—Revised,* and was found to have a verbal I.Q. of 114, a performance I.Q. of 126, and a full scale I.Q. of 120. This would place his reading expectancy at a beginning college freshman level ($1.20 \times 10) + 1$, or grade 13 reading expectancy.

John was given the *Woodcock Reading Mastery Tests—Revised, Form G*. His grade scores follow:

Word Identification	9.0
Word Attack	9.7
Word Comprehension	10.0
Passage Comprehension	4.9
Total Reading	8.4

These results show that word recognition was not John's basic problem. His pronunciation of common words, ability to work out the pronunciation of new words, and his understanding of the meanings of words was adequate. A comparison of his general reading vocabulary, science-mathematics vocabulary, social studies vocabulary, and humanities vocabulary showed each to be reasonably well developed. John's comprehension of passages, on the other hand, was very poor. Since the *Woodcock Reading Mastery Tests—Revised* are individually administered and allow adequate time for each response, John's poor passage comprehension was judged to be the result of a basic comprehension problem, not simply a reflection of his generally slow reading rate.

John's oral and silent reading ability was then appraised by informal techniques (Chapter 8). He was found to read orally and silently at approximately the same rate—about ninety words a minute. He could read seventh-grade material aloud without excessive word-pronunciation errors; but when he answered questions about the content, even of fourth-grade material, he was inaccurate and asked to be allowed to reread to find the answers. This he could do reasonably well. John was a word-by-word reader who gave no indication of reading in thought units and had little sense of sentence organization. His eye-voice span was limited to one or two words.

In silent reading, John could be seen to make many eye fixations per line of print, and he made many large regressions. This indicated that in silent reading John was using much the same single-word techniques that he had used in oral reading. The examiner also noted that while John was reading silently he was, in fact, reading aloud to himself. This showed up in lip movements and other indications of excessive vocalization. John was reading silently, word-by-word, vocalizing what he read, and then rereading to understand the meaning of what he had read.

The answers to the diagnostic questions raised in Chapter 7 indicated the following:

1. Is John correctly classified as a disabled reader? The results of the diagnosis showed that he was definitely a disabled reader. John had a limiting condition that would have to be overcome before he could become an able reader and achieve educationally in keeping with his intellectual capacity. John's tendency to withdraw in the classroom was felt to be a symptom, and not the cause, of his problem. Rather it led one to believe that he was aware of his reading inadequacy.

2. What is the nature of the training needed? The remedial program designed

for John had the following components: (1) practice in rapid recognition of phrases, including flash drills, as discussed in Chapter 14; (2) prepared oral reading, with emphasis on proper phrasing and oral expression of sentence meaning to improve reading in thought units; (3) steps to overcome the vocalization John used in reading activities; (4) use of context clues and other meaning clues as an aid to comprehension (see chapter 14).

3. Who can most effectively give the remedial work? On the basis of the diagnosis, it was decided that work with an individual remedial teacher, plus a reading-improvement class, was the best arrangement that could be made for John during the summer period.

4. How can improvement be brought about most efficiently? At the start, the clinician selected high interest-low reading level materials. These materials required reading ability of about the end of fourth-grade level, but had the interest level and format of a seventh-grade book. In addition, independent reading of suitable materials, such as those discussed in Chapter 9, was encouraged. The remedial teacher gave John many opportunities to do prepared oral reading with emphasis upon proper phrasing and oral expression of sentence meaning, both to improve oral reading and to develop phrasing. This was thought to be justified in spite of John's vocalization tendencies, since lack of reading by thought units and sentence meaning is more limiting to total reading growth than is vocalization. The remedial teacher developed exercises to help train him in locating thought units within sentences, as described in Chapter 14. Flash drills, using flash cards, were developed for rapid phrase-recognition exercises.

The teacher of the reading improvement class was informed of the findings of the diagnosis, and she adjusted her instruction for John in order to achieve the same remedial objectives. Her help was especially effective in helping John to overcome his tendency to withdraw when working in groups.

John took home relatively easy books for independent reading. He was told to read these books as rapidly as he could for three minute periods, as measured by the timer on the electric stove. Then he was to note, for each 15-minute period, the number of pages read, such as: from the top of the page 21 to the middle of page 29. He was also told to write, in not more than three short sentences, the major ideas presented. Each day he would bring the results of his independent reading to the remedial teacher. Using his "major ideas" sentences as notes, he would discuss the independent reading he had done at home the day before. He also kept a daily rate chart, calculated on the results of his final 15-minute timed period of reading. John was, of course, free to read the books taken home for leisurely, untimed reading, and he was encouraged to do so. During his home reading, as in all other reading activities, John was told to try to limit vocalization. This home practice was reinforced by the flash drills used to develop phrase recognition, which also helped in overcoming vocalization.

5. Does the child have any limiting conditions that must be considered? John was not limited in any sensory or physical way that would contribute to the complexity of his reading problem. His tendency to withdraw in school situations and

his lack of confidence, while thought to be a direct outgrowth of his reading frustrations, were taken into account in formulating the remedial plans. John's confidence was bolstered by the acceptance of himself and his reading problem by the remedial teacher. His withdrawal tendencies were recognized quickly by the high school corrective-reading teacher. At the very start of instruction, she provided John with a story to report on about delivering the mail on skis and encouraged him to tell about his own skiing experiences. This approach quickly established John favorably among his classmates.

6. Are there any environmental conditions that might interfere with progress in reading? The environment in which John was placed during this summer period was thought to be ideal. His grandparents were cooperative and knowledgeable. They made certain that he had an enjoyable summer vacation including opportunities to swim and play tennis with his classmates. They also provided John with a suitable place for leisure reading and took a healthy interest in what he was reading.

Results.   John was given remedial instruction as outlined previously, and he also enrolled in the reading improvement class for the ten-week period. The results were thought to be outstanding. Of course, John was an able boy with no limiting physical conditions and was helped under ideal circumstances. His problems were of a type in which rapid correction often takes place. Nonetheless, the results were gratifying to all persons concerned.

The *Woodcock Reading Mastery Tests—Revised, Form H* were repeated at the end of the ten-week period, with the following results:

Word Identification	9.3
Word Attack	9.4
Word Comprehension	10.8
Passage Comprehension	10.7
Total Reading	10.5

The limiting condition of word-by-word reading and his excessive vocalization had been overcome. John was now able to couple his skill in word recognition with his able intellect to read slightly better than a typical beginning tenth-grade student, even though he was still not reading up to his reading expectancy level. John had also overcome the insecurity in reading situations which had previously inhibited his performance. This gain in confidence undoubtedly helped to improve his measured reading capabilities. John's interest in reading and his ability to concentrate on what he was reading developed to the point that, while reading a book on his way to school on the bus one morning, he missed his stop and rode all the way to the downtown area before he looked up from his book to check on his whereabouts.

An informal evaluation showed that, John was able to read high school material for varied purposes at from 300 to 400 words a minute, with a high degree of accuracy. It was felt, at the end of the session, that his reading ability would no longer interfere with his future progress.

SUMMARY

A good speed of reading is that rate at which material is comprehended according to the purpose for which it is being read. For the proficient reader especially, speed of reading is fairly specific to the particular reading situation, materials, and purposes. In general, the goal is to comprehend at as fast a rate as possible. Some details discussed in achieving this goal are (1) rate of comprehension that avoids dawdling, (2) rate to fit material read, (3) rate to fit purpose, (4) flexibility in adapting rate to materials and purposes, (5) relation of rate to comprehension, (6) role of eye movements in different rates, and (7) norms for speed of reading. General methods for determining deficiencies in rate of reading include standardized tests and informal tests. Each type of test should supplement the other in diagnosis.

A complete diagnosis of difficulties in speed of reading must include an analysis of possible limiting conditions, such as the basic word-recognition skills and basic comprehension abilities which preclude rapid reading. These must be corrected before the specific types of inefficient rates can be overcome. The specific rate problems discussed include the overanalytical reader, the word-by-word reader, the reader with faulty habits, the reader with faulty eye movements, the reader with excessive vocalization, and the inflexible reader.

The program for improving rate of reading must include (1) use of appropriate materials, (2) proper incentives to develop and maintain motivation, and (3) techniques for increasing rate.

Two general techniques are used to increase speed of reading. The first is working against time with proper materials and adequate motivation. The second is using various machines. Just as much gain in speed can be obtained by the well-organized, less-complicated, and less-expensive procedures as by machines.

An essential part of any program for speeding up reading is to develop flexibility in adjusting rate to materials and purposes. Ineffective oral readers need to be given material that is relatively easy for them to read and they must have ample opportunity to prepare. The major problems in oral reading are inappropriate eye-voice span, a lack of proper phrasing, unfortunate rate and timing, and frustration in oral reading. Some children benefit from efforts to help them develop fluency in oral reading and some benefit from their own guided attempts at oral reading improvement.

STUDY QUESTIONS

1. How should reading rate be assessed?
2. What incentives should be considered when trying to help a student improve his reading speed?
3. What is meant by "a flexible reader"? What characteristics of the reading task determine the appropriate reading rate?

4. What are the causes of poor oral reading? What are some general practices which promote good oral reading?

SELECTED READINGS

BURMEISTER, L. E. *Reading Strategies for Secondary School Teachers,* Chap. 10. Reading, MA: Addison-Wesley Publishing Co., Inc., 1974.

DURKIN, D. *Teaching Young Children to Read,* 4th ed., Chap. 6. Boston: Allyn & Bacon, 1987.

HARRIS, A. J., AND E. R. SIPAY. *How to Increase Reading Ability,* 8th ed., Chap. 14. New York: Longman, Inc., 1985.

HILL, W. R. *Secondary School Reading: Process, Program, Procedure,* Chap. 12. Boston: Allyn & Bacon, 1979.

McCORMICK S. *Remedial and Clinical Reading Instruction,* Chap. 17. Columbus, OH: Charles E. Merrill Publishing Company, 1987.

TONJES, M. J., AND M. V. ZINTZ. *Teaching Reading Thinking Study Skills in Content Classrooms,* 2nd ed., Chap. 5. Dubuque, IA: Wm. C. Brown Publishers, 1987.

17

Encouraging Continued Growth in Reading

After a child has overcome a reading handicap sufficiently to allow him to discontinue the concentrated remedial program, he should be put into classroom situations where he will gain increasing independence in reading. He must be aided and assisted carefully by the classroom teacher. This child needs the support and encouragement necessary to ensure that he will continue to make reading gains, and he also needs opportunities to gradually develop real self-sufficiency and independence in reading.

If the results of remedial training are to become permanent and if continuous growth in reading is to occur in the classroom, the child should

1. Develop a permanent interest in reading
2. Establish independence in using reading
3. Continue to progress in reading after remediation

These three essentials will be discussed in the following sections.

DEVELOPING A PERMANENT INTEREST IN READING

Throughout a remedial treatment program, as discussed in this book, attention was given to the independent reading of the disabled reader. The development of reading interests and the desire to use reading as a source of information and enjoyment were considered essential to reading growth. If remedial instruction is to establish permanent learning, an appreciation of reading as a worthwhile activity must be cultivated.

Of great importance in establishing a continuing appreciation for and utilization of reading is to provide the child with selections and materials which appeal to his interests. Whether in the remedial reading setting or in the classroom, nothing is more important to ensuring continued growth in reading than maintaining strong motivation. There is ample evidence from both clinic and classroom to show that children make greater progress in their reading when they can read about things that are highly interesting to them.

According to recent research by Greenlaw (1983), children at the primary level select as most preferred, books that are classified as funny; followed by make-believe, books about people, and animal stories; real things, rhyme, and mystery books were third most popular. Fairy tales, sports, and how-to-do-it books were least often chosen. Books selected by upper-level children as most preferred included adventure, jokes/humor, and informational books. Second most popular were fantasy, mystery, sports, and the supernatural. How-to-do-it, biography, historical fiction, and poetry were chosen third most frequently, science fiction and romance were least often chosen. October issues of the *Reading Teacher* and the *Journal of Reading* provide current bibliographies of books most preferred by children and young adults.

When Wolfson, Manning, and Manning (1984) had fourth-grade children respond to a reading interest inventory, they found that more boys expressed interest than girls in reading about adventure, machines and applied science, and animals. More girls, however, expressed interest in the multi-ethnic, family life and children, and fine and applied arts categories of reading. Boys and girls showed little or no difference in interest in fantasy, sports, social studies, famous people, and plants. Fantasy was the most popular category studied among boys and girls combined, whereas plants were not a popular topic for either.

A review of research on children's leisure reading interests by Greaney (1980) reveals that children at the end of elementary school read the most, girls read more books than boys do, children from higher socioeconomic classes read more than children from lower socioeconomic classes, good students read more and better-quality materials than do poor students, and many poor readers at the secondary level seem to have abandoned reading. Mellon (1987) studied the leisure reading of rural secondary students. She found that over 25% of low-achieving students indicated on a questionnaire that they did no leisure reading. Further, twice as many males as females said that they did not read in their spare time. The two most frequently given reasons for not reading were working after school and hatred of reading. Among males who did leisure reading the three preferred types of reading were magazines, sports and sports biographies, and comic books. For females the three preferred categories were romance, mystery, and magazines.

In general, the research suggested differences in reading preferences depending upon the age and sex of the reader. A decline in leisure reading with age accompanied by the complete rejection of reading by many older, poor-achieving students is a cause for concern.

Identifying Specific Interests of a Disabled Reader

Studies of children's reading interests are valuable for suggesting what types of books might appeal to children of a certain age and sex, and also what books might appeal to a given child. However, in teaching an individual child, especially one who is resistant to reading, it becomes necessary to identify and evaluate his own particular interests.

Questionnaires. Information may be gained from simple questionnaires. Often the best questionnaire is one devised by the teacher herself, for it can apply specifically to a particular child or group of children. With reading-disabled children, the teacher must often read the items of the questionnaire to the child and write in his responses.

Interview. As the remedial teacher works with a disabled reader, she should be alert to the child's interests. When the child seems to be comfortable in the remedial-reading setting, the teacher should have a relaxed conversational interview with the child. Informal conversation, recommended by Norton (1987, p. 101), is a simple, natural, and effective way to uncover a child's interests.

The interview may supplement the questionnaire, or for some children, substitute for it. During the interview, every effort is made to help the child feel comfortable so he will want to talk freely about his activities in and out of school, the kind of reading he likes, his favorite television programs, and so on. The teacher may use a mimeographed outline to guide her interview and to record the information. It should not be used if it breaks the rapport between teacher and pupil. Jotting down such items as favorite sports, movies, books, or suggestions for future reading does not ordinarily disturb a child. But sometimes the relaxed personal give-and-take of a quiet interview is ruined by following a mimeographed schedule. Although an interview may be time-consuming, so much information is usually gained that it is worthwhile.

Observation. A relatively simple and effective way to find out what a child's interests are is to watch his daily activities in and out of school. When children are free to express themselves in talk, play, drawing, and other activities, the alert teacher finds many opportunities to jot down an anecdotal note for later reference. The child who draws dogs is probably interested in reading about dogs. The child who loves to play doctor usually enjoys reading about doctors. Many possible reading interests are discovered in this way.

Methods for developing the desire to read. Children with reading disabilities, nearly all of whom, at the start of remedial treatment, dislike reading, present special difficulties. The first problem is to identify the pupil's interest patterns as previously described. His introduction to voluntary reading should be with a book on a topic of paramount interest to him. The book should be easy to read, short, well-written, and have lots of pictures. More books should be supplied as needed. The first several books may all be on one subject, perhaps animals, if they are what he likes. It is important to keep within the area of his known interests until the habit of voluntary reading is established, even if they are very narrow. He may refuse to read anything but animal stories, or space stories, or gangster stories. But in time, his interests may be expanded gradually. The main problem with disabled readers is to teach them to read at an appropriate level. Enrichment and expansion of interests can come gradually.

To develop an interest in reading, conditions in the classroom, resource center, and at home must be favorable to reading. Reading is encouraged in school settings by (1) teachers who are enthusiastic about books, (2) classrooms and resource rooms that are full of well-selected, easily accessible books, (3) providing enough time to look through, choose, and read books, (4) specific recommendations given by teachers and peers, and (5) teachers who read aloud every day. For more information about school settings that encourage reading see Hickman (1983). To learn more about reading aloud to children, *The Read Aloud Handbook* (Trelease, 1985) is highly recommended. Reading is encouraged at home by (1) parents who are supportive of reading, (2) available books and magazines that are appropriate to the child's reading level and interests, (3) parents who converse with their child about what the child has read, and (4) parents who read aloud to their children. To be effective, these activities must be spontaneous, rather than staged to snare the child into reading. Many children want to be like their parents in ways that are genuine and worthwhile. Under such favorable conditions, most children will lengthen their leisure-time reading and broaden their reading interests.

Although the real motivation for reading must come from the child himself, the teacher, having appraised intrinsic motivations, can help the child pursue established interests and discover new ones. The child is not born with interests. They are acquired, including those in reading, and can be encouraged by training. One interest can lead to another. For example, a child may be interested in baseball. This may lead to reading newspaper accounts of baseball games, which in turn may lead to reading biographies of baseball heroes, which may lead to reading about—who knows what? Some suggestions for developing and extending permanent interests in reading are discussed in the following sections.

Build interest by reading to disabled readers. The remedial teacher who reads stories aloud with real enthusiasm so that they fascinate children will have little difficulty in stimulating interest in reading. An entertaining story which the teacher has read to a group will be reread by many pupils when it is placed in the reading corner and when attention is called to it. Similarly some of the more advanced readers among the pupils may read aloud to the group a selection from a story which they have prepared to read. When this is done, the reader is motivated to do his best, and his listeners become interested in the story and will probably wish to read it all.

Build interests free from skill-development instruction.   There should be a clear-cut distinction between reading done in the remedial program to develop skills and abilities and reading to expand interests, much of which is achieved during the time set aside for personal reading. McKee (1948) emphasizes this point when he says "methods used to help children build an abiding interest in good reading material and a taste for such material must be inherently informal," enabling children to approach a selection as something to be enjoyed in its own right. There is no surer way to stifle expanding interests than to stop the ongoing enjoyment of a story or selection in order to engage in drill upon a fundamental of reading or to attempt to extract an analysis of content, plot, or characterization. It is unwise to probe and quiz, implying that nothing can be learned unless the teacher asks questions and the children answer them. When a child needs help in recognizing a word or comprehending a concept, it should be given freely and quickly so that he can continue to communicate with the author actively and with interest.

To instill in a child the interest and desire to do extensive reading—to be a reader—is a paramount goal of any reading program. The beauty and the wonder is lost when reading becomes nothing more than a forced and unpleasant classroom exercise. All the reading skills combined are of little use to the one who does not read.

Present systematic lessons.   Lessons designed to expand reading interests should be planned carefully and systematically. Recommending systematic planning, Burton and Larrick (1961) state

> Emphasis on the pleasures of reading in the elementary school does not mean a *laissez-faire* policy of "surround them with books and sit back." Instead, it means careful planning to provide for individual differences in an atmosphere that encourages children to wonder and to seek, to contemplate and to evaluate.

Based upon knowledge of each child's reading abilities and interests, the remedial teacher can arrange experiences to expand interests. One way is to integrate the ideas found in reading with the children's daily experiences. Careful integration of ideas requires thought and attention. Any subject contains a potential for deepening and expanding reading interests. It is often assumed that the development of reading interests is limited to reading juvenile fiction. Such an assumption should not be made. It should be recognized that at the present time children's interests are being expanded beyond juvenile fiction. It is equally important to recognize that children are interested in the wonders of the world about them. The concept of children's literature has broadened to include materials from many fields, both factual and fictional.

Use hobbies to stimulate reading interests.   Teachers have found that allowing pupils time in school to pursue hobbies is worthwhile. One child's enthusiasm may spark others' interest in a particular hobby. Often the teacher can suggest some type of related reading which will be valuable to the young enthusiasts. Especially at the secondary level, many students participate in optional after-school activities which stimulate strong interest in reading. Books directed toward specialized interests such as *How to Stay Alive in the Woods* or *Step-By-Step Jewelry* often have great appeal to students who devote their time and energy to such areas.

Other methods of stimulating interest in reading include (1) displays of book jackets and book advertisements, (2) a book club with its own student officers, (3) carefully organized and regularly changed book exhibits in a corridor case, (4) an attractive wall chart on which each student can list books he has read, and (5) *very brief* book reports. Children most enjoy informal book chats presented to a few classmates who share similar interests. In general the enthusiastic teacher who promotes "real" reading and plans systematically for developing interests will find she is rewarded.

Perhaps the most effective incentive for broadening interests comes from feeling the enthusiasm of the teacher and of other pupils for stories and books not dealing with what one thought was the only interesting area. Judicious use of all the methods discussed above can be applied to expand reading interests as well as to deepen them. The alert teacher will know which method or methods to use with a particular pupil.

We have pointed out the strong influence of a teacher's enthusiasm. It is well-known that the teacher who is most successful in developing an interest in reading in a specific area is one who herself is interested in that material, lives it, appreciates it, and shares her enjoyment with the children whom she teaches. It should also be noted that interaction among students often generates reading interests which are almost unlimited.

General statement.   The goal of continued growth in reading by a particular pupil will have been achieved when he has acquired broad and permanent interests and desirable tastes. Although growth in reading interests and tastes is gradual, proper guidance throughout the grades can accomplish much. Besides providing strong motivation for learning to read, interests determine what is read and how much is read voluntarily.

There is no such thing as a criterion of good taste which is applicable to all children. Improvement in taste is relative to the level of a particular pupil. Although improvement is slow, well-organized guidance can lead to discrimination and improved choice of reading materials for all children. The gains will be large for some pupils, small for others. A remedial program to broaden interests and cultivate tastes is essentially the same as a sequential program. The main difference is that the remedial program is more intensive and more highly individualized.

ESTABLISHING INDEPENDENCE IN USING READING

When a child begins remedial reading instruction he is often insecure, lacking self-confidence and independence. An important part of helping such a child improve his reading is helping him to become increasingly more independent.

Developing Initial Independence

In initial remedial reading instruction, it is often wise to intersperse short, easily accomplished reading activities with other types of activities which are more appealing to reading-disabled children. Eventually as a student gains in confidence and in reading skill, it becomes desirable to devote more of the instructional period to reading. In addition, the student should be asked to read increasingly longer selections and should be given less direct teacher assistance for the purpose of increasing the student's reading independence. Allowing a student to take an appropriate book home to read is a similar aid to independence. Although oral reading instruction is valuable for many reading-disabled children, silent reading must receive a good deal of emphasis in order to help establish skills for independence in reading. Allowing a student to make his own reading selections from among available choices fosters independence in reading, as does allowing him to use reading for his own reasons. The independent reader reads books of his own selection for such reasons as for pure enjoyment, because his friends are talking about a certain book, or because he needs information for a project or activity.

The older student benefits from some direct instruction in functional reading of such materials as newspapers, telephone books, television guides, catalogs, and promotional pamphlets. Most students enjoy reading these materials, especially when they are allowed to read according to their own interests and learn to use the materials in an independent manner to gather useful information.

Learning to Use Library Resources

Reading-disabled children often do not make successful use of the school library and therefore can profit from direct assistance in library usage as a part of their remedial instruction. The organization of the library and library procedures can be discussed with the disabled reader on an individual basis by the school librarian. The reading teacher can help the child successfully practice such procedures as using the card catalog, finding a book, and checking out books, until the student becomes quite skillful and confident in obtaining books from the library.

Use of the public library should also be encouraged. Often upon the remedial reading teacher's suggestion, parents take their reading-disabled children to the public library and assist them in book selection and in obtaining a library card. With encouragement from the school and from the home, such children can become proficient in the use of both the school and the public library and begin to use both with independence.

Exploring Other Sources of Reading Material

When the other children in the school make purchases of inexpensive editions of well-liked books through the school book club, the disabled readers should be assisted to do so, too. The remedial reading teacher can compile an appropriate list of choices for the child who reads poorly, and his parents can encourage him to choose a book or two.

In addition, parents can point out to their reading-disabled children the many displays of books and magazines in stores. If a child shows an interest in a magazine from a store display shelf, a parent should feel free to buy it for the child even though it may seem too advanced. Although the child may not be able to read every word or even to understand every idea in the magazine, it is a step toward independence in reading to have a magazine of one's own.

It is also beneficial for poor readers to be introduced to a bookstore and to see the many different books offered for sale such as attractive oversized picture books, inexpensive paperback books, and fat hardcover books. It is good for the child to observe that people come to the store to select and purchase books. Perhaps when looking through the books in the store, the child might decide that he wants a book of his own. Such a decision is part of reading independence.

CONTINUING PROGRESS IN READING AFTER REMEDIATION

When a child has shown sufficient growth in reading to enable him to discontinue remedial assistance, it is important that planning between the remedial teacher and the classroom teacher be done in order to accomplish a smooth transition for the child. During remediation a good deal of communication between the classroom teacher and the remedial reading teacher served to coordinate efforts on the child's behalf. At the termination of remediation, the remedial teacher will want to share some insights and suggestions with the classroom teacher that can help her assist the child to continue to grow in reading.

The classroom teacher should support the child so he can maintain confidence in his reading now that he will be without the reassurance of the remedial teacher. The classroom teacher should also be alert to signs of difficulty in reading so that the child does not experience immediate frustration in classroom reading situations. In some instances, children may revisit the remedial reading teacher once a week or twice a month for the purpose of a little additional supportive attention. On occasion these children benefit from being enrolled in a summer program designed to enhance reading improvement.

It is also important for parents to continue to be encouraging of their child's reading efforts and to continue to be aware of and supportive of their child's reading program. Communication with the classroom teacher is beneficial. Occasionally parents can continue to provide home assistance in reading under the classroom teacher's guidance. Sometimes they will want to communicate to the teacher about signs of tension they detect in their child or to mention how much better their child seems to like school now that his reading is more successful.

When a disabled reader has overcome the reading difficulties that were impeding his reading and educational growth, when he has developed a real desire to read, and when he has established independence and self-sufficiency in the use of reading as a tool of learning at his level of reading expectancy, then his chances for continuing growth in reading become excellent. If, in addition, his teachers continue to give instruction suited to his individual learning characteristics, his successful reading development will be practically ensured. Such diagnostic teaching in classrooms and resource centers will make possible success for many students who otherwise would be unable to realize their complete educational potential. Such teaching takes the highest level of professional dedication, but therein lies the educational future of many children.

STUDY QUESTIONS

1. How can one identify specific interests of disabled readers?
2. What can be done to help poor readers develop an interest in reading?
3. Why is effort made to insure continuing progress in reading after remediation so essential?

SELECTED READINGS

HARRIS, A. J., AND E. R. SIPAY, Eds. *Readings on Reading Instruction*, 3rd ed., Chap. 12. New York: Longman, Inc., 1984.

ROSER, N., AND M. FRITH, Eds. *Children's Choices*, Newark, DE: International Reading Association, 1983.

TRELEASE, J. *The Read Aloud Handbook*, 2nd ed. New York: Viking Penguin, 1985.

References

ALLEN, P. D., AND J. D. WATSON, eds. (1976). *Findings of Research in Miscue Analysis: Classroom Implications*. Urbana, IL: National Council of Teachers of English.

ARAM, D. M., B. L. KELMAN, AND J. E. NATION. (1984) "Preschoolers with Language Disorders: Ten Years Later." *Journal of Speech and Hearing Research, 27,* 232–45.

AUSTIN, M. C., C. L. BUSH, AND M. H. HUEBNER. (1961). *Reading Evaluation*. New York: Ronald Press.

AUSTIN, M. C. AND C. MORRISON. (1963). *The First R*. New York: Macmillan Publishing Co.

BACKMAN, J. (1983). "The Role of Psycholinguistic Skills in Reading Acquisition: A Look at Early Readers." *Reading Research Quarterly, 18,* 466–79.

BAKKER, D. J., J. TEUNISSEN, AND J. BOSCH. (1976). "Development of Laterality." *In* R. M. Knights and D. J. Bakker, eds., *The Neuropsychology of Learning Disorders: Theoretical Approaches.* Baltimore: University Park Press.

BALOW, B., R. RUBIN, AND M. J. ROSEN. (1975). *"Perinatal Events as Precursors of Reading Disability." Reading Research Quarterly, 11,* 36–71.

BANNATYNE, A. (1974). "Diagnosis: A Note on Recategorization of the WISC Scaled Scores." *Journal of Learning Disabilities, 7,* 272–73.

BARNITZ, J. G. (1980). "Syntactic Effects of the Reading Comprehension of Pronoun Referent Structures by Children in Grades Two, Four, and Six." *Reading Research Quarterly, 15,* 268–89.

BARR, R. AND M. SADOW. (1985). *Reading Diagnosis for Teachers*. New York: Longman, Inc.

BELDIN, H. O. (1976). *Differences between Good and Poor Readers*. Paper presented at the annual meeting of the College Reading Association, Miami Beach, October 1976.

BENDER, L. (1957). "Specific Reading Disability as a Maturational Lag." *Bulletin of the Orton Society, 9,* 9–18.

BERRES, F. B., J. C. COLEMAN, W. S. BRISCOE, AND F. M. HEWETT. (1967). *The Deep Sea Adventure Series*. Menlo Park, CA: Addison-Wesley Publishing Company.

BETTS, E. A. (1957). *Foundations of Reading Instruction.* New York: American Book Company.

BIRCH, H. G., AND J. D. GUSSOW. (1970). *Disadvantaged Children: Health, Nutrition, and School Failure.* New York: Grune and Stratton, Inc.

BLACHMAN, B. A. (1984). "Relationship of Rapid Naming Ability and Language Analysis Skills to Kindergarten and First-Grade Reading Achievement." *Journal of Educational Psychology, 76,* 601–22.

BLACK, F. W. (1971). "An Investigation of Intelligence as a Causal Factor in Reading Problems." *Journal of Learning Disabilities, 4,* 139–42.

———. (1973). "Neurological Dysfunction and Reading Disorders." *Journal of Learning Disabilities, 6,* 313–16.

———. (1974). "Self-Concept as Related to Achievement and Age in Learning Disabled Children." *Child Development, 45,* 1137–40.

———. (1976). "Cognitive, Academic, and Behavioral Findings in Children with Suspected and Documented Neurological Dysfunction." *Journal of Learning Disabilities, 9,* 182–87.

BLAHA, J. (1982). "Predicting Reading and Arithmetic Achievement with Measures of Reading Attitudes and Cognitive Styles." *Perceptual and Motor Skills, 55,* 107–14.

BLAIR, J. C., M. E. PETERSON, AND S. H. VIEHWEG. (1985). "The Effects of Mild Sensorineural Hearing Loss on Academic Performance of Young School-Age Children." *Volta Review, 87,* 87–93.

BLAKE, M. E. (1985). "The Relationship between Field Dependence-Independence and the Comprehension of Expository and Literary Text Types." *Reading World, 24,* 53–62.

BLANCE, E., AND A. COOK. (1973). *Monster Books.* Glendale, CA: Bowmar/Noble Publishers, Inc.

BLANCHARD, J. S., G. E. MASON, AND D. DANIEL. (1987). *Computer Applications in Reading* (3rd ed.). Newark, DE: International Reading Association.

BLOOMFIELD, L., AND C. BARNHART. (1961). *Let's Read: A Linguistic Approach.* Detroit: Wayne State University Press.

BOCKMILLER, P. R. (1981). "Hearing-Impaired Children: Learning to Read a Second Language." *American Annals of the Deaf, 126,* 810–813.

BOND, G. L. (1935). *The auditory and speech characteristics of poor readers.* Teachers College, Columbia University.

———. (1976). "Employ More Diagnostic Teaching in the Classroom." *Reading Improvement, 13,* 35–39.

———. AND R. DYKSTRA. (1967). *Coordinating center for first grade reading instruction programs.* Final Report of Project No. X-001, Contract No. OE-5-10-264. Minneapolis, MN: University of Minnesota.

BOND, G. L., AND E. B. WAGNER. (1966). *Teaching the child to read* (4th ed.). New York: Macmillan.

BONING, R. A. (1978). *Specific Skills Series.* Baldwin, NY: Barnell Loft., Ltd.

BORMUTH, J. R. (1967). "Comparable Cloze and Multiple-choice Test comprehension Scores." *Journal of Reading, 10,* 295.

BROCK, H. (1982). "Factor Structure of Intellectual and Achievement Measures for Learning Disabled Children." *Psychology in the Schools, 19,* 297–304.

BROWN, D. A. (1982). *Reading Diagnosis and Remediation.* Englewood Cliffs, NJ: Prentice-Hall, Inc.

BROWN, J. I., J. M. BENNETT, AND G. HANNA. (1981). *Nelson-Denny Reading Test.* Chicago: Riverside Publishing Company.

BROWN, V. L., D. D. HAMMILL, AND J. L. WIEDERHOLT. (1986). *Test of Reading Comprehension, Revised.* Austin, TX: ProEd.

BRUECKNER, L. J., AND G. L. BOND. (1955). *Diagnosis and Treatment of Learning Difficulties.* New York: Appleton-Century-Crofts, 1955.

BRYAN, T. H., AND J. H. BRYAN. (1978). *Understanding Learning Disabilities,* 2nd ed. Port Washington, NY: Alfred Publishing Company, Inc.

BUCHANAN, C. D. (1963, 1964). *Programmed Reading.* New York: McGraw-Hill Book Co.

BURKE, C. M. (1973). Preparing Elementary Teachers to Teach Reading. *In* K. S. Goodman, ed., *Miscue Analysis: Applications to Reading Instruction.* Urbana, IL: National Council of Teachers of English.

BURMEISTER, L. E. (1974). *Reading Strategies for Secondary School Teachers.* Reading, Ma.: Addison-Wesley Publishing Co. Inc.

BUROS, O. K., Ed. (1985). *The Ninth Mental Measurements Yearbook.* Highland Park, NJ: The Gryphon Press.

BURTON, D. L., AND N. LARRICK. (1961). Literature for Children and Youth. *In Development in and through Reading,* Sixtieth Yearbook of the National Society for the Study of Education, Part I. Chicago: University of Chicago Press.

BUTTERY, T. J., AND G. E. MASON. (1979). "Reading Improvement for Mainstreamed Children who Are Mildly Mentally Handicapped." *Reading Improvement, 16,* 334–37.

CAMP, B. W., AND S. G. ZIMET. (1975). "Classroom Behavior during Reading Instruction." *Exceptional Children, 42,* 109–10.

CARBO, M. (1983). "Research in Reading and Learning Style: Implications for Exceptional Children." *Exceptional Children, 49,* 486–94.

————. (1985). "Research in Learning Style and Reading: Implications for Instruction." *Theory into Practice, 23,* 72–76.

CARNER, R. L. (1981). "Physiological Variables and Reading Disability." *Journal of Research and Development in Education, 14,* 24–34.

CEGELKA, J. A., AND W. J. CEGELKA. (1970). "A Review of Research: Reading and the Educable Mentally Retarded." *Exceptional Children, 37,* 187–200.

CHALFANT, J. C., AND M. A. SCHEFFELIN. (1969). *Central Processing Dysfunctions in Children: A Review of Research.* Washington, D.C.: U.S. Government Printing Office.

CHANDLER, E. W. (1971). *Cowboy Sam Series.* Westchester, IL: Benefic Press.

CHAPMAN, J. (1979). "Confirming Children's Use of Cohesive Ties in Text: Pronouns." *The Reading Teacher, 33,* 317–22.

CHAPMAN, J. W., P. A. SILVA, AND S. M. WILLIAMS. (1984). "Academic Self-Concept: Some Developmental and Emotional Correlates in Nine-Year-Old Children." *British Journal of Educational Psychology, 54,* 284–92.

CHOMSKY, C. (1969). *The Acquisition of Syntax in Children from 5 to 10.* Cambridge, MA: M. I. T. Press.

CLYMER, T. W. (1952). *The Influence of Reading Ability on the Validity of Group Intelligence Tests.* Unpublished doctoral dissertation, University of Minnesota.

COHEN, S. A. (1969). *Teach Them All to Read.* New York: Random House.

————, and T. COOPER. (1972). "Seven Fallacies: Reading Retardation and the Urban Disadvantaged Reader." *The Reading Teacher, 26,* 38–44.

COLE, L. (1938). *The Improvement of Reading.* New York: Holt, Rinehart, and Winston.

CRANE, J. A. (1950). *Reading Difficulties as a Social Work Problem.* Unpublished masters thesis, McGill University.

CRITCHLEY, M. (1970). *The Dyslexic Child.* Springfield, IL: Charles C. Thomas.

CRUICKSHANK, W. M., ed. (1971). *Psychology of Exceptional Children and Youth,* 3rd ed. Englewood Cliffs, NJ: Prentice-Hall, Inc.

CTB/McGRAW-HILL. (1985, 1986). *California Achievement Tests.* Monterey, CA: Author.

————. (1985, 1986). *California Achievement Tests, Reading.* Monterey, CA: Author.

CUMMINS, J. P., AND J. P. DAS. (1980). "Cognitive Processing, Academic Achievement, and WISC-R Performance." *Journal of Consulting and Clinical Psychology, 48,* 777–79.

DALE, E., AND J. CHALL. (1948). "Formula for Predicting Readability." *Educational Research Bulletin, 27,* 11–20 and 37–45.

DALGLEISH, B. W. J., AND S. ENKELMANN. (1979). "The Interpretation of Pronominal Reference by Retarded and Normal Readers." *British Journal of Educational Psychology, 49,* 290–96.

DECHANT, E. V. (1981). *Diagnosis and Remediation of Reading Disabilities.* Englewood Cliffs, NJ: Prentice-Hall, Inc.

————. AND H. P. SMITH. (1977). *Psychology of Teaching Reading,* 2nd ed. Englewood Cliffs, NJ: Prentice-Hall, Inc.

DeHIRSH, K., J. J. JANSKY, AND W. S. LANGFORD. (1966). *Predicting Reading Failure: A Preliminary Study.* New York: Harper & Row.

DEIGHTON, L. C., AND A. B. SANFORD. (1964). *Macmillan Spectrum of Books.* New York: Macmillan Publishing Co., Inc.

DEREVENSKY, J. L. (1978). "Modal Preferences and Strengths: Implications for Reading Research." *Journal of Reading Behavior, 10,* 7–23.

DOLCH, E. W. (1945). *A Manual for Remedial Reading,* 2nd ed. Champaign, IL: Garrard Press, 1945.

DOLCH, E. W. (1951). *Psychology and Teaching of Reading,* 2nd ed. Champaign, IL: Garrard Press, Publishers.

————. (1960). *Teaching Primary Reading,* 3rd ed. Champaign, IL: The Garrard Press, Publishers.

DUANE, D. D. (1983). "Neurobiological Correlates of Reading Disorders." *Journal of Educational Research, 77,* 5–15.

DUNN, R., G. E. PRICE, K. DUNN, AND W. SAUNDERS. (1979). "Relationship of Learning Style to Self Concept." *The Clearing House, 53,* 155–58.

DURKIN, D. (1976). *Teaching Young Children to Read,* 2nd ed. Boston: Allyn and Bacon, Inc.

————. (1987). *Teaching Young Children to Read,* 4th ed. Boston: Allyn and Bacon, Inc.

DURRELL, D. D. (1955). *Improving Reading Instruction.* New York: Harcourt Brace Jovanovich.

————, AND J. H. CATTERSON. (1980). *Durrell Analysis of Reading Difficulties,* 3rd ed. San Antonio, TX: The Psychological Corporation.

EAMES, T. H. (1935). "A Frequency Study of Physical Handicaps in Reading Disability and Unselected Groups." *Journal of Educational Research, 29,* 1–5.

EARLE, R. A. (1976). *Teaching Reading and Mathematics.* Newark, DE: International Reading Association.

EBERLY, D. W. (1972). *How Does my Child's Vision Affect his Reading?* Newark, DE: International Reading Association.

EDMIASTON, R. K. (1984). "Oral Language and Reading: How Are They Related for Third Graders?" *Remedial and Special Education, 5,* 33–37.

EKWALL, E. E. (1986). *Ekwall Reading Inventory,* 2nd ed. Rockleigh, NJ: Allyn and Bacon, Inc.

ELDREDGE, A. R. (1981). "An Investigation to Determine the Relationships among Self-Concept, Locus of Control, and Reading Achievement." *Reading World, 21,* 59–64.

ENGELMANN, S. (1974). *Corrective Reading.* Chicago: Science Research Associates, Inc.

ENGLE, P. L. (1975). "Language Medium in Early School Years for Minority Language Groups." *Review of Educational Research, 45,* 283–325.

ENGLEHARDT, R. M. (1965). "Speed Is not a Nasty Word." *Journal of Reading, 8,* 330–31.

EVANS, R. V. (1979). "The Relationship between the Reading and Writing of Syntactic Structure." *Research in the Teaching of English, 13,* 129–135.

FEATHERSTONE, W. B. (1951). *Teaching the Slow Learner,* rev. ed. New York: Bureau of Publications, Teachers College, Columbia University.

FELDHUSEN, J. F., J. R. THURSTON, AND J. J. BENNING. (1970). "Longitudinal Analysis of Classroom Behavior and School Achievement." *Journal of Experimental Education, 38,* 4–10.

FERNALD, G. M. (1971). *Remedial Techniques in Basic School Subjects.* New York: McGraw-Hill Book Company.

FLETCHER, J. M., P. SATZ, AND R. J. SCHOLES. (1981), "Developmental Changes in the Linguistic Performance Correlates of Reading Achievement." *Brain and Language, 13,* 78–90.

FOSTER, G. G., J. H. REESE, C. R. SCHMIDT, AND W. F. ORTHMAN. (1976). "Modality Preference and the Learning of Sight Words." *Journal of Special Education, 10,* 253–58.

FRIES, C. C. (1963). *Linguistics and Reading.* New York: Holt, Rinehart, and Winston.

FROST, B. P. (1965). "Some Personality Characteristics of Poor Readers." *Psychology in the Schools, 2,* 218–20.

GARDNER, E. F., H. C. RUDMEN, B. A. KARLSEN, AND J. C. MERWIN. (1982, 1983, 1984). *Stanford Achievement Tests.* San Antonio, TX: The Psychological Corporation.

GATES, A. I. (1947). *The Improvement of Reading,* 3rd ed. New York: Macmillan Publishing Company, Inc.

————, A. S. McKILLOP, and E. C. Horowitz. (1981). *Reading Diagnostic Tests,* 2nd ed. New York: Teachers College Press.

GAVER, M. V. (1961). "Effectiveness of Centralized Library Services in Elementary Schools (Phase 1)." *Library Quarterly, 31,* 245–56.

GENEVA MEDICO-EDUCATIONAL SERVICE. (1968). "Problems posed by Dyslexia." *Journal of Learning Disabilities, 1,* 158–71.

GENTILE, L. M., AND M. M. McMILLAN. (1987). *Stress and Reading Difficulties: Research, Assessment, Intervention.* Newark, DE: International Reading Association.

GILLET, J. W., AND C. TEMPLE. (1986). *Understanding Reading Problems,* 2nd ed. Boston: Little, Brown, and Company.

GILLINGHAM, A., AND B. W. STILLMAN. (1960). *Remedial Training for Children with Specific Disability in Reading, Spelling, and Penmanship.* Cambridge, MA: Educators Publishing Service, Inc.

GLAVIN, J. P., AND F. R. ANNESLEY. (1971). "Reading and Arithmetic Correlates of Conduct-Problem and Withdrawn Children." *Journal of Special Education, 5,* 213–19.

GLAZER, S. M., AND L. M. MORROW. (1978). "The Syntactic Complexity of Primary Grade Children's Oral Language and Primary Grade Reading Materials: A Comparative Analysis." *Journal of Reading Behavior, 10,* 200–203.

GOODMAN, K. S., ed. (1973). *Miscue Analysis: Applications to Reading Instruction*. Urbana, IL: National Council of Teachers of English.

————, AND Y. M. GOODMAN. (1980). *Linguistics, Psycholinguistics, and the Teaching of Reading*, 3rd ed. Newark, DE: International Reading Association.

GOODMAN, Y. M., AND C. M. BURKE. (1972). *Reading Miscue Inventory: Procedure for Diagnosis and Evaluation*. New York: Macmillan Book Company, Inc.

————, AND D. J. WATSON. (1977). "A Reading Program to Live With: Focus on Comprehension." *Language Arts, 54,* 868–79.

GRAUBARD, P. S. (1971). "The Relationship between Academic Achievement and Behavior Dimensions." *Exceptional Children, 37,* 755–56.

GRAY, R. A., J. SASKI, M. E. McENTIRE, AND S. C. LARSEN. (1980). "Is Proficiency in Oral Language a Predictor of Academic Success?" *The Elementary School Journal, 80,* 260–68.

GREANEY, V. (1980). "Factors Related to Amount and Type of Leisure Time Reading." *Reading Research Quarterly, 15,* 337–57.

GREENLAW, M. J. (1983). "Reading Interest Research and Children's Choices." *In* N. Roser and M. Frith, eds. *Children's Choice: Teaching with Books Children Like.* Newark, DE: International Reading Association.

HALPERN, H. G. (1984). "An Investigation of Reading and Conceptual Tempo Measures." *Reading World, 24*(1), 90–96.

HAMMILL, D. (1972). "Training Visual Perceptual Processes." *Journal of Learning Disabilities, 5,* 39–46.

————, AND S. C. LARSEN. (1974). "The Relationship of Selected Auditory Perceptual Skills and Reading Ability." *Journal of Learning Disabilities, 7,* 429–35.

HAMMILL, D. D., AND G. McNUTT. (1980). "Language Abilities and Reading: A Review of the Literature on their Relationship." *The Elementary School Journal, 80,* 269–77.

HARE, B. A. (1977). "Perceptual Deficits Are not a Cue to Reading Problems in Second Grade." *Reading Teacher, 30,* 624–27.

HARKER, W. J. (1985). *Classroom Strategies for Secondary Reading,* 2nd ed. Newark, DE: International Reading Association.

HARRIS, A. J. (1970). *How to Increase Reading Ability,* 5th ed. New York: David McKay Company, Inc.

————, AND M. D. JACOBSON. (1972). *Basic Elementary Reading Vocabularies.* New York: Macmillan Publishing Co., Inc.

HARRIS, A. J., AND E. R. SIPAY. (1975). *How to Increase Reading ability,* 6th ed. New York: David McKay.

————. (1980). *How to Increase Reading Ability,* 7th ed. New York: Longman, Inc.

————, eds. (1984). *Readings on Reading Instruction,* 3rd ed. New York: Longman, Inc.

————. (1985). *How to Increase Reading Ability,* 8th ed. New York: Longman, Inc.

HARRIS, W. J., AND D. R. KING. (1982). "Achievement, Sociometric Status, and Personality Characteristics of Children Selected by their Teachers as Having Learning and/or Behavior Problems." *Psychology in the Schools, 19,* 452–57.

HART, B. 0. (1976). *Teaching Reading to Deaf Children.* New York: Alexander Graham Bell Association for the Deaf.

HEGGE, T. G., S. A. KIRK, AND W. D. KIRK. (1945). *Remedial Reading Drills.* Ann Arbor, MI: Wahr.

HEILMAN, A. W., T. R. BLAIR, AND W. H. RUPLEY. (1986). *Principles and Practices of Teaching Reading,* 6th ed. Columbus, OH: Charles E. Merrill Publishing Company.

HELFELDT, J. P. (1983). "Sex-Linked Characteristics of Brain Functioning: Why Jimmy Reads Differently." *Reading World, 22,* 90–96.

HENK, W. A., J. P. HELFELDT, AND J. M. PLATT. (1986). "Developing Reading Fluency in Learning Disabled Students." *Teaching Exceptional Children, 18,* 202–206.

HERBER, H. L. (1965). "Reading Study Skills: Some Studies." *Reading and Inquiry, 10,* 94–96.

————. (1978). *Teaching Reading in Content Areas,* 2nd ed. Englewood Cliffs, NJ: Prentice-Hall, Inc.

HERBERT, D. J. (1968). "Reading Comprehension as a Function of Self Concept." *Perceptual and Motor Skills, 27,* 78.

HERMANN, M. A. (1987). *Tiger's Tales: A Reading Adventure* (computer program). Pleasantville, NY: Sunburst Communications, Inc.

HEWETT, F. M., AND F. D. TAYLOR. (1980). *The Emotionally Disturbed Child in the Classroom: The Orchestration of Success.* Boston: Allyn and Bacon, Inc.

HICKMAN, J. (1983). "Classrooms that Help Children Like Books." *In* N. Roser and M. Frith, Eds.

Children's Choices: Teaching with Books Children Like. Newark, DE: International Reading Association.

HIERONYMUS, A. N., H. D. HOOVER, AND E. F. LINDQUIST. (1986). *Iowa Tests of Basic Skills.* Chicago: The Riverside Publishing Company.

HILL, W. R. (1979). *Secondary School Reading: Process, Program, Procedure.* Boston: Allyn and Bacon, Inc.

HOOD, J. (1978). "Is Miscue Analysis Practical for Teachers?" *The Reading Teacher, 32,* 260–66.

HOSKINS, S. B. (1986). "Text Superstructures." *Journal of Reading, 29,* 538–43.

HUELSMAN, C. B., JR. (1970). "The WISC Subtest Syndrome for Disabled Readers." *Perceptual and Motor Skills, 30,* 535–50.

IDOL, L. (1987). "Group Story Mapping: A Comprehension Strategy for both Skilled and Unskilled Readers." *Journal of Learning Disabilities, 20,* 196–205.

ISOM, J. B. (1968). "Neurological Research Relevant to Reading." *In* H. K. Smith, Ed. *Perception and Reading.* Newark, DE: International Reading Association.

JOBE, F. W. (1976). *Screening Vision in Schools.* Newark, DE: International Reading Association.

JOHNS, J. L. (1985). *Basic Reading Inventory,* 3rd ed. Dubuque, IA: Kendall/Hunt Publishing Company.

JOHNSON, D. J., AND H. R. MYKLEBUST. (1967). *Learning Disabilities: Educational Principles and Practices.* New York: Grune & Stratton.

JOHNSON, M. J., R. A. KRESS, AND J. J. PIKULSKI. (1987). *Informal Reading Inventories,* 2nd ed. Newark, DE: International Reading Association.

JORM, A. F., D. L. SHARE, R. MATTHEWS, AND R. MACLEAN. (1986). "Behavior Problems in Specific Reading Retarded and General Reading Backward Children: A Longitudinal Study." *Journal of Child Psychology & Psychiatry & Allied Disciplines, 27,* 33–43.

KALUGER, G., AND C. J. KOLSON. (1978). *Reading and Learning Disabilities,* 2nd ed. Columbus, OH: Charles E. Merrill Publishing Company.

KARLSEN, B. A. (1954). *A Comparison of Some Educational and Psychological Characteristics of Successful and Unsuccessful Readers at the Elementary School Level.* Unpublished doctoral dissertation, University of Minnesota.

KARLSEN, B. A., R. MADDEN, AND E. F. GARDNER. (1984). *Stanford Diagnostic Reading Test* 3rd ed. Chicago: The Psychological Corporation Harcourt Brace Jovanovich, Publishers.

KASS, C. E. (1966). "Psycholinguistic Disabilities of Children with Reading Problems." *Exceptional Children, 32,* 533–39.

KAUFMAN, A. S. (1975). "Factor Analysis of the WISC-R at 11 Age Levels between 6 ½ and 16 ½ Years." *Journal of Consulting and Clinical Psychology, 43,* 135–47.

_____, AND N. L. KAUFMAN. (1985). *Kaufman Test of Educational Achievement, Brief Form.* Circle Pines, MN: American Guidance Service, Inc.

_____. (1985). *Kaufman Test of Educational Achievement, Comprehensive Form.* Circle Pines, MN: American Guidance Service, Inc.

KAVALE, K. A. (1981). "The Relationship between Auditory Perceptual Skills and Reading Ability: A Meta-Analysis." *Journal of Learning Disabilities, 14,* 539–46.

_____. (1982). "Meta-Analysis of the Relationship between Visual Perception Skills and Reading Achievement." *Journal of Learning Disabilities, 15,* 42–51.

KENDLER, J. P. (1972). "Is There Really a WISC Profile for Poor Readers?" *Journal of Learning Disabilities, 5,* 397–400.

KENT, C. E. (1984). "A Linguist Compares Narrative and Expository Prose." *Journal of Reading, 28,* 232–36.

KEPHART, N. C. (1971). *The Slow Learner in the Classroom,* 2nd ed. Columbus, OH: Charles E. Merrill Publishing Company.

KIRK, S. A. (1940). *Teaching Reading to Slow-Learning Children.* Boston: Houghton Mifflin Company.

_____, AND J. ELKINS. (1975). "Characteristics of Children Enrolled in the Child Service Demonstration Centers." *Journal of Learning Disabilities, 8,* 630–37.

KIRK, S. A., AND J. J. GALLAGHER. (1986). *Educating Exceptional Children,* 5th ed. Boston: Houghton Mifflin Company.

KIRK, S. A., J. M. KLIEBHAN, AND J. W. LERNER. (1978). *Teaching Reading to Slow and Disabled Learners.* Boston: Houghton Mifflin Company.

KIRK, S. A., J. J. McCARTHY, AND W. D. KIRK. (1968). *The Illinois Test of Psycholinguistic Abilities,* rev. ed. Urbana, IL: University of Illinois Press.

KLEIN, R. S., S. D. ALTMAN, K. DREIZEN, R. FRIEDMAN, AND L. POWERS. (1981). "Restructuring

Dysfunctional Attitudes toward Children's Learning and Behavior in School: Family-Oriented Psychoeducational Therapy.'' *Journal of Learning Disabilities, 14,* 15–19.

KNOX, G. E. (1953). ''Classroom Symptoms of Visual Difficulty.'' *In Clinical Studies in Reading: II* (Supplementary Educational Monographs no. 77), Chicago: University of Chicago Press.

KOGAN, N. (1980). ''Cognitive Styles and Reading Performance.'' *Bulletin of the Orton Society, 30,* 63–78.

KOZLOWSKI, L. J. (1968). ''Identifying Visual Problems by Teacher Observation.'' *In Clinical Studies in Reading: III* (Supplementary Educational Monographs no. 97), Chicago: University of Chicago Press.

LAFFEY, J. L., AND R. SHUY, Eds. (1973). *Language Differences: Do They Interfere?* Newark, DE: International Reading Association.

LAPP, D., AND J. FLOOD. (1978). *Teaching Reading to Every Child.* New York: Macmillan Publishing Co., Inc.

LARSEN, J., C. E. TILLMAN, J. J. ROSS, P. SATZ, B. CASSIN, AND W. WOLKIN. (1973). ''Factors in Reading Achievement: An Interdisciplinary Approach.'' *Journal of Learning Disabilities, 6,* 636–44.

LIN-FU, J. S. (1971). *Vision Screening of Children.* Washington, DC: U.S. Government Printing Office.

LLOYD, H. M. (1965). ''What's Ahead in Reading for the Disadvantaged?'' *The Reading Teacher, 18,* 471–76.

LUNDSTEEN, S. W. (1976). *Children Learn to Communicate.* Englewood Cliffs, NJ: Prentice-Hall, Inc.

LUNSTRUM, J. P., AND B. L. TAYLOR. (1978). *Teaching Reading in the Social Studies.* Newark, DE: International Reading Association.

LYLE, J. G. (1970). Certain Antenatal, Perinatal, and Developmental Variables and Reading Retardation. *Child Development, 41,* 481–91.

MACGINITIE, W. H. (1978). *Gates-MacGinitie Reading Tests,* 2nd ed. Chicago: Riverside Publishing Company.

MARGOLIS, H., N. PETERSON, AND H. S. LEONARD. (1978). ''Conceptual Tempo as a Predictor of First-Grade Reading Achievement.'' *Journal of Reading Behavior, 10,* 359–62.

MARTIN, H. P. (1971). ''Vision and its Role in Reading Disability and Dyslexia.'' *The Journal of School Health, 41,* 468–71.

MARZANO, R. J., P. J. HAGERTY, S. W. VALENCIA, AND P. P. DISTEFANO. (1982). *Reading Diagnosis and Instruction.* Englewood Cliffs, NJ: Prentice-Hall, Inc.

MCCARTHY, J. J., AND S. A. KIRK. (1961). *The Illinois Test of Psycholinguistic Abilities.* Urbana, IL: University of Illinois Press.

MCCONAUGHY, S. H. (1985). ''Good and Poor Readers' Comprehension of Story Structure across Different Input and Output Modalities.'' *Reading Research Quarterly, 20,* 219–32.

MCCORMICK, S. (1987). *Remedial and Clinical Reading Instruction.* Columbus, OH: Charles E. Merrill Publishing Company

MCDERMOTT, J. C. (1983). ''Physical and Behavioral Aspects of Middle Ear Disease in School Children.'' *Journal of School Health, 53,* 463–66.

MCGINNIS, D. J., AND D. E. SMITH. (1982). *Analyzing and Treating Reading Problems.* New York: Macmillan Publishing Co., Inc.

MCKEE, P. (1948). *The Teaching of Reading in the Elementary School.* Boston: Houghton Mifflin Company.

MCKINNEY, J. D., J. MASON, K. PERKERSON, AND M. CLIFFORD. (1975). ''Relationship between Classroom Behavior and Academic Achievement.'' *Journal of Educational Psychology, 67,* 198–202.

MCLEOD, J. (1965). *Some Psychological and Psycholinguistic Aspects of Severe Reading Disability in Children.* Unpublished doctoral dissertation. University of Queensland, Australia.

MCMICHAEL, P. (1979). ''The Hen or the Egg? Which Comes First—Antisocial Emotional Disorders or Reading Disability?'' *British Journal of Educational Psychology, 49,* 226–38.

MEIGHEN, M. (1972). *The New Phonics We Use.* Des Moines, IA: Meredith Press.

MELLON, C. A. (1987). ''Teenagers Do Read: What Rural Youth Say about Leisure Reading.'' *School Library Journal, 33,* 27–30.

MILLER, W. H. (1982). *Reading Correction Kit,* 2nd ed. West Nyack, NY: Center for Applied Research in Education, Inc.

MINNESOTA EDUCATIONAL COMPUTING CORPORATION. (1985). *Word Munchers.* St. Paul, MN: Minnesota Educational Computing Corporation.

MONROE, M. (1932). *Children who Cannot Read.* Chicago: University of Chicago Press.

MOORE, D. W., AND 0. P. WIELAND. (1981). "WISC-R Scatter Indexes of Children Referred for Reading Diagnosis." *Journal of Learning Disabilities, 14,* 511–14.

MOORES, D. F. (1982). *Educating the Deaf: Psychology, Principles, and practices,* 2nd ed. Boston: Houghton Mifflin Company.

MUESER, A. M. (1981). *Reading Aids through the Grades,* 4th ed. New York: Teachers College Press.

MYERS, P. I., AND D. D. HAMMILL. (1976). *Methods for Learning Disorders,* 3rd ed. New York: John Wiley and Sons, Inc.

NASLUND, R. A., L. P. THORPE, AND D. W. LEFEVER. (1983, 1984). *SRA Achievement Series.* Chicago: Science Research Associates, Inc.

NEUMAN, S. B. (1986). "The Home Environment and Fifth Grade Student's Leisure Reading." *Elementary School Journal, 86,* 335–43.

NEWCOMER, P. L., AND D. D. HAMMILL. (1976). *Psycholinguistics in the Schools.* Columbus, OH: Charles E. Merrill Publishing Company.

NORTON, D. E. (1987). "Evaluating and Selecting Literature for Children." *In Through the Eyes of a Child: An Introduction to Children's Literature,* 2nd ed. Columbus, Oh: Charles E. Merrill Publishing Company.

PARADISE, L. V., AND C. BLOCK. (1984). "The Relationship of Teacher-Student Cognitive Style to Academic Achievement." *Journal of Research and Development in Education, 17,* 57–61.

POOSTAY, E., AND I. E. AARON. (1982). "Reading Problems of Children: The Perspectives of Reading Specialists." *School Psychology Review, 11,* 251–56.

PRENDERGAST, M. A., AND D. M. BINDER. (1975). "Relationships of Selected Self Concept and Academic Achievement Measures." *Measurement and Evaluation in Guidance, 8,* 92–95.

PRENTICE ASSOCIATES, INC. (1986). *Trickster Coyote.* Bridgeport, CT: Queue, Inc.

PRESCOTT, G. A., I. H. BALOW, T. P. HOGAN, AND R. FARR. (1985). *Metropolitan Achievement Tests.* San Antonio, TX: The Psychological Corporation.

PRICE, G. E., R. DUNN, AND W. SAUNDERS. (1981). "Reading Achievement and Learning Style Characteristics." *The Clearing House, 54,* 223–26.

QUANT, I. (1972). "Self-concept and Reading." Newark, DE: International Reading Association.

QUINN, L. (1981). "Reading Skills of Hearing and Congenitally Deaf Children." *Journal of Experimental Child Psychology, 32,* 139–61.

RAABE, J. A. (1974). *Preprimary Readers.* Cleveland: Modern Curriculum Press, Inc.

RABINOVITCH, R. D. (1962). "Dyslexia: Psychiatric Considerations." *In J. Money, ed. Reading Disability: Progress and Research Needs in Dyslexia.* Baltimore: Johns Hopkins Press.

RAGLAND, G. G. (1964). *The Performance of Educable Mentally Handicapped Students of Differing Reading Ability on the ITPA.* Unpublished doctoral dissertation, University of Virginia.

RAMBEAU, J., AND M. RAMBEAU. (1962). *The Morgan Bay Mysteries.* Menlo Park, CA: Addison-Wesley Publishing Company.

REDENCE, J. E., AND R. S. BALDWIN. (1978). "The Relationship of Cognitive Style and Phonics Instruction." *Journal of Educational Research, 72,* 44–52.

REID, D. K. AND W. P. HRESKO. (1981). *A Cognitive Approach to Learning Disabilities.* New York: McGraw-Hill, Inc.

REUTZEL, D. R. (1985). "Reconciling Schema Theory and the Basal Reading Lesson." *The Reading Teacher, 39,* 194–97.

RIST, R. C. (1970). "Social Class and Teacher Expectations: The Self-Fulfilling Prophecy in Ghetto Education." *Harvard Educational Review, 40,* 411–51.

ROBERGE, J. J., AND B. K. FLEXER. (1984). "Cognitive Style, Operativity , and Reading Achievement." *American Educational Research Journal, 21,* 227–36.

ROBERTS, T. (1983). "Factors of Intelligence in the Reading Comprehension of Learning Disordered/Reading Disordered Youngsters." *Reading Improvement, 20,* 91–95.

ROBINSON, H. M. (1972). "Visual and Auditory Modalities Related to Methods for Beginning Reading." *Reading Research Quarterly, 8,* 7–39.

ROSENBLUM, D. R., AND M. I. STEPHENS. (1981). "Correlates of Syntactic Development in Kindergarteners: Deficiency vs. Proficiency." *Brain and Language, 13,* 103–17.

ROSENTHAL, A. S., K. BAKER, AND A. GINSBURG. (1983). "The Effect of Language Background on Achievement Level and Learning among Elementary School Students." *Sociology of Education, 56,* 157–69.

ROSER, N., AND M. FRITH, eds. (1983). *Children's Choices: Teaching with Books Children Like.* Newark, DE: International Reading Association.

ROSWELL, F., AND G. NATCHEZ. (1971). *Reading Disability: Diagnosis and Treatment,* 2nd ed. New York: Basic Books, Inc., Publishers.

ROURKE, B. P. (1975). 'Brain-behavior Relationships in Children with Learning Disabilities.' *American Psychologist, 30,* 911–20.

RUBIN, D. R. (1982). *Diagnosis and Correction in Reading Instruction.* New York: Holt, Rinehart and Winston.

RUDDELL, R. B. (1979). "Early Prediction of Reading Success: Profiles of Good and Poor Readers." *In* M. L. Kamil and A. J. Moe, Eds. *Reading Research: Studies and Applications.* Twenty-eighth Yearbook of the National Reading Twenty-eighth Yearbook of the National Reading Conference.

RUGEL, R. P. (1974). "WISC Subtest Scores of Disabled Readers: A Review with Respect to Bannatyne's Recategorization." *Journal of Learning Disabilities, 7,* 48–64.

RUPLEY, W. H., AND T. R. BLAIR. (1979). *Reading Diagnosis and Remediation: A Primer for Classroom and Clinic.* Chicago: Rand McNally Publishing Company.

———. (1983). *Reading Diagnosis and Remediation: Classroom and Clinic,* 2nd ed. Boston: Houghton Mifflin Company.

RUTHERFORD, W. L. (1967). "Vision and Perception in the Reading Process." *In* J. A. Figurel, Ed. *Vistas in Reading.* Newark, DE: International Reading Association.

RYSTROM, R. (1973). "Reading, Language, and Nonstandard Dialects: A Research Report." *In* J. L. Laffey and R. Shuy, eds. *Language Differences: Do They Interfere?* Newark, DE: International-Reading Association.

———. (1977). "Reflections of Meaning." *Journal of Reading Behavior, 9,* 193–200.

SANNOMIYA, M. (1984). "Modality Effect on Text Processing as a Function of Ability to Comprehend." *Preceptual and Motor Skills, 58,* 379–82.

SATTLER, J. M. (1974). *Assessment of Children's Intelligence* (revised reprint). Philadelphia: W. B. Saunders Company.

SAVAGE, J. F., AND J. F. MOONEY. (1979). *Teaching Reading to Children with Special Needs.* Boston: Allyn and Bacon, Inc.

SEARLS. E. F. (1985). *How to Use WISC-R Scores in Reading/Learning Disability Diagnosis.* Newark, DE: International Reading Association.

SEATON, H. W. (1977). "The Effects of a Visual Perception Training Program on Reading Achievement." *Journal of Reading Behavior, 9,* 188–92.

SEIGLER, H. G., AND M. D. GYNTHER. (1960). "Reading Ability of Children and Family Harmony." *Journal of Developmental Reading, 4,* 17–24.

SERWATKA, T. S., D. HESSON, AND M. GRAHAM. (1984). "The Effect of Indirect Intervention on the Improvement of Hearing-Impaired Student's Reading Scores." *The Volta Review, 86,* 81–86.

SEWELL, T. E., AND R. A. SEVERSON. (1975). "Intelligence and Achievement in First-Grade Black Children." *Journal of Consulting and Clinical Psychology, 43,* 112.

SILVA, P. A., D. CHALMERS, AND I. STEWART (1986). "Some Audiological, Psychological, Educational and Behavioral Characteristics of Children with Bilateral Otitis Media with Effusion: A Longitudinal Study." *Journal of Learning Disabilities, 19,* 165–69.

SIMONS, H. B. (1973). "Black Dialect and Learning to Read." *In* J. L. Johns, ed. *Literacy for Diverse Learners.* Newark, DE: International Reading Association.

SMITH, F. (1973). *Psycholinguistics and Reading.* New York: Holt, Rinehart and Winston.

SMITH, F. (1978). *Reading Without Nonsense.* New York: Teachers College Press

SMITH, P. L., AND M. FRIEND. (1986). "Training Learning Disabled Adolescents in a Strategy for Using Text Structure to Aid Recall of Instructional Prose." *Learning Disabilities Research, 2,* 38–44.

SORNSON, H. H. (1950). *A Longitudinal Study of the Relationship between Various Child Behavior Ratings and Success in Reading.* Unpublished doctoral dissertation, University of Minnesota.

SPACHE, G. D. (1953). "A New Readability Formula for Primary-Grade Reading." *Elementary School Journal, 52,* 410–13.

———. (1963). *Toward Better Reading.* Champaign, IL: Garrard Publishing Company.

———. (1965). *A Study of a Longitudinal First Grade Reading Readiness Program* (Cooperative Research Project 2742). Tallahassee, FL: Florida State Department of Eduation.

———. (1970). *Good Reading for the Disadvantaged Reader.* Champaign, IL: Garrard Publishing Company.

———. (1975). *Good Reading for the Disadvantaged Reader: Multi-Ethnic Resources.* Champaign, IL: Garrard Publishing Company.

————. (1976). *Diagnosing and Correcting Reading Disabilities*. Boston: Allyn and Bacon, Inc.

————. (1976). *Investigating the Issues of Reading Disabilities*. Boston: Allyn and Bacon, Inc.

————. (1978). *Good Reading for Poor Readers*, rev. ed. Champaign, IL: Garrard Publishing Company.

————. (1981). *Diagnostic Reading Scales*. Monterey, CA: CTB/McGraw-Hill.

————, AND E. B. SPACHE. (1986). *Reading in the Elementary School*, 5th ed. Boston: Allyn and Bacon, Inc.

SPACHE, G. D., & C. E. TILLMAN. (1962). "A Comparison of the Visual Profiles of Retarded and Non-Retarded Readers." *Journal of Developmental Reading, 5*, 101–9.

STEVENS, D. 0. (1971). "Reading Difficulty and Classroom Acceptance." *The Reading Teacher, 25*, 52–55.

STRICKLAND, D. S., J. T. FEELEY, AND S. B. WEPNER. (1987). *Using Computers in the Teaching of Reading*. New York: Teachers College Press.

SULLIVAN ASSOCIATES. (1973). *The Programmed Reading Series*. New York: McGraw-Hill.

SWANSON, B. (1984). "The Relationship of First Graders' Self Report and Direct Observational Attitude Scores to Reading Achievement." *Reading Improvement, 21*, 170.

————. (1982). "The Relationship between Attitude toward Reading and Reading Achievement." *Educational and Psychological Measurement, 42*, 1303–4.

TELFORD, C. W., AND J. M. SAWREY. (1981). *The Exceptional Individual*, 4th ed. Englewood Cliffs, NJ: Prentice Hall, Inc.

TEMPLETON, S., AND S. MOWERY. (1985). "Readability, Basal Readers, and Story Grammar: What Lies beneath the 'surface'?" *Reading World, 24*, 40–47.

THAYER, J. A. (1970). "Johnny Could Read—What Happened?" *Journal of Reading, 13*, 501–6 and 561.

THELEN, J. N. (1984). *Improving Reading in Science*, 2nd ed. Newark, DE: International Reading Association.

THONIS, E. W. (1976). *Literacy for America's Spanish Speaking Children*. Newark, DE: International Reading Association.

TINKER, M. A., AND C. M. McCULLOUGH. (1975). *Teaching Elementary Reading*, 4th ed. Englewood Cliffs, NJ: Prentice-Hall, Inc.

TONJES, M. J., AND M. V. ZINTZ. (1987). *Teaching Reading Thinking Study Skills in Content Classrooms*, 2nd ed. Dubuque, IA: Wm. C. Brown, Publishers.

TRELEASE, J. (1985). *The Read-Aloud Handbook*. New York: Penguin Books.

VENEZKY, R. L., AND R. S. CHAPMAN, (1973). Is Learning to Read Dialect Bound? *In* J. L. Laffey and R. Shuy, eds. *Language Differences: Do They Interfere?* Newark, DE: International Reading Association.

VERNON, M. D. (1960). *Backwardness in Reading*. New York: Cambridge University Press.

————. (1969). *Visual Perception and its Relation to Reading*. Newark, DE: International Reading Association.

VICK, M. L. (1973). "Relevant Content for the Black Elementary School Pupil." *In* J. L. Johns, Ed. *Literacy for Diverse Learners*. Newark, DE: International Reading Association.

WALBERG, J. J., AND S. TSAI. (1985). "Correlates of Reading Achievement and Attitude: A National Assessment Study." *Journal of Educational Research, 78*, 159–67.

WASSON, B., P. BEARE, AND J. WASSON. (1988). *Behavioral Characteristics of Good and Poor Readers*. Moorhead, MN: Moorhead State University, Department of Education.

WATTENBERG, W. W., AND C. CLIFFORD, (1966). "Relationship of Self-Concept to Beginning Achievement in Reading." *Childhood Education, 43*, 58.

WEINBERG, W., AND A. REHMET. (1983). "Childhood Affective Disorder and School Problems. *In* D. F. Cantwell and G. A. Carlson, Eds. *Affective Disorders in Childhood and Adolescence: An Update*. New York: SP Medical & Scientific Books.

WEINTRAUB, S. (1972). *Auditory Perception and Deafness*. Newark, DE: International Reading Association.

————, AND R. J. COWAN. (1982). *Vision/Visual Perception: An Annotated Bibliography*. Newark, DE.: International Reading Association.

WHARRY, R. E., AND S. W. KIRKPATRICK, (1986). "Vision and Academic Performance of Learning Disabled Children." *Perceptual and Motor Skills, 62*, 323–36.

WIESS, M. J. (1982). "Children's Preferences for Format Factors in Books." *The Reading Teacher, 35*, 400–406.

WILKERSON, A. (1971). *The Foundations of Language.* London: Oxford University Press.

WILSON, R. M., AND C. J. CLELAND. (1985). *Diagnostic and Remedial Reading for Classroom and Clinic,* 5th ed. Columbus, OH: Charles E. Merrill Publishing Company.

WITTY, P. (1953). *How to Become a Better Reader.* Chicago: Science Research Associates.

WOLFSON, B. J., G. MANNING, AND M. MANNING. (1984). "Revisiting what Children Say their Reading Interests Are." *Reading World, 23,* 4–10.

WOODCOCK, R. W. (1973). *Woodcock Reading Mastery Tests.* Circle Pines, MN: American Guidance Service, Inc.

————. (1986). *Woodcock Reading Mastery Tests, Revised.* Circle Pines, MN: American Guidance Service, Inc.

————, AND M. B. JOHNSON. (1977). *Woodcock-Johnson Psycho-Educational Battery.* Hingham, MA: Teaching Resources.

WOODS, M. L., AND A. J. MOE. (1985). *Analytical Reading Inventory,* 3rd ed. Columbus, OH: Charles E. Merrill Publishing Company.

YOUNG, F. A. (1963). "Reading Measures of Intelligence and Refractive Errors." *American Journal and Archives of American Academy of Optometry, 40,* 257–264.

ZINKUS, P. W., M. I. GOTTLIEB, AND M. SCHAPIRO. (1978). "Developmental and Psychoeducational Sequelae of Chronic Otitis Media." *American Journal of Diseases of Children, 132,* 1100–1104.

ZINTZ, M. V. (1981). *Corrective Reading,* 4th ed. Dubuque, IA: Wm. C. Brown Company Publishers.

Author Index

Subject Index